STAR WARS®

THE ESSENTIAL GUIDE TO CHARACTERS

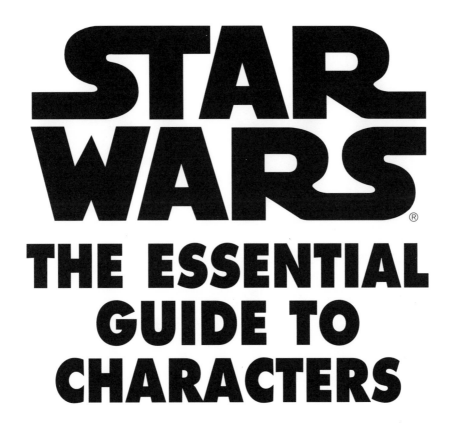

STAR WARS®

THE ESSENTIAL GUIDE TO CHARACTERS

ANDY MANGELS

BXTREE

First published in the UK in 1996 by Boxtree Limited, Broadwall House, 21 Broadwall, London, SE1 9PL

First published in the USA in 1995 by Ballantine Books, a division of Random House, Inc., New York.

ISBN 0 7522 0109 3

Interior and Cover design by Michaelis/Carpelis Design Associates, Inc.

10 9 8 7 6 5 4 3 2 1

Printed and bound in Great Britain by Redwood Books, Trowbridge, Wiltshire.

A CIP catalogue entry for this book is available from the British Library

I don't remember when I first saw *Star Wars*, but the initial time
I was going to see *The Empire Strikes Back* is burned into my mind.

The first friend I'd ever had who accepted me for who and what I was,
Dustyn C. Halverson,
was killed a half hour before we left to see the film,
Wednesday, July 16, 1980.

Years later, two friends would join me at the head of the line
to see *Return of the Jedi,* on May 25, 1983.

Will Goetter, Dan Traeger, and I went to Norm's News to sneak a
peek at who the "other" was in the Marvel comic adaptation.
An acquaintance, holding our place, got interviewed on the news.

For
Dusty Halverson
Will Goetter
Dan Traeger

Friendship is forever.

ACKNOWLEDGMENTS

I always wondered how so many people could fit on an acknowledgment page, and now I know. Many people deserve thanks for their assistance and answers in this project: I might not be writing this if it hadn't been for Bob Woods, editor of Topps' *Star Wars Galaxy* magazine. His assignment of a Boba Fett biography in their premiere issue got me the attention of Lucasfilm's Lucy Autrey Wilson. Knowing talent, she assigned me this book. Big thanks go to the two of them.

Sue Rostoni of Lucasfilm is one of the most pleasant and helpful editors I've ever worked with, and her prompt return of phone calls endeared her to me all the more; Kelly Macsisak was the best research assistant anyone could ask for, and she gets mucho gratitude; Bill Smith at West End Games not only filled in the gaps for the incredible line of *Star Wars* gaming and resource material, but endured many fact-checking phone calls.

Lots of people helped with research, and they deserve many thanks: Bruce Doering of *A Media Blitz* in Portland is the Northwest's best *Star Wars* source; Jamie Macsisak of *Claustrophobic Comics and Chaos* in Portland helped with comic research and loaned me his wife; Tammy Campbell, R.B. "Doggy" Hiatt, Kehvan M. Zydhek, and Dave Galvan helped with other research; authors Stephen J. Sansweet, Kevin J. Anderson, Rebecca Moesta, Tom Veitch, and Timothy Zahn all gladly answered questions when needed; my ex-partner Jim Carlson supported me throughout much of this project.

Thanks for research materials go to Len Brown of Topps cards, Neweleen Trebnik at Prima Publishing, Ryder Windham and Peet Janes at Dark Horse Comics, Allan Kausch at Lucasfilm, and Dan Madsen at *Star Wars Insider* magazine.

My editors at Ballantine helped make this book look great; artist Mike Butkus helped breathe visual life into the characters.

And thanks to the Force behind the *Star Wars* galaxy, George Lucas, without whom my adolescence would have been much more miserable. He offered me hope.

INTRODUCTION

In today's culture, the amount of trivial information stored in our minds is phenomenal. Our media gets more sophisticated every day, allowing even more data to find its way to the back recesses of the brain. Science-fiction and fantasy fans have often been accused of having a little *too* much interest in the trivial, a little too much identification with the fictional, a little too much obsession with the facts behind the fantasies.

For those accusers, this book is a testament to fiction and fantasy. If you're not into that, go read another book. Of course, if you do, you'll be missing out on the more exciting picture, the tapestry on the wall that examines the lives of heroes and villains, of Empires and Rebellions . . .

A Long Time Ago In a Galaxy Far, Far Away . . .

With that phrase, George Lucas launched the public into the first *Star Wars* movie. It was a science-fiction world unlike anything seen before on film or television. Humanoids and aliens lived and worked side by side. Spaceships and dwellings reflected lives lived; no sterile and pristine settings existed on the planets with names like Tatooine and Yavin.

And yet, there was familiarity to it all. Inspired by Japanese film and movie serials, Lucas's creation was full of black-hearted (and black-armored) villains and wide-eyed, innocent heroes and heroines. The evil Empire was opposed by the noble Alliance, and those who didn't choose sides might get caught in the middle.

But into that familiar mix, the creator threw a host of exciting ingredients. A sarcastic and mercenary smuggler was pressed into reluctant heroism. The fresh farmboy was pulled into training in an ancient order of galactic guardians, only to have his teacher killed almost immediately. The robotic sidekicks not only had personality, but they bickered. And the "helpless" female who needed rescuing was the best shot of the bunch. (Check it out. Princess Leia *never* misses.)

As we all know, *Star Wars* was a success. The public wanted more. A comic book series from Marvel flourished. Then a novelized sequel, *Splinter of the Mind's Eye*, hit the stands. A *Star Wars Holiday Special* popped up on TV. But the demand only increased. Toys and costumes and mugs and records and model kits were all snapped up as we bought into the fantasy.

Two more movies followed, and various spin-offs emerged. More novels were written, children's books were published, and the *Droids* and *Ewoks* got their own cartoon series. The comics continued, and "far, far away" was kept close to us. But eventually, the public moved on to other pursuits, and the lumbering fantasy beast that was *Star Wars* went into hibernation—for a time.

Several years ago, the creature awoke, and again the public embraced it. In the last few years, *Star Wars* has been revitalized. Dozens of new novels and comics have been published, with the first generation of fans sharing the adventure with their children. Unlike other films of the '70s, the *Star Wars* trilogy never dated. It existed in its own time, with its own rules, independent of us. And thus, it appeals to the new generation as much as to the old.

In the course of the almost twenty years since *Star Wars* premiered, the galaxy has become a much busier place. Take a quick flip to the back of this book and check out the Bibliography, and then come back here. Don't start into the book itself . . . yet.

You're back? Good. Now were you amazed to find out just how much has been written about *Star Wars*? There's probably a lot there you didn't know about. *Bingo. That's* why you're holding this book in your hands.

When I started work on this project, my objective was pretty broad-based, and awfully daunting. I had to read or watch or listen to every bit of licensed *Star Wars* fiction (and much of the nonfiction) and catalogue it. Lucasfilm representatives and I worked out a list of characters who we felt had played a major role in the *Star Wars* galaxy. Most were from the trilogy, while others were from the novels, the role-playing games, and the cartoons or TV movies.

I took that vast amount of information and condensed it into concise biographies for each of the characters, weaving characters' lives in and out of their many adventures. Many stories aren't specifi-

cally reflected in this book, although careful readers will find some relatively obscure references. As new authors and artists have had input into the world first created by George Lucas, the people, places, and things in that world have multiplied. For example, did you know that Ben Kenobi's brother played a significant role in *Star Wars*? Did you know that Chewbacca has a wife and child?

And what about the nonpivotal players? Well, you'll find an entry for just about every alien that appeared in the Mos Eisley cantina and in Jabba's palace. You'll meet the children of Han Solo and Princess Leia, and the next generation of Jedi Knights (as well as the Jedi of thousands of years past). Heck, you'll even find out the name of the "Look, sir—droids" stormtrooper in the desolate wastes of Tatooine!

I've worked hard to make sure this book covers the essentials for the characters you've grown to know and love. Although the entries do reveal plot details of the original stories, I have tried to make sure that they don't seem to try to replace the stories themselves. You can read the character biographies here, and then go to the sources to find out more. Think of this book as a tasty dessert; it's fun to devour, but you'll want to eat the main course, as well.

As George Lucas creates the next *Star Wars* trilogy—prequels to *Star Wars: A New Hope*—a *new* tapestry is being created. This one will have threads of the old, woven in with exciting and vibrant new colors. But even before the new films premiere, there's a whole galaxy waiting for your exploration . . . a galaxy of heroes, villains, aliens, and droids.

Like any good explorer, you should enter that galaxy—even a fictional one—with knowledge.

Some would call that knowledge trivial.

We call it essential.

Come on and strap yourself in. I'll be your guide.

—Andy Mangels
Portland, OR
May 1995

TABLE OF CONTENTS

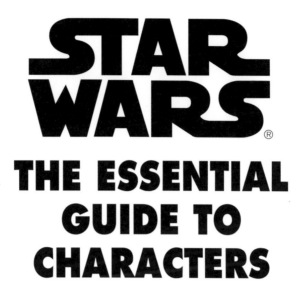

STAR WARS®

THE ESSENTIAL GUIDE TO CHARACTERS

ADMIRAL ACKBAR

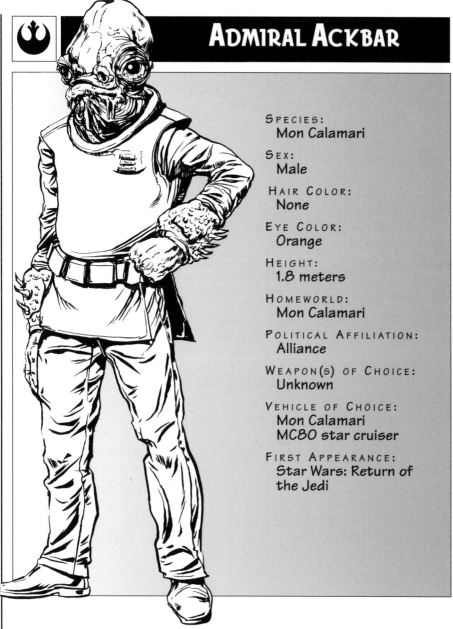

SPECIES:
Mon Calamari

SEX:
Male

HAIR COLOR:
None

EYE COLOR:
Orange

HEIGHT:
1.8 meters

HOMEWORLD:
Mon Calamari

POLITICAL AFFILIATION:
Alliance

WEAPON(S) OF CHOICE:
Unknown

VEHICLE OF CHOICE:
Mon Calamari MC80 star cruiser

FIRST APPEARANCE:
Star Wars: Return of the Jedi

For the Empire, slavery and racism were standard operating procedure. When they attempted to take the watery world of Mon Calamari and capture one of its leaders, Ackbar, they learned that sometimes procedure just won't work.

The planet was almost entirely covered by water, and its two main species had coped with survival in different ways. The Mon Calamari—who had adopted the name of their world—were air breathers who built tremendous floating cities, while the Quarren were largely water breathers, and preferred to live in the ocean depths. Ackbar was a peaceful man, content to lead the citizens of Mon Calamari's Coral City.

Over time, the Mon Calamari made contact with the Quarren, and the two species began a symbiotic relationship. The Quarren mined the deep-sea ores on the planet, while the Calamari created the civilization's floating cities. Each city had multiple levels, extending both above and below water. The Quarren lived in the lower levels, and the Calamari lived above. While the Quarren swam to move around the planet, the Calamari used wavespeeders to get from city to city, and submersible devices to explore the oceans.

For millennia, the Mon Calamari and Quarren lived peaceful lives. The Calamari developed a highly evolved and civilized culture. Their art, music, literature, and science were all important to them; they eventually developed space travel to explore new worlds and make friends with other civilizations, as they had done with the Quarren. Floating space platforms and spaceship facilities orbited the planet, mirroring life on the surface below.

The first time a Mon Calamari ship met an Imperial ship, the Calamari made overtures of peace and free trade, but the Imperials were more interested in slaves and Mon Calamari technology. They began an invasion, and when the peaceful people protested, Emperor Palpatine ordered the destruction of three of their floating cities. The Emperor wanted to send a clear message across the galaxy as to the fate of all those who opposed his New Order . . . especially the "inferior" alien species.

The plan backfired.

The Mon Calamari began using their technology to create weaponry and battleships. They eventually drove the Empire away, but at great cost to their cities and leadership.

Ackbar had been one of the first Mon Calamari enslaved by the Empire. He was initially taken to be an interpreter and personal servant for a fleet officer on a flagship. Soon after, he was presented as a gift to Grand Moff Tarkin, who was in charge of Oversector Outer, which included almost all of the Outer Rim Territories. Tarkin reported only to the Emperor.

Playing the role of a dutiful slave, Ackbar was able to learn much about the Empire and its military, from its basic command structures to its battle tactics. He studied secret military documents and listened to Tarkin's theories on war and his "rule by fear" doctrine. Ackbar also learned of a Rebellion against the Empire, for Tarkin was always muttering about his new superweapon that would allow him to crush the Rebellion.

As the Grand Moff was en route from the Governor's palace on Eriadu to the completed Death Star, his ship was attacked by Rebels. Following a firefight with Admiral Motti's Star Destroyer, the Rebels escaped with Tarkin's servant, Ackbar.

Pledging his aid to the Rebellion, Ackbar returned to Mon Calamari to help convince his people to support his rescuers. Even as his people began making and designing new weapons and assault ships for the Alliance, Ackbar was looking for even more ways to get involved.

With their salmon-colored skin, webbed fingers, chin-tentacles, and bulbous eyes, Ackbar and his Calamari workers sometimes presented comical pictures, but their sincerity and drive convinced everyone that they represented the "spirit" of the Rebel Alliance.

The main Mon Calamari star cruisers were handcrafted by dedicated technicians and engineers. Most had originally been space liners that were converted into combat starships. Their cylindrical shapes were covered by pods, bulges, and bumps, all of them containing some essential element. The cruisers looked more organic than mechanical, allowing the Calamari to turn their weapons of war into works of art.

Made a commander in the Alliance, Ackbar wanted to create an answer to the Empire's deadly new Nebulon-B frigate, which maintained twenty-four laser batteries, heavy shielding, and two TIE fighter squadrons, which made it more than a match for traditionally lightly armed Rebel starfighters. Ackbar went to the Roche system to deal with a renowned species of brilliant ship designers, the insectoid Verpine. Code-named Shantipole, the project would lead to the development of an oddly shaped, two-crewed B-wing starfighter.

Working with Ackbar and other Calamari, the peaceful Verpine were able to create several prototypes of the B-wing. Despite a betrayal by Salin Glek, Ackbar's Quarren lieutenant, the Empire was unable to capture the new ships. Several days after the B-wings were delivered, Ackbar was promoted to admiral by Alliance leader Mon Mothma.

Following the Battle of Yavin, the Bothans had joined the Alliance at about the same time as the Mon Calamari had. One of their leaders, Borsk Fey'lya, was brought into the power structure of the emerging Alliance, but he didn't like the amphibious Mon Calamarians, and Fey'lya especially didn't like having to compete for power. For his part, though, the peaceful Ackbar did his best to ignore the Bothan, or to work with him when necessary.

Shortly before the Alliance moved to establish Echo Base on Hoth, a bulk freighter in which Ackbar and several of his top technicians were travelling was struck down by Imperials. The Mon Calamari launched escape pods before their ship was destroyed, and ended up stranded on the mist-covered world of Daluuj. Han Solo, Luke Skywalker, Princess Leia Organa, and their droids, R2-D2 and C-3PO, set out on a rescue mission to save Ackbar and his fellow Calamari before the Imperials got to them. With the help of some giant, energy-eating water-worms, the Alliance heroes all escaped Daluuj in the *Millennium Falcon*.

Ackbar began receiving more and more responsibility from Mon Mothma. He became one of her top two advisors, and she made him the commander of the entire Rebel fleet. Although the promotion had been made entirely based on Ackbar's skills and character, it carried much political weight. The Empire had practiced racism, slavery, and genocide against nonhuman species; now the Alliance was not only embracing them, but allowing them positions of great power. The weight on Ackbar's shoulders was great.

When Bothan spies discovered the location of a second Death Star, Ackbar and the other military tacticians developed the plans for a surprise attack on the battle station. General Han Solo would lead a strike team down to the forest moon of Endor to destroy the source of the Death Star's protective energy shields. Meanwhile, General Lando Calrissian would lead the squads of X-wing, Y-wing, A-wing, and B-wing starfighters, and Mon Calamarian battle cruisers against the battle station itself.

Ackbar's plan would have worked except

that the Death Star was already operational, and Solo's team was unable to immediately incapacitate the shields. Several of the Rebel command ships and frigates were destroyed, while Alliance fighter ships had to deal with the Imperial TIEs and Star Destroyers.

Ackbar ordered a withdrawal, but General Calrissian talked him into taking the battle *closer* and destroying the Star Destroyers. Both fervently hoped that Solo's team would succeed down on Endor. A bloody and destructive battle followed, but finally, the Alliance ships were victorious. Wedge Antilles and Lando Calrissian helped destroy the second Death Star, with Emperor Palpatine and Darth Vader on board.

The Empire was severely crippled, but not dead. The day after destroying the second Death Star, Wedge Antilles captured an Imperial drone ship carrying a plea for assistance from the Bakuran system. Admiral Ackbar and Mon Mothma agreed to dispense a strike team to go to the aid of Bakura, which was under attack by the reptilian Ssi-ruuk. Ackbar put Luke in command of a team of five Corellian gunships, Wedge Antilles's Rogue Squadron of X-wings, and a corvette.

The Rebels were victorious at Bakura, and over the years they would aid other planets in need and make many successful attacks on the survivors of the Empire. Ackbar preferred to personally lead important assaults, but this was gradually overtaken by his need to plan defense procedures, and by his responsibilities to the New Republic. He was named commander-in-chief of all New Republic military operations, and he served on the Provisional Council and the ruling Inner Council of the New Republic, helping to forge the new galactic government. Fey'lya's rivalry with Ackbar continued unabated, and meetings of the Councils were often taken up by the debates between the two.

The Alliance established a number of new headquarters prior to settling on a permanent residence. These included bases on

the moon of Endor and the forest planet of Arbra. For a short time, Mothma and Ackbar established a private strike team of the Alliance's most daring heroes, calling it the Senate Interplanetary Intelligence Network—SPIN. The team consisted of Leia Organa, Luke Skywalker, Han Solo, Chewbacca, Lando Calrissian, R2-D2, and C-3PO. Ackbar and Mothma personally assigned them missions.

Ackbar himself aided Luke Skywalker on a mission to Mon Calamari, where they helped save the massive whaladons from rampant hunting and harvesting by Captain Dunwell. The SPIN strike force had a variety of adventures, eventually leading to the discovery—and destruction—of the Lost City of the Jedi. Mon Mothma eventually disbanded the special group as missions of more importance came into place.

Eventually the New Republic Council decided to move its headquarters to Coruscant's Imperial City, once the seat of Emperor Palpatine. Mon Mothma and the others felt it the correct message to send to the galaxy; the Empire was dead and conquered, and the New Republic sat benevolently in its place, headquartered in the Imperial Palace.

While the Provisional Council was trying to deal with its political issues and struggles, the war against the Empire was still skirmishing on the outer edges of the

galaxy—and sometimes in the heart of it. Mothma, Ackbar, Fey'lya, and Leia Organa Solo formed a smaller group, called the Inner Council, that helped provide the immediate, day-to-day decisions needed by the New Republic.

One of the most pressing issues to face the Inner Council was the appearance of Grand Admiral Thrawn and his fleet. Mothma and Ackbar oversaw the battle at Sluis Van shipyards and the resulting battle for control over the *Katana* Dreadnaught fleet, then faced an attack on Coruscant as Thrawn released invisible, "cloaked" asteroids into orbit, stopping Alliance ships from leaving the planet.

In the midst of these attacks, Ackbar was *arrested* and charged with treason. Thrawn had planted false evidence in Ackbar's credit accounts, and Fey'lya had implicated Ackbar for both the credit issues and for supposed military mismanagement at the Battle of Sluis Van. Ackbar was cleared through evidence gathered by a smuggler named Ghent, and he resumed his duties and helped lead the fleet to victory over Thrawn's forces in the battle at the Bilbringi Shipyards.

Soon after Thrawn's defeat, six Imperial Starfleet commanders joined with survivors of the Emperor's Ruling Circle to stage an assault on Coruscant. They succeeded in driving the New Republic away, and recaptured the planet. Later, the New Republic placed their headquarters on the Fifth Moon of Da Soocha in the Cyax system. There, Ackbar and the other Inner Council leaders dealt with the "resurrected" clone of the Emperor and his attacks on Mon Calamari, led by the ghastly World Devastators. Although the Rebels did manage to stop the Devastators, the death toll was high.

Soon after, Ackbar helped plan a New Republic attack on the Imperial centers on Byss. The attack was partially successful, but not before the Da Soocha Pinnacle Base was destroyed by the Emperor-clone's Galaxy Gun. The New Republic had abandoned the base shortly before the attack, and Ackbar and the other leaders relocated again, this time to the abandoned floating space city of Nespis VIII.

Within months the New Republic forces attacked the Imperial City on Coruscant yet again, and succeeded in driving the remnants of the Empire away. The New Republic Council returned to the chambers of the Senate and resumed their attempts at restructuring an intergalactic government.

After the battles against the mad Jedi clone Joruus C'Baoth and the equally mad clones of Emperor Palpatine, Leia and Han realized the danger to which their young, Force-powerful children would be exposed if they remained with their parents at any of the Rebel bases. If someone using the dark side of the Force came near the children, the offspring could be warped permanently.

Admiral Ackbar and Luke scouted out a faraway world called Anoth, which could support life. A heavily guarded facility was constructed in which the woman known as Winter would teach the Solo children and take care of them. No one except Luke, Ackbar, and Winter knew Anoth's location.

Unknown to Ackbar, his chief starship mechanic, a Mon Calamari named Terpfen, was secretly a spy. Terpfen had been tortured by the Imperials, and organic circuitry had been placed into his brain, forcing him to spy for them. He reported to Caridian Imperial Ambassador Furgan.

Terpfen was told to sabotage Ackbar's own modified B-wing fighter. Ackbar took Leia to the windy planet of Vortex, where she planned to meet with the winged Vors. His B-wing malfunctioned and Ackbar crashed the ship into the towering, crystalline Cathedral of the Winds. The Vors' greatest artistic treasure was destroyed, and Ackbar held himself responsible.

Back on Coruscant, Ackbar faced the Council. Terpfen had found nothing wrong with the ship's system, so the blunder was blamed on Ackbar's piloting error. Ackbar resigned his commission, and left for a quiet retirement on Mon Calamari.

He made a quick stop on Anoth to see Winter, not realizing that Terpfen had tracked his ship to betray the planet's location to Furgan. Ackbar returned to Mon Calamari, and promptly disappeared, sequestering himself in a small dwelling in the seatree thickets under the water, where he had lived when he was younger. There he began using his technical knowledge to measure the tectonic disturbances in Mon Calamari's crust.

A short time later, when Admiral Daala attacked the floating cities with her Star Destroyers, Ackbar was called upon to help protect his planet for the third time. His quick thinking and strong tactics saved the day. He used a partially constructed ship, the *Startide*, as a battering ram, driving the ship and its spacedock into the Star Destroyer *Manticore*. Daala's two remaining ships withdrew as Rebel battleships

responded to the attack on Mon Calamari. Despite the recognition of his heroism, Ackbar still chose to remain on his home planet, to help strengthen its defenses.

Weeks later, everything changed. Terpfen had overridden his programming and confessed his hand in the sabotage of Ackbar's ship and the betrayal of Anoth's location. Ackbar, Leia, and Terpfen arrived on Anoth in time to help Winter stop Furgan and his forces from kidnapping the infant Anakin Solo. Ackbar was also able to stop Terpfen before he could kill himself over his betrayals.

Ackbar returned to Coruscant and regained his rank. He also brought the Mon Calamari healer Cilghal to help heal the dying Mon Mothma. A short time later, Admiral Ackbar asked Winter to accompany him to the planet Vortex for the reopening of the Cathedral of the Winds. She expressed her happiness that Ackbar had returned to the Alliance. Since the Solo children had been returned to Coruscant, he in turn, expressed his own pleasure that Winter would no longer be exiled on Anoth.

Ackbar and the white-haired beauty would enjoy each others' company a lot over the coming years, both in their tasks for building the New Republic, and in private. With many more missions and successes in his future, Admiral Ackbar would go down in history as one of the galaxy's greatest military leaders.

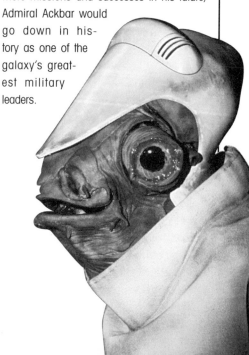

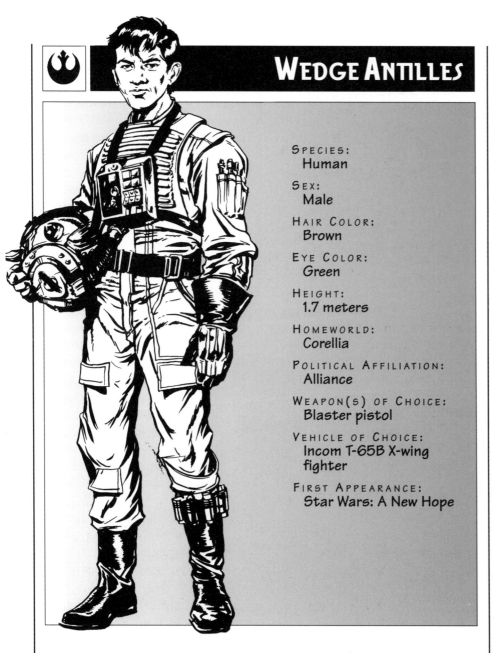

WEDGE ANTILLES

SPECIES:
Human

SEX:
Male

HAIR COLOR:
Brown

EYE COLOR:
Green

HEIGHT:
1.7 meters

HOMEWORLD:
Corellia

POLITICAL AFFILIATION:
Alliance

WEAPON(S) OF CHOICE:
Blaster pistol

VEHICLE OF CHOICE:
Incom T-65B X-wing fighter

FIRST APPEARANCE:
Star Wars: A New Hope

One of the New Republic's most dependable fighter pilots began his service early in the Rebellion, and Wedge Antilles would see more combat time than most seasoned veterans could ever claim.

Wedge's parents managed a fueling depot in outer Gus Treta, a spaceport in the Corellian system. Wedge was in school when he heard the news: his parents had been killed in an explosion caused by a pirate ship fleeing from authorities. His upper division schooling almost complete,

Wedge was left with a huge settlement from the insurance companies, as well as a reward for his part in the indirect disposal of the wanted felons.

Orphaned and alone, Wedge bought a Corellian stock light freighter and tried to start his own legitimate shipping business. In the Corellian system, though, smuggling was the rule, and Wedge was the exception. If he was forced to smuggle, Wedge decided that it would be for something he believed in, so he began smuggling weapons for the Alliance, and eventually got

caught up in the fervor of the Rebellion.

Having learned about mechanics by watching the workers at his father's fueling station, Wedge repaired ships for the Rebels. He also started training in the use of the T65B X-wing fighters, and through simulations and three real battle engagements, became an expert combat pilot. Most of the wingmen who flew with him kidded him about his age, but at sixteen years old, he was already better than most of them.

Wedge was one of the X-wing fighter pilots to fly against the first Death Star. During General Jan Dodonna's debriefing, he expressed his concern over the small size of the target—the battle station's exhaust port. A newcomer, Luke Skywalker, noted that he used to hit womp rats the same size in his T-16 skyhopper on Tatooine. That didn't do much to allay Wedge's fears.

Wedge was teamed up with Skywalker in the X-wing Red Squadron; Wedge was Red Two, Luke was Red Five, Biggs Darklighter was Red Three. When the Death Star came into view, the pilots were shocked. "Look at the size of that thing," Wedge gasped, before Red Leader reprimanded him.

Wedge acquitted himself well in the battle above the Death Star, swooping to the surface to destroy defense towers, and helping blast a TIE fighter that was on the tail of Luke's X-wing. When Red Leader's first strike team was killed on their approach down the Death Star trench, Luke, Biggs, and Wedge started their own run. Luke led, with the other two pilots as wingmen.

Despite evasive maneuvers, Wedge's ship was hit in an attack by Darth Vader and two TIE fighters, forcing him to abort and skim off into space. Then, Biggs's X-wing was destroyed in a blast from Vader's ship. Wedge watched from space as Luke Skywalker completed his run alone. Amazingly, his missiles did find their mark, and the Death Star was destroyed.

Wedge joined Luke over the next several

years as part of Rogue Squadron, which consisted of some of the most elite young pilots the Alliance had to offer. When the Alliance moved its base to the icy planet of Hoth, Wedge and Rogue Squadron learned how to handle combat snowspeeders, custom-modified Incom T-47 repulsorlift speeders. The training proved very useful, as the Imperials eventually attacked Hoth, launching All Terrain Armored Transports—AT-ATs—toward the Rebels' Echo Base.

During the battle, many of Rogue Squadron tried their best, but the twelve two-person snowspeeders lost many of their gunners in the battle. Wedge was backed up by his own gunner, Wes Janson. They were the first to successfully trip a walker, causing it to explode.

Wedge's snowspeeder was hit in the ensuing battle, and he and Janson had to abandon it. Neither was seriously injured. Wedge and Luke both arrived back at the base and loaded supplies into their X-wings. Janson piloted a Y-wing, and the ships escorted one of the last transports, piloted by their friend Tarrin, from Echo Base. Wedge and Janson put into use a tactic called the "Tallon split," which, in conjunction with Luke's hidden attack from underneath the transport, allowed them all to escape the fire of an orbiting Star Destroyer. Luke peeled off and agreed to

meet them later at the rendezvous point.

With Luke off on missions for the Alliance—including one to rescue Han Solo—Wedge assumed control of Rogue Squadron, finding more top-notch pilots to replace those lost on Hoth. He was promoted to commander, and his squadron was directly attached to protect the Headquarters Frigate. His squadron chose to continue to fly X-wings, passing up the B- and A-wings for the ships they knew best. Wedge named Rogue Squadron "Red Group," harkening back to the battle against the first Death Star. He and Luke were the only survivors, and it seemed a fitting testament to the sacrifice of the other pilots.

When the attack against the second Death Star was planned, two leaders were set to work under Admiral Ackbar's direct orders: General Calrissian as Gold Leader, and Wedge Antilles as Red Leader. Ready to assault the battle station, the Rebel fleet found themselves having to engage Imperial fighters above the moon of Endor. Until the Death Star's shields went down, no one could approach it. In the battle, Wedge and his team helped take out the Star Destroyer that functioned as the main communications ship. He also helped stop the TIE fighters from destroying a medical frigate.

Once the shields were down, the Rebels were freed to make their attack runs. Wedge went down the main reactor shaft first,

followed by the *Millennium Falcon*, several other X-wings, and a mob of enemy TIE fighters.

Both Wedge and the *Falcon* made it to the reactor core. Wedge targeted the power regulator in the north tower, launching concussion missiles, and Lando torpedoed the main reactor. Then the two ships had to retrace their perilous flight through the Death Star superstructure, even as it collapsed and exploded around them. With milliseconds to spare, Wedge and the *Falcon* escaped the shaft into open space. Behind them, the battle station blew up.

Wedge was a hero to the Alliance, but while the Empire had fallen, the battles continued. The day after the destruction of the Death Star, Wedge Antilles joined a patrol above the forest moon of Endor. He intercepted an ancient Imperial drone ship, accidentally activating its self-destruct mechanism. To stop the sequence, he had to thrust his hand in between two crystals before they could touch and explode. Luke Skywalker helped rescue his

friend; although the Corellian lost a lot of blood and oxygen, he was able to recuperate in the bacta tank at the Med Center.

The ancient drone ship contained a message from an Imperial base at the far-off world of Bakura. The world was being invaded by the reptilian Ssi-ruuk. Wedge accompanied Luke's strike force to Bakura, leading his twelve-person Rogue Squadron, and aided in the battle against the Ssi-ruuk fleet.

Wedge turned down promotion after promotion, preferring to stay with the Rogues, and Admiral Ackbar recognized the importance of the group. The elite group received their orders directly from Ackbar's office in the New Republic Provisional Council. Besides launching strikes on leftover Imperial strongholds, Rogue Squadron also performed elite escort duties for ambassadors such as Mon Mothma or Princess Leia Organa Solo.

Five years after the Battle of Endor, Wedge and his Rogue Squadron were pulled into the battle for the Sluis Van shipyards, facing Grand Admiral Thrawn's forces. The reappearance of the dreaded Imperial leader led to a host of battles and dangerous escort missions for the Rogues, including a deadly firefight for possession of the legendary *Katana* Dreadnaught fleet. During that battle, Wedge and his crew helped destroy the *Peremptory*, one of the most powerful surviving Star Destroyers in the Imperial fleet.

The Rogues would later be involved in pitched battles near Filve and at the Bilbringi Imperial Shipyards. With the help of a coalition of smugglers, Rogue Squadron and the other Rebel fighters were victorious at Bilbringi. Wedge's tactics and leadership were impeccable during the battle.

In the year following Thrawn's defeat, Wedge finally accepted a promotion to general, even though he knew it would separate him from Rogue Squadron some of the time.

He did retain rights to command his old squadron when he wanted to, though. Wedge and Lando Calrissian—himself recently reinstated as a general in the New Republic—were given command of the captured Star Destroyers *Liberator* and *Emancipator*.

At this point the Empire had retaken Coruscant from the Alliance, but various

factions were warring with each other, so Wedge, Lando, and Luke took the *Liberator* to Coruscant in an attempt to finish off the Imperials. They ended up crashing planetside, with only Luke's Jedi powers saving their lives. The Rebels holed up in Imperial City until help arrived in the familiar shape of the *Millennium Falcon*.

The crises weren't over though. Back at the Alliance's Pinnacle Base on the Fifth Moon of Da Soocha, Wedge and Lando were assigned to take the *Emancipator* to Mon Calamari to help fight the Empire's World Devastators. Although they brought full complements of X-wing fighters and

speeder transports with them, Lando and Wedge soon lost their second Star Destroyer. A redirected World Devastator began to eat their ship, and they ejected in escape pods. They were picked up by the frigate *Antares Six*, where they watched as reinforcements arrived, some flying in the new E-wings. On board the *Falcon*, R2-D2 used stolen control codes to immobilize the Devastators. The New Republic forces were victorious, but at great cost to the environs of Mon Calamari.

Months later, Wedge and Lando commanded a military strike at Byss, the current seat of the Empire's power. They and their troops stowed away aboard a set of S-1 Viper Automadon war droids, which were conveyed onto Byss by unknowing Imperials. The Republic heroes attacked, but the Imperials retaliated with powerful turbolasers and then released chrysalis beasts, which would overcome the Viper Automadons.

Wedge and Lando's troops were rescued by a trio of smuggler's ships. Next stop was New Alderaan, where they were to help halt the invading Imperials who threatened the lives of Han and Leia's children. Finally, the smugglers and assorted Republic heroes and troops arrived at the Auril system, where the abandoned floating space city of Nespis VIII was serving as a temporary base.

Within months, the Alliance again attacked the Imperial City on Coruscant, and succeeded in driving away the remnants of the Empire. Wedge again commanded Rogue Squadron for the final attack on Coruscant.

During the cleanup of Imperial City, Wedge took a more grounded commission. Commanding a crew of two hundred workers and four multistory construction droids, Wedge's demolition team made good progress. They also found an old Imperial interrogation center. Wedge summoned Luke, Leia, and Ackbar, and the four of them made a surprising discovery: holographic paddles that allowed anyone to measure the aura of Force users! This would aid Luke's search for Jedi students immensely, and in the initial tests, Wedge confirmed what he always suspected: that he had no affinity for the Force.

When he got a little crazy from all the demolition, Wedge decided to pilot a transport carrier filled with colonization specialists, sociologists, survival instructors, and lots of supplies and shelters. They picked up the Eol Sha survivors and transported them to Dantooine, helping them start life anew. Directly afterward, he took a supply ship to Yavin Four, and visited for a short time with Luke.

He shared the news from Coruscant with his Jedi friend, also discussing the new assignment he faced; Wedge Antilles was to be scientist Qwi Xux's bodyguard and escort. She had recently fled the Empire and joined the Alliance, and Wedge quickly became impressed by Qwi's intelligence and honesty, even as he was smitten by her naïveté, her beauty, and her ethereal nature. He supported her when she went to the New Republic Assembly, urging them to dispose of the deadly superweapon known as the Sun Crusher, which she had helped to design.

Kyp Durron was drafted to fly the Sun Crusher to Yavin, accompanied by Wedge and Qwi in an armored Alliance transport. As the trio watched the deadly weapon disappear into the heart of the gas giant Yavin, Wedge felt great relief. Soon thereafter, they dropped Kyp off on the Yavin Four moon, where he was to begin his Jedi training with Luke.

Wedge and Qwi Xux went to Vortex to watch the repair work on the crystal Cathedral of the Winds. Wedge worked with the cleanup crews while Qwi walked through the glassy debris, watching the lacy-winged Vors as they navigated the strong winds. When Qwi played music on

one of the broken crystals, a Vors leader confronted her. There was to be no more music until the cathedral was finished.

Wanting to help her find peace, Wedge took Qwi to the undeveloped paradise world of Ithor. There, they were surprised to find themselves greeted by Momaw Nadon, the "Hammerhead" Herd leader of the floating city *Tafanda Bay*. At Mon Mothma's request, he did everything he could to make their stay a pleasant and comfortable one. Over the next week, Wedge and Qwi explored the beautiful world, sight-seeing, watching Ithor's four moons rise, and exploring both the planet and each other. Tentatively, they began to fall in love.

The morning after he had finally gotten up the nerve to kiss Qwi, Wedge was horrified to find her slumped on the floor in her room. Filled with the dark side of the Force, Kyp Durron had visited her the night before and filleted her memories, removing anything that could be remotely connected to the Sun Crusher or the other weapons she had created at the Maw Installation. His mindwipe had erased most of her life.

Returning to Coruscant, Wedge asked to lead the strike team that was going to raid the Maw Installation. He took control of the escort frigate *Yavaris*, and brought Qwi Xux

along with him. They had been working to restore her memories, but it was difficult. Wedge hoped that the trip to the Maw would help. Even without her memories, Qwi's brilliant computations, as well as data tapes from the Sun Crusher, provided the fleet with a clear path inside.

Inside the Maw, the installation's personnel did not put up much of a fight. Wedge and Qwi Xux followed Page's Commandos and the other Rebels into the installation, overrunning it quickly. But then the mission went awry in almost every way possible. Maw director Tol Sivron stole a Death Star prototype and exited the Maw, returning later in the heat of battle. Meanwhile, Admiral Daala had returned to the Maw to destroy it with her only surviving Star Destroyer, the *Gorgon*. Daala pressed into attack, using turbolasers and TIE fighters to fight the raiding Rebel forces and the installation's own gamma assault shuttles, piloted by escaped Wookiee slaves.

Qwi was unable to retrieve vital weapons plans from the installation's computer system, and as the battle intensified and the reactor cores began to shut down, Wedge and the other Rebels knew their time was running out. Wedge, Qwi, Luke, and Rebel troops escaped off the installation in a transport shuttle minutes before the reactor asteroid went critical. They traveled out of the Maw while behind them, it appeared that Daala had guided her *Gorgon* into the destructive explosion.

Later, Qwi and Wedge attended the reopening of the Cathedral of the Winds on Vortex. With Wedge's support and love, Qwi would build a new life and new memories.

Wedge continues to work diligently with General Garm Bel Iblis on air defense, and with Admiral Ackbar, General Carlist Rieekan, and General Jan Dodonna in Alliance High Command. Having survived and triumphed at so many battles, General Wedge Antilles and his Rogue Squadron will likely have many top-flight adventures for years to come.

BODO BAAS

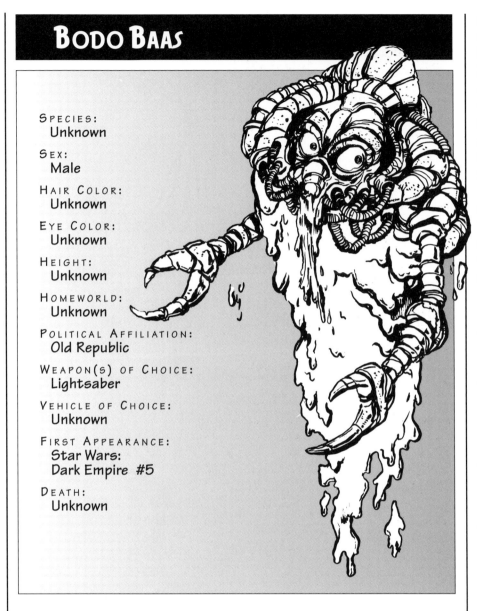

SPECIES:
Unknown

SEX:
Male

HAIR COLOR:
Unknown

EYE COLOR:
Unknown

HEIGHT:
Unknown

HOMEWORLD:
Unknown

POLITICAL AFFILIATION:
Old Republic

WEAPON(S) OF CHOICE:
Lightsaber

VEHICLE OF CHOICE:
Unknown

FIRST APPEARANCE:
Star Wars:
Dark Empire #5

DEATH:
Unknown

Bodo Baas was part of the Jedi group that lived in the Adega system, six hundred years before the destruction of the first Death Star. Eventually becoming a Jedi Master, Bodo inherited one of the several Jedi Holocrons passed down through generations. As had other Masters before him, Bodo recorded his stories and those of the other Jedi in the Holocron.

The glowing cube of the Holocron could be activated by the touch of someone in tune with the Force. Several Holocrons existed, each with its own interactive "Gatekeeper." Bodo Baas became the Gatekeeper of his Holocron.

During the great purge of the Jedi, Emperor Palpatine had Bodo Baas executed, and the Holocron in the Jedi's belongings eventually passed into his grasp. Although Palpatine was able to unlock many of the mysteries of the Holocron, deeper levels were reserved only for those Jedi Knights using the light side of the Force.

Six years after the destruction of the second Death Star, Princess Leia Organa Solo gained Bodo Baas's Jedi Holocron when she confronted the clone of Emperor Palpatine, on Byss. She and several other Rebels escaped Byss on the *Millennium Falcon*, while her brother, Luke Skywalker, stayed behind to help destroy Palpatine's clone and all his auxiliary clone bodies. Aboard the *Falcon*, Leia activated the Holocron, listening to Baas's version of the tale of the corrupted Jedi Ulic Qel-Droma.

Later, Leia activated the Holocron again, asking Bodo to tell her of Skywalker's future. The ancient Jedi Master revealed that although the Force allowed glimpses of the future, this one was cloaked in mists and shadows.

Bodo Baas had an ancestor who was a previous Holocron Gatekeeper and an early Jedi named Vodo-Siosk Baas. Vodo-Siosk had been the Jedi Master who trained Exar Kun and many others. When Kun betrayed and killed Vodo-Siosk, the Master's spirit became one with the Force, and his stories became a part of the Jedi Holocrons. Vodo-Siosk's specific Holocron was used thousands of years later by Luke Skywalker on the moon of Yavin Four, but Exar Kun's spirit, trapped on the planet, destroyed the cube. Shortly thereafter, Vodo-Siosk's spirit joined with Skywalker and his Jedi initiates to bind and destroy Exar Kun forever.

It is unknown whether or not Princess Leia's Holocron, with Master Bodo Baas as Gatekeeper, is still in the hands of the Alliance. Even if it is not, as long as there are other Holocrons in the galaxy, the wisdom and prophecies of the Jedi will never be lost.

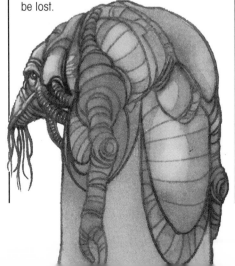

PONDA BABA/DR. EVAZAN

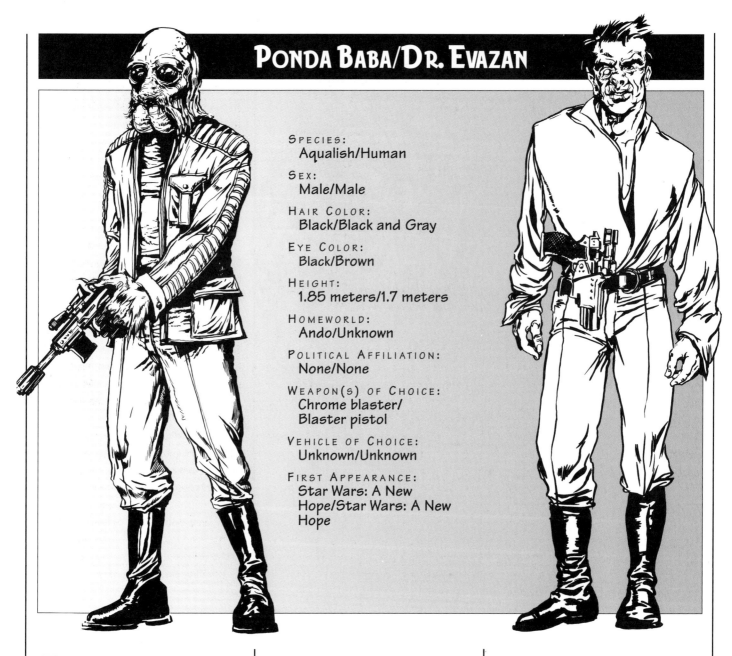

SPECIES:
Aqualish/Human

SEX:
Male/Male

HAIR COLOR:
Black/Black and Gray

EYE COLOR:
Black/Brown

HEIGHT:
1.85 meters/1.7 meters

HOMEWORLD:
Ando/Unknown

POLITICAL AFFILIATION:
None/None

WEAPON(S) OF CHOICE:
Chrome blaster/
Blaster pistol

VEHICLE OF CHOICE:
Unknown/Unknown

FIRST APPEARANCE:
Star Wars: A New
Hope/Star Wars: A New
Hope

The crimes of Dr. Evazan and Ponda Baba are well known throughout the galaxy. The mad doctor and his partner have managed to survive for years with their murderous ways, despite one very close call with a Jedi.

Ponda Baba was an Aqualish smuggler and pirate. Like all of his tusked people back on Ando, he was antisocial, obnoxious, and aggressive. Belonging to a group that comprised only ten percent of Ando's inhabitants, Baba was of the Quara race, a group of fingered Aqualish that survived in the swamps and wetlands of the planet.

Baba roamed the spaceways, robbing and murdering. When some of his victims posted a bounty, hunter Jodo Kast took it. While repairing his Corellian light freighter, Baba was surprised by Kast, but got away.

Dr. Evazan is an insane medical practitioner, fond of "creative surgery." He likes to take things apart and put them back together differently, preferring the victims to scream. When he applied to the Imperial Academy on Caridia, the Imperials had him institutionalized on the Delarian Prison Planet. Evazan easily escaped to the Hindsaar system.

There, he bought a forged "personal surgeon" license and set up a private practice. Practice didn't make perfect in this case, as hundreds of his patients ended up with horrible scarring, and several dozen died. Evazan moved from system to system, using various aliases, including "Dr. Cornelius" and "Roofoo." Over the years, he also engaged in slaving, assassination, illegal cyborging, and many other crimes.

More than a dozen systems—including Anoat—posted death-sentence notices for

Evazan. Victims and their families have put out a million-credit bounty on him, but few have even come close to collecting. Jodo Kast almost caught Evazan in the Corellian system, but only succeeded in heavily scarring his face with a blaster shot. The doctor's life was saved by Ponda Baba and a well-timed bolt from his freighter.

Although Baba himself had planned to turn Evazan in, he realized how valuable the human could be. The two became partners in crime. They traveled together to Tatooine, where they often took on spice-smuggling runs for Jabba the Hutt. While looking for trouble, the pair would often spend time at the Mos Eisley cantina.

On one fateful day at the cantina, Ponda Baba picked the wrong person to harass. Drunk, Baba shoved young Luke Skywalker. When Luke tried to smooth matters, Dr. Evazan threatened him, bragging that he had the death sentence in twelve systems.

"I'll be careful," Luke said.

"You'll be dead," Evazan snarled, not noticing the brown-robed old man who had appeared next to the young farm boy. The man, Obi-Wan Kenobi, attempted to calm Baba and Evazan. When the duo attacked anyway, Obi-Wan ignited his lightsaber, slicing Evazan's chest and cutting off Baba's right arm at the elbow joint.

Baba and Evazan fled Mos Eisley and Tatooine and became lost in the endless spaceways of the galaxy. Surgical mutilations began showing up in victims on raided merchant ships, rumors of the mad doctor and his Aqualish friend abounded.

Evazan attempted to graft a bionic arm onto Ponda Baba, but botched the surgery and was soon on the run from his onetime partner.

Baba tracked Evazan back to Mos Eisley, where he had set up a small illegal cyborging operation called the Cutting Edge Clinic. Evazan was now using the name "Dr. Cornelius," but there was no disguising the massively scarred, squinty face.

Ponda forced Evazan to promise him a top-of-the-line bionic arm, and the doctor

gave him a more functional temporary arm until a better one could be produced. An uneasy alliance was formed again, with Ponda acting as Evazan's bodyguard.

The two returned to Ando, where Evazan moved into a castle keep on an isolated isle. There, the doctor took in a deadly, gelatinous Meduza as his pet watch animal. Somehow, Evazan convinced the Andoan senate to give him research grants for his promised medical breakthroughs.

When a senator visited to check up on the progress, Evazan took him to his laboratory. He had modified an Imperial transmogrify unit normally used for reprogramming droids; now it theoretically could transfer the electronic elements of the mind from body to body, effectively giving the mind immortality.

While the senator watched, shocked, Evazan stunned a handsome young human and brought him to the labs. Evazan hoped to transfer his own mind into this new, healthy body, but the transfer machine still needed to be tested, and Ponda wanted to be the subject. If the doctor could put Ponda's mind into that of the hapless Andoan senator, Baba would get his arm back, and governmental power as well.

Strapping the two Aqualish in, Evazan made the transfer. While he waited for the "new" Ponda Baba to regain conscious-

ness, the doctor went to look at the young human body whose mind he would soon replace with his own. He found the stunned "man" was wearing a holoshroud, and that the human in his keep was a bounty hunter named Gurion Silizzar, who had an armed thermal detonator in his hand.

Seven members of the hunter's family had been destroyed by Evazan's experiments, and he meant to exact his revenge. Gurion took the doctor to the roof, where his mother's ship was to touch down. Evazan's pet Meduza attacked the hunter, allowing the doctor to disarm his foe. Gurion fell off the tower to his death, and Evazan barely caught hold of the rooftop edge.

Footsteps neared the edge, and Evazan was surprised to see his grudging partner. But the transfer had put the senator into Ponda's body. The senator set the thermal detonator and walked away. As Gurion's friends neared in their ship, the top of the castle exploded.

Had the Silizzar family stayed, they would have witnessed Dr. Evazan extract himself from a gooey mass. The Meduza had cushioned him as he dropped from the tower just before the explosion.

Ponda Baba was missing, but Dr. Evazan was buoyed by hope. His device had worked—after a fashion—and there would doubtless be a next time!

BARADA

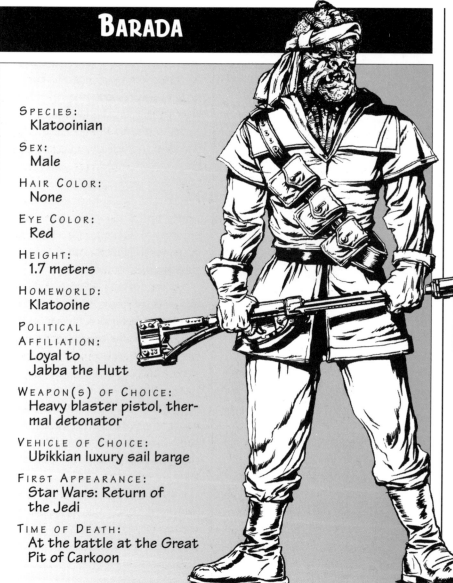

SPECIES:
Klatooinian

SEX:
Male

HAIR COLOR:
None

EYE COLOR:
Red

HEIGHT:
1.7 meters

HOMEWORLD:
Klatooine

POLITICAL AFFILIATION:
Loyal to Jabba the Hutt

WEAPON(S) OF CHOICE:
Heavy blaster pistol, thermal detonator

VEHICLE OF CHOICE:
Ubikkian luxury sail barge

FIRST APPEARANCE:
Star Wars: Return of the Jedi

TIME OF DEATH:
At the battle at the Great Pit of Carkoon

One of the most loyal and hardworking creatures in Jabba the Hutt's palace was Barada, a Klatooinan. His loyalty would last until his death at the hands of the Rebellion's greatest heroes.

On Klatooine, parents demanded respect. Barada, a disrespectful son, was sold into indentured servitude to a garage owner. That same owner lost his business to Jabba over a game of sabacc—a game Jabba had rigged, although no one would accuse him of it. Barada, the brown-skinned, leathery Klatooinian with the skull crest, was now Jabba's, along with the garage.

Barada had been using his earnings to buy his freedom, and was only 2,000 credits short when Jabba took over his contract. Recognizing Barada's incredible mechanical talents, Jabba devised a way to keep Barada indentured forever—he charged the Klatooinian the exact same amount for room and board as he was paying him. Since Barada couldn't get any outside work, he was not able to pay off his contract.

Jabba put Barada in charge of his repulsorpool, taking care of the different vehicles that the Hutt and his workers used. Barada serviced the repulsor sleds that allowed Jabba personal mobility, as well as landspeeders and desert skiffs. The biggest vehicle he maintained was Jabba's huge Ubikkian luxury sail barge.

Barada was largely a loner, but he got along well with Ephant Mon. The hulking beast confided in the mechanic and sought his advice. Since Ephant was Jabba's behind-the-scenes spy, watching for conspiracies or betrayals, Barada was one of the more well-informed denizens of Jabba's palace.

When Jabba had captured Han Solo, Chewbacca, and the Jedi Luke Skywalker, he decided to throw them to the Sarlacc in the Great Pit of Carkoon. Barada and several others loaded the trio of prisoners onto a sand skiff.

Jabba, though, had underestimated the Jedi. The young man freed himself and his friends with his shining emerald lightsaber. Barada was the first one killed in the fight that followed, his body falling into the mouth of the Sarlacc. In death, Barada was finally free of Jabba the Hutt.

BOLLUX/BLUE MAX

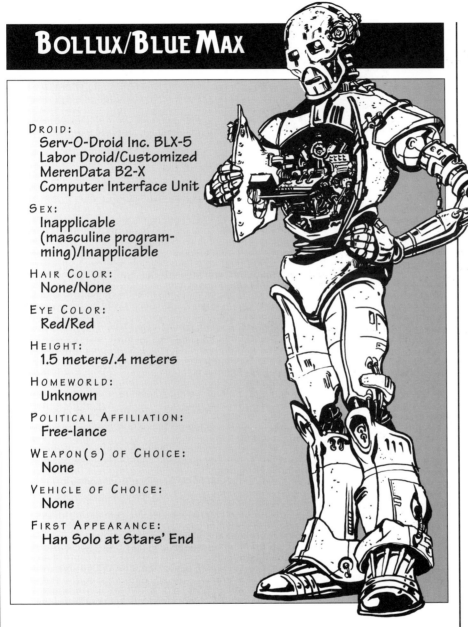

DROID:
Serv-O-Droid Inc. BLX-5
Labor Droid/Customized
MerenData B2-X
Computer Interface Unit

SEX:
Inapplicable
(masculine program-
ming)/Inapplicable

HAIR COLOR:
None/None

EYE COLOR:
Red/Red

HEIGHT:
1.5 meters/.4 meters

HOMEWORLD:
Unknown

POLITICAL AFFILIATION:
Free-lance

WEAPON(S) OF CHOICE:
None

VEHICLE OF CHOICE:
None

FIRST APPEARANCE:
Han Solo at Stars' End

Although they could function autono-mously, the droids Bollux and Blue Max were symbiotically linked. Both had personality programs allowing them to feel emotions, especially in the times they served with Han Solo, and his partner, Chewbacca.

Bollux was a century-old BLX-5 heavy-industrial droid who was activated at the Fondor shipyards. Through a series of coin-cidences and omissions, BLX-5 never had frequent memory wipes like other droids. This allowed BLX-5 to develop a more com-plex personality.

Via structural modifications and system upgrades, his personality continued to evolve. He was pleasant and performed excellently. BLX-5 worked for the Republic's military constructing trenches and forti-fications, then in a heavy-gravity mining colony, before he became obsolete and was sold off.

BLX-5 ended up in the service of the outlaw tech, Doc, on his asteroid base in the Corporate Sector. Doc's daughter, Jessa, constantly upgraded his subsystems, and gave BLX-5 the nickname of "Bollux."

As the Empire arose, the Corporate Sector was largely untouched, but that didn't stop Imperial technology from showing up. Doc got his hands on a stolen advanced computer system, a cube that had more memory and systems than most starship computers.

The minicomputer was colored a multi-layered blue, and Doc called it "Blue Max." It had several protrusions and telescoping appendages, with a red photoreceptor mounted on top. Doc reprogrammed Blue Max with a new per-sonality—perky, chipper, and somewhat obtrusive. It contrasted well with Bollux's slow, measured drawl.

As Blue Max was limited in its ability to move, Doc and Jessa installed it in Bollux's chest cavity. Bollux could open his plas-tron chest cavity, exposing the little computer, and, if needed, could remove Blue Max as a separate unit.

Doc disappeared, and Jessa hired the smuggler Han Solo to find him, insisting that Solo take the two droids along. They aided him greatly on the mission, which ended in near disaster at the Stars' End Penal Facility on Mytus VII.

Bollux, who had long ago become a "free" droid, chose to remain with Solo. Blue Max came with him, although both still planned to return to Doc and Jessa. The droids aided Solo when he was blackmailed into accepting a slaving run from a slaver named Zlarb, and eventually helped Corporate Sector Assistant Auditor General Fiolla to catch the leader of the slavery ring. They also proved themselves invaluable when Solo and an old friend, Badure, tried to find the long-lost Xim treasure ship called *Queen of Ranroon.*

Bollux and Blue Max stayed with Solo for many other adventures, yet when the Corellian ventured back into the Outer Rim and into Imperial territory, the two droids did not accompany him. Their fate is unknown.

BOSSK

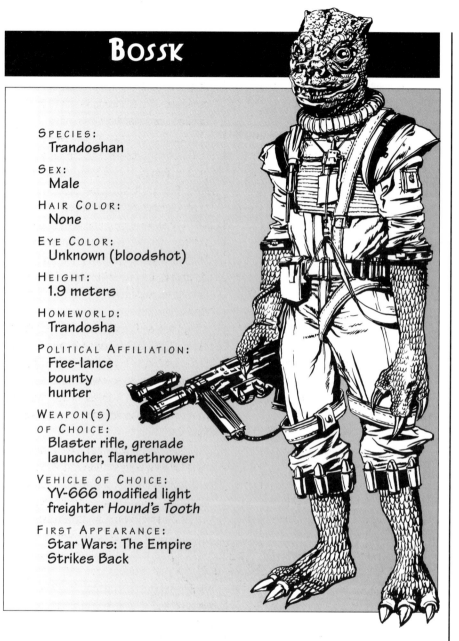

SPECIES:
Trandoshan

SEX:
Male

HAIR COLOR:
None

EYE COLOR:
Unknown (bloodshot)

HEIGHT:
1.9 meters

HOMEWORLD:
Trandosha

POLITICAL AFFILIATION:
Free-lance bounty hunter

WEAPON(S) OF CHOICE:
Blaster rifle, grenade launcher, flamethrower

VEHICLE OF CHOICE:
YV-666 modified light freighter *Hound's Tooth*

FIRST APPEARANCE:
Star Wars: The Empire Strikes Back

Although his species hates Wookiees, the reptilian bounty hunter named Bossk hates one Wookiee in particular. Chewbacca and his Corellian friend Han Solo have humiliated Bossk too many times, and he means one day to have his revenge.

Bossk is a Trandoshan, a three-toed, three-fingered reptilian. Like the rest of his species, he has the ability to regenerate lost limbs and can see in the dark by using the portion of his eyes that responds to infrared light. His home planet is in the same solar system as Kashyyyk, the Wookiee world. Bossk hates the hairy beasts, as do most of the Trandoshans.

The Wookiees owed much of their pain to the Trandoshans. The reptiles used to hunt them, skinning them for their pelts. But the worst transgression came when a Trandoshan dignitary convinced the Empire to use Wookiees as their slave labor. After the Empire subjugated, enslaved, and occupied much of Kashyyyk, the Trandoshans offered to hunt down any Wookiees that had escaped.

When his liege lord suggested he become a bounty hunter who specialized in Wookiee captures and kills, Bossk was more than happy to do so. He outfitted himself with protective body armor and a variety of weapons. His favorite weapon was his blaster rifle, which hung from an elaborate sling fastened around his neck and under his left arm.

Bossk gained great fame for his success in hunting Wookiees, but his most wanted target persistently refused to present himself. A giant named Chewbacca—allied with a Corellian smuggler named Han Solo—had gained a high amount of respect in the galaxy's underworld, and Bossk decided to bring him down. Meanwhile, he continued the hunts, and in addition to the many Wookiees he trapped and killed, he made twelve captures, delivering eight to their enemies alive.

Finally, Bossk got his shot at Chewbacca. He had heard news that a group of renegade Wookiees had set up a safe colony on Gandolo IV, a remote Outer Rim world. The Trandoshan went to the Imperial governor of the sector, to be paid in advance, and then he armed himself for the trip to Gandolo IV. There, he found his prey.

Chewbacca was helping the small group of Wookiees settle on the rocky moon. Bossk and his thugs surrounded the Wookiee camp, outnumbering and easily capturing the poorly armed creatures. Bossk had little time to gloat over his victory, though, as Chewbacca was not alone. Han Solo had dropped his copilot on Gandolo IV, then he visited an old girlfriend in a nearby system. Now he returned, the *Millennium Falcon*'s scanners picking up the bounty-hunter ships even before he got in visual range.

Solo dove the *Falcon* toward the planet, catching Bossk and his thugs by surprise, as they had the Wookiees. Solo flew in low over the Wookiee colony, buzzing the hunters and strafing the ground with laser fire. He couldn't hit the bounty hunters full on, as they had the bound Wookiees in their midst.

Intending to pursue the *Falcon*, Bossk and his thugs boarded their own ship, leaving two guards behind. But Han Solo had

other plans. As soon as the entry ramp was raised on Bossk's ship, Han pulled the *Falcon* directly above it, lowered the landing gear, and touched down directly on top of the other ship!

The hunter's craft buckled under the strain, its own landing gear caving in, its hydraulics shot, and its interiors sparking and exploding. Bossk's people tried in vain to get the emergency hatches open. Meanwhile, Chewbacca and the other Wookiees broke free of their binders and overcame the two guards.

Chewbacca and Solo agreed to help the Wookiees find a new, safe colony, refusing to kill the humiliated Bossk before they left.

The hunters finally freed themselves from the crushed shell that had been their ship; it had taken them days to cut their way out with blasters and a few hand torches. A week later, the group was picked up by a small out-world hauler carrying a load of nerf manure.

Years later, Bossk would get another chance at the Wookiee and the brash Corellian. Shortly before the Battle of Hoth, Boba Fett gathered several fellow bounty hunters, including Bossk, Dengar, and a newer hunter named Skorr, to find Han Solo.

They captured him, along with Luke Skywalker and Chewbacca, aboard the pirate Raskar's ship. Bringing the Rebels to the planet Ord Mantell, the hunters were taken by surprise when Luke used his Force powers to engineer the trio's escape.

When Darth Vader put out an open call for bounty hunters to find the *Millennium Falcon*, Bossk immediately went to the Super Star Destroyer *Executor*. There, he found he had competition from five other bounty hunters: Boba Fett, IG-88, Dengar, Zuckuss, and 4-LOM. Thinking he had the inside track on where the *Falcon* was located, Bossk took off with some temporary partners—bounty hunters who hadn't made Vader's cut.

Much later, Bossk found out that Boba Fett had indeed succeeded in tracking the *Falcon* and in procuring the carbon-frozen body of Han Solo to deliver to Jabba the Hutt. Chewbacca had escaped, though, aided by the Baron Administrator of Bespin's Cloud City.

Following the Alliance's daring mission to rescue Han Solo on Tatooine, Bossk and IG-88 moved on to the hunter's world of Keyorin, where they accepted bounty from the small-time crime boss, Drebble, for Lando Calrissian's head. Coincidentally, Lando had accompanied Han and Chewbacca to Keyorin. A confrontation soon followed, but the Alliance heroes were victorious yet again.

Now fifty-eight standard years old, Bossk is willing to sacrifice Chewbacca's pelt for a quick kill if he ever sees the Wookiee again. Meanwhile, there is a whole galaxy of bounties to pursue, and Bossk is just the Trandoshan to collect.

C-3PO

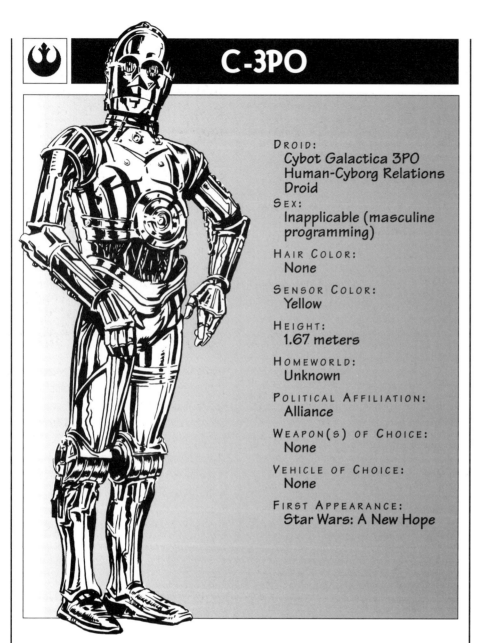

DROID:
Cybot Galactica 3PO Human-Cyborg Relations Droid

SEX:
Inapplicable (masculine programming)

HAIR COLOR:
None

SENSOR COLOR:
Yellow

HEIGHT:
1.67 meters

HOMEWORLD:
Unknown

POLITICAL AFFILIATION:
Alliance

WEAPON(S) OF CHOICE:
None

VEHICLE OF CHOICE:
None

FIRST APPEARANCE:
Star Wars: A New Hope

For all his prissy manners and compulsive odds-quoting, C-3PO is about as self-aware as a droid can get. Perpetually paired with a brash astromech droid, he and his partner, R2-D2, make up the Alliance's most famous droid team.

C-3PO is a Cybot Galactica 3PO Human-Cyborg Relations Droid. He was activated 112 years before his adventures with the Rebel Alliance, and his first job was said to be programming binary load lifters. A protocol droid whose main functions are etiquette and translation, he is outfitted with a TranLang Communication module, and is fluent in over six million galactic languages. These range from the obvious and common dialects to obscure and archaic languages from forgotten systems.

He was designed to work closely with humans, his form and speech mirroring theirs in most ways. His voice is pleasant, with a slightly clipped accent and a precise tone that always somehow suggests the edge of panic.

Threepio has apparently been fitted with extensive personality modules in his AA-1 VerboBrain, allowing him to experience emotions and feelings almost as much as the humans and aliens he interacts with. Indeed, he seems to take unusual pleasure in worrying, complaining, whining, and arguing. His two favorite topics of discussion are how difficult his life is, and how much trouble Artoo has caused him. Although his creativity circuits were designed with parameters to assure accurate translations, the lack of periodic memory wipes has enabled Threepio to develop his talent for interpretation and embellishments more fully than most protocol droids.

C-3PO is bipedal, with a largely gold-colored body, though for some unexplained reason, his right leg is silver from the knee joint to the tip of the foot. He is equipped with two visual photoreceptors and audio sensors, olfactory sensors, a vocabulator speech/sound system, energy transducers, and pelvic servomotors. Broadband antenna receivers allow him to communicate with similiarly-equipped droids, and to receive transmissions. Because of his elaborate multijointed construction, Threepio requires frequent lubrication baths to keep his locomotion systems operating efficiently.

C-3PO has long been paired with a tripodal utility astromech droid named R2-D2. Artoo is designed to operate in deep

R2-D2

DROID:
Industrial Automaton R2-Series Astromech Droid

SEX:
Inapplicable (masculine programming)

HAIR COLOR:
None

SENSOR COLOR:
Red

HEIGHT:
.96 meters

HOMEWORLD:
Unknown

POLITICAL AFFILIATION:
Alliance

WEAPON(S) OF CHOICE:
Small arc welder, small buzz saw

VEHICLE OF CHOICE:
Incom T-65B X-wing fighter

FIRST APPEARANCE:
Star Wars: A New Hope

space, interfacing with fighter craft and computer systems to augment the capabilities of ships and their pilots. He monitors and diagnoses flight performance, maps and stores hyperspace data, and pinpoints technical errors or faulty computer coding. He is also well versed in starship repair for hundreds of styles of spacecraft.

He converses in an information-dense, low-redundancy electronic language that sounds to the untrained ear like beeps, boops, chirps, and whistles. Although he can understand most forms of human speech, R2-D2 must have his own communications interpreted by another droid or computers.

Artoo has a domed head, which can rotate 360 degrees. The dome has infrared receptors, electromagnetic-field sensors, a register readout and logic dispenser, dedicated energy receptors, radar eye, heat and motion detectors, and a holographic recorder and projector built into it. His cylindrical body has many doors that open, revealing hidden instruments, including a storage/retrieval jack for computer linkup, auditory receivers, flame-retardant foam dispenser, electric shock prod, high-powered spotlight, grasping claw, laser welder, circular saw, and a cybot acoustic signaler.

The meter-high droid has two treaded "legs" running down opposing sides of his body. A third treaded leg can be extended to provide extra stability in rough terrain. He also has flotation devices that allow him to stay near the surface if he is plunged into water or other liquid. A periscoping visual scanner helps guide him if he is submerged.

Threepio and Artoo have developed an odd relationship over the years. The protocol droid is a fussy mother hen, constantly cajoling, belittling, or arguing with his squat counterpart. Artoo is loyal, inventive, and sarcastic, coolly egging Threepio on without seeming to do so. To watch the two droids together, one would expect them to deprogram each other, given half a chance, but in truth, the two have come to learn that they can depend on each other with their "lives."

One of the earliest known "masters" for Threepio and Artoo was a notorious smuggler who abandoned them on the arid, salty planet Ingo, where they were soon adopted by the young speeder racer Thall Joben. He and his mechanic, Jord Dusat, were prim-

ing their superspeeder, the *White Witch*, for races at Boonta. Thall had made an enemy out of the evil gang leader, Tig Fromm, and his father, Sise Fromm. With the help of Threepio, Artoo, and starship pilot Kea Moll, Thall was able to fend off Fromm's attacks. Even when the gangster hired the notorious bounty hunter Boba Fett, the droids helped save the day, and Thall set them free.

The two droids were assigned a new master by the Intergalactic Droid Agency, and found themselves serving drinks at Doodnik Cafe in the rough mining town of Tyne's Hokey. Fired after a short while on the job, Threepio and Artoo were auctioned off to Jann Tosh, and soon came in contact with an amnesiac android prince—Mon Julpa of the planet Tammuz-an. They helped Prince Julpa regain his memory and joined Jann and pilot Jessica "Jess" Meade in returning Julpa home. Later, they helped Jess and Jann stop Kybo Ren and the pirates of Tarnooga. When Jann was accepted into the Academy, he freed the droids.

They soon had a new master, Mungo Baobab, a trading merchant with bigger aspirations, and Threepio and Artoo were helpful in his many adventures in the Roon

system. Still later the droids were sold to a Master Wena, but he put them up for auction. A junk trader from the Kalarba system bought them, and they were shipped off to Hosk Station. There they had a run-in with the bounty-hunter droid IG-88, but escaped to the surface of Kalarba and were taken in by the Pitareeze family, whom they helped in bringing to justice the infamous Olag Greck.

Years later, the droids came into galactic prominence *completely* by accident. Serving under their master, Captain Colton, they were two of many droids owned by the Royal House of Alderaan. Threepio was assigned to the royal family, where he enjoyed endless state dinners and affairs until a social *faux pas* at the annual Emperor's Ball almost got him dismantled. Trying to pay a compliment to what he thought was a shiny, new, black GuardDroid, Threepio was introduced to the fury of the black-robed Darth Vader.

So he was demoted to preschool duty for a year, but finally ended up in the labor pool, where he was reassigned to work with Artoo. They were then both assigned to report to Captain Antilles on the *Tantive IV* as it embarked on a secret mission to intercept stolen Imperial data.

When they reported for duty, Antilles gave them a voice override with the actuating code of "Epsilon Actual." They were ordered to restrict and protect all references to Princess Leia Organa's presence on the ship. R2-D2 was sent onto the hull of the ship to pretend he was making repairs; Threepio was assigned to maintain contact with Artoo through a tranceiver. As the *Tantive IV* had to enter a restricted system to gain the data, the "needed repairs" provided an alibi in the event they were apprehended.

Despite their ruse, the *Tantive IV* was nearly caught by the Imperial Star

Destroyer *Devastator*, and Artoo was brought back into the ship just before it jumped into hyperspace, escaping the Imperials; the next stop was to be Tatooine, but the Star Destroyer followed them. Attacked by the *Devastator*, the *Tantive IV* made a second desperate run for freedom, but this time it was caught in a tractor beam. Knowing the Imperials would board the ship, Leia told Antilles to stall them at all costs.

Leia hurriedly placed the stolen data inside R2-D2, then she ordered him to find Obi-Wan Kenobi in the Tatooine deserts, and to bring him back to Alderaan. C-3PO stumbled upon the princess and the smaller droid just as Leia was finishing her instructions. Moments later, with laser fire erupting in the corridors, Artoo got into an escape pod. Panicking, Threepio joined him, and the two jettisoned to the planet below.

On Tatooine, Threepio became angry with Artoo, whose talk of a "secret mission" and "plans" seemed to make absolutely no sense. The little astromech droid wanted to go one way, but Threepio thought the other way was best. When Artoo rolled along on his own, the fussy protocol droid decided to split from his longtime partner. "Go that way," he yelled. "You'll be malfunctioning within a day, you nearsighted scrap pile!"

Threepio trudged through the sandy Dune Sea, and eventually caught a glint from a moving object. Thinking it a transport, he waved and yelled. It *was* a transport: a Jawa sandcrawler. Threepio was fitted with a restraining bolt and tossed into a filthy storeroom full of metallic scrap and partially working or immobile droids. Meanwhile, Artoo was spotted by Jawas as well, was shot with a disrupter gun, and was sucked up into the sandcrawler.

Long hours later, Threepio was cheered when he was reunited with his counterpart. "Do you think they'll melt us down?" he asked Artoo. That wasn't the intention, though. The Jawas stopped at the Lars homestead, intent on selling the moisture farmer whatever they could.

Because Threepio could communicate with moisture vaporators, Owen Lars bought him, as well as a red R5 unit. The smaller droid malfunctioned, though, giving Threepio a chance to pitch for Artoo. Soon the two droids were being cleaned up by their new master, a young man named Luke Skywalker.

As he scraped carbon scoring from Artoo's innards, Luke activated part of the holomessage Princess Leia had recorded for Obi-Wan Kenobi. Luke wanted to hear the whole message, but Artoo refused, telling him that for that to occur, the restrain-

ing bolt would have to be removed. Luke did so, but the holo *disappeared*. Artoo bleeped innocently, but Threepio was livid. He promised their master he would work on his counterpart while Luke was at dinner.

But Artoo had other plans, and he took off into the desert, searching for Kenobi. Luke came back and found Threepio hiding, ashamed of Artoo's behavior, but it was too dark to catch the little droid. The next morning, though, Luke and Threepio took off in the landspeeder, locating Artoo out in the Jundland Wastes. Before they could get him into the landspeeder and back to the farm, a group of Tusken Raiders attacked. In the scuffle, Threepio fell off a ledge, breaking his arm off at the elbow joint.

Luke and the droids were rescued by the strange hermit, Ben Kenobi, who imitated the cry of a krayt dragon to scare away the Raiders. Ben admitted that he *had been* Obi-Wan Kenobi, long ago, and he took the trio back to his home. There, Luke reattached Threepio's arm, and saw the entire holo from Princess Leia—a plea asking for help from Kenobi, the last of the Jedi.

Unknown to Luke, Ben, or the droids, Imperial troops were scouring the desert for Artoo and Threepio. They found the Jawas, and after they got their information, they

killed them, then proceeded to the Lars homestead. The droids weren't there either, so they killed Owen and Beru, ransacking and destroying their home.

Meanwhile, Luke agreed to take Ben and the droids to Anchorhead. On the way, they passed the destroyed sandcrawler. Luke realized that the same troopers who had attacked the crawler might well have gone to his home, and he sped off in his landspeeder, leaving Ben and the two droids to help clean up the dead Jawas. When Luke returned, he was grimly ready to join Kenobi on his mission across the galaxy.

The resulting adventures were the wildest that Threepio and Artoo had experienced. They were taken on the *Millennium Falcon* to Alderaan, and then were captured by the Empire's fearsome battle station, the Death Star. Luke and the *Falcon*'s pilots, Han Solo and Chewbacca, attempted a rescue mission to save Princess Leia, while Kenobi tried to destroy the station's tractor beam. Artoo and Threepio had to fend for themselves among the Imperials.

In the escape from the Death Star, Kenobi sacrificed himself so the others

could leave. They journeyed to the moon of Yavin Four, site of the Rebel Alliance's base. There, the information stored in Artoo was revealed: it was the technical readouts of the Death Star. Alliance technicians formulated a plan to strike at the station's sole weakness. Scores of starfighters would have to make an attack run on the station, then score a direct hit on a two-meter thermal exhaust port.

Artoo volunteered to fly in Luke Skywalker's X-wing, replacing the generic astrogation droid they would have otherwise given him. Threepio had to stay behind, worriedly watching the battle screens with Princess Leia, General Jan Dodonna, and other Alliance tacticians.

Using his Force talents, Skywalker was able to destroy the station, thanks in part to some timely intervention from the *Millennium Falcon*. Artoo was hit by a laser blast, but Threepio was assured he could be saved. Indeed he was. Days later, at a ceremony honoring Luke, Han, and Chewbacca's bravery, Threepio

and Artoo stood on the dais with the Alliance dignitaries. Both of them sparkled and gleamed, their systems running more optimally than ever.

Threepio and Artoo became an integral part of the Alliance, working with the quartet that had been nicknamed "the Heroes of Yavin": Luke, Han, Chewbacca, and Leia. As the Rebellion picked up steam, the droids were pulled farther apart by their responsibilities. Artoo generally traveled with Luke in his X-wing, while Threepio was either with Princess Leia or making a nuisance of himself in the *Millennium Falcon*. Of course Threepio didn't believe he was a nuisance, but more than once Han Solo considered feeding him to mynocks.

The droids accompanied Leia and Luke on their diplomatic meeting on Circarpous, aiding them when they had to make an unscheduled landing on the jungle planet of Mimban. Over the next several years, they traveled back to Tatooine several times, adventured on the gambling palace known as the Wheel, and helped in the search to find a new Rebel base.

The Alliance relocated to Hoth, but the base was discovered by an Imperial probe droid and the Rebels were forced to flee into space; Threepio went with Han, Chewie, and Leia on the *Falcon*, while Artoo went with Luke. Threepio ended up being shot by stormtroopers and dismembered by Ugnaughts on Bespin's Cloud City, while Artoo suffered many "indignities" at the Force powers of Jedi Master Yoda on Dagobah.

Reunited after the events on Bespin, the Rebel heroes concentrated on the mission to rescue Han Solo, who had been imprisoned at Jabba the Hutt's palace on Tatooine. Lando Calrissian, posing as skiff guard Tamtel Skreej, helped make way for Threepio and Artoo when they arrived to deliver a message from Luke to Jabba. Threepio seemed startled to learn that Skywalker was giving him and Artoo to Jabba as gifts. The protocol droid func-

tioned as Jabba's new translator, while Artoo was reduced to performing menial labor until the rescue attempt erupted in violence above the Great Pit of Carkoon. Artoo turned the tide by giving Luke his Jedi lightsaber, which had been hidden inside the droid's dome.

Amazingly, Threepio was the next to act as the savior of the Alliance heroes. Luke, Han, Chewie, and the droids were captured on the forest moon of Endor as they moved to destroy an Imperial shield-generator bunker. There, the furry little Ewoks saw Threepio as their golden god, especially when Luke levitated the droid using Force talents.

Threepio proved his master story-telling abilities that evening, with the tale of the battle between the Alliance and the Empire. The Ewoks were convinced that they should help Threepio and his friends, and their aid allowed the Rebels to overrun the bunker and destroy the shield, which in turn enabled Alliance starfighters to destroy the second Death Star high in orbit above Endor.

Over the years that followed, Artoo became an integral component of Luke Skywalker's life. He interfaced so closely with Luke's X-wing that the ship's computer became his own personal domain, and without him the Alliance techs and computers couldn't even communicate with the X-wing's computer system.

C-3PO became an almost constant presence at the side of Princess Leia. As her diplomatic and ambassadorial duties increased with the rise of the New Republic, the well-mannered protocol droid played an essential part in negotiations and truce building.

The adventures didn't end with the fall of the Empire though. Threepio and Artoo participated in the battle against the Ssi-ruuk, and helped with the truce at Bakura. They joined the main Alliance heroes as part of the short-lived Senate Interplanetary Intelligence Network—SPIN—and their missions included infiltrating an Imperial enclave on Kessel.

Eight years after he had first met Han Solo, Threepio helped the Corellian to win Leia back from the Hapan Prince Isolder, while Artoo helped Luke and Isolder track the others to Dathomir. Han did marry Leia shortly thereafter, but despite his well-intended actions, Threepio was still "persecuted" by the Corellian general.

Threepio and Artoo were heavily involved in the Alliance's move to Coruscant, and later in the battle against the Imperial Grand Admiral Thrawn and the mad Jedi clone Joruus C'Baoth. Threepio was called upon to tell stories again, this time to the fearsome Noghri assassins, who looked upon Leia as the important "Lady Vader." Finally, both droids helped destroy Mount Tantiss on Wayland.

When the clone of Emperor Palpatine surfaced and brought Luke under his dark-side influence, Artoo began to get very worried. Technicians began removing his files and replacing them with something else. He soon realized it was Master Control Signals, which would later aid the New Republic forces in shutting down the massive World Devastators as they ravaged Calamari. For Luke had not really fallen to the dark side at all!

During a second Alliance relocation to Coruscant, Threepio adopted a strange new role: nanny droid. He was put in charge of Leia and Han's rambunctious and clever twins, Jacen and Jaina Solo. Despite his best efforts, it was difficult to handle the children; time and again they hoodwinked and teased him.

Artoo accompanied Luke on his searches for Jedi recruits, and on a spy mission at the Imperial Correctional Facility on Kessel. He went with his master to the moon of Yavin Four, and helped him set up his new Jedi academy there. When Kyp Durron and the spirit of Exar Kun, the Dark Lord of the Sith, struck Luke down, Artoo faithfully watched over Skywalker's catatonic body, protecting him and the other Jedi students.

While R2-D2 languished on Yavin Four, C-3PO was finally released from service to the twins, but the alternative was little better. As part of the New Republic strike force to raid the

Empire's Maw Installation, Threepio was pressed into service coordinating a team of assault shuttles piloted by Wookiee slaves, in what may have been the most terrifying and exhilarating experience of Threepio's sentient life.

As the New Republic expanded and grew, the Empire's forces dwindled. The droids accompanied their masters on missions to Plawell, to destroy the *Eye of Palpatine* battle station, and to rescue the kidnapped Solo children from the rogue dark-side adept, Hethrir. Artoo continued his duties at the Jedi academy, where even Threepio assisted at times, programming the Miniaturized Translator Droid, Em Teedee, for the young Wookiee initiate, Lowbacca. Unfortunately for Lowbacca and those around him, Em Teedee had more than a little of Threepio's personality and vocal mannerisms.

Due to their lack of memory wipes, both Threepio and Artoo have developed strong personalities. They have grown and learned from their experiences, gaining a wisdom and insight not generally seen in droids. Their limits of self-awareness and personality growth have not yet been reached. Probably the only pair of bickering droids to be feted as heroes throughout the galaxy, C-3PO and R2-D2 are invaluable assets to their masters, to the New Republic, and to the cause of freedom.

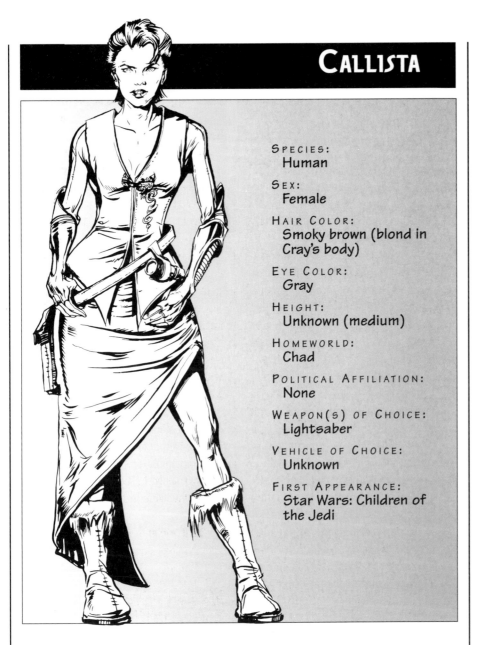

CALLISTA

SPECIES:
Human

SEX:
Female

HAIR COLOR:
Smoky brown (blond in Cray's body)

EYE COLOR:
Gray

HEIGHT:
Unknown (medium)

HOMEWORLD:
Chad

POLITICAL AFFILIATION:
None

WEAPON(S) OF CHOICE:
Lightsaber

VEHICLE OF CHOICE:
Unknown

FIRST APPEARANCE:
Star Wars: Children of the Jedi

Only through the power of the Force was Callista able to keep herself alive . . . within the computer banks of one of the Emperor's deadly weapons!

Callista lived with her family on the watery world of Chad, sharing the planet with the fun-loving, mousy Chadra-Fan. They herded sea cows in a deep-water ranch, moving with the herds along the Algic Current. Callista had strong powers in the Force, but wasn't aware of them until she instinctively used them one winter to free herself from a floe of pack ice.

Years later, Callista met Geith, another who was strong in the Force. Drawn to the Moonflower Nebula, Geith and Callista found one of Emperor Palpatine's experimental weapons: a space station known as the *Eye of Palpatine*. Geith and Callista were killed trying to destroy it.

But through the Force, Callista did not allow her spirit to die. Her essence resided in the gunnery computer, preventing anyone else from activating the deadly weaponry, and the project was abandoned. She existed in a dreamlike suspension for nearly thirty years, her memories becoming fainter.

Throughout the galaxy, Palpatine's Jedi purge had been completed, and a Rebellion had sprung up to fight the evil Empire. Many more superweapons were developed, and the Jedi slowly began to rise again. Eight years after the destruction of the second Death Star, Callista was awakened by new stirrings in the Force. Luke Skywalker had come aboard the *Eye* to destroy the Emperor's weapon forever. Sick from an earlier attack, Luke saw Callista in his dreams.

Callista felt a connection to the Jedi Master, and reached out to apologize for not properly disposing of the battle station in the years past. Though Nichos Marr and Cray Mingla, two of Skywalker's former students, had accompanied him to the *Eye*, only Luke sensed the presence on the station, but he was unable to make contact on his own until she communicated with him through the ship's computer system.

Callista aided the trio in the destruction of the *Eye*, explaining the weaknesses to Nichos and Cray, who planned to sacrifice themselves. Luke could not bear to say good-bye to the woman he now loved, but the only way to save her computer-generated life was to leave the station intact.

Shortly before the explosion that destroyed the *Eye*, Luke and the droid Threepio jettisoned away in a shuttle, leaving behind Cray, Nichos, and Callista. The shuttle rendezvoused with Mara Jade's ship, *Hunter's Luck*, where Luke was welcomed back by Leia, Han, and Chewbacca. Mara picked up one more passenger, intercepting an escape pod from the *Eye*. Luke opened the pod, expecting to find Cray, but as his once-student smiled up at him, he recognized Callista!

Callista and Cray had utilized their last strength in the Force to put Callista's essence into Cray's body. Bereft of her Force powers, Callista was together with Luke at last.

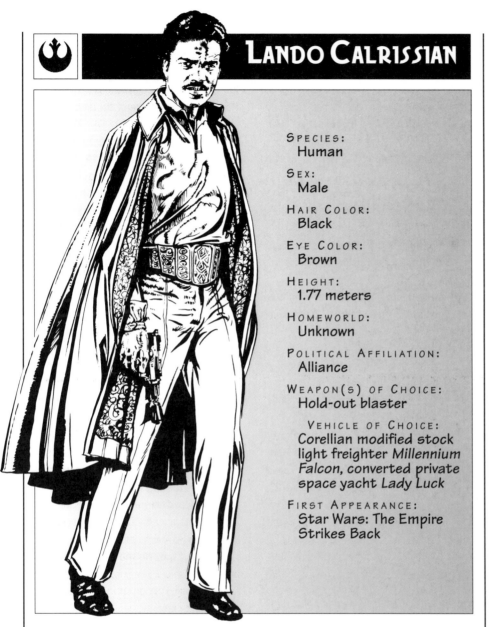

LANDO CALRISSIAN

SPECIES:
Human

SEX:
Male

HAIR COLOR:
Black

EYE COLOR:
Brown

HEIGHT:
1.77 meters

HOMEWORLD:
Unknown

POLITICAL AFFILIATION:
Alliance

WEAPON(S) OF CHOICE:
Hold-out blaster

VEHICLE OF CHOICE:
Corellian modified stock light freighter Millennium Falcon, converted private space yacht Lady Luck

FIRST APPEARANCE:
Star Wars: The Empire Strikes Back

Con artist and smuggler . . . Lando Calrissian never thought he'd also earn titles like leader and war hero. He never dreamed the Empire would force him to betray an old friend, either.

Little is known about the history of the charming and roguish gambler—his past is generally a well-guarded secret. It is known that, at least five years prior to the *Millennium Falcon*'s assault on the first Death Star, Lando experienced many of his own adventures in the Corellian freighter.

He had used the *Falcon* to store precious life crystals from Rafar V, gaining the enmity of a supposed sorcerer named Rakus Gepta. During that time period, Lando traveled with a droid named Vuffi Raa, and amassed a sizable fortune from the life crystals, 173,000 credits gained from a sabacc game against a Corporate Sector Authority cop, and a reward of gemstones and precious minerals, so Calrissian was a man of considerable resources.

Over the years, Lando had befriended a raucous Corellian smuggler, Han Solo, whose partner, a huge Wookiee named

Chewbacca, made sure that Solo never came to harm. The friends crossed and double-crossed each other over time, but never with any truly disastrous effects. Lando, Han, and Chewie even undertook smuggling missions together. Then one night on Bespin, Lando and Han played a high-stakes game of sabacc, and when it was over, Han was the new owner of the *Millennium Falcon*.

Lando took his remaining fortunes and embarked on a galaxywide tour. He again hit success when he returned to Bespin and challenged Baron Administrator Raynor to a game of all-or-nothing sabacc. Raynor was the inept controller of Bespin's Cloud City, a mining and gambling center infamous throughout the galaxy. Lando was inconspicuously aided by a cyborg aide named Lobot, and he won Cloud City, becoming its new Baron Administrator. He kept Lobot as his chief aide.

In addition to his public duties, Lobot proved equally adept at handling Calrissian's more clandestine operations. Some of those included smuggling, while others involved surreptitiously aiding the Rebellion.

On the whole, Lando was doing very well running Cloud City and its Tibanna gas-mining operation. Profits and produc-

tion were up, and the constituents were happy. Shady business dealings were common, but violence was kept down by a strong police presence. Lando was becoming respectable, and so was his city.

But Lando was soon to get a jolt, brought about by the arrival of Imperial forces and the Dark Lord of the Sith, Darth Vader. Meeting with Lando, Vader "persuaded" him to help trap Han Solo. If the Baron Administrator helped him, the Imperials would never again bother Bespin or Cloud City. If he didn't help, Lando could say good-bye to his future. The gambler agreed to betray Solo.

Having escaped from Imperial forces in the Hoth system, Han Solo brought his damaged *Millennium Falcon* to Cloud City for repairs. Lando welcomed Han and his companions, promising that his techs would get right to work on the *Falcon*'s troublesome hyperdrive. While he played the cordial and dashing host, flirting with Leia and showing off what a successful businessman he had become, Lando was setting Solo up for a fall.

When Vader actually took Han prisoner, his deal with Lando began to go sour. Han was tortured and frozen in a carbonite block, then given to the bounty hunter, Boba Fett, to be taken to Jabba the Hutt. Chewie and Leia were to be retained by Vader. Lando outwardly capitulated to the Dark Lord's demands, but inwardly, he was planning his next move.

When it became clear that his beloved city was to become an armed camp, Lando ordered Lobot to assemble a dozen of Calrissian's personal guards to rescue Leia, Chewie, and a dismembered C-3PO. As the troopers and their prisoners neared the phalanx of Cloud City guards, Lando gave the command "Code Force Seven," and Lobot had the men draw their weapons on the six surprised Imperials.

After a brief altercation wherein Chewbacca tried to strangle Lando, the administrator convinced the Rebels they could save Han from Boba Fett. They arrived

too late, and Lando knew they had to flee the city. He utilized the public-address systems to announce that Imperial takeover was imminent, urging the Cloud City citizens to evacuate. He then helped Leia and Chewie escape in the *Falcon*, and even managed to save Luke Skywalker, who was on the verge of plummeting from the floating metropolis.

Later, when a decision was made for a small strike force to retrieve Han Solo from the Tatooine desert palace of Jabba the Hutt, Lando took the role of a skiff guard named Tamtel Skreej. He surveyed the palace, sending messages and layouts back to the other members of the team. It was easy to spy on Jabba; half of the courtesans in the palace were doing so.

One by one, the players came to the palace: first Leia, disguised as a bounty hunter named Boushh, brought Jabba a "captive" Chewbacca; and finally Luke Skywalker.

On a skiff over the Great Pit of Carkoon, Lando revealed himself and helped Han, Chewie, and Luke fight off the guards. Lando was knocked off the skiff and toward the Sarlacc, but Han saved his life. The Alliance heroes blew up Jabba's sail barge and soared away to freedom.

Back at the New Republic's headquarters, Lando was given the rank of general, in recognition of his reputation as a soldier of fortune and his role in the Battle of Taanab. When a leader was needed for the starfighter assault on the second Death Star, Lando volunteered. Han and Chewie were planning a simultaneous raid on the moon of Endor, to destroy the Death Star's shields, so Han turned control of the

Millenium Falcon over to Lando.

Lando picked a Sullustan named Nien Nunb as his copilot in the assault against the battle station. General Calrissian was Gold Leader, in charge of the attack, working under Admiral Ackbar. The Rebel fleet engaged the Imperials above the moon of Endor, waiting until the Death Star's shields went down, and they were freed to make their attack runs. Wedge Antilles led the way down the main reactor shaft, followed by Lando and Nien Nunb in the *Falcon*, and several X-wings and TIE fighters.

The *Falcon* and Wedge Antilles's X-wing fighter made it to the reactor core. Wedge targeted the power regulator and Lando torpedoed the main reactor, then the two ships had to retrace their perilous flight through the Death Star superstructure, even as it collapsed and exploded around them. With milliseconds to spare, Wedge and the *Falcon* escaped the shaft into open space. Behind them, the Death Star blew up.

Lando was a hero to the Alliance, but while the Empire had fallen, their battles continued. So when Lando asked Solo and the Alliance for help in liberating Cloud City from Imperial Control, they had to decline. Han and many of the others were called to help dispel an invasion on Bakura, while Lando meandered his way back to Bespin, trying to figure out a way to get the city back on his own. He hoped the Empire would have left following the death of the Emperor, but it didn't seem likely.

Surprisingly, the Imperials *had* left, but only because of a revolt by the Ugnaughts, who hated the Empire. When Lando returned, the mining center appeared deserted, but he found out differently when Lobot attacked him. The cyborg's motivation-

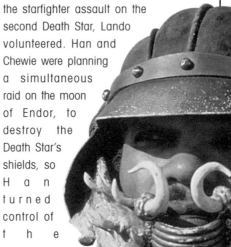

al programming capsule had been damaged by the rebellious Ugnaughts. Fortunately, Lando managed to remove the damaged capsule and repair it, for he needed Lobot to help him disarm bombs that the Ugnaughts had planted on the city.

The Imperials hadn't yet given up, though, and when they returned, they *literally* threw Lando out. He was saved from free-fall by Lobot, who used a set of life-jets. Teaming with the rebellious Ugnaughts, Lando and Lobot staged a raid on Cloud City, only to find Luke Skywalker and Lieutenant Shira Brei there, already engaging the Imperial troops. Once the Imperials were defeated, Lando broadcast that Cloud City was no longer under the Empire's control. Former citizens joined with newcomers to revive the city.

Lando had Lobot completely repaired, and the cyborg aided in the running of Cloud City whenever Lando was off flying missions with the Rebellion. For a short time Mon Mothma established a private strike team of the Alliance's most daring heroes, calling it the Senate Interplanetary Intelligence Network—SPIN. The team consisted of Leia, Luke, Han, Chewbacca, Lando, R2-D2, and C-3PO. At first, Lando only worked with SPIN when it was convenient, although he remained informed through Han. His Baron Administrator duties on Cloud City kept him busy, but the conflict was not to continue.

Zorba the Hutt, father of Jabba, arrived on the city and challenged Lando for a part of the city Jabba had owned. Lando, believing Zorba to be a poor gambler, challenged him in turn to an all-or-nothing game of sabacc. Lando didn't know that there were ultraviolet images on the sabacc cards that Zorba could see. He lost the city, and Zorba sent him packing.

Lando quickly landed on his feet, taking a job as the Baron Administrator of Hologram Fun World, a dome-covered amusement park floating on a helium gas cloud near the Zabian star system. When Han and Leia visited the park, Zorba the

Hutt's thugs and bounty hunters attacked, trashed the place, and kidnapped Leia. Lando joined Han on the successful mission back to Tatooine to save Leia.

Mon Mothma eventually disbanded the SPIN group, and Lando resigned his commission and went back to the private sector. He established a mining operation on the dark side of Nkllon, a planet in the Athega system. The system's sun was so hot that anything caught in its direct light would fry, so Lando had his people design giant, umbrellalike, reflective shieldships. The mining operation itself was known as Nomad City, and its mobile capacity allowed it to constantly stay on Nkllon's dark side.

Lando based the plans for Nomad City on those that Cloud City founder Lord Ecclessis Figg originally had drafted for Bespin mining machines. The majority of Nomad City was constructed from the hulk of an Imperial *Dreadnaught*-class cruiser and those of captured AT-AT walkers scavenged after the Battle of Endor. The operation was adept at mining rare and valuable ores—Hfredium, Kammris, Dolovite, and others—and Lando had another successful

scheme on his hands. Because the Alliance had aided him in starting up the endeavor, Lando provided them with ores at a deep discount.

Several years passed, and then the Empire attacked Nkllon, acting on Grand Admiral Thrawn's orders, stealing fifty-one of Lando's mole miners. Seeking revenge against the Empire, Lando joined Han, Leia, Chewbacca, and Luke on a mission that led him to become embroiled in the fight against the Grand Admiral *and* the mad Jedi Joruus C'Baoth. Lando helped find Alliance founder Garm Bel Iblis and the *Katana* Dreadnaught fleet, enlisted their aid, and participated in the battle for the fleet.

The damage the Imperials inflicted finished Nomad City, though, leaving Lando twenty days before the crippled city would be exposed to the superhot sun's rays and destroyed. Although Iblis offered the Alliance's assistance, Lando knew he had to evacuate his people; the city itself was doomed.

As it happened, the Alliance was still in trouble with Thrawn and his forces. After a quick trip to Coruscant, Lando was involved in the strike force that traveled to Wayland to destroy the Emperor's Spaarti cloning cylinders and facility at Mount Tantiss.

Lando lost the Nkllon mining project in another sabacc game—though it could be argued that he lost on purpose—and again found himself between jobs. Ackbar owed Calrissian some favors, so Lando was reinstated as a general in the New Republic. Together he and General Wedge Antilles commanded the Star Destroyers *Liberator* and *Emancipator*.

At this point Coruscant was again in Imperial hands, but Imperial factions were warring with each other, so Lando, Wedge, and Luke took the *Liberator* to Coruscant to finish off the Imperials. They ended up crashing planetside, with only Luke's Jedi powers saving their lives. The Rebels holed up in Imperial City until help arrived in the familiar shape of the *Millennium Falcon*.

Back at Pinnacle Base on the Fifth Moon

of Da Soocha, Lando and Wedge were assigned to take the *Emancipator* to the planet Mon Calamari to help fight the Empire's World Devastators. Although they helped bring in full complements of X-wing fighters and speeder transports, Lando and Wedge soon lost their second Star Destroyer; as a redirected World Devastator began to eat their ship, they ejected in escape pods. They were picked up by the frigate *Antares Six,* where they watched as reinforcements arrived and R2-D2 used stolen control codes to immobilize the Devastators. The New Republic forces were victorious, but at great cost to the environs of Calamari.

A short time later, Lando and Wedge planned to strike at Byss, the seat of the Empire's power. They and their troops stowed away aboard a set of commandeered S-1 Viper Automadon war droids, which were conveyed onto Byss by the Imperials. The Republic heroes attacked, but the Imperials released chrysalis beasts, which would overcome the Viper Automadons.

The Republic troops were rescued by three smuggler's ships: Shug Ninx's *Starhook VII,* the *Bespin Bandit,* and Lo Khan's *Hyperspace Marauder.* The smugglers then went to New Alderaan, to help stop the invading Imperials who threatened the lives of Han and Leia's children. Finally, the smugglers and assorted Republic heroes and troops settled at the Auril system's abandoned floating space city of Nespis VIII, which served as their base.

The relocation was only temporary though; within months, the Alliance attacked the Imperial City on Coruscant yet again and succeeded in driving away the remnants of the Empire. Luke Skywalker and the droids combed Imperial records, looking for potential Jedi candidates for his academy. Lando helped them find one, a boy named Tymmo who was a regular winner at the Umgullian blob races. But Tymmo was not a Force user; he was a con artist and the runaway consort of the Duchess Mystal of Dargul. For capturing him, Lando was presented with a million-credit reward.

With credits in his accounts again, Lando helped Luke on a spy mission at the Imperial Correctional Facility on Kessel, where Leia thought Han and Chewie might be prisoners. They had been, but the Corellian and his partner had escaped even as Lando and Luke looked for clues as to their whereabouts.

Lando and Luke confronted prison administrator Moruth Doole, then barely escaped on the *Millennium Falcon.* A battle between the *Falcon* and Kessel's ragtag defense fleet turned deadly with the emergence of the Sun Crusher and three Star Destroyers from the swirling gases outside the black-hole cluster known as the Maw. Luckily, the Sun Crusher was being piloted by Han, Chewie, and a young Kyp Durron.

Shortly thereafter, in an angry confrontation, Lando and Han replayed their game of sabacc for the *Falcon.* Lando won, but he made a deal with Han: once Solo had helped Calrissian get his new ship, a modified yacht called the *Lady Luck,* back from Kessel, Han could have the *Falcon.* They did so, and as the two prepared to take Kyp Durron to Yavin Four, they picked up another passenger: the lovely smuggler Mara Jade. Lando had always liked her, but even his best manners yielded nothing but her contempt.

Yet another game of sabacc took place, and the *Falcon* reverted to Han. It wasn't to last for long though. One more game was played after they picked up Mara Jade

from Yavin Four, and this time, Lando soundly won the freighter. With a flourish and a sparkle meant for Mara's eyes, Lando presented Han with the *Falcon,* free and clear.

Lando helped Han stop the rogue Kyp Durron in the Sun Crusher, then enlisted his friend's help in liberating the Kessel Correctional Facility from Doole. Still holding credits he had from Tymmo's capture, Lando planned on reopening the glitterstim spice mines of Kessel, teaming with Mara Jade and her Smugglers' Alliance to distribute the expensive spice. Rather than use the slave/prisoner labor that the Empire and Moruth Doole had used in the pitch-black mines, Lando hired Nien Nunb and other Sullustans to run the installation, while droids worked the mines.

Nineteen years after the betrayal at Bespin, Lando Calrissian opened GemDiver Station, a sprawling, corusca-gem-mining industrial station in orbit around Yavin's gaseous surface, and once again, Lobot was his assistant. Lando allowed Han's twin children, Jacen and Jaina Solo, to come to the station on a field trip from Luke's Jedi academy, accompanied by Lowbacca and his droid, Em Teedee, and Imperial ships struck while the children were on board. Tamith Kai, a Dathomirian Nightsister, wanted the young Jedi children, and she would stop at nothing to get them.

GemDiver Station was boarded and the children and Lowbacca were captured. Lando offered to help in the mission to find the twins and the Wookiee, but Luke Skywalker and Tenel Ka were already tracking them, so Lando and Lobot turned their attention to finding the best ways to protect the station so that an invasion or pirate attack could never happen again.

Whatever schemes lie in Lando Calrissian's future, over the years, he has learned responsibility, loyalty, and pride. The New Republic can gamble on the full support of the roguish Lando Calrissian. They'll win it every time.

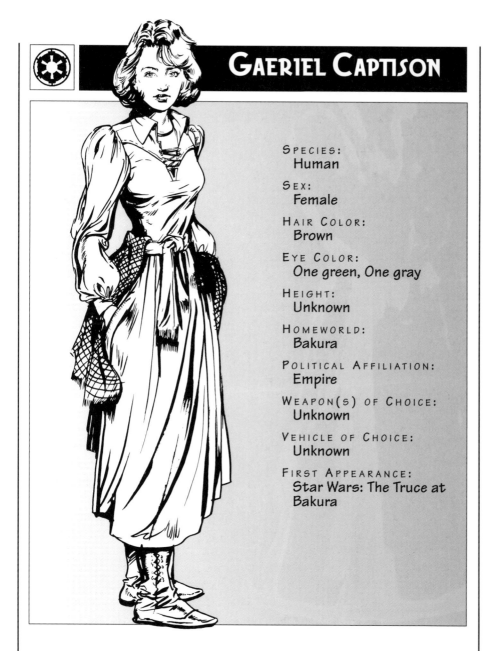

GAERIEL CAPTISON

SPECIES:
Human

SEX:
Female

HAIR COLOR:
Brown

EYE COLOR:
One green, One gray

HEIGHT:
Unknown

HOMEWORLD:
Bakura

POLITICAL AFFILIATION:
Empire

WEAPON(S) OF CHOICE:
Unknown

VEHICLE OF CHOICE:
Unknown

FIRST APPEARANCE:
Star Wars: The Truce at Bakura

Gaeriel Captison had lived a hard-knock life under the control of the Empire. Faced with an invasion of her world and a choice between Imperial or Alliance help, Gaeriel made the choice that would help her people most.

Gaeriel was an Imperial senator from Bakura, a planet on the edge of the Outer Rim whose economy was largely based on the export of repulsorlift components, exotic fruits, candy, and liqueur.

Gaeriel was the daughter of a senator. Growing up around politicos, she grew used to hearing the never-ending bickering and political machinations. Because no two senators could ever cooperate, Bakura fell quickly when the Empire attacked.

In resultant uprising against the Imperial forces, Gaeriel's parents were killed, as were thousands of Bakurans. Gaeriel was raised by her aunt and uncle, Tiree and Yeorg Captison. Her uncle was allowed to stay on as prime minister, but the role was largely ceremonial. Gaeriel was elected to the senate, and spent a year training at Imperial Center, doing postgraduate work in govern-

ment. She finally returned to the Bakuran capital city of Salis D'aar to fill her post, just in time for tragedy to strike again.

The reptilian Ssi-ruuk invaded, and Imperial Commander Pter Thanas marshalled his troops to try to stop them before they came planetside. A deadly battle crippled much of the Bakuran defense fleet, even though the losses to the Ssi-ruuk battle droids were equally heavy. In the midst of the battle, several ships from the Rebel Alliance showed up, offering aid.

Gaeriel was skeptical, especially when Leia Organa turned the mission into a diplomatic one, as well. Leia told the Bakurans that, just days before, the Emperor had been killed and his second Death Star destroyed, but Gaeriel had seen what happened to those who opposed the Empire.

As an aid to Bakura's Imperial Governor Wilek Nereus, Gaeriel learned that the Ssi-ruuk would leave peacefully if the Bakurans handed over the intriguing Jedi Knight, Luke Skywalker. However, fearful of what the Ssi-ruuk could do with Jedi Force powers at their disposal, Nereus had no intention of giving the Ssi-ruuk everything they wanted. The governor had egg pods from trihoic larvae hidden in Luke's food; they would quickly burrow their way into his heart and kill him, but not before he infected the Ssi-ruuk. When Gaeriel learned of Nereus's treachery, she told Luke about the larvae, allowing him to protect himself. After the Ssi-ruuk were defeated, Gaeriel resigned from her Imperial service. Nereus himself was killed, and Commander Thanas defected, turning his remaining ships over to the Rebels.

Gaeriel now aids her uncle, the prime minister, in reviving Bakura from the damage inflicted by its Imperial masters. She helped draft the truce by which her world joined the Alliance, and knows that one day, Bakura will repay the debt of their freedom.

JORUUS C'BAOTH

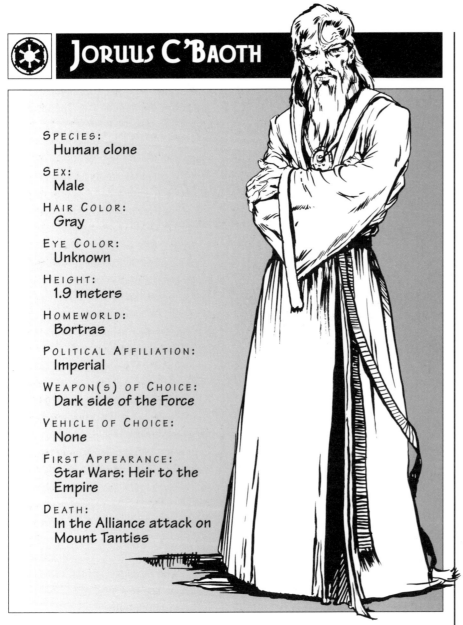

SPECIES:
Human clone

SEX:
Male

HAIR COLOR:
Gray

EYE COLOR:
Unknown

HEIGHT:
1.9 meters

HOMEWORLD:
Bortras

POLITICAL AFFILIATION:
Imperial

WEAPON(S) OF CHOICE:
Dark side of the Force

VEHICLE OF CHOICE:
None

FIRST APPEARANCE:
Star Wars: Heir to the Empire

DEATH:
In the Alliance attack on Mount Tantiss

The name of Jorus C'Baoth was once held in high regard in the circles of the Jedi and those with power in the Force. Decades later, his clone, Joruus C'Baoth, would also be powerful in the Force . . . but his madness served the dark side.

The first Force user to use that surname was Jorus C'Baoth, born on the planet Bortras in the Reithcas sector. Bright, and strong in the Force, Jorus began his studies at Mirnic University at age seventeen. Upon his graduation, he came to the Jedi Training Center on Kamparas, where he trained for two years before a Jedi Master took him on as a private student. After another two years, Jorus was bestowed the title of Jedi Knight. He advanced once more—after twelve years of service to the Force—to the status of Jedi Master.

Jorus was a strong supporter of the Old Republic, traveling as part of a demilitarization observation group on Ando, serving as a member of the Senate Interspecies Advisory Committee, and even acting as a personal Jedi advisor to the ambitious young Senator Palpatine. C'Baoth also joined the Jedi task force that assembled to oppose the Dark Jedi insurrection on Bpfassh. He was part of the delegation to Alderaan when problems with selecting a new viceroy cropped up; the eventual decision led to the ascendancy of the Organa family.

Other elements of C'Baoth's record are equally impressive. He helped the Jedi Master Tra's M'ins mediate the Duinuogwuin-Gotal conflict and served as ambassador-at-large to the Xappyh sector. It was Jorus's support of the Old Republic's Outbound Flight Project that led to his disappearance. He was one of six Jedi Masters who left Yaga Minor in search of intelligent life outside the galaxy proper.

Jorus C'Baoth never returned. When the ship exited Old Republic space, a young man named Thrawn destroyed it, working under Senator Palpatine's orders. The time for his New Order to strike was soon, Palpatine knew, and ridding himself of six Jedi Masters at once was too good an opportunity to pass up.

Five years after the fall of Palpatine's Empire and the destruction of the second Death Star, a white-haired, long-bearded man calling himself Joruus C'Baoth—note the differently spelled first name—was found on the planet Wayland. Palpatine had cloned Jorus, intent on bending him to the dark side. Unfortunately, the early clones that led to the second C'Baoth tended toward mental instability. They were grown too fast and were susceptible to "clone madness."

Joruus protected the Wayland facility known as Mount Tantiss, a secret Imperial facility used for cloning purposes and weapons storage. The storehouses were filled with plundered art treasures, Spaarti cylinders used for cloning, and a working prototype of a cloaking device. Over the many years he guarded the facility, C'Baoth slowly lost his mind, becoming irrevocably insane. However, it was a charismatic insanity, so it allowed him to fool even Luke

Skywalker for a short time.

With his memories clouded, this C'Baoth did not even remember his original mission, nor his service to the Emperor Palpatine. He served himself alone; his goal became the founding of a new order of Dark Jedi, trained to rule the galaxy, with himself as their master.

When Grand Admiral Thrawn found C'Baoth at Wayland, the clone had already killed many of the people on the planet, controlling their lives with his powers, and sometimes, controlling their deaths. C'Baoth subjugated what still survived of the three species on the planet—human, Psadan, and Myneyrsh—creating his own kingdom and singular society at the base of Mount Tantiss.

Thrawn managed to recruit C'Baoth, convincing him to help rebuild the Empire by promising him more Jedi to turn to the dark side. First would be Luke Skywalker, then his pregnant sister, Leia Organa Solo, and finally, her unborn twins. C'Baoth knew that Mara Jade, the "Emperor's Hand," would also one day bow down to him.

Skywalker, seeking a Jedi who could help further his training, eventually found the "Master" in his acquired High Castle on the planet Jomark, but he soon realized that C'Baoth was not the teacher he sought. When he left to help Mara Jade rescue the smuggler Talon Karrde, Luke planned to return to C'Baoth's side, to heal the Jedi Master and pull him back from the frayed edges of the dark side.

Joruus wielded many dark side powers that Luke had already seen, and many that he had not. Like Palpatine, C'Baoth could strike with a bluish, dark-Force lightning that could kill. He was able to manipulate people like puppets, completely subjugating their minds. He could enhance coordination between people, linking even those who were light-years apart.

The tension between C'Baoth and Grand

Admiral Thrawn increased over time, as the dark side Master began retreating more and more into a world of half-remembered conversations and worlds that never were. In addition, Thrawn had failed to capture Luke or Leia, and the Jedi was growing impatient with him. C'Baoth saw himself as the new leader of the revitalized Empire; Thrawn was only the means to that end. At times, this fantasy became all too powerful: Once, C'Baoth mind-controlled every crew member of Thrawn's Star Destroyer *Chimaera*, just to make a point to the Grand Admiral and Captain Pellaeon.

Eventually, C'Baoth returned to Mount Tantiss with a squad of Imperials. He killed their leader, General Freja Covell, by taking over his mind so forcefully that the officer's brain tissue shut down. In the Spaarti cloning cylinders, Joruus had created a clone of Luke Skywalker using tissue from the Emperor's prize sample B-2332-54—Luke's hand, which had been lopped off in the Bespin lightsaber duel between Skywalker and Darth Vader.

Since C'Baoth had finally realized that he

could not turn Luke to the dark side, he unleashed the evil clone, known as Luuke Skywalker, for an attack on the original. Using the very lightsaber Luke had lost on Cloud City, the clone pressed the attack. But Mara Jade killed Luuke, thus fulfilling her destiny as ordained long ago by the Emperor.

C'Baoth lost control, his dark-Force powers raging against the Jedi and Jedi-to-be. He attacked Luke and Mara using blue lightning and collapsed rubble from the ceiling, planning to replace the clone of Luke and grow another clone of Mara Jade. "I have foreseen that Mara Jade will kneel before me," he said. "One Mara Jade . . . or another."

Mara freed herself first, charging C'Baoth with Leia's lightsaber. She used it to deflect his corona of lightning, but was overcome by a blinding hail of rocks. Leia, who had accompanied them, linked her mind with Mara's, allowing her to see where she was going. Exhausted and in pain, Luke used the Force to free the savage vornskrs that were leashed nearby. The growling creatures ran for Joruus, distracting the evil clone and his magics. Mara Jade charged and killed C'Baoth with a thrust of the lightsaber. Joruus C'Baoth was finally and truly dead.

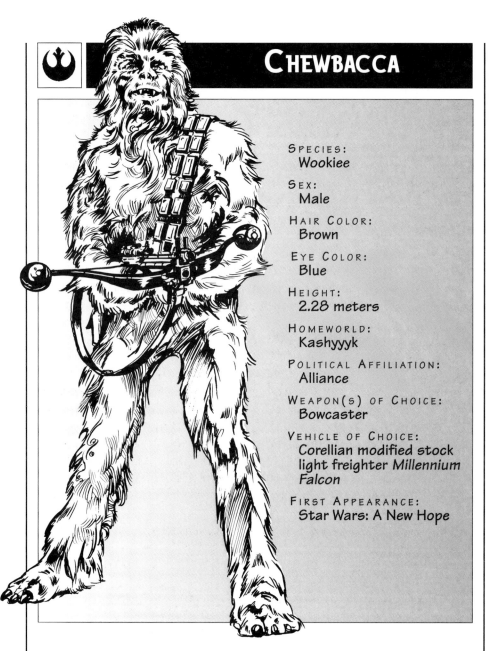

CHEWBACCA

SPECIES:
Wookiee

SEX:
Male

HAIR COLOR:
Brown

EYE COLOR:
Blue

HEIGHT:
2.28 meters

HOMEWORLD:
Kashyyyk

POLITICAL AFFILIATION:
Alliance

WEAPON(S) OF CHOICE:
Bowcaster

VEHICLE OF CHOICE:
Corellian modified stock light freighter Millennium Falcon

FIRST APPEARANCE:
Star Wars: A New Hope

Few sane inhabitants of the galaxy would argue with a muscular, two-meter-tall creature covered with fur and baring a mouthful of sharp teeth. Chewbacca the Wookiee doesn't mind if they argue, though. He always wins.

Chewbacca is a member of the Wookiee species native to the arboreal jungle planet of Kashyyyk. These bipedal creatures are intelligent and friendly, and remain firmly committed to those they like and trust. And when their anger is aroused, a Wookiee can be very dangerous.

Proficiency at hand-to-hand combat is an important part of Wookiee life. Arguments are often settled by stomping and chanting aggressively, but when they are mad enough to fight, the fur *really* flies. An opponent who is not a Wookiee may find their arms or legs ripped off, or their armor crushed—with them inside.

Kashyyyk is a beautiful world, with giant wroshyr trees whose tops grow together so densely that it's possible to walk on the top of the foliage. Although some buildings have been created in higher-ground areas,

the multiple layers of Kashyyyk's ecosystem have made it possible to leave much of the planet's surface untouched. The Wookiees themselves live in houses high in the trees. Family clusters are part of larger tree communities, which in turn are part of a larger tree city.

Although their homes and many of their personal items are handcrafted, the Wookiees are not antitechnology. They have an aptitude for high-tech repair, starship piloting and/or mechanics, and even droid programming. They also have mastered most of the high-tech energy weapons, from blasters and disruptor rifles, to shipboard blaster cannons.

Chewbacca, like many of his people, uses a more archaic weapon known as a bowcaster. The handcrafted crossbow-style weapon was created by Wookiees, and requires tremendous strength to load and cock. It shoots explosive energy quarrels that are targeted by using a telescopic sight. Chewbacca wears a bandolier slung from his left shoulder, which holds quarrels and energy packs for his bowcaster.

Chewbacca was born two hundred years prior to the Battle of Yavin. His father was a strange-looking, shorter, gray-furred Wookiee named Attichitcuk, although most of his tribe-family called him "Itchy."

Perhaps it was the carved spaceship Itchy created for his son that sparked the offspring's imagination; at an early age, Chewbacca exhibited a natural talent toward mechanics and piloting.

He was also a champion-level player of a hologame that features little holographic creatures fighting for gameboard supremacy. His best friend, Salporin, knew better than to play the game with Chewie.

As he grew into adolescence, Chewbacca learned to fly almost every craft on the planet. He grew restless, struck by wanderlust, so at the tender age of fifty standard years, Chewie left Kashyyyk and began exploring the galaxy. He traveled for 140 years—give or take a few—before the fun abruptly ended. Oblivious to the political climate that had been sweeping the galaxy, Chewbacca was enraged when he was captured by slavers. He killed five of them with his bare hands before he was finally subdued and sold to the Imperials.

For while Chewbacca had been off exploring the galaxy, the Empire had arrived. Many Wookiees had been enslaved, as their great strength made them excellent laborers. Others were hunted by the reptilian Trandoshans, whose planet lay in the same system as Kashyyyk. It had been the Trandoshans who had convinced the Empire of the value of Wookiee slaves, causing it to be declared illegal for free Wookiees to travel the space lanes.

At a hard-labor camp, an Imperial officer named Han Solo saved Chewbacca's life, in the process destroying his own promising military career. The young Corellian was courtmartialed and drummed out of the Empire. When he exited, he found that Chewbacca had become his shadow. At first Han was annoyed, but then he grew to understand.

Chewbacca had established a "life debt" to Han Solo. This custom was essentially an oath of allegiance to a person or persons who had saved a Wookiee's life. Once a life debt was undertaken, a Wookiee would serve at the person's side from one end of the galaxy to the other. Wookiees did not see this as a form of slavery, but more a personal choice to repay the honor of a gift beyond measure, and honor is an all-important concept to Wookiees.

Later, Chewbacca would expand his life debt to create an "honor family," including in it Princess Leia Organa, and Han and Leia's children. He would gladly risk his life for any of them, and often did.

Han came to appreciate the Wookiee's company and life-saving gestures, and to count him as a friend. Soon after the end of his military service, Han embarked on a smuggling career, taking Chewbacca on as his partner. At first they ran with Roa's gang, but later they hooked up with fellow Corellian Shug Ninx, his partner Salla Zend, and the gambler Lando Calrissian.

When Han won the modified freighter *Millennium Falcon* from Lando, he and Chewie gained their own fast new ship. Smuggling was easier with the *Falcon*, and "captain" Han and "first mate" Chewie modified it constantly, usually in Shug Ninx's spacebarn on the smuggler's moon of Nar Shaddaa.

Chewbacca's language is a series of grunts, growls, snuffles, barks, and terrifying roars. His vocal abilities won't allow him to speak Basic—very few Wookiees can—but he does understand it. Han did learn to understand the Wookiee's language, although he himself sounds remarkably stupid if he tries to speak it.

Han eventually went back to Kashyyyk with Chewbacca, to meet his people, and was surprised when Chewie married a female Wookiee named Mallatobuck. She had been taking care of Attichitcuk ever since the Empire's initial slave runs, when both of them had been left behind as undesirables.

During a later visit, Chewie was excited to learn that Malla was pregnant. She bore a chunky little light-furred Wookiee, and he

was named Lumpawarrump, or "Lumpy" for short. Chewbacca visited his family as often as he could, and his family, designated as an honor family, was looked after by other Wookiees.

Han and Chewie grew tired of the Empire, and Han was getting nervous about Salla Zend, who was pressuring him to settle down. Without warning, they departed on the *Falcon* for the more lawless Corporate Sector. There, Han and Chewie did runs for crime lords and smuggler barons such as Big Bunji and Ploovo Two-For-One, as well as for the Corporate Sector Authority. They were joined on their adventures by the droid Bollux and his miniature supercomputer companion, Blue Max.

After destroying the prison asteroid's Stars' End Tower, fighting Zlarb and his slavers, scuffling with Fiolla, the beautiful assistant auditor general of the CSA, and facing down the gunman Gallandro, Han and Chewie decided to take a break and return to Imperial space.

Han Solo's reputation grew as his more daring exploits made the rounds of the cantinas and reached the crime lords. Han began taking on smuggling jobs from Jabba the Hutt and others, and as Han's reputation grew, Chewbacca also became famous. His strength, head-sized fists, loaded bowcaster, and reputedly violent temper kept all but the most tenacious—or drunk—assailants away from Han.

On one of Han's spice-smuggling runs for Jabba the Hutt, the Imperials stopped his ship. In order to avoid arrest, Han jettisoned his shipment, intending to pick it up later. Unfortunately, by the time he was able to return, the spice was gone. Han and Chewie both knew Jabba was *not* going to be happy.

Before they went to Tatooine to face Jabba, the two returned to Kashyyyk to celebrate Chewbacca's two hundredth birthday. During the visit, Lumpy got lost in the lower levels of the trees, but Chewbacca rescued him in time for the surprise party the tree-family had arranged.

Finally, the meeting with Jabba couldn't be delayed any longer. Han and Chewie landed at Docking Bay 94 at the Mos Eisley spaceport. On the way to see Jabba, they stopped in at Chalmun's cantina, where an old man and a farm boy questioned them about passage to Alderaan. Han got a funny feeling about the fellow, but for 17,000 credits, Han wouldn't ask questions. That would be enough to pay Jabba off *and* get back to business.

Han and Chewie never made it to Jabba, as they were swept up in much more than they had bargained for. The old man's droids were wanted by the Empire, and Alderaan was destroyed by the huge Imperial Death Star battle station. The *Falcon* was pulled into the station, but Han and Chewie managed to hide themselves and their passengers in smuggling compartments. When the old man left to disable the tractor beam, the kid, Luke Skywalker, talked Han and Chewie into rescuing a very rich princess. Amazingly, the rescue worked . . . after a fashion. The *Falcon* got off the station and escaped into hyperspace, headed for Rebel headquarters with Princess Leia Organa on board.

Though Solo wanted nothing to do with the anti-Imperial Rebellion, Chewbacca played conscience to Solo's heartlessness

when the Rebels went up against the Death Star in what seemed a suicide attack. Han and the Wookiee brought the *Falcon* into battle just in time to save Luke Skywalker from disintegration. Luke's torpedo found its mark and destroyed the Death Star. Han, Chewie, and Luke were all fêted as heroes.

Solo didn't plan to stay with the Rebellion, although events would soon transpire that would lead him back to aid his new friends. A pirate raid, led by Crimson Jack, left Han penniless and unable to repay Jabba. With the Hutt's bounty hanging over his head, the Rebellion suddenly seemed a safer place than the smuggling underworld.

Shortly after the Battle of Yavin, Han and Chewie attempted to return to Kashyyyk for Life Day, an important Wookiee celebration that occurred every three years. Even while they themselves were dodging blockades and TIE fighters, Chewie's family was facing Imperials in their own home. Two stormtroopers, a technician, and a commander searched the home looking for evidence of Rebel sympathies. While a quick-thinking human trader helped Malla and Itchy fool the Imperials, Chewbacca and Han finally arrived and took care of the Imperials. The celebration, at the Tree of Life, commenced shortly thereafter.

Life in the Alliance proved good for Chewbacca's sense of worth. He could identify with the Rebels' honor, and he certainly had no affection for the Empire. Once he had helped convince Han to join up with the Rebels full time—more or less—they helped free other worlds and other species, learning the finer points of life on the *real* edge of the Empire; while smuggling was all but tolerated by many Imperial officials, rebellion certainly wasn't.

Shortly before the Rebels relocated to Hoth, C-3PO and R2-D2 once again accompanied Han and Chewie back to Kashyyyk, where they discovered the tribal Elder had canceled the Life Day celebration. The Orga root that was their special food was found in the lower levels of the trees, and Imperial patrols down below had made the predators angry and hungry. After Chewie got in a fight with the elder, he and Han, along with the droids, ventured down to the eighth level. There, they were witnesses when the sentient plants finally attacked the Imperial troopers and scientists who were also searching for the Orga root. They helped save a female biologist named Gyla Petro, and Chewie calmed the plants down enough to acquire the Orga root. The Life Day ceremonies were celebrated after all.

Soon thereafter, the Empire discovered the Rebel's Echo Base on Hoth, and Lando Calrissian betrayed Han to Darth Vader and the bounty

hunter, Boba Fett. To his horror, Chewbacca was forced to watch the Corellian frozen in a block of carbonite. Over the following months, Chewbacca, Lando, Luke Skywalker, and Princess Leia all worked to find Han and in turn the best way to rescue him. Their daring plan involved a gradual infiltration of Jabba the Hutt's palace. The rescue worked, and Han was reunited with his friends.

All too soon, another assault against the Empire was being readied. Solo, who had finally accepted a commission in the Alliance, was to lead a strike force onto the forest moon of Endor to disable a shield generator. That would allow the Alliance's starfighters to attack and destroy the second Death Star, under construction above the moon. Working with the native Ewoks—small bearlike creatures—Chewbacca helped defeat the Imperials, gaining access to the shield bunker for Han, Leia, and the droids. The mission was a success.

After the fall of the Empire, Chewbacca, Han, and Lando went to Kashyyyk in the *Falcon* and Lando's *Cobra*, but quickly discovered that slavers had returned to the world, led by the N'Gai colloquially known as "Knife." With the help of Malla's blacksheep older brother, Vargi, Knife was cleaning out the families of Chewbacca's treeclan. Lando and Han helped save Chewie and his family, although Knife escaped in Lando's ship.

As the years passed, Chewbacca divided his time between his family and his travels with Han and the Alliance. He assisted in the mission to Bakura, worked with the short-lived Senate Interplanetary Intelligence Network—SPIN—team, and argued with Han about his romantic overtures when he kidnapped Leia to Dathomir. For once Chewie the conscience was wrong, and soon after the adventures on Dathomir, Han and Leia were married.

Five years after the destruction of the second Death Star, the Alliance faced the return of the brilliant and ruthless Grand Admiral Thrawn and his Imperial forces.

Chewie helped protect the pregnant Leia by taking her to Kashyyyk, where they were attacked by the deadly Noghri. He helped Leia convince the Noghri that the Empire, not the Alliance, was their real enemy. Chewie participated in the destruction of Mount Tantiss on Wayland, as well as in the battles against Thrawn's forces.

Chewbacca aided Han on various missions against the reborn Emperor Palpatine, first rescuing Lando and Wedge Antilles's strike teams on Coruscant, then escaping from Nar Shaddaa along with Shug Ninx and Salla Zend, and finally making a run to save Luke Skywalker from the clutches of the Emperor on Byss When Han and Leia returned to Nar Shaddaa, Chewie was able to capture the helmet of Boba Fett. He kept it in the *Falcon*'s cockpit, a trophy more prestigious than any he had ever claimed.

In the time between adventures and missions, Chewbacca was a devoted "uncle" to Han and Leia's three children, supplementing the stuffy C-3PO as their caretaker. But adventuring certainly didn't cease. After his escape from the glitterstim-spice mines of Kessel, Chewie was instrumental in freeing a horde of Wookiee slaves from the Empire's Maw Installation. He helped Han and Leia search for the Jedi hiding place known as Plett's Well, and helped Leia rescue her children when the Firrerreon named Hethrir kidnapped them.

Twenty-three years after he first met Luke Skywalker in the noisy Mos Eisley cantina, Chewbacca brought him a new Jedi student; his own nineteen-year-old nephew, Lowbacca. The young Wookiee had strong ties to the Force, and his training quickly commenced at the Jedi academy on Yavin Four.

Chewbacca spends a lot more time with his own family these days, but his extended family of the Rebellion is still very important to him. As long as they need Han, the *Millennium Falcon*, and Chewie himself, the good-natured and loyal Wookiee will stand ready to fight for the cause of freedom.

QUEEN MOTHER TA'A CHUME

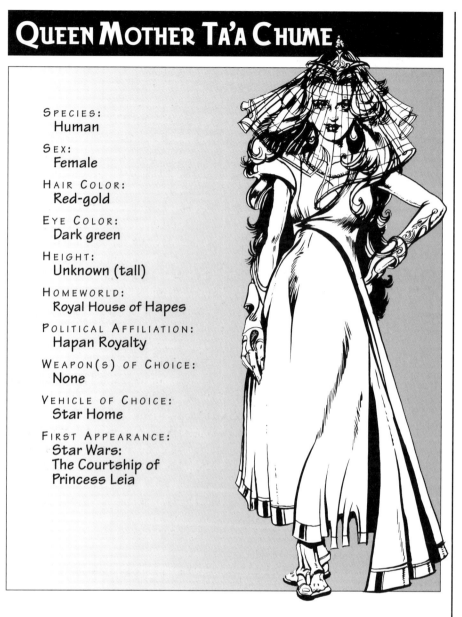

SPECIES:
Human

SEX:
Female

HAIR COLOR:
Red-gold

EYE COLOR:
Dark green

HEIGHT:
Unknown (tall)

HOMEWORLD:
Royal House of Hapes

POLITICAL AFFILIATION:
Hapan Royalty

WEAPON(S) OF CHOICE:
None

VEHICLE OF CHOICE:
Star Home

FIRST APPEARANCE:
Star Wars:
The Courtship of
Princess Leia

The sixty-three worlds of the Hapes cluster were founded by a group of male pirates called the Lorell Raiders. For over a century, they staked out trade routes of the Old Republic, seizing ships and cargo. When they found a beautiful woman, they would take her to the hidden worlds of Hapes.

As the planet Hapes evolved and the pirates retired or were captured, the women came to hold dominance over the men. A matriarchy was established; for four thousand years, the queens ruled not only Hapes, but the entire cluster. Women made up the core of the elite, men played secondary roles as fathers and laborers.

Queen Mother Ta'a Chume is one of a long line of beautiful people, emitting an aura of slender grace, and looks much younger than her years. Calm and composed, Ta'a Chume is veiled in public, as are many of the nobility of Hapes.

Unfortunately for her, Ta'a Chume did not have a female heir. Her first son was weak and pacifistic, and she arranged his assassination. Her second son, the stunningly handsome Prince Isolder, would have to find a royal wife who both befitted him and could provide him many heirs of his own.

The first woman Isolder loved was Lady Ellian, who was conveniently murdered. Ta'a Chume played the role of sorrowful mother, but in time, she steered Isolder toward other women. When he fell in love with New Republic Ambassador Leia Organa, Ta'a Chume had had enough. This Leia was weak and a political pacifist. The Hapan dynasty would collapse in a year under her rule.

Even so, Isolder and ambassadors from the sixty-three Hapes worlds traveled to Coruscant to shower Leia with gifts. But inside her space citadel, the Star Home, the queen was plotting. She hired assassins to take the Rebel woman, but they were foiled by Prince Isolder himself.

Ta'a Chume's other schemes to assassinate Leia backfired. Luke confronted the queen about the attempts, and her son put together the clues that tied the queen to the deaths of his dead brother and first love.

But for the queen, the worst turn of events was that Isolder changed his mind, and was to marry a common woman named Teneniel Djo. She was one of the witches on the arid world of Dathomir, had no royal lineage, and wore animal and lizard skins. But Tenenial Djo was not common, nor weak, and she proved it to Ta'a Chume.

Not that it mattered; Isolder had had enough of Ta'a Chume's schemings and was going forward with the marriage with or without her permission. Ever one to hold her head up in pride, Ta'a Chume relented.

Years later, Isolder and Teneniel would have a female child, Tenel Ka. Grandmother Ta'a Chume doted on the child as best she could, trying to rescue her from her mother's wild ways. The battle of grandma's will versus free will would go on for quite some time.

SALACIOUS CRUMB

SPECIES:
Kowakian lizard-monkey

SEX:
Male

HAIR COLOR:
Reddish brown

EYE COLOR:
Yellow

HEIGHT:
.7 meters

HOMEWORLD:
Unknown

POLITICAL AFFILIATION:
Loyal to
Jabba the Hutt

WEAPONS OF CHOICE:
None

VEHICLE OF CHOICE:
None

FIRST APPEARANCE:
Star Wars: Return of the
Jedi

DEATH:
On Jabba the Hutt's
sail barge

Salacious Crumb was a brown, leathery-skinned Kowakian lizard-monkey. The bizarre scrawny little creature seemed only slightly sentient, but his stupidity was partially an act. Although he mainly spoke in cackles and laughs, Salacious was intelligent enough to survive his tough job as Jabba's court jester.

Crumb had met Jabba on the Kwenn space station. Oblivious to the Mantilorrian rat catchers pursuing a scampering, cackling little beast, Jabba didn't notice when the creature escaped into his ship. Crumb

hid himself away in Jabba's own shipboard quarters, eating a greenish goo from Jabba's feeding bowl.

When the Hutt did discover the intruder, he was surprised, and tried to snatch Crumb up and eat him—after all, Crumb *was* sitting in his food. The lizard-monkey was too quick, darting to the ceiling struts, the bowl on his head like a dripping green blast helmet.

Bib Fortuna and Bidlo Kwerve burst into the room, arguing about something trivial, and Crumb dumped the bowl of food on their heads, slopping green goo all over them. An angry Bidlo tried to shoot the cackling creature, but only green ooze squirted from his pistol, glopping onto Fortuna's face.

Jabba laughed so hard that his whole body shook. He called Salacious Crumb down to him and offered him a job and a future. Crumb's duty was to make Jabba laugh. Every day. Without fail.

When Luke Skywalker appeared before Jabba to petition the release of his friends—Han Solo, Leia Organa, and Chewbacca—Crumb cackled loudly. So did Jabba. The laughter stopped a short time later when Skywalker managed to kill Jabba's other pet, the rancor.

Crumb accompanied his master as they traveled to the Great Pit of Carkoon. But everything went wrong, starting with Skywalker's escape, and ending with the death of Jabba the Hutt. Even the lizard-monkey wasn't safe from harm; as he pulled the eye sensor out of the translator droid C-3PO, the astromech-droid R2-D2 zapped Crumb with an electrical shock.

Salacious Crumb didn't have to worry, though. As soon as the Rebels escaped the sail barge, it blew up, killing him and everyone aboard.

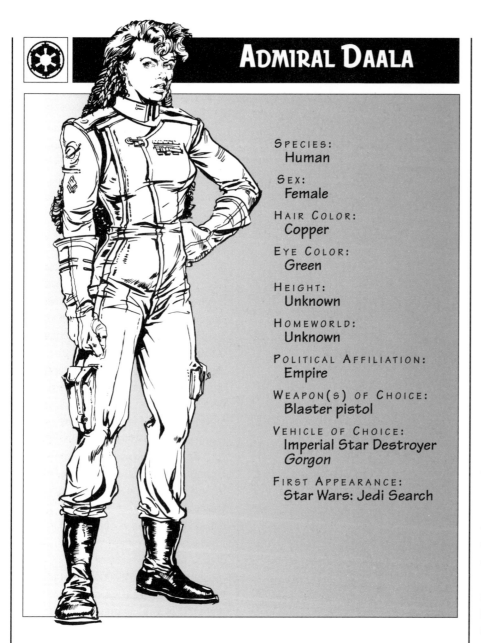

ADMIRAL DAALA

SPECIES:
Human

SEX:
Female

HAIR COLOR:
Copper

EYE COLOR:
Green

HEIGHT:
Unknown

HOMEWORLD:
Unknown

POLITICAL AFFILIATION:
Empire

WEAPON(S) OF CHOICE:
Blaster pistol

VEHICLE OF CHOICE:
Imperial Star Destroyer
Gorgon

FIRST APPEARANCE:
Star Wars: Jedi Search

A beautiful woman with striking features, Admiral Daala was the ruthless commander of a fleet of Star Destroyers, and the one-time lover of one of the most evil men in the Empire. Forgotten in a remote sector of space for over a decade since the Battle of Yavin, Daala emerged to wreak destruction.

As a young woman, Daala had attended the Imperial Academy on Caridia, one of the most grueling of training grounds for military service. She was an excellent strategist, a fierce combatant, and excelled in every curriculum. Still, despite her outstanding talents, sexism gripped the Empire, supported wholly by Emperor Palpatine.

Upon Daala's graduation, the Academy assigned her to difficult and thankless assignments, promoting less-qualified men above her time and again. She created a false persona in the computer networks, and set out to create a name for herself. Several of the radical ideas caught the eye of Moff Tarkin, who traveled to Caridia to find this brilliant tactician.

Daala was quickly assigned to Tarkin's personal staff, and was brought to the Oversector Outer, which included almost all of the Outer Rim Territories. They became lovers, despite the fact that he had a wife on Phelarion, and their intelligence and ruthless drive complemented each other fiercely. Eventually Tarkin became the first Grand Moff, with unlimited decision-making power in priority sectors, reporting only to the Emperor.

The ambitious Tarkin wanted to keep Daala hidden from the Emperor, and assigned her to command a secret project, deep in the black-hole cluster outside Kessel, in an area known as the Maw. As the Navy's first female admiral, Daala would command both the project and four Star Destroyers. Tarkin took her to watch the construction of the Destroyers in the orbiting Kuat Drive Yards, impressing upon her the power he was granting.

The Maw Installation was intended as a super-think tank where the most brilliant scientists and theoreticians could convene and create new weapons. Daala knew that Tarkin kept both her and the installation a secret from Emperor Palpatine, protecting and using her. Only he and those stationed at the Maw knew about the installation's existence. Tarkin could take credit for any destructive devices created.

When the installation's construction was completed, the workers and architects left the sector, but Daala personally reconfigured their navicomputer. All the builders were sucked into a nearby black hole, leaving no loose ends.

It was at the Maw that administrator Tol Sivron, top Imperial designer Chief Bevel Lemelisk, and Omwat designer/engineer Qwi Xux created the plans for the first Death Star. They built a prototype, winning Tarkin's accolades. When the Emperor approved the Death Star plans, Tarkin took Lemelisk from the Maw to supervise construction.

Tarkin often returned to the Maw Installation to see his lover. The final time, he challenged the scientists to create a weapon that *surpassed* the Death Star. He gave them nine years to complete the task, then said good-bye to Daala. She was given strict orders not to leave the Maw, nor allow anyone else to do so.

Over the intervening years, Daala enforced a strict military code. The only break from protocol was the length of her copper hair; she had arrived with stubble—part of the Academy's humiliation efforts—but grew it out, until it reached her hips.

Her own Star Destroyer was the *Gorgon*, captained by Captain Kratas. The other ships under her command were the *Manticore*, the *Basilisk*, and the *Hydra*. Daala's total command was over 180,000 people.

Daala did not take another lover, saving herself for Tarkin, who had given her the opportunity no one else would have dared to. The installation received no news of the galaxy beyond the Maw, as the swirling space field blacked out all external HoloNet transmissions.

Eleven years passed. Daala knew the men were restless, and she had news and weaponry to report. Then, an Imperial shuttle burst into the Maw, and delivery seemed imminent. Daala was surprised to find that it contained not Imperials, but Han Solo, Chewbacca, and Kyp Durron, newly escaped from the Kessel spice mines.

Daala and Captain Kratas interrogated Solo, finding out about Tarkin's death, the destruction of both Death Stars, and the fall of the Empire. Consulting with chief administrator Tol Sivron and top designer Qwi Xux, Daala planned to unleash upon an unsuspecting galaxy her—and Tarkin's—ultimate weapon: the Sun Crusher!

Unfortunately for Daala, Han Solo appealed to Qwi Xux's conscience, and the scientist freed Han, Kyp, and Chewbacca. The quartet stole the only working model of the Sun Crusher. The resulting space battle left the *Hydra* sucked into a black hole, while the remaining three Destroyers chased the Sun Crusher outside the Maw. Daala's ships engaged much of the Kessel fleet, wreaking havoc before vanishing into hyperspace.

Daala retreated to the Cauldron Nebula to plan tactics against the Alliance. She moved her ships to wait at the end of the Corellian Trade Spine, a heavily traveled shipping lane. They captured a Corellian corvette on its way to Dantooine, released it, and traced the Alliance frequencies when the ship reported the attack. Daala had the ship destroyed shortly after the transmission ended.

She traveled to Dantooine, where the inhabitants of Eol Sha had been relocated by Luke Skywalker and the Alliance. Dispatching six AT-ATs, Daala ordered the destruction of the entire colony.

Her next target was Calamari, the site of an Alliance starship-construction facility. Two of her Star Destroyers attacked the water planet from space, their turbolasers causing devastating damage on the floating cities. When Admiral Ackbar pulled the fleet of B-wing defenders to fight the two Destroyers, Daala ordered the third Destroyer, the *Manticore*, to move in and destroy the shipyards. What she didn't know was that Ackbar was planning

to trap them. He used a partially constructed ship, the *Startide*, as a battering ram, driving the ship and its spacedock into the *Manticore*, resulting in a brilliant double explosion.

When Rebel battleships responded to the attack on Calamari, Daala withdrew the *Gorgon* and the *Basilisk* back into the Cauldron Nebula. There, she decided to use Ackbar's own tactics against him, to make a lightning attack on Coruscant, the Alliance base, and drive the *Basilisk* into the city.

Unfortunately for Daala, Kyp Durron had resurrected the Sun Crusher. As the admiral prepared to lead her ships to Coruscant, Kyp launched sun-destroying torpedoes into the cluster of blue-giant stars at the heart of the Cauldron Nebula. Although Daala ordered an immediate withdrawal, the cataclysmic explosion of the nebula destroyed the *Basilisk*.

The *Gorgon* barely escaped, losing much of its shields and firepower. Daala ordered the ship on a blind jump into hyperspace, but many of the systems were destroyed, and took weeks to repair. They limped back to the Maw Installation just as the Alliance was raiding it.

The battle was raging within the Maw when a new Death Star prototype, piloted by the inept bureaucrat Tol Sivron, and the Sun Crusher, piloted by Kyp Durron, both entered the fray. Although Daala requested assistance from the Death Star, Sivron refused. The admiral downloaded the weapon plans from the installation's computers, and then set what appeared to be a suicide course into the installation. As the Imperial research facility blew up, Daala's ship disappeared.

But the *Gorgon* again survived and limped away, unnoticed. The admiral addressed her crew, telling them they were headed toward the Core systems, where they would ally themselves with one of the powerful Imperial warlords. With the weapon plans from the Maw Installation, Daala and her crew would be irreplaceably important to the rebuilding of the Empire.

FIGRIN D'AN (AND HIS BAND)

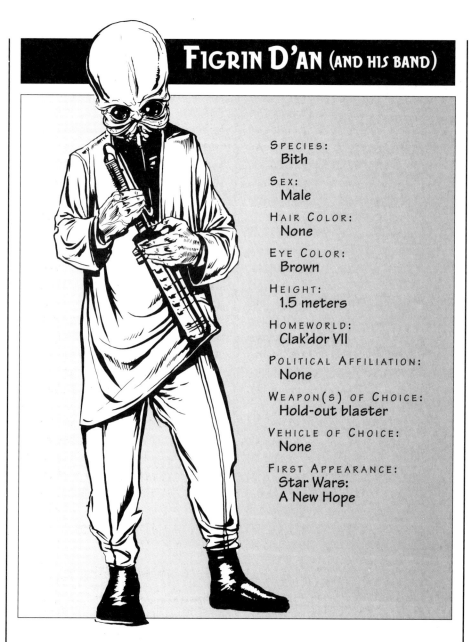

SPECIES:
Bith

SEX:
Male

HAIR COLOR:
None

EYE COLOR:
Brown

HEIGHT:
1.5 meters

HOMEWORLD:
Clak'dor VII

POLITICAL AFFILIATION:
None

WEAPON(S) OF CHOICE:
Hold-out blaster

VEHICLE OF CHOICE:
None

FIRST APPEARANCE:
**Star Wars:
A New Hope**

Imperial, Rebel, bounty hunter, quarry, native, alien . . . as long as he and his band get paid, the Bith musician Figrin D'an only sees what he needs to see.

Figrin is a native of Clak'dor VII, a small planet orbiting the large white star Colu in the Mayagil Sector. His people, the Bith, live on the boggy world, devastated generations before by a chemical war. They are highly advanced on the evolutionary scale, and their oversized craniums hold larger, complex brains. The regions controlling aptitude in the arts and sciences are especially well developed, but the brain centers for fear, aggression, and other instinctual animal responses are small and atrophied.

The Biths' bodies are unusual, as well. Their five-fingered hands have fully opposable thumbs and little fingers. Their large, lidless eyes can focus on tiny details for hours. Their respiratory system extracts every usable molecule from each breath, expelling tiny amounts of waste gasses through the skin.

The Bith society is structured, advanced, and peaceful. Their mating is completely arranged by computer, with no possibility for birth defects. Political leaders are chosen by an analytical computer program.

Musically creative, Figrin gathered five other Biths to play with him in an intergalactic jizz band called "Figrin D'an and the Modal Nodes." Because of his mean riffs on the Kloo horn, Figrin was nicknamed "Fiery Figrin." The Bith bandleader also played hot percussion on his gasan string drum. Doikk Na'ts played the Dorenian Beshniquel—commonly called a "Fizzz"—and Tedn and Ickabel both played Fanfars. Nalan played the Bandfill, complete with horn bells, while Tech controlled the sound with an Ommni Box. A sometime backup band member, Lirin Car'n, also played the Kloo horn.

Despite atrocities he's seen on many worlds, Figrin is politically neutral on the subject of the Empire and the Alliance. As long as they leave him alone to play his music, earn his money, and play sabacc, Figrin doesn't care who's in charge.

His neutrality doesn't mean he can't be bought. Figrin is more than happy to dispense valuable information for the right price. He won't accept outright bribery, though, preferring to gamble with the questioner. With each win for the Bith, he gives

the loser a bit of information. His motto is simple: "The more you lose, the more you win."

Eventually, Figrin and his band came to Tatooine, where they were hired by a powerful Tatooine fixture, Jabba the Hutt. The gang lord used to call the Bith group his "favorite band." Playing for Jabba and his court was an honor—not to mention well paying—but the musicians were careful. They knew what had happened to some of Jabba's other "favorites" over the years.

The band eventually did incur the wrath of the Hutt gang lord when they accepted a onetime contract to play at Lady Valarian's wedding reception. A Devaronian named Labria had talked the Whiphid bride-to-be out of using Max Rebo's band and into using the Modal Nodes. Lady Valarian had agreed, less from his recommendation than for the fact that they were Jabba's band. The morning of the nuptials, Labria informed Jabba that the band was playing at the

Whiphid wedding. In return, Jabba's "least favorite spy" was granted immunity for a slight he had made against the Hutt. One of the band, Doikk, soon got news from Kodu Terrafin, one of the Hutt's courier pilots; Jabba was angry. Very angry.

Still, the band could earn its 3,000 credits and leave the planet if it played its cards—and its songs—right.

Despite Jabba's thugs sprinkled throughout the crowd, all was going smoothly at the reception, when suddenly an argument between the bride and groom led to a full-fledged meleé, with Imperial stormtroopers arriving shortly thereafter. It seemed the place was being raided for illegal gambling, as well!

As they escaped, Doikk and Figrin saved

the life of an ugly human bartender, Wuher, who earlier had complimented them on their music. He pulled them into a cantina owned by a Wookiee named Chalmun, who offered them a two-season contract. Chalmun hoped that the live music in his cantina would bring in more peaceful locals. Figrin agreed, figuring the band could find a way off world and away from Jabba soon enough.

Then Labria, who had helped arrange the day's events far more than anyone would ever know, challenged Figrin to a game of sabacc. By the time they were finished playing, Labria owned all of the musicians' instruments except Doikk Na'ts's Fizzz. The band wouldn't be able to leave the planet until Figrin D'an bought the instruments back from the Devaronian.

It was while playing at the cantina that the band witnessed the brawl involving Dr. Evazan, Ponda Baba, the young Luke Skywalker, and his companion, Ben Kenobi, who made quick work of the two thugs. Nobody cared, but the band had hardly missed a beat. Eventually, Figrin D'an and the Modal Nodes did recover their instruments and depart Tatooine. They were soon lost in the millions of lounge clubs and revues throughout the galaxy.

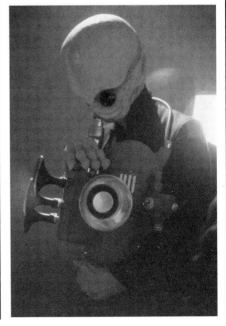

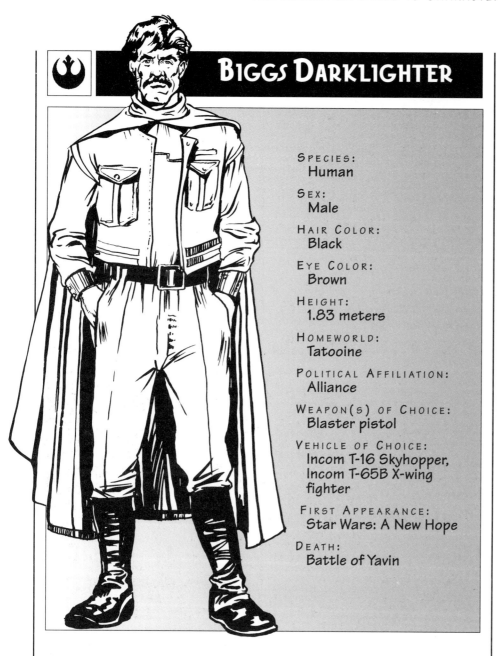

BIGGS DARKLIGHTER

SPECIES:
Human

SEX:
Male

HAIR COLOR:
Black

EYE COLOR:
Brown

HEIGHT:
1.83 meters

HOMEWORLD:
Tatooine

POLITICAL AFFILIATION:
Alliance

WEAPON(S) OF CHOICE:
Blaster pistol

VEHICLE OF CHOICE:
Incom T-16 Skyhopper,
Incom T-65B X-wing
fighter

FIRST APPEARANCE:
Star Wars: A New Hope

DEATH:
Battle of Yavin

Raised a privileged child on Tatooine, Biggs Darklighter was the son of food magnate Huff Darklighter, a generous but distant man. The elder Darklighter owned dozens of moisture farms, and bought water from other moisture farmers at cut-rate prices. He used some to irrigate his own subterranean crops and sold the rest at a high profit.

As a teenager, Biggs spent much of his time in the town of Anchorhead, where he met young Luke Skywalker. Despite the fast friendship that developed, an undercurrent of competition kept their lives charged. Biggs and Luke raced landspeeders and skyhoppers, all the while planning to enter the Imperial Space Academy together. They also planned to buy a spaceship after graduation, though they did not have a plan for its use.

The two often raced skyhoppers through Beggar's Canyon in the Jundland Wastes "tagging" womp rats. Luke was a better shot in his used Incom T-16 skyhopper, but Biggs was a better pilot in his newer model. Biggs "threaded" his way through a small opening in a sixty-meter spindle of rock known as the Stone Needle, giving him near-legendary status among Anchorhead residents. Others who ran the Wastes with Biggs and Luke were the jealous Fixer, sexy Camie, and tagalongs Deak and Windy. Sometimes they were joined by Tank, another hopeful pilot.

Biggs and Luke also engaged in another semidangerous sport, "invented" by Fixer. Sandsurfing involved the participants being dragged behind a sand skiff, while wearing repulsor disks on their feet. Fixer was in constant competition with Biggs and Luke, and engineered a dangerous obstacle course in an attempt to prove himself better than they. On a jump over the Great Pit of Carkoon, Fixer was knocked unconscious and fell toward the grasping tentacles of the Sarlacc. Biggs and Luke worked together to save Fixer's life, and not wanting the stunt to be duplicated, they acceded that Fixer was the "king of the sandsurfers."

Biggs's father arranged his son's commission into the Academy, and Tank was also accepted, but Luke's uncle, Owen Lars, kept his nephew behind for "another season." A short time before Biggs departed, the Anchorhead gang had a celebration and race in Beggar's Canyon. The adventure ended in battle when a clan of Tusken Raiders attacked. When Biggs was wounded by a Raider's gaderffii stick, Luke was forced to pilot him to safety through the treacherous Diablo's Cut.

While in the Academy, Biggs and several classmates made contact with the Rebellion while on a trip to the planet Bestine—not to be confused with Bestine, the capitol of Tatooine. The group made plans to join the forces fighting the Empire as soon as possible. Upon his graduation, the twenty-four-year-old Biggs was assigned to a non-combat post as first mate on the merchant ship *Rand Ecliptic*.

A week after his commission, Biggs made a final trip to his native Tatooine. There, he and Luke had an unexpected reunion at Fixer's shop in Tosche power sta-

Red Leader's first strike team was killed on its approach down the Death Star trench, Luke, Biggs, and Wedge Antilles started their own run. Luke led, with the other two pilots as backup.

Unfortunately, Darth Vader and two TIE fighters dogged the trio. First, Wedge's ship was hit and he had to abort, and then Biggs's X-wing was destroyed in a blast from Vader's ship. Luke Skywalker choked back remorse over the loss of his friend and completed the run alone. His missiles destroyed the Death Star.

Shortly after the Battle of Yavin, Luke returned to Tattooine. He found that the Darklighters had left the planet, and that their lands had been bought by Baron Orman Tagge, a brother to a general killed

tion. Luke told him of a space battle above Tatooine, but Biggs assured him it was just ships refueling. Later, in private, Biggs told Luke that he was going to join the Rebellion, then bade his friend good-bye. The next morning, he departed Tatooine.

A few short weeks later, Biggs and his executive officer, Derek "Hobbie" Klivian, made contact with Rebellion spies while at the Imperial Navy Yard in the central Bestine system. Aided by their Captain Heleisk— himself a Rebel spy—the two young officers staged a mutiny aboard the *Rand Ecliptic* and stole it, escaping from the Navy Yards with a valuable ship- ment of rubindun ore.

Biggs was a great help to the Rebellion, piloting an X-wing fighter in several space battles. He was united with his friend Luke Skywalker on the Fourth Moon of Yavin as

the battle against the first Death Star was about to begin. Both childhood friends were flying with the X-wing Red Squadron, Biggs as Red Three, Luke as Red Five.

In the battle above the surface of the Death Star, Biggs narrowly escaped death when a TIE fighter on his tail was destroyed by Luke's X-wing. He later destroyed several TIEs himself, and when

aboard the Death Star. Fixer and Camie, now married, lived in the Darklighter estate.

Today, Luke still keeps alive the memory of Biggs Darklighter, the friend who gave all to the cause in which he believed.

DENGAR

SPECIES:
Human

SEX:
Male

HAIR COLOR:
Unknown

EYE COLOR:
Unknown

HEIGHT:
1.8 meters

HOMEWORLD:
Unknown

POLITICAL AFFILIATION:
Free-lance bounty hunter

WEAPON(S) OF CHOICE:
Blaster file, concussion grenades, vibroblade

VEHICLE OF CHOICE:
Unknown

FIRST APPEARANCE:
Star Wars: The Empire Strikes Back

crystal swamps of Agrilat. Even though Solo had been accepted into the Imperial Academy of Caridia, he couldn't refuse the challenge.

The swoop race was one of the most-watched events in the Corellian system, and the two racers seemed evenly matched—until the final stretch. Solo sped to a lower altitude, zooming through the dangerous underbrush, pulling ahead slightly. Dengar decided to go one better and swooped closer to the swamps, taking an even lower approach. As he cleared the last bit of foliage before the straightaway to the target, Dengar didn't realize Solo was directly above him.

Dengar pulled his swoop up and crashed into Solo's main repulsor fin. The impact left him badly burned, with major cranial trauma. While he was recovering, he also received word he had been kicked out of professional swoop racing for engaging in the illegal race with Solo. Dengar's life was destroyed, and he held Han Solo responsible.

Although he eventually healed, Dengar carried a burning hatred for Solo. For a time, he worked as a gladiator, but eventu-

When Darth Vader put out a call for bounty hunters to find Han Solo, one of his obvious choices was the armored Dengar. This particular hunter had a long-standing grudge against Solo, and his hunt would be personal.

When he was a young adult, Dengar had been a successful swoop jockey on the popular Ferini team. Swoops were dangerous repulsorlift bikes, and Dengar had been racing them since his childhood, becoming a cult hero throughout the Corellian system. With the Ferini team, he became even more

popular, gaining endorsement contracts and ever higher wages and winnings. But the controlled world of professional, tour swoop racing was not what held Dengar's attention.

The private tour called to Dengar—wild and dangerous, and with one major challenge. A young Corellian named Han Solo had become a popular swoop jockey on the private circuit, and Dengar was constantly compared to him. Finally, tired of the comparisons, Dengar challenged Solo to a winner-takes-all race across the dangerous

ally, he found another calling: The Empire wanted him as an assassin. They would train him and provide him with equipment that might help balance his mind—unstable since the accident. Records about Dengar's time in service to the Empire—and subsequent departure—have not yet been found.

When he learned there was a galaxy-wide bounty on Solo's head, he decided to become a bounty hunter. Outfitting himself with body-protecting blast armor and major weaponry, Dengar eventually came into the employ of Jabba the Hutt. The ex-racer's success ratio over the following decade was debatable. Of the twenty-three bounties he captured, only six were alive.

Shortly before the Battle of Hoth, Boba Fett gathered several other hunters, including Bossk, Dengar, and Skorr, to find Han Solo. The hunters captured him aboard the pirate Raskar's ship, along with Luke Skywalker and Chewbacca. While bringing the trio to the planet Ord Mantell, the hunters were taken by surprise when Luke used his Force powers to engineer the Alliance members' escape.

Events soon conspired to bring Dengar into the service of Darth Vader on the Super Star Destroyer *Executor*. Baba Fett, Bossk, IG-88, Zuckuss, and 4-LOM were assigned to track down the *Millennium Falcon*. Unfortunately for Dengar and the others, Fett was the one who succeeded in tracking the *Falcon* to the Bespin system, and who received not only the bounty, but also the carbon-frozen body of Han Solo to deliver to Jabba the Hutt.

Months later, Dengar arrived on Tatooine, making his way to Jabba's palace and the endless partying there. Too drunk on Zeltron spiced wine, he missed the excitement when the execution party left to dispose of Luke, Han, and Chewbacca. He soon learned that Jabba was dead, and the sail barge wrecked.

A short time later, Dengar set out to search for Jabba's body among the wreckage of the sail barge near the Great Pit of Carkoon. The hunter had figured that Jabba would have kept an identi-chip with him—one that was needed to open the mysterious and hopefully treasure-filled vaults deep in the palace. Instead of Jabba, Dengar found Boba Fett, devoid of armor and covered in scars and fibers from the Sarlacc. Dengar took Fett back to the palace, and spent the next month nursing him back to health using Jabba's medical droids. During that time, Dengar was also constantly traveling to Mos Eisley on mysterious business. When Fett was well enough, the two set off in Dengar's ship, bound for Nar Shaddaa, the spaceport moon that functioned as the smuggling center of the galaxy.

Six years after the death of Jabba the Hutt, Solo and his now-wife Leia went to Nar Shaddaa, where Han was surprised to find that Boba Fett and Dengar were waiting for him in his quarters. Dodging a hail of blaster fire, Leia and Han made it off world, escaping to Byss in Salla Zend's *Starlight Intruder*.

Fett and Dengar followed in Fett's *Slave II*, snatching their prey's coordinates and jumping into hyperspace. Although the *Slave II* arrived at Byss before the *Starlight Intruder*, only Salla's ship was cleared to get through the planetary security shields. The shields closed, locking out Fett's ship and breaking off a control rudder. As they spun away, trying to regain control of the ship, Dengar angrily told Fett this was the last time he'd ever work with him.

Dengar's current whereabouts are unknown, but his bounty-hunting days are far from over. In the back of his mind, the hunter knows that, one day, he will cause Solo as much pain as the Corellian has caused him.

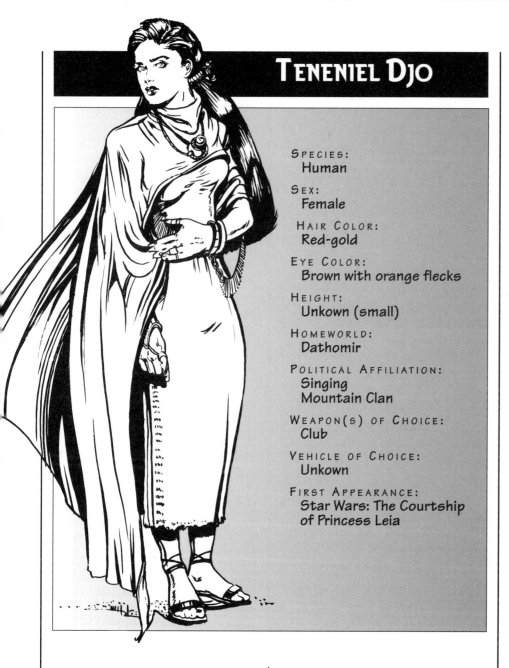

TENENIEL DJO

SPECIES:
Human

SEX:
Female

HAIR COLOR:
Red-gold

EYE COLOR:
Brown with orange flecks

HEIGHT:
Unkown (small)

HOMEWORLD:
Dathomir

POLITICAL AFFILIATION:
Singing
Mountain Clan

WEAPON(S) OF CHOICE:
Club

VEHICLE OF CHOICE:
Unkown

FIRST APPEARANCE:
Star Wars: The Courtship
of Princess Leia

Luckily for Teneniel Djo, the first Jedi she whacked on the head with a club was Luke Skywalker. With a romantic style like that, it's no surprise the Dathomirian witch became betrothed to a Hapes prince.

Teneniel Djo was part of a long line of Force-using Nightsisters on Dathomir. Part of the Singing Mountain Clan, Teneniel is the daughter of Allaya Djo, who led the clan until her death, after which her grandmother Augwynne Djo took control. But unknown to Teneniel, the clan was looking to her to be their next queen.

The clan's women conducted the business, while the men acted as servants or mates. Women of the Singing Mountain Clan rode savage rancor beasts, taming them through kindness and magic songs. In order to use their magic—which they did not realize was a part of the Force—the clans of Nightsisters chanted and sang . . . all except for the evil Gethzerion. She was the only one who knew she could tap into the Force without ritual.

Many of Teneniel's aunts had been pulled to the dark side, led by the grotesque Gethzerion. The evil Nightsisters tried to convert the women of the Singing Mountain Clan; when refused, the Nightsisters launched attacks.

Patrolling the deserts of Dathomir one day, Teneniel found two men poking around an ancient Chu'unthor spaceship. Sensing that one was stronger in magic, she attacked, tied the two up, and walked them back toward her clan village. She was certain that the blondish magic user would be her new husband; the other was nice looking, but purely ornamental.

The blond freed himself and his companion with some kind of shining sword. Teneniel discovered that she had captured a Jedi named Luke Skywalker, along with Hapes ruler, Prince Isolder. Luke and Isolder agreed to accompany Teneniel back to the village, hoping she could help them find the missing Han Solo and Princess Leia.

Luke and Isolder were reunited with Leia, Han, Chewbacca, and the droids, R2-D2 and C-3PO. The Alliance heroes, Teneniel, and Isolder became involved in a raid on an Imperial prison fortress, and were attacked by Gethzerion and the full clan of evil Nightsisters. As if matters weren't grim enough, a rogue Imperial warlord named Zsinj began firing on the planet from his Star Destroyer, the *Iron Fist*.

During the battles that followed, Teneniel and Isolder fell in love. When he asked her to be his wife, she initially resisted. Would his people accept her even though she was not of royal lineage? He assured her they would—even his traitorous mother, Queen Ta'a Chume. Isolder and his new bride-to-be returned to Hapes, leaving Leia and Han to plan their own nuptials, and Luke to nurse the bump on his head.

Prince Isolder and Teneniel Djo eventually had a daughter, Tenel Ka, whose powers in the Force were strong enough to get her accepted into Luke Skywalker's Jedi academy. The next heir to the Hapes throne may well be a Jedi Knight.

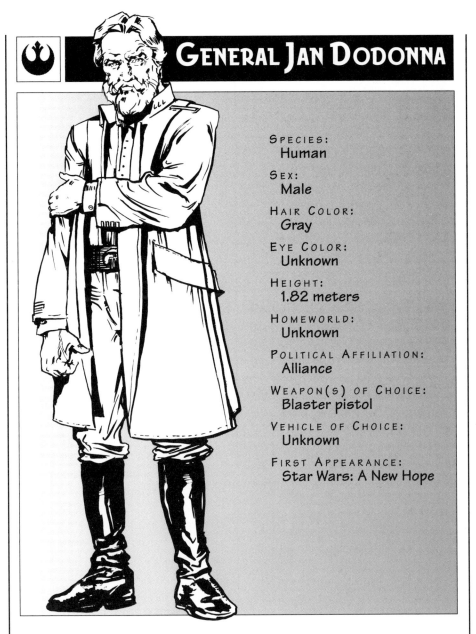

GENERAL JAN DODONNA

SPECIES:
Human

SEX:
Male

HAIR COLOR:
Gray

EYE COLOR:
Unknown

HEIGHT:
1.82 meters

HOMEWORLD:
Unknown

POLITICAL AFFILIATION:
Alliance

WEAPON(S) OF CHOICE:
Blaster pistol

VEHICLE OF CHOICE:
Unknown

FIRST APPEARANCE:
Star Wars: A New Hope

While the brash and flashy victories of Alliance heroes such as Luke Skywalker, Han Solo, or Wedge Antilles give credit to the young members of the Alliance, it was the aging General Jan Dodonna who planned the preemptive strike against the first Death Star.

Gray-bearded and grizzled, Dodonna appears to be an Academy professor, yet he is one of the most brilliant military tacticians in the galaxy. He was one of the first Star Destroyer captains in the days of the Old Republic. He and his best friend, Adar Tallon, were infamous for their knowledge and execution of interstellar battle tactics; Tallon was proficient in ship-to-ship combat, while Dodonna specialized in logistics and siege aspects of war.

When he believed that Tallon had died, the combat tactician retired. The new emperor Palpatine's New Order began shortly thereafter, and Dodonna's Imperial Navy record was examined. It was felt that he was too old to be "retrained" for service to the Empire, so his execution was ordered.

The Alliance reached him first, begging him to aid their cause. At first he refused, his body tired and fighting spirit weakened. But when Imperial troops arrived to assassinate him, Dodonna forced his way to safety on the Rebel ship. Taking command as in the days of old, he efficiently and fiercely dealt with the Imperial troops.

After several months of exercise, study of new technology, and examination of the galaxy's political situations, Dodonna was reborn as one of the Alliance's strongest and most important military commanders, answering only to Mon Mothma and the Alliance Council. Working under him were Commander Willard at the base on the moon of Yavin Four, and General Rieekan, who would later distinguish himself in service at the Hoth base.

Dodonna came to regret much of his past work. Many of the siege weapons and battle plans he had developed were used by the Empire, especially in the Siege of Dalron Five and the infamous Project Asteroid.

Princess Leia Organa arrived on Yavin Four with the readouts and schematics for the super-sized battle station called the Death Star tucked inside the memory systems of an R2 droid. There was little time to spare. The Death Star had tracked her to Yavin Four, and was en route.

Overnight, Dodonna and several other scientists and tacticians studied the readouts and mapped strategies. Though he had not been involved in the development of the Death Star, it was Dodonna alone, in the wee hours of morning, who finally struck upon the chink in its armor. He called a meeting, klaxons warning and waking everyone in the Massassi temple that housed the Rebel base.

All available Alliance dignitaries, technicians, and Rebel starfighter pilots convened in the temple's central briefing room of the Rebel headquarters. Dodonna addressed the gathering and pointed out the reactor shaft, the Death Star's only design flaw. A photon torpedo, properly targeted, could cause a chain reaction and destroy the entire battle station. As he wrapped up the briefing, he announced that the Death Star would be in range of Yavin Four within thirty minutes. "Man your ships," he told the departing pilots, "and may the Force be with you."

During the ensuing battle Dodonna watched a computerized main tactical display that homed in on the ships. As Base One, the general and his men helped guide the attack teams as much as they could. Princess Leia watched as well, worriedly; her new friend and rescuer, Luke Skywalker, was fighting with the fleet, as were countless others the princess had known. Dodonna comforted her as best he could, given the tense circumstances.

Although he didn't receive medals like those given to Skywalker and the heroic smuggler, Han Solo, Dodonna watched the victory ceremony from the main stage. He stood proudly as the amassed troops of the Rebellion cheered. He knew that many of them cheered for him, as well.

Over the following year, as the Alliance searched for a new base, Dodonna commanded the defense of Yavin Four. When he received news of Darth Vader's new Super Star Destroyer, *Executor*, Dodonna knew that the base would be its first major target. One of the Alliance members on the mission to help destroy the *Executor* was Dodonna's own son, Vrad. The rest of the fleet was destroyed, but Vrad managed to escape in a Rebel scoutcraft.

Back on Yavin, as an evacuation to the icy planet of Hoth was imminent, Dodonna received the distressing news that his son was dead. But then Vrad showed up, his fighter badly damaged. He and Luke volunteered for what was thought to be a suicide mission. They were going to attack the *Executor* with a fighter and a power gem that would disrupt the Destroyer's energy shields.

Although Vrad cracked under the pressure, dumping Luke on an asteroid and planning to escape from the Rebellion and the Empire, his ship was fired upon by the *Executor*. Realizing he could never escape,

Vrad made a suicide run on the Destroyer, causing minimal damage. When Luke returned to Yavin Four, he did not tell the general about his son's cowardice. It was bad enough that the general had lost his son.

The blow crippled the old man's confidence. His last act as general was to promote Luke Skywalker to commander. Then, as the last transport left Yavin, Dodonna ducked out of the ship.

Leaving the great Massassi temple that had been the actual command center for the Rebellion, Dodonna set a series of concussion charges in one of the other temples. Broadcasting his farewell to the Alliance, he allowed a fleet of TIE bombers to home in on his signal. As they arrived to attack, he set off the charges, destroying the fleet and the temple.

But he did not die. Critically wounded, he was unable to fend off an Imperial attack team and was captured. Later, receiving news that the general was alive but imprisoned, the Rebels dispatched an assault team to rescue him. The brilliant tactician rejoined the Alliance, but much of his fire had been dampened. Due to his injuries, he was forced to walk with a cane.

He was reunited with his friend, Tallon, who had been hiding for years but had been convinced to join the Rebellion. Still, Dodonna chose to go into semiretirement, only advising the Inner Council on certain missions. His impromptu group of retired advisors included Tallon, Pashna Starkiller, and Vanden Willard, who jokingly called themselves the "gray cadre." Six years after the destruction of the second Death Star, Dodonna was instrumental in advising the attacks on the new Imperial World Devastators from Pinnacle Base on the Fifth Moon of Da Soocha.

General Dodonna continued to live with honor and to sacrifice for the ideals in which he so strongly believed. His tactics and battle plans would lead the Alliance to many more victories.

MORUTH DOOLE

SPECIES:
Rybet

SEX:
Male

HAIR COLOR:
None

EYE COLOR:
Whitish

HEIGHT:
Unknown (short)

HOMEWORLD:
Unknown/based on Kessel

POLITICAL AFFILIATION:
None

WEAPON(S) OF CHOICE:
Blaster

VEHICLE OF CHOICE:
Various spacecraft

FIRST APPEARANCE:
Star Wars: Jedi Search

DEATH:
Star Wars: Champions of the Force

Moruth Doole was a squat Rybet, froglike in appearance, with green, slimy-looking skin. He preferred to wear clothing made of the skins of other reptiles, his favorite being a waistcoast. During his period of mating readiness, he sported a bright yellow cravat. The clothing made him look buffoonish, but his secret life was no laughing matter.

Doole was an official in one of Kessel's gigantic prison complexes, the Imperial Correctional Facility. There, the Empire used prison slaves to mine the glitterstim spice, a powerful drug that sold for high amounts in an unrefined form. Doole would skim the black-market spice from the Imperial production quotas, and would buy spice mined on other parts of the planet to have it smuggled off world. He also sold maps and access codes for Kessel's energy shields.

Whenever spice veins began to run dry, Doole would step in as a prison official and double-cross his business partners. Reporting "newly discovered" illegal mines, Doole would seed the raiding parties with his own men, who made sure that anyone who could provide evidence of Doole's double life was murdered.

Doole employed a variety of smugglers, including the Corellian Han Solo. Doole's favor always went to the highest bidder, though, and he had no qualms about turning one of his smugglers over to authorities if paid the right amount.

Shortly before the battle against the first Death Star, Han Solo was making a smuggling run of spice, transporting it to the Tatooine palace of the gangster Jabba the Hutt. Doole provided Imperial tariff ships with Solo's coordinates, and when the *Falcon* came out of hyperspace, they were waiting. Before the *Falcon* was boarded, Solo jettisoned the spice, escaping punishment for the contraband material. Solo was unable to retrieve his cargo—cargo that Jabba had paid for in advance, so Jabba put a bounty on Solo's head. Doole had successfully double-crossed Solo, and had been paid by both the tariff officials and Jabba.

But the Hutt's men had infiltrated the mining operation and Jabba, suspecting Doole's double-cross, put a contract out on the Rybet. A sadistic bounty hunter fried one of his overlarge, lanternlike eyes, half blinding the other before Skynxnex, Doole's assistant, killed him.

About to be exposed, Doole and those loyal to him staged a prison revolt. The warden had been one of Jabba's employees, but half the guards were being paid by Doole. With the Empire in chaos over the destruction of the first Death Star, Doole's takeover of the Kessel facilities went unnoticed. Over the next several years, Doole managed to dispose of the other slave lords on the planet, taking over other mining and prison facilities. Doole's biggest opponent could have been the ruthless Trioculus, Lord Overseer and Supreme Slavelord in the mines on the opposite side of Kessel, but the three-eyed mutant was busy with his own plans to take over the Empire. When Trioculus was killed, Doole's planetary takeover was complete. He assembled a ragtag defense fleet made of spaceships of all kinds, and moved the spice-mining operations into full swing.

To compensate the loss of vision, Doole had a mechanical focusing device created. Without the device, he was almost blind. He took the warden's headquarters and transformed them into "Doole's Place." The warden himself had been sent to the spice mines to work, and when he was exhausted, Doole implanted spice grubs in the man's body. As the grubs burrowed through the warden's insides, Doole had the convulsing man encased in carbonite, and the warden became a wall hanging in his own office.

To serve his mating needs, Doole had dozens of female Rybet slaves shipped to Kessel from his home planet. He kept them caged in a secure wing, and the dozens of offspring he fathered were kept in their blind larvaelike states in the spice-processing area, working in total darkness to package the spice for shipment.

Seven years after the Battle of Endor, Han Solo and Chewbacca returned to Kessel and were shot down by Moruth Doole's ships. Solo had come to the planet as an Alliance ambassador, but soon found himself Doole's prisoner. The Rybet administrator was afraid the Alliance would try to take control of the spice-mining operations, and wanted to send a message to them. The fact that the "spy" was Han Solo was an unexpected bonus.

Doole used pure glitterstim to read Solo's mind. Horrified, he found that Solo was telling the truth and that he really *was* there as an ambassador. Afraid that his hasty actions would be interpreted as a declaration of war on the Alliance, Doole ordered all information about the *Falcon* and its inhabitants erased from the records. Then, he had Han and Chewbacca sent into the deepest spice mines of Kessel, where they would slave away until their deaths.

When Leia Organa Solo then contacted Doole, the Rybet "commissioner" disavowed any knowledge of the *Falcon* or the ambas-

sadors from the Alliance. He suggested that perhaps Solo and his ship had been sucked into the black-hole cluster known as the Maw. Leia's suspicions were aroused, yet she had no proof of wrongdoing. Doole himself had concerns that his answers had seemed too rehearsed, and he decided to have Han Solo killed.

Doole dispatched Skynxnex to kill the troublesome Corellian. Unfortunately for the hit man, Solo, Chewbacca, and Kyp Durron, a spice-mine worker, had an escape plan. Skynxnex followed them deep into the mines, but was killed by the giant spice-producing spiders that lived there. Solo and his partners escaped. Stealing an Imperial cargo shuttle Solo managed to escape Kessel and its defense fleet, only to be pulled into the Maw.

Doole's relief at seeing Solo disappear turned to frustration soon enough. Luke Skywalker and Lando Calrissian, posing as rich investors, landed on Kessel. They tricked Doole into giving R2-D2 access to his computer banks, allowing the little droid to search for information about Solo and the *Falcon*, but Artoo could find nothing.

Doole toured Skywalker and Calrissian through the spice-mining operations, and showed them the defensive garrison on Kessel's moon. There, Lando and Luke recognized the stripped-down *Falcon*. Confronting Doole with the truth, the two Alliance heroes were surprised as he escaped. Lando piloted the *Falcon* out into Kessel orbit, the Rybet's defense fleet in pursuit.

Unbeknownst to Doole, Imperial Admiral Daala had a top-secret fleet and weapons-design center inside the Maw. Solo, Chewbacca, and Kyp Durron had managed to steal Daala's most powerful weapon, a ship known as the Sun Crusher. Daala's Star Destroyers pursued the Sun Crusher out of the Maw, and ran directly into Doole's Kessel defense fleet.

In the ensuing battle, the *Falcon* and the Sun Crusher both escaped into hyperspace, ninety percent of Doole's fleet was

destroyed, and the rest of the ships fled. Daala's ships fired their turbolasers on Kessel, targeting factories and facilities. The planet was devastated, and Doole was without most of his defense force. Others left or escaped as they could. In the following months, the New Republic did send relief ships to Kessel, evacuating most of the inhabitants, the correctional facility prisoners, and the slaves working the spice mines. Doole became more and more paranoid, retreating into the towers and offices of the correctional facility.

Ironically, Lando Calrissian really had been looking to invest in spice mining. Now that Kessel was abandoned. Calrissian planned to team with the Smugglers' Alliance, run by Mara Jade, to distribute the spice throughout the galaxy. Lando and Han Solo returned to Kessel, where the Smugglers' Alliance had already set up on the garrison moon. When they flew down to the planet's surface, Mara Jade told Lando of the one small problem they still faced: Moruth Doole had remained holed up inside the prison in a high-security cell, and was using its defense capabilities to keep everyone out.

Mara Jade called on a friend, Ghent, to get her and her partners inside the prison. Seeing the smugglers and Alliance members break in, Doole panicked and put his escape plan into motion. First, he armed the immature Rybet larvae that were still faithful to him, then he holed up in a room, shielded and waiting.

Unfortunately for Doole, all the elements of destruction came together at once. The blind larvae fired at his voice rather than at the incoming smugglers. Squealing, Doole hit a trapdoor and was flung into an escape tunnel through the spice mines.

As Han Solo listened, the last sound he heard from Doole was a high-pitched scream when the glitterstim-producing energy spiders speared the traitorous Rybet on their legs, and Doole became a feast for a larger predator.

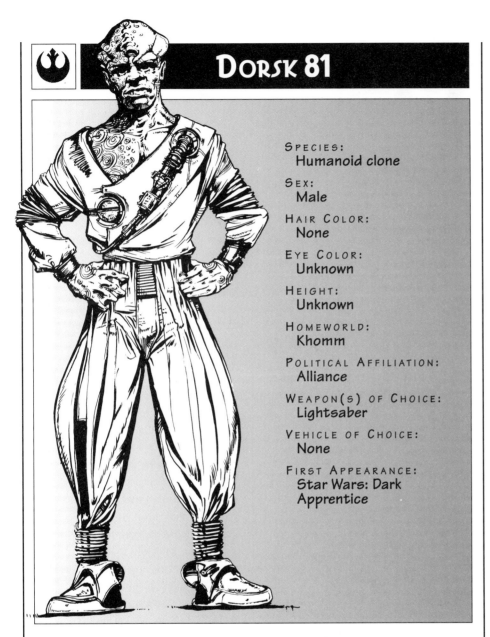

DORSK 81

SPECIES:
Humanoid clone

SEX:
Male

HAIR COLOR:
None

EYE COLOR:
Unknown

HEIGHT:
Unknown

HOMEWORLD:
Khomm

POLITICAL AFFILIATION:
Alliance

WEAPON(S) OF CHOICE:
Lightsaber

VEHICLE OF CHOICE:
None

FIRST APPEARANCE:
Star Wars: Dark Apprentice

On Dorsk 81's bureaucratic home planet, Khomm, all members of the family units were genetically identical, bred to carry on the societal status quo. A thousand years before Emperor Palpatine, the Khomm people felt that their society and their genetics had reached perfection. To prevent undesirable changes, they froze evolution, cloning their people rather than risking genetic abnormalities.

Thin and bald, with smooth green-and-yellow skin, Dorsk 81 is the eighty-first reincarnation of the original Dorsk. What was different about Dorsk 81 was his mind and spirit, and his ability to feel the Force flowing through him. He felt he was a failure to his race, until he heard about the New Republic's plan to rebuild the Jedi Knights.

Seven years after the destruction of the second Death Star, Luke Skywalker set up his Jedi academy on Yavin Four, teaching his students in the ancient Massassi temple that had once housed the Rebel base. Dorsk 81 came to Luke, seeking guidance.

Dorsk 81 became one of the first twelve trainees to receive Skywalker's training.

Other trainees included the Bespin gas prospector Streen, the angry Gantoris, the Dathomirian witch Kirani Ti, the musician Tionne, and Jedi son Kam Solusar. Later, Kyp Durron, Nichos Marr, Cray Mingla, and the Mon Calamari ambassador Cilghal joined them.

Although he did well at his studies, Dorsk exhibited problems eating the food, even natural foods brought from the Yavin forests. For his people had always eaten highly processed food.

During one training session, when Luke had the students float in an underground lake, bubbles of volcanic gas came from below. Despite Luke's insistence that Jedi could block out heat or cold, Dorsk panicked. Gantoris helped him hold on until the bubbling stopped. A few days later, Gantoris was killed by the spirit of the evil Sith lord Exar Kun.

Kun called to Kyp Durron, as well. High atop the temple, Kyp used powers from the dark side of the Force. Together they drove Luke's spirit from his body, trapping him just out of sync with reality.

Dorsk and the others tried to protect Luke's body, for though it contained no life, neither was it dead. When Kun summoned monstrous winged creatures, Dorsk was among the trainees that aided Jacen and Jaina Solo in driving them off.

Although he was filled with unreasoning fear, Dorsk 81 joined the other trainees in luring Kun into the room where Skywalker's body lay, there surrounding him. Kun attempted to prey on their weaknesses to escape, noting Dorsk's sense of failure to his people. However, Dorsk had learned from Luke that his differences made him *stronger*. Using their combined powers the students destroyed Exar Kun for all time, and freed Luke's spirit.

Although his particular talents in the Force have not manifested themselves, Dorsk 81 has learned that he is part of the larger framework of the Force, and one of the cornerstones for a new generation of Jedi Knights!

KYP DURRON

SPECIES:
Human

SEX:
Male

HAIR COLOR:
Dark brown

EYE COLOR:
Unknown

HEIGHT:
Unknown

HOMEWORLD:
Deyer Colony of Anoat

POLITICAL AFFILIATION:
Alliance

WEAPON(S) OF CHOICE:
Lightsaber (violet and white)

VEHICLE OF CHOICE:
Sun Crusher

FIRST APPEARANCE:
Star Wars: Jedi Search

Alliance hero Luke Skywalker had been a young man when he helped save the galaxy from the Empire, but there was an even younger teenager with a strong connection to the Force. Kyp Durron, whose life had been full of tragedy due to the Empire, gained the ultimate weapon—the power of the dark side—to use against it.

Kyp was born on the Deyer Colony of the Anoat system. The Deyer colonists lived on raft cities anchored in a complex of ter-raformed lakes. Kyp's parents had been out-spoken politicians, who had tried to make Emperor Palpatine realize the need for moderate actions instead of the drastic ones he employed against the Rebels and their sym-pathizers. They protested during the anniversary of the Ghorman Massacre, and again when the Death Star destroyed the peaceful planet of Alderaan.

One night, the stormtroopers crashed into the Durron home. Kyp's fourteen-year-old brother, Zeth, was sent to the Imperial Academy on Caridia, one of the most grueling training grounds for military service.

Shackled with stun cuffs, Kyp was led off with his parents.

Eight-year-old Kyp and his parents were sent to one of Kessel's gigantic prison complexes, the Imperial Correctional Facility, where the Empire used prison slaves to mine glitterstim spice, a powerful drug that sold for high amounts in an unrefined form. During the years of the Rebellion's battle against the Empire, Kyp worked, forgotten, down in the dark glitterstim mines. When a Rybet administrator, Moruth Doole, took over the Kessel facilities, Kyp's parents were executed. Alone, he continued to mine, end-lessly passing his days in the blackness.

Several years passed until an old woman named Vima-Da-Boda was sent to the correctional facility. Vima, who had been a Jedi Knight in the days of the Old Republic, was soon drawn to Kyp Durron. She could feel his incredibly strong aptitude for the Force, and trained Kyp to use some lesser Force skills. But one day, the Imperials came and took her away; Kyp Durron never saw her again.

Seven years after the Battle of Endor, Han Solo and Chewbacca came to Kessel and were shot down by Moruth Doole's ships. The Rybet administrator had Han and Chewbacca sent into the deepest spice mines, to slave away until their deaths. There, Kyp and Solo became friends.

Han soon discovered the eighteen-year-old Kyp's great aptitude for the Force, which gave him abilities that helped them escape. Stealing an Imperial cargo shuttle, they managed to flee Kessel and its defense fleet, only to be pulled into the Maw, a secret Imperial weapons-creation site presided over by Admiral Daala.

Daala's men captured the shuttle and brutally interrogated Solo, Chewbacca, and Durron. When Solo appealed to the willowy scientist Qwi Xux's conscience, she decided to help them escape. Kyp, Han, Chewbacca, and Qwi commandeered her ultimate weapon-ship, the Sun Crusher. Using his Force powers, Kyp piloted the Crusher through the Maw and out to freedom.

Back at the Rebel base on Coruscant, Luke Skywalker tested Kyp's Jedi power potential. What he discovered was the strongest Force presence he had known since his Masters, Obi-Wan Kenobi and Yoda. Luke invited Kyp to join him as a Jedi trainee on the moon of Yavin Four.

Although his skills were great, Kyp felt they were not enough. In Daala's dungeon at the Maw, he had promised himself that he would never again be weak. Between his impatience and desire for revenge against the Empire, he was ripe pickings for a servant of the dark side: Exar Kun, the long-dead Dark Lord of the Sith, whose spirit was trapped in a Massassi temple. Durron began secretly training with Kun.

As he trained with both Luke Skywalker and Exar Kun, Kyp became ever more annoyed at Luke's peaceful, patient ways. He confronted Luke several times, barely holding his rage in check. When Mara Jade arrived on the planet, Kyp heard for the first time how much destruction Admiral Daala was wreaking on the outside. He stole Mara's Z-95 Headhunter spaceship and headed for the moon of Endor.

On Endor, Kyp sought out the funeral pyre of Darth Vader. Luke had told the students that Vader, a Dark Lord of the Sith, had reformed in the end. Kyp thought this meant that Sith Lords could still use the light side of the Force, and he grasped that thought as a way to ward off the intrusive influence of Exar Kun, who pulled the student toward the dark side. Kyp was determined that he would be the new Dark Lord of the Sith, filled with righteous vengeance.

That vengeance first manifested itself on Ithor, where Kyp broke into Qwi Xux's quarters and waited for her in the dark. When she returned from a day trip with Wedge Antilles, Kyp used the Force to fillet her memories, removing anything that could be remotely connected to the Sun Crusher or the other weaponry she had created at the Maw Installation.

He returned to Yavin Four in the darkness of night, landing atop the Massassi temple where he and the other Jedi had trained. As dawn broke, he felt Exar Kun's power join his. Together, they used the Force to raise the Sun Crusher from its gassy crypt in Yavin's heart and the superweapon, gleaming and new, came to rest on the temple top.

When Luke Skywalker rushed to confront him, Kyp derided the Jedi. Durron decided to use the Sun Crusher to destroy the Empire himself, and as Luke ignited his lightsaber to stop him, Kyp called forth dark-side lightning, striking his Master. Exar Kun's spirit joined in, and together they split Luke's essence apart from his body, setting it adrift in the same netherspace that Kun himself inhabited.

In the Cauldron Nebula, Kyp found his most hated enemy, Admiral Daala, with her Star Destroyers *Gorgon* and the *Basilisk*. As Daala prepared to lead her ships in an attack on Coruscant, Kyp launched sundestroying resonance torpedoes to blow up the cluster of blue-giant stars at the heart of the nebula, all the while taunting Daala over the communications systems. Although the admiral realized the peril and ordered an immediate withdrawal, the cataclysmic explosion of the nebula caught the *Basilisk* full on, destroying it completely. As the nebula died behind him, Kyp took off to find his next target.

That target was the Imperial Academy on Caridia, where Kyp hoped to learn the whereabouts of his brother, Zeth, before he destroyed the Imperial system. The Imperial ambassador Furgan attempted to bluff Kyp with faked news of Zeth's death, even as his fighters scrambled and attacked. Kyp easily fought off the fighters and launched a resonance torpedo into Caridia's sun.

While he waited to witness the Academy's destruction, Kyp was surprised to hear another hail from the Imperials. They had found his brother—alive—and would have him soon. As the chronometer counted off the fleeting minutes, Kyp flew the Sun Crusher to the Academy, where he would meet Lieutenant Dauron and his brother on a roof.

Dauron battered Zeth while Kyp moved in, and Zeth blasted the Imperial. As Kyp attempted to draw the staggering Zeth up to the ship with its tractor beam, Caridia's sun exploded, destroying everything in the system. Zeth was immediately incinerated along with all the Imperials still left at the Academy. Kyp's Force powers locked in, helping him steer the ship and ride the waves of the explosion.

Back at the Rebel base on Coruscant, Han Solo departed aboard the *Millennium Falcon*, hoping to appeal to Kyp as his friend, and seeking to stop the carnage that lay in the Sun Crusher's wake. He and Lando Calrissian soon found that Durron had destroyed a red-dwarf star, the site of several orbiting starship-construction yards and weapons depots.

Aboard the *Falcon*, Han and Lando received the signal for the Sun Crusher and, surprisingly, they caught the ship in their tractor beam. Angered, Kyp planned to launch one of the torpedoes into the *Falcon*. Han tried to talk to him while Lando used override codes to shut down the Crusher's power. Even more angry, Kyp used the Force to reactivate the ship. In his mind, he could hear the spirit of Exar Kun, telling him to avenge himself at any cost.

Suddenly, Kun's spirit screamed and disappeared. Luke's students had destroyed the spirit back on Yavin Four. Free from Kun's influence, Kyp depowered the ship and surrendered to Han.

Having been seduced by the dark side himself, Luke was more than willing to give Kyp a second chance. If he could be cleansed and trained, Kyp Durron had the potential to become one of the greatest of the New Order of Jedi Knights.

EMPEROR'S ROYAL GUARDS

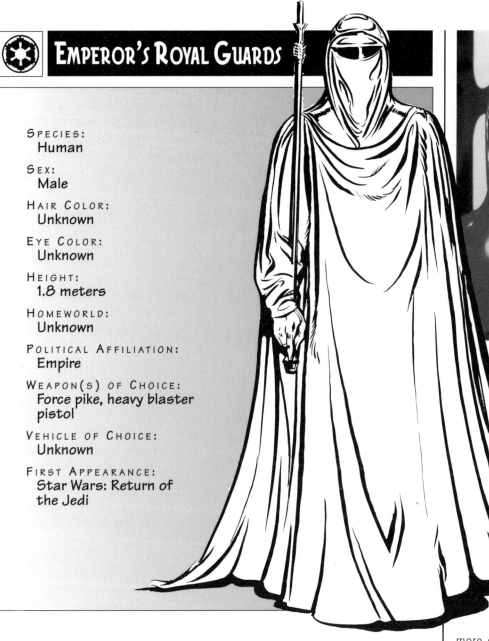

SPECIES:
Human

SEX:
Male

HAIR COLOR:
Unknown

EYE COLOR:
Unknown

HEIGHT:
1.8 meters

HOMEWORLD:
Unknown

POLITICAL AFFILIATION:
Empire

WEAPON(S) OF CHOICE:
Force pike, heavy blaster pistol

VEHICLE OF CHOICE:
Unknown

FIRST APPEARANCE:
Star Wars: Return of the Jedi

Tall and imposing in their blood red cloaks and helmets, the Emperor's Royal Guards were the most mysterious—and deadly—of the Empire's soldiers.

The elite Royal Guards were once stormtroopers, handpicked for their size, strength, intelligence, and loyalty, lavished with the costliest equipment and the best training. They were fitted for red battle armor, different from all other Imperial armor, the designs based partially on the uniforms of the Mandalore system's Death Watch and the Sun Guards of the Thyrsus system.

The exact number of Royal Guard members has never been known to any but the top Imperial brass and Emperor Palpatine. The Royal Guard reported to the Emperor, and the Emperor only. A handful of the Guards accompanied the Emperor at all times, traveling with him in his private shuttles.

The Royal Guard was completely devoted to the Emperor, and would gladly have laid down their lives for him. However, it is rumored that not one single Royal Guard was ever killed in battle. Their main weapons were two-meter force pikes, which looked deceptively harmless, but in the hands of a Guard, were almost as lethal as the heavy blaster pistols concealed beneath their robes. The most elite members had been tapped to become Imperial Sovereign Protectors, watching over the palaces and monasteries Palpatine used, and his special clone vats on Byss. The Sovereign Protectors' red armor was more ceremonial than even the Royal Guards'.

The ranks of the Royal Guard seemed to have dissipated or been reassigned following Emperor Palpatine's death. When the Emperor's first clone was activated, six years after the destruction of the second Death Star, only the Sovereign Protectors appeared active. Perhaps the remnants of the Guards became the fanatically evil Dark Siders that later served the Emperor's additional clones. Or perhaps, without their Emperor to lead them, the Royal Guards committed suicide; no one knows.

DAVIN FELTH

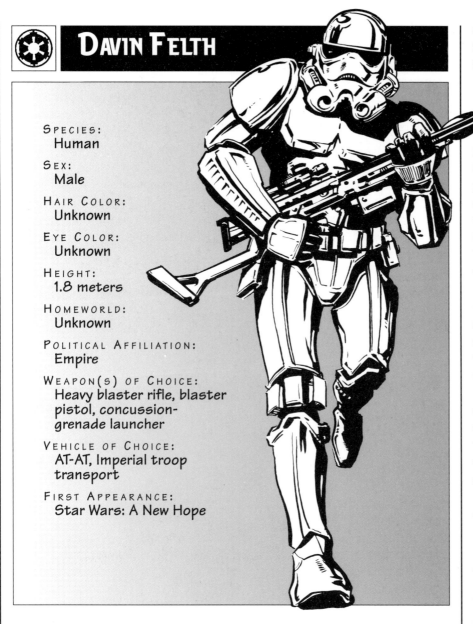

SPECIES:
Human

SEX:
Male

HAIR COLOR:
Unknown

EYE COLOR:
Unknown

HEIGHT:
1.8 meters

HOMEWORLD:
Unknown

POLITICAL AFFILIATION:
Empire

WEAPON(S) OF CHOICE:
Heavy blaster rifle, blaster pistol, concussion-grenade launcher

VEHICLE OF CHOICE:
AT-AT, Imperial troop transport

FIRST APPEARANCE:
Star Wars: A New Hope

Indistinguishable from one another in their black-and-white armor, their skull-like helmets glaring, stormtroopers are a weapon of fear and an example of complete, unquestioning conformity. But for Davin Felth, a trooper on Tatooine, mindlessness came to an end when he came face to face with the Force and the Rebellion.

Like other stormtroopers, Davin wears a set of white plastisteel protective armor over a black, two-piece, temperature-control body glove. The eighteen-piece outer shell includes an energy source and control devices. In theory, the armor forms an antiblaster cocoon, but the number of blasted troopers throughout the galaxy belies that "fact." Stormtrooper helmets contain automatic polarized lenses, breathing filters, and comlink units. The belt packs house specialized survival equipment, concentrated rations, emergency batteries, and a spare hand-held comlink.

Although the Caridian training leaves all stormtroopers capable of surviving on any livable planetary surface, some elite troops are also trained in specialized units such as the lightly armored seatroopers for underwater worlds, cold-assault snowtroopers for frozen climates, and the ultralite zero-g stormtroopers for space work.

The Imperial Navy controls stormtrooper training and assignments in the Imperial Starfleet, although the Imperial Army uses navy-trained troopers to precede their own ground forces. Troopers act as security troops and assault troops in times of conflict, or as honor guards for Imperial dignitaries and ranking officials. Their unswerving devotion to the Emperor is fanatical.

Davin Felth joined the ranks of the Empire as an eighteen-year-old; like many others, he had the desire to serve his government, gain usable skills, and work toward a command position. Although he had looked forward to the experience of the Imperial Academy, within thirty seconds of arriving on the military training planet of Caridia, his enthusiasm disappeared. For the next six months, Davin did whatever was necessary to survive, to make his superiors happy, to become a stormtrooper. His roommates were the tall, red-headed Geoff f'Tuhns, and the smaller, muscular Mychael Ologat.

Despite the many discomforts of Academy life, Davin excelled and was placed with other top recruits in the special training for Colonel Veers's All Terrain Armored Transport detachment.

Davin was one of the few who finished the AT-AT training. On a dry run, during which he commanded one of these massive machines, Davin was surprised when four fighters attacked him. Resisting panic and brilliantly planning his strategies, the trooper destroyed the four ships. Shortly thereafter, he found out that the ships had been simulations, and that he had been tested by Colonel Veers. The officer pulled Felth aside from the others, questioning his tactics: the young man had revealed potential flaws in the AT-AT design!

Oddly enough, rather than rewarding the

exceptional student, Veers had him immediately assigned to a stormtrooper unit. Sent to the arid planet of Tatooine, Davin was assigned the number 1023, as stormtroopers were not referred to by name. He was issued the armor of the desert-sands stormtroopers, commonly called sandtroopers.

Davin was then reassigned by Captain Terrik to the scout unit Zeta. Terrik led the Zeta unit, and oversaw Alvien and Drax squads. Their task was a search-and-destroy mission to find an escape pod that had jettisoned from a Rebel ship.

Imperial computers were already mapping trajectories for the pod as the troopers touched down in the desert. Giant dewback lizards had been grav-lifted in to help the sandtroopers cover more territory among the dunes. Hours passed, and they continued their search of the endlessly shifting terrain. After one false alarm, it was Davin who found the escape pod, and moments later he found something even more important: a piece of an R2 unit. "Look, sir—droids," he told Terrik.

Zeta unit followed a set of wandering tracks that eventually led them to a giant ore hauler that the Tatooine natives, the Jawas, used as their home and mobile droid-scavenging facility. Davin and his fellow troopers searched the sandcrawler but could find no sign of any R2 units, nor the protocol droid they were also seeking.

Terrik questioned the Jawa leaders, however, ascertaining that two such droids had been sold to a moisture farmer named Owen Lars.

As his men moved on, Terrik ordered the stormtroopers to fire on the Jawa sandcrawler and kill all inside, then plant evidence that would make it appear that the roving Tusken Raiders had attacked the diminutive scavengers. Davin's heart was heavy; he hadn't joined the Imperials to kill innocent beings.

Davin and the other troopers boarded cargo skiffs and quickly thereafter arrived at the Lars homestead. After the troopers had

ransacked the house and garages looking for the droids, the feisty moisture farmer did the unthinkable: he spit on Captain Terrik, cursing him. Davin knew what was to come. As he boarded the skiff to go to the Mos Eisley spaceport, Davin tried to block out the carnage that followed; troopers mowed down the farmer and his wife, razing their homestead with laser fire. Davin asked himself what he would do if he was asked to kill in this fashion.

Once they arrived at the busy spaceport, Alvien squad was assigned to checkpoints of entrances to the city. Drax and Zeta squads' job was to patrol and search door to door. Felth questioned a gigantic hairy Talz, Muftak, then conferred with his superior, Lieutenant Alima.

While on patrol, Davin and his backup, 1047, responded to screams issuing from a cantina. Davin inspected the bar, seeing an old man and a young boy leaving as he entered. Nothing in the establishment seemed out of the ordinary, though, and Davin returned to the streets.

Shortly afterward, a crazed Jawa made an abortive attack on the troopers. Trooper 1047 fired, killing the creature and making Davin wonder once again about the overpowering presence of death he was facing as a stormtrooper. Was this what the Empire was about?

Later in the day, a call through the comlink brought all the troopers to Docking Bay 94, where the droids had been found. In the firefight that followed, Davin recognized the men from the bar, including an athletic-looking smuggler and a Wookiee. His superiors said they were Rebels. Could these few individuals have caused the Empire so much trouble?

As the fighting went on, Davin was forced to make a decision. Captain Terrik had drawn a bead on the smuggler from the

cantina and was sure to kill him. Striking back against the man who had poisoned his life with evil, Davin made the captain his first kill.

As the freighter took off and the troopers retreated, Davin was filled with a new sense of purpose—he had found a new cause. The Rebels were right—the Empire *was* evil. But maybe, by leaking information to the Rebellion from within the ranks of the Empire, the stormtrooper named Davin Felth—*not* 1023—could regain his drive and reclaim his life.

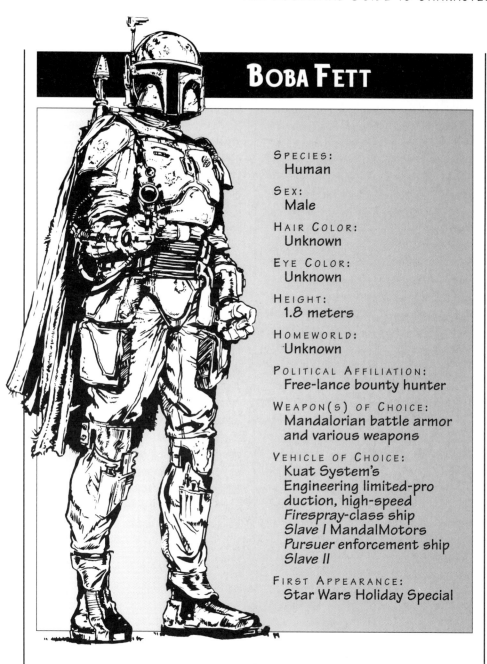

BOBA FETT

SPECIES:
Human

SEX:
Male

HAIR COLOR:
Unknown

EYE COLOR:
Unknown

HEIGHT:
1.8 meters

HOMEWORLD:
Unknown

POLITICAL AFFILIATION:
Free-lance bounty hunter

WEAPON(S) OF CHOICE:
Mandalorian battle armor and various weapons

VEHICLE OF CHOICE:
Kuat System's Engineering limited-pro duction, high-speed Firespray-class ship Slave I MandalMotors Pursuer enforcement ship Slave II

FIRST APPEARANCE:
Star Wars Holiday Special

The most notorious and fearsome bounty hunter in the galaxy is also the most mysterious. Many legends and stories have arisen over the years, but few facts are known of the man called Boba Fett, or of his inextricable link to Han Solo.

Long before Luke Skywalker journeyed off Tatooine to fulfill his destiny as a Jedi, Boba Fett was known as Journeyman Protector Jaster Mereel. Years past, the ugly young law-enforcement officer on the world of Concord Down had killed another protector, and though the dead man had been

corrupt, disgracing his office and uniform, Mereel was still imprisoned for the murder. Against the wishes of his pleader, the arrogant young man remained unrepentant to the trial court, and Jaster Mereel was exiled from Concord Down, stripped of all he owned.

Mereel's adoption of the name Boba Fett, and the manner in which he acquired his rare battle armor, are tales lost in time, remembered by no living being except for Fett himself.

Fett wears the armor of the

Mandalorians, a group of evil warriors who were defeated by the Jedi Knights during the Clone Wars. Fett's modified Mandalore armor includes a helmet that has a mac-robinocular viewplate, motion and sound sensors, infrared capabilities, an internal comlink with his ship, the *Slave I*, and a broadband antenna for intercepting and decoding transmissions. Wrist gauntlets house lasers, a miniature flame projector, and a fibercord whip/grappling device; a backpack jet pack includes a turbo-projected magnetic grappling hook with twenty-meter lanyard. Fett also carries knee-pad rocket dart launchers, spiked boots, a concussion-grenade launcher, and a Blas Tech EE-3 rifle. Braided Wookiee scalps hang over his right shoulder to complete the outfit.

Beyond Fett and Fenn Shysa, the only other living person known to wear the Mandalorian armor is Jodo Kast, an ambitious young bounty hunter who patterned his career after that of Boba Fett. Prowling the Outer Rim Territories, Kast wears armor with much of the same external weaponry that Fett utilizes. It is unlikely, however, that he has as much hidden weaponry and modified circuitry in his suit. In the past, Kast has allowed people to believe he *was* Fett, adding even greater mystery to the legends surrounding the older hunter.

Throughout his life, Fett has worked as a mercenary, a soldier, a personal guard, an assassin, and, most frequently, as a bounty hunter—the most expensive bounty hunter in the known systems. He collected 150,000 credits for the capture of pirate Feldrall Okor, and took a record 500,000 credits when he caught the religious Ffib heretic Nivek'Yppiks for the Lohrans.

Fett has worked on retainer for Jabba the Hutt and others of the Hutt clan, as well as for the Empire, and has crossed paths with the Rebellion's greatest heroes more than a few times over the years. Fett is slow and methodical and as unpredictable as the shifting sands of Tatooine. He rarely loses his quarry, and has, thus far, shown no

remorse for their fate. Fett has been known to work with other bounty hunters, but his motives may have been to show the others up; Fett has always emerged as the one who catches the prize.

Sometime in the years before the Battle of Yavin, Boba Fett had his first meeting with R2-D2 and C-3PO. On the desert Planet of Ingo, the droids had become the property of speeder racer Thall Joben and his friends, Kea Moll and Jord Dusat. Joben had angered the criminal Fromm gang, and Sise Fromm traveled to the Boonta speeder races to find them. There, Sise hired the mysterious, armor-clad bounty hunter to kill the young racing team, a job Fett took on as a favor owed Fromm, even though Fromm himself was wanted by intergalactic crime lord Jabba the Hutt. After the contract to kill Joben was finished, Fett noted that all debts were paid.

Fett's robot, BR-17, befriended C-3PO and turned him against R2-D2 while Fromm's gang put a bomb in Joben's racing ship, the *White Witch*. Fett chased Thall and Kea, but they escaped, joining in the speeder race. At the same time, C-3PO learned of the treachery of BR-17—who was then crushed by falling machinery—and discovered the bomb planted on the *Witch*.

Unaware of the bomb, Fett followed Joben into the race and attempted to stop him, using every weapon at his disposal. When he tried magnets, Fett accidentally pulled the bomb onto his own speeder and had to escape at the last minute before it blew up. Angry at the loss of his droid and his speeder, Fett took Fromm and his gang hostage, to turn them over to Jabba the Hutt. He expected a great reward for the corpulent trio of villains.

Several years later, shortly after the Battle of Yavin, Luke Skywalker took R2-D2, C-3PO, and a Y-wing fighter to go look for Han Solo. The Corellian was due back from his search for an invisibility talisman, a mystic item the Empire also sought. When Luke crash-landed on a red-water moon in the Panna system, he was *rescued* by the mysterious Boba Fett.

Luke was felled by a strange sleeping virus that had also knocked out Han, so Fett and Chewbacca snuck into the Imperial-guarded city to get an antidote. While there, Boba contacted Darth Vader, who called him the "best bounty hunter in the galaxy." It was at this point that the droids intercepted Fett's message that he planned to capture the Rebels and claim the talisman.

Back at the *Millennium Falcon,* following a harrowing chase by stormtroopers, Boba administered the antidote to Han and Luke. Still groggy, Han didn't recognize Boba, and didn't object when Luke offered the hunter a place in the Rebellion. C-3PO and R2-D2 interrupted, telling the Rebels of Fett's transmission to Vader. Fett rocketed away, vowing vengeance.

Prior to the Rebels' establishment of the Hoth base, Fett reappeared in pursuit of "the Mole," a man wanted for leaving the service of Darth Vader. Piloting a TIE fighter, Fett was chased down by Luke Skywalker in an X-wing. Luke chased the mercenary's ship through the ice canyons of the frozen world of Ota, and both ships crashed. Fett got the drop on Luke, but both of them were captured by the apelike Snogars. The Snogars' city was growing colder, and they were convinced the off worlders could restore their heat-providing machines.

Meanwhile, Han, Chewie, Leia Organa, and the droids had come to Ota to find Luke. While Luke and Boba made a break from the Snogars, Han himself was captured. Ever the opportunist, Boba agreed to go with Luke to rescue Han, planning to capture the smuggler for profit.

In a wild sequence of events, the Rebels and the Mole were caught between the Snogars and Fett. When Fett tried to take *both* the Mole and Han prisoner, the Mole used a giant magnet to pin the bounty hunter to the wall. The Rebels and the Mole made their respective escapes, Fett swearing vengeance yet again.

Fett sometimes used his bounties against each other. Once, for example, Fett found out that the magician, Magwit, was performing at a small frontier settlement in the wastelands. The dwarf had a minor Imperial bounty on his head, but Fett knew Magwit could help him in acquiring

another bounty; Gorga the Hutt had hired Fett to bring in the notorious space pirate Bar-Kooda. Fett forced Magwit to buy his freedom by smuggling the hunter in his magic props. Magwit was "captured" and taken aboard Bar-Kooda's massive pirate vessel, *Bloodstar*, where the savage carnivore demanded the magician's final performance. Magwit's most impressive trick used a hoop to cause objects to appear and disappear. The hoop was connected to a short-range matter transmitter, with Fett waiting on the other side. Working in concert with Magwit, the hunter pulled Bar-Kooda through the hoop and escaped, causing carnage along the way. Magwit survived via a speedy exit, and true to his word, Fett gave the magician his freedom.

Shortly before the Battle of Hoth, Jabba the Hutt hired Fett to find Han Solo. Working both sides of the fence, Fett met Darth Vader mask to mask for the first time. For reasons unknown to either of them an instant sense of mutual respect was born, and the bounty hunter agreed to work with Dengar, Bossk, and a rookie bounty hunter named Skorr. But on the planet Ord Mantell, the wily Han Solo, Luke, and Chewie escaped Fett's clutches, heading back to the newly established Rebel base on Hoth.

Despite his failure to capture Solo and the other Rebels, Fett was once again summoned to work with Vader. One of the six bounty hunters instructed to find the *Millennium Falcon*, Fett succeeded in tracking the ship to the Bespin system. There, he aided Vader in capturing the Rebel leaders

and exacted his price in the capture of Han Solo.

Unfortunately for Han, Vader wanted to use him as the test subject for the carbonite-freezing process. Solo survived, and Fett took the quick-frozen Corellian to his ship for transport to Jabba the Hutt's Tatooine palace. On the way to board the *Slave I*, he exchanged shots with the wary Luke Skywalker, who was attempting to save his friends.

As he neared Tatooine, Fett was angered to find that IG-88, one of Vader's other bounty hunters, had tracked him. Fett used evasive maneuvers and his weaponry to blow up the starfighter *IG-2000* and its pilot. He continued on his way, delivering to Jabba his Han Solo "wall sculpture," and collecting his bounty. Arguing that the carbonite piece was actually art from the hands of Darth Vader, Fett was able to talk Jabba into raising Solo's bounty from 100,000 credits to 250,000.

For the following year, Boba was steadily employed, and a constant presence in Jabba's court. Although the Hutt would never admit it, he was afraid that the Alliance would retaliate for the capture of Solo, so he gave Fett assignments to keep him around, knowing how valuble the hunter was. One such job offered a 100,000 credit bounty to capture a live krayt dragon to be placed in battle with the Hutt's monstrous rancor.

When Luke, Leia, and Chewie came to Tatooine and were all captured while trying to rescue Han, Jabba sentenced them to death in the Great Pit of Carkoon. But Jabba had not counted on Skywalker's Jedi powers or initiative, and the Rebels broke free. In the battle that followed, Fett's backpack was hit and he flew, out of control, into the mouth of the Sarlacc.

Fett somehow escaped the Sarlacc, crawling away from the pit and lapsing into a painful oblivion. A short time later the bounty hunter Dengar, who had also been in Jabba's employ, set out to search for the Hutt's body. Instead, he found Boba Fett, devoid of armor and covered in scars and fibers from the Sarlacc. Dengar nursed Fett back to health, using Jabba's medical droids. A month later, Fett was well enough to travel, and since the Alliance had confiscated the *Slave I*, the two hunters set off in Dengar's ship for the spaceport moon of Nar Shaddaa, the smuggling center of the galaxy.

Boba had a little-used backup ship on Nar Shaddaa: The *Slave II* was a MandalMotors *Pursuer* enforcement ship, and few sentients in the galaxy even knew that Fett had one. The hunter used this to his advantage, knocking out old enemies who thought him dead, and collecting bounties quickly, sometimes working with the tagalong Dengar. Meanwhile, the Alliance let the *Slave I* sit on Grakouine, gathering dust.

Wary of another encounter with Solo and Skywalker, Fett decided to buy his ship back legally. With the help of an old employer, Crystalboy, he used a system of dummy corporations, paper trails, and forged requisition forms, eventually getting the *Slave I* as part of a "surplus liquidation" deal. Fett repaired the ship and put it in orbit around Nar Shaddaa. He would use it again, but for now, he was profiting more from the anonymity the *Slave II* and his "death" had given him.

It wasn't long before the galaxy realized Fett was alive. When he captured an infamous pirate, Feldrall Okor, Fett took a page from the plan Princess Leia had used when she had infiltrated Jabba's palace. He presented Feldrall to Imperial Governor Isis, but when she balked at his bounty price, he charged a thermal detonator. As tense seconds ticked by, the governor argued, while Fett calmly upped his price. Ultimately, the governor trusted her fortunes more than she trusted Fett's sanity, and she gave the hunter his ransom.

Six years after the death of Jabba the Hutt, Han and Leia went to Nar Shaddaa, the galactic smuggling center. There, Han was surprised to find that Boba Fett and

Dengar were waiting for him in his quarters. Fett told Solo that the Sarlacc had found him "indigestible," adding that the descendants of Jabba the Hutt wanted Han and Leia, dead or alive!

In a hail of blaster fire, Leia and Han made it off world, escaping in Salla Zend's *Starlight Intruder*. Fett and Dengar followed

in the *Slave II*, snatching the *Intruder*'s coordinates and jumping into hyperspace. Although the *Slave II* arrived at Byss before the *Starlight Intruder*, only Salla's ship had been cleared to get through the planetary security shields, which closed, locking out Fett's ship and breaking off a control rudder. As they spun away, trying to regain control of the ship, Dengar angrily informed Fett this was the last time he'd ever work with him. Although he was grateful to Dengar for saving him back on Tatooine, Fett was glad to be rid of the other hunter.

When Han and Lei again returned to Nar Shaddaa seeking the Jedi Master Vima-Da-Boda, they were afraid Fett might be lying in wait. In fact, two Imperial Dark Side

Warriors were attempting to blackmail the bounty hunter into working for them. They claimed knowledge of his past—that Fett had been a stormtrooper who had murdered his superior officer. Fett rejected their attempts and fought back as the two warriors attacked him. He escaped even as Solo's *Millennium Falcon* prepared to touch down.

Fett bided his time, and when the *Falcon* prepared to depart, the *Slave I* rushed forward on a suicidal run. Fett expected Han to turn tail; instead, the Corellian used his freighter to clip the *Slave I*'s stabilizer. Although Fett lost some control, he was still able to blast the *Falcon*, causing the ship to lose all sensor frequencies.

The bounty hunter tracked the *Falcon* to the lower levels, where he ambushed Leia and Han shortly after they found Vima-Da-Boda. In turn, he was ambushed by Chewbacca. During the ensuing firefight, Boba shot Chewbacca in the side, but the Wookiee managed to rip off Boba's helmet and send him spiraling into the roof high above.

Fett recovered quickly enough to board the *Slave I* and pursue the *Falcon* through the floating space debris of the spaceport moon. Scoring a hit on the freighter, Fett figured he finally had his bounty. He was surprised when Solo piloted the *Falcon* into an interstellar gas cloud. His ship's sensors were useless, so Fett hung back, waiting for several days before the *Falcon* reemerged. Unfortunately for Fett, Solo had beefed up his firepower and used it to play havoc with the *Slave I*. Fett's ship spun out of control into the gas cloud.

Though Fett disappeared, and has not reappeared on Han Solo's trail, new reports of the bounty hunter's adventures have surfaced throughout the galaxy. Han Solo knows that one day, he will once again—perhaps for the final time—face the toughest and most feared bounty hunter in space—Boba Fett.

BORSK FEY'LYA

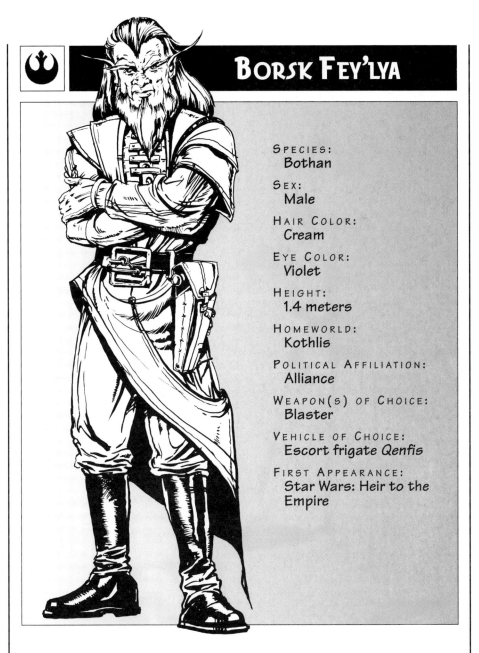

SPECIES:
Bothan

SEX:
Male

HAIR COLOR:
Cream

EYE COLOR:
Violet

HEIGHT:
1.4 meters

HOMEWORLD:
Kothlis

POLITICAL AFFILIATION:
Alliance

WEAPON(S) OF CHOICE:
Blaster

VEHICLE OF CHOICE:
Escort frigate Qenfis

FIRST APPEARANCE:
Star Wars: Heir to the Empire

Borsk Fey'lya has been a boon to the New Republic since just before the Battle of Endor, despite his hunger for power in the Provisional and Inner Councils.

Fey'lya is Bothan, a species of short, furry beings from the planet Bothawui, although he himself grew up on the colony of Kothlis. Bothans communicate not only vocally, but also with their fur. It ripples when they speak, emphasizing points or showing emotions in ways only they completely understand. His people are power hungry, and Fey'lya is no exception.

Joining with the Rebellion just after the Battle of Yavin, Borsk Fey'lya and his faction arrived at about the same time as the Mon Calamari. The Bothans didn't like the amphibious Calamarians, and Fey'lya was constantly jockeying against Ackbar for greater position. Ackbar did his best to ignore the Bothan, only working with him when necessary.

Four years after the destruction of the first Death Star, Fey'lya's people discovered a horrible secret—the Empire was building a *new* battle station. Breaking the Imperial codes, the Bothans uncovered the location and operational schedule of the new Death Star, and many died in the attempt to get the plans back to the Alliance.

Although his motives were at times weighted to aid the Bothan people, Fey'lya became an effective Alliance administrator. His rivalry with the promoted *Admiral* Ackbar continued unabated though. To the distress of some of the other Alliance leaders, the Bothan also became one of Mon Mothma's most trusted advisors.

Half a decade later, Fey'lya managed to implicate Ackbar in a plot of treason, for supposed military mismanagement at the Battle of Sluis Van. Ackbar was cleared shortly thereafter. Meanwhile, the Bothan himself—and his top aide, Tav Breil'lya—aided the rogue Corellian senator Garm bel Iblis, who was waging his own personal war against the Empire, but even so, Fey'lya felt he must remain true to the Alliance.

His downfall began when Rebel troops tried to take the long-missing *Katana* fleet. During the battle Fey'lya felt the tide turning, and ordered the withdrawal of the escort frigate *Qenfis,* thus trapping Han Solo, Lando Calrissian, and Wedge Antilles's Rogue Squadron. Though they escaped, Leia and Talon Karrde managed to expose the Bothan's disregard for even his own people. While his soldiers continued the battle, Fey'lya was put under military arrest and sent to Coruscant to face the Provisional Council.

The Council pardoned him, and he retained his seat, though he lost much of the respect and support he had enjoyed. In the weeks following, he was insistent that the Alliance destroy the Mount Tantiss cloning facility on Wayland, even agreeing to pay Talon Karrde 70,000 credits to make sure it was obliterated. Fey'lya offered vague explanations of weaponry the Emperor had developed, but Leia was suspicious; Fey'lya was hiding something.

During the following years, Councillor Fey'lya's power continued to diminish so that today his fate is unknown.

BIB FORTUNA

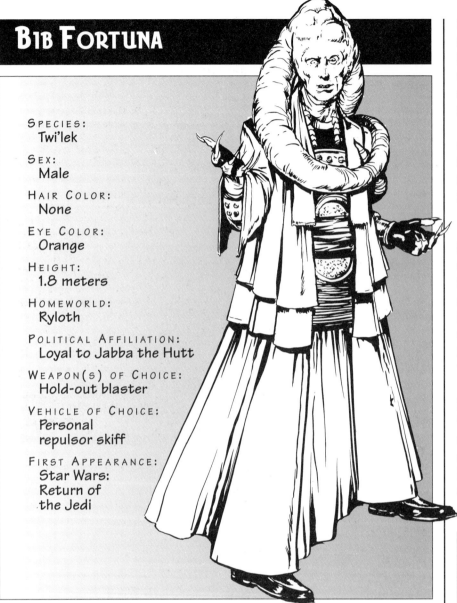

SPECIES:
Twi'lek

SEX:
Male

HAIR COLOR:
None

EYE COLOR:
Orange

HEIGHT:
1.8 meters

HOMEWORLD:
Ryloth

POLITICAL AFFILIATION:
Loyal to Jabba the Hutt

WEAPON(S) OF CHOICE:
Hold-out blaster

VEHICLE OF CHOICE:
Personal repulsor skiff

FIRST APPEARANCE:
Star Wars: Return of the Jedi

Empire, as well as that of smugglers and slavers. Angry at the death and slaving Bib Fortuna had brought on their people, a court of his peers ordered his death, and he escaped, swearing to one day take his revenge.

Adaptation was a way of life on Ryloth, and the Twi'lek soon began to allow ryll trade. Even some harvesting of Twi'lek slaves was permitted. Often, the heads of the clans would sell their own people off to gain wealth or protection.

Even with a Twi'lek bounty on his head, the notorious Bib Fotuna soon got an interesting offer. The Tatooine gang lord, Jabba the Hutt, wanted to enter into the glitterstim spice–smuggling trade, and he wanted Fortuna to work for him as his production and transport agent. Jabba's people would handle the distribution, but it was the Twi'lek's job to bring in the spice.

Jabba was a demanding boss who tended to kill anyone who made a mistake. Very few in the upper levels of Jabba's hierarchy ever lived long, but Fortuna was canny and didn't fail or disappoint. But the Imperial Navy started intercepting the spice shipments, and Jabba began to get angry.

Fortuna knew that if he stayed at that

Ambitious and obsequious at the same time, Jabba the Hutt's majordomo, Bib Fortuna, had as grating a personality as his master's. With Fortuna to set an example, it was no surprise that many people in the galaxy referred to the Twi'lek people as "worm heads."

Fortuna's species lived on the hard twilight world of Ryloth, where one side of the planet was always hot, arid day, while the other side always maintained a cool, moist night. Most of the Twi'lek lived in the darker area, in complex cities, their families part of city clans.

Like all his people, Fotuna had twin tentacular appendages coming from the back of his pointed skull. The appendages, called *lekku*—or sometimes "head-tails"—were used for cognitive functions and communication, as well as for sensual pleasures.

With no space-travel capabilities of their own, the Twi'lek seemed to have little to offer the galaxy. Bib Fortuna, however, became one of the foremost "clandestine exporters" of the addictive chemical ryll, used largely in the Corporate Sector. Ryll trade eventually caught the attention of the job, he'd soon be dead, so he requested a more important position in Jabba's organization. Surprisingly, the Hutt agreed, making the Twi'lek one of his lieutenants. Jabba used them to help conduct his business, and to fawn and bow to him, Fortuna didn't mind bowing his head—and his head-tails; after all, it was just a job.

Fortuna eventually got his revenge on his homeworld, going there with a host of attacking slaver ships. In the burning rubble of one home, he found the last descendent of a great Twi'lek house. He took the child, Nat Secura, knowing that when he finally returned to his planet again, to conquer it, Nat's lineage and support would ease the "transition." By the time Fortuna left Ryloth, with Nat in tow, seven cities were in ruin, their citizens taken as slaves.

Jabba was impressed by Fortuna's organizational and management skills, and the Twi'lek was brought into the inner circle of Jabba's chosen few. Fortuna ambitiously planned to wrest the position of majordomo from the aging Naroon Cuthus, but he had to bide his time. And he had to compete with the grubby Corellian smuggler, Bidlo Kwerve. Jabba knew that one of them would eventually triumph over the other, and he would have his new majordomo.

Fortuna did outsmart Kwerve when the two of them presented Jabba with a gift: a monstrous giant known as a rancor. While canniness on the Twi'lek's part led to caution, Kwerve's greed led him to a "greater reward" as the first rancor snack.

From that moment on, Fortuna was almost always at Jabba's side, constantly whispering to him through dagger-sharp teeth. Fortuna counseled him on almost every decision, but also knew when to back off and let the Hutt take control. And at every opportunity, the Twi'lek made himself both invaluable and worshipful.

On another trip back to Ryloth, Fortuna stumbled upon Oola, the daughter of a clan head. The beautiful young Twi'lek was a seductive dancer, her head-tails caressing and accentuating her ceremonial moves.

Fortuna kidnapped her and took her to his smuggling complex. Later, he presented her as a gift to Jabba. The Hutt was smitten with his gift, but the beautiful Twi'lek refused to dance. Fortuna berated her and the Gamorrean guards beat her.

Fearful that this might lead to his downfall, Fortuna had to deal with surprises that began popping up. Two droids arrived at the palace, gifts of faith from a man claiming to be a Jedi Knight. Then, the bounty hunter Boussh arrived to collect the

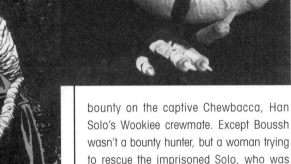

bounty on the captive Chewbacca, Han Solo's Wookiee crewmate. Except Boussh wasn't a bounty hunter, but a woman trying to rescue the imprisoned Solo, who was frozen in carbonite.

The last straw came when the Jedi Luke Skywalker showed up, using a Jedi mind trick on Fortuna, forcing him to allow the young man entrance. In the court room, to the hoots of the crowd, Luke threatened Jabba with destruction if he didn't let all of his friends free. Jabba fed the Jedi to his rancor, only to watch in horror as the young man killed the prize beast.

Jabba was angry, and scheduled the execution of Solo, Skywalker, and Chewbacca in the Great Pit of Carkoon. But Jabba had underestimated the Rebels, who had infiltrated the palace more than any had realized. When Skywalker launched the escape attempt, Fortuna ran to his private skiff, hidden nearby.

Bib Fortuna has never been seen again.

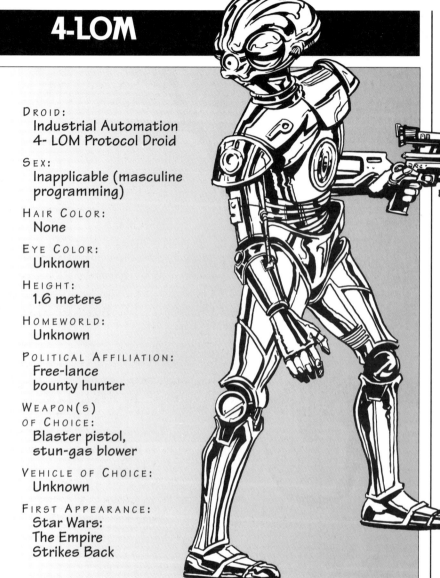

4-LOM

DROID:
Industrial Automation
4- LOM Protocol Droid

SEX:
Inapplicable (masculine programming)

HAIR COLOR:
None

EYE COLOR:
Unknown

HEIGHT:
1.6 meters

HOMEWORLD:
Unknown

POLITICAL AFFILIATION:
Free-lance bounty hunter

WEAPON(S) OF CHOICE:
Blaster pistol, stun-gas blower

VEHICLE OF CHOICE:
Unknown

FIRST APPEARANCE:
Star Wars: The Empire Strikes Back

In the history of the galaxy, it is quite extraordinary for a droid to change the level of its own self-awareness, particularly to the degree of personal transformation that 4-LOM achieved prior to its becoming one of the galaxy's fiercest bounty hunters.

4-LOM was a late-model protocol droid serving as a valet and human-cyborg relations specialist on the passenger liner *Kuari Princess*. With a TranLang III Communication module giving it knowledge of more than seven million languages, 4-LOM acted as an interpreter between the rich guests and the ship's computer. The droid was entirely aware of what the guests—and their possessions—were doing at all times.

As entertainment, the protocol droid began engaging the main computer in a series of games, simulating how best to steal valuables. The games became serious, though, when the droid and the computer began to alter each others' programming. Soon, unexplained and perfectly executed thefts had the *Kuari Princess* owners worried. No one suspected 4-LOM, the benevolent and passive droid.

Eventually, 4-LOM's altered programming allowed it more sentience, and it became bored with the ease with which it robbed from the space liner's guests. Off ship, the protocol droid became a master thief and information broker for many of the galaxy's most powerful crime lords, including Tatooine's Jabba the Hutt.

Jabba realized that 4-LOM would make an excellent bounty hunter, but the droid reminded him that its programming would not allow him violent actions. Jabba offered the droid a deal: he would refit, reprogram, and rebuild 4-LOM in exchange for its services. The droid agreed, and Jabba soon had the smartest bounty hunter in the galaxy working for him.

The crime lord paired 4-LOM with a Gand hunter named Zuckuss, whose intuition and ability to outguess his opponents worked perfectly in combination with 4-LOM's analytical skills. For a time, they were two of Jabba's favorite hunters.

A year after the destruction of the Empire's first Death Star, Darth Vader sent out a call for bounty hunters to find Han Solo, whose capture he believed would lure Luke Skywalker to him. Jabba sent 4-LOM and Zuckuss as "nonofficial emissaries." They arrived on Vader's Super Star Destroyer *Executor*, finding that four other bounty hunters had also been chosen for the hunt: Boba Fett, Dengar, IG-88, and Bossk.

Unfortunately for the paired hunters, Boba Fett was the one who tracked the *Falcon* to the Bespin system. Fett received not only the bounty from Vader, but also the carbon-frozen body of Han Solo to deliver to Jabba the Hutt.

Pleased to have Solo hanging on his wall, Jabba did not have his own hunter pair killed for their failure. The droid and the Gand were much too useful. 4-LOM and Zuckuss would have many more successful missions in their future.

GALLANDRO

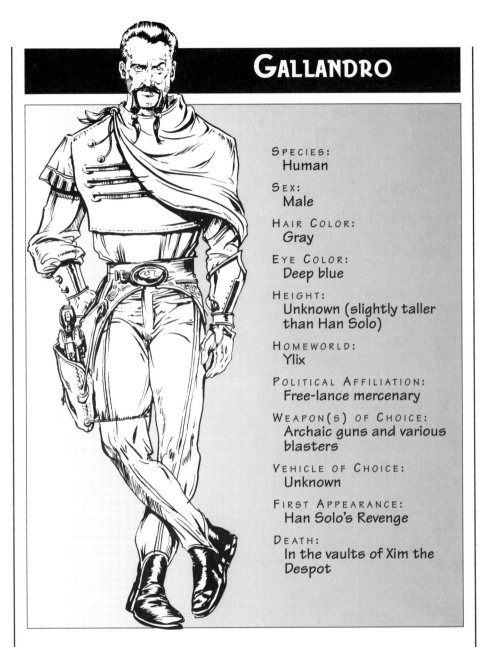

SPECIES:
Human

SEX:
Male

HAIR COLOR:
Gray

EYE COLOR:
Deep blue

HEIGHT:
Unknown (slightly taller than Han Solo)

HOMEWORLD:
Ylix

POLITICAL AFFILIATION:
Free-lance mercenary

WEAPON(S) OF CHOICE:
Archaic guns and various blasters

VEHICLE OF CHOICE:
Unknown

FIRST APPEARANCE:
Han Solo's Revenge

DEATH:
In the vaults of Xim the Despot

One of the most merciless gunmen in the galaxy, Gallandro learned at an early age to be cold, heartless, and later, quick on the draw.

Gallandro was a commoner on the backwater planet of Ylix, a world besieged by revolutionaries and terrorists from Goelitz, a rival colony in a nearby system. Attacks were common, but they never affected young Gallandro until the day he saw his parents murdered before his eyes.

Gallandro grew up in orphanages, and joined the planetary militia as soon as he was old enough. Hatred for the Goelitz burned in his breast and he became an exemplary soldier. While he became a hero to some, others were disturbed by his lack of conscience. He volunteered for increasingly hazardous assignments, becoming addicted to danger and conflict.

When the war against the Goelitz ended, Gallandro became a mercenary, hiring out as a bodyguard, soldier, bounty hunter, or assassin. All the while, he practiced his quick draw.

Gallandro's exploits became legendary.

He single-handedly hijacked the *Quamar Messenger* on its maiden run, and flew with Marso's Demons. He incurred the wrath of the Assassin's Guild but when he killed half their Elite Circle, they decided to leave him alone. The gunman gained the death mark on over a hundred worlds, but he was too tough for anyone to take down.

Odumin, a powerful sector manager for the outlying Corporate Sector Authority, made Gallandro an offer. Odumin wanted the Malorm Family dead. Not only would he offer good pay, but a general amnesty, as well. Gallandro finished the job easily. Impressed, Odumin brought Gallandro onto his staff of operatives. On retainer, Gallandro began living life better. Then he met his match in a young Corellian pilot named Han Solo.

After a brief altercation on the planet Ammuud, Han and Gallandro faced each other aboard the *Millennium Falcon* while it was held in the tractor beam of an Espo *Victory*-class Destroyer. Han tricked his opponent into grabbing a rigged security case, which sent neural shocks up Gallandro's right arm. Knowing he couldn't draw as well with his left hand, a humiliated Gallandro acceded to Solo.

Gallandro encountered Solo only once more. The gunman was working for J'uoch at a mining operation on Dellalt. Solo and his partners arrived on the planet in search of the Xim treasure ship *Queen of Ranroon*. During a battle against a group of rogue robots, Gallandro and Han saved each others' lives, but once Han found the treasure, all truces were off.

In a duel, Gallandro was faster. Han was disabled, but Gallandro didn't know that Xim had installed a no-weapons system in part of the chambers.

Dozens of lasers shot toward Gallandro at the speed of light, igniting his body in a flaming inferno. And so the fastest gunman in the galaxy met his match.

YARNA D'AL' GARGAN

SPECIES:
Askajian

SEX:
Female

HAIR COLOR:
Dark brown

EYE COLOR:
Unknown

HEIGHT:
Unknown

HOMEWORLD:
Askajia

POLITICAL AFFILIATION:
None

WEAPON(S) OF CHOICE:
None

VEHICLE OF CHOICE:
None

FIRST APPEARANCE:
Star Wars: Return of the Jedi

One thing that could be said in Jabba's favor was that he didn't have unrealistic standards of beauty. He found it in many races and species, including in the corpulent, six-breasted dancer Yarna d'al' Gargan.

The daughter of a tribal chieftain on the desert planet of Askajia, Yarna often danced for the honor of her tribe. The Askajian could retain and store water in their bodies, swelling in preparation for dry seasons and droughts. Yarna was married to Nauteg, and mothered a quartet of cublings.

When a slave-raiding party swept through Yarna's village, one of the cublings was killed, and the remaining three were taken by the slavers, along with Yarna and Nauteg, to Tatooine and the palace of Jabba the Hutt.

The cubs were sold to Mos Eisley's Imperial prefect, Eugene Talmont, but the worst of Yarna's losses was yet to come, for Nauteg stood up to Jabba, defiantly telling him he would not allow his family to be enslaved. Annoyed, Jabba opened the trap-door beneath Nauteg's feet, and Yarna's husband fell into the rancor pit. As the screams of her husband reached out to her, Yarna knew that if she ever wanted to see her cubs again, she must do whatever it took to survive.

Yarna became one of the dancers in Jabba's court, undulating to the jeers of those assembled. Despite the cruelty of the onlookers, Jabba never treated Yarna as anything but beautiful. Sometimes he had her wear warty face patches so she would remind him of his own mother. Perhaps out of that memory, Jabba had her sign an indentured-service contract that would allow her to eventually earn her freedom.

The other dancers came to look on Yarna as a mother figure, but she found it difficult to bond completely with any of them. Jabba killed them all too quickly. Eventually, Bib Fortuna presented Jabba with a graceful Twi'lek girl named Oola, who he said was a spectacular dancer. Horrified when she saw the sluglike Hutt, Oola refused to dance.

When Oola wouldn't give in to Jabba's amorous advances, Yarna tried to warn her not to resist Jabba. At first Jabba was amused by Oola's struggles, but by the third day of Oola's confinement, Jabba had had enough. Oola finally performed a beautiful dance, but as the dance ended, the Twi'lek girl again refused Jabba's molestations.

Yarna had to turn away as Jabba fed the girl to the rancor. She didn't have long to contemplate though; the arrival of a young man claiming to be a Jedi set the palace in an uproar.

Soon Jabba was dead, choked by a chained Alderaanian woman, and Yarna saw her chance. She was free from Jabba's contract, free to take goods she had stolen from the palace and buy back her children. And finally, she was free from the nightmare.

GARINDAN

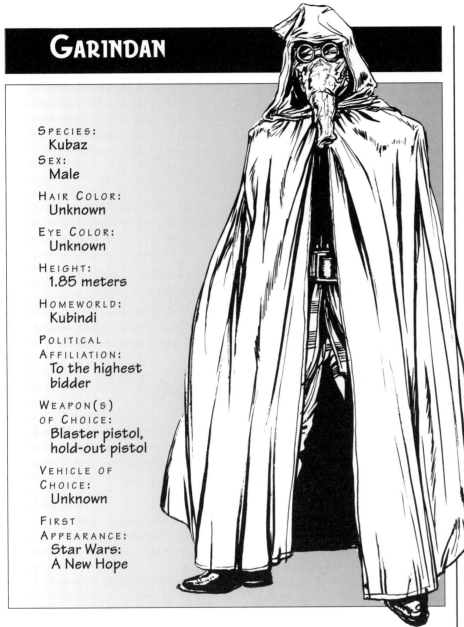

SPECIES:
Kubaz

SEX:
Male

HAIR COLOR:
Unknown

EYE COLOR:
Unknown

HEIGHT:
1.85 meters

HOMEWORLD:
Kubindi

POLITICAL AFFILIATION:
To the highest bidder

WEAPON(S) OF CHOICE:
Blaster pistol, hold-out pistol

VEHICLE OF CHOICE:
Unknown

FIRST APPEARANCE:
Star Wars: A New Hope

for information, he can produce the credit chits immediately.

The information Garindan gathers is available . . . for a price. His only allegiances are to himself; the fact that the local Imperial prefect pays him well only means that Garindan hasn't found a better offer. Even Jabba the Hutt was wary of Long Snoot finding out too much about his business transactions. Garindan bided his time, knowing that he would eventually acquire facts about Jabba and his operations, information that could make him wealthy.

One assignment from the Imperial prefect nearly cost the Alliance its future, when Garindan was hired to find the missing droids C-3PO and R2-D2. He found them with the old wizard Obi-Wan Kenobi and a young farmboy. Long Snoot trailed them from the cantina to Docking Bay 94, where they were meeting with Han Solo to charter the *Millennium Falcon*. Using his comlink, Garindan brought stormtroopers to the bay. Only a combination of luck and skill allowed Solo to get his passengers and his ship safely out of the firefight that followed.

Garindan's current whereabouts are unknown, but it is unlikely that he stayed on Tatooine amidst the turbulence following Jabba the Hutt's death. After all, information can be bought and sold anywhere in the galaxy, if one knows where to look.

The greatest spy at Mos Eisley spaceport is the mysterious creature Garindan, also known as "Long Snoot," due to his long, prehensile, trunklike nose. He wears dark goggles, as his large eyes are very sensitive to the red wavelengths of light. He is a Kubaz from the arid planet of Kubindi, and has the rough-textured, greenish black skin and bristly head hair of his species. Like his people back home, Garindan eats insects, largely exotic delicacies shipped in from the Ku'Bakai system. On Tatooine, he is almost always hooded and under a heavy robe, leading inhabitants to speculate wildly on his species and planet of origin.

Rumors abound that Garindan is fabulously wealthy. He's rarely seen with large amounts of credits, but when called upon to pay

GARTOGG

SPECIES:
Gamorrean

SEX:
Male

HAIR COLOR:
None

EYE COLOR:
Blue

HEIGHT:
1.8 meters

HOMEWORLD:
Gamorr

POLITICAL
AFFILIATION:
Loyal to
Jabba the Hutt

WEAPON(S)
OF CHOICE:
Vibro-ax

VEHICLE OF CHOICE:
None

FIRST APPEARANCE:
Star Wars:
Return of the Jedi

The planet Gamorr is a pleasant planet with an unpleasant dominant species. The Gamorreans are forever at war with anyone who will fight. The males train from birth in warfare and weaponry; as adults, their time is spent pillaging other Gamorrean clans while the women slave at home. These porcine creatures are experts at using ancient weapons, as using a blaster on Gamorr is considered declassé.

When their species was discovered by trade ships, the Gamorreans quickly became popular as slave workers. However, given their violent disposition, even the more unsavory business-creatures of the galaxy recognized that the Gamorreans would be better used as guards, soldiers, and mercenaries. Although a few Gamorreans tried their hand at bounty hunting, their bulk and lack of stealth usually led to failure.

Gartogg was one of twelve Gamorreans who came to Tatooine at the request of Jabba the Hutt. As was their custom, the Gamorreans engaged their employer in personal combat before they agreed to work. Jabba boasted he'd take them all on at once, but only if they were blindfolded, as was Hutt tradition in such dominance fights. Of course, once the pigs were unable to see, Jabba had dozens of his thugs beat the Gamorreans mercilessly. The nine who survived were awed at the "fighting proficiency" of the Hutt crime lord.

The leader of the guards was the tough Ortugg, also a Gamorrean, whose time was spent alternately watching the Quarren Tessek for Jabba, and harassing the simple Gartogg. Gartogg and the others served as palace sentries. Although the guards could understand many alien tongues, their vocal anatomy forced them to speak in Gamorrese, which sounded to the average non-Gamorrean listener like a series of grunts, squeals, and snorts.

While the rescue attempt to free Han Solo was being launched by a team of Rebels, Gartogg had his own problems. Bodies were piling up in the lower levels of the palace, and he wanted to solve their murders. His sleuthing duties would save his life, as they kept him from getting to ride the ill-fated sail barge to dispose of Jabba's prisoners at the Great Pit of Carkoon.

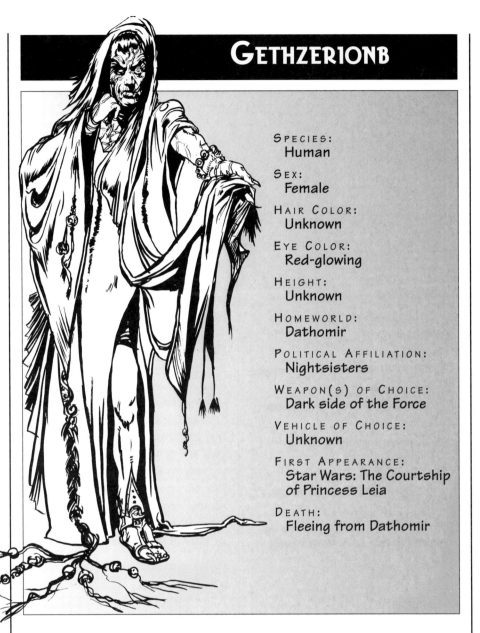

GETHZERIONB

SPECIES:
Human

SEX:
Female

HAIR COLOR:
Unknown

EYE COLOR:
Red-glowing

HEIGHT:
Unknown

HOMEWORLD:
Dathomir

POLITICAL AFFILIATION:
Nightsisters

WEAPON(S) OF CHOICE:
Dark side of the Force

VEHICLE OF CHOICE:
Unknown

FIRST APPEARANCE:
Star Wars: The Courtship of Princess Leia

DEATH:
Fleeing from Dathomir

If the term "witch" ever truly applied to anyone, it certainly applied to Gethzerion.

The clannish people of the dry planet of Dathomir followed female leaders and rulers, with males acting as servants or mates. Fewer than a hundred of the people still lived, and many of them had been killed or imprisoned by Gethzerion, one of the evil Nightsisters.

The Nightsisters were Force wielders whose genes had been developed via selective breeding to assure power. The majority of them believed they had to chant, sing, or perform rituals and spells to use their magic. Only Gethzerion realized they could use their Force talents without the rituals; she used her "powerful" solo magic to intimidate and force her will on others. Gethzerion's clan was aggressive, her followers attacking the sisters of the other clans.

When he was alive, Emperor Palpatine had known of Gethzerion. He allowed her twisted usage of the dark side of the Force as long as she was trapped on Dathomir, where an Imperial penal colony housed political prisoners. Knowing the extent of her powers, though, he decided it would be dangerous to let her get off planet, so Palpatine ordered the orbiting airfield destroyed, in the process stranding many of his own people. Gethzerion took over the colony, enslaving many of the survivors.

For years, no one came to Dathomir. Imperial Commander Zsinj was assigned to watch the planet as he traveled the Quelii Sector in his Star Destroyer, the *Iron Fist*. Palpatine died and the Empire was in chaos; Imperial leaders became warlords, each fighting for their own piece of the power. In the four years following the Emperor's death, Zsinj became one of those warlords.

When Han Solo crashed the *Millennium Falcon* on Dathomir, Zsinj contacted Gethzerion. The warlord wanted Solo for the Hapan bounty on his head, while the Nightsister wanted a ship that would take her off planet. She offered the service of the dark Nightsisters—as well as the prisoners Han Solo and Princess Leia Organa—if Zsinj would provide her a ship.

The main obstacles to Gethzerion's plan were the young Teneniel Djo of the Singing Mountain Clan, and a Jedi named Luke Skywalker. Force storms Gethzerion conjured up and Zsinj's orbital nightcloak—which was causing Dathomir's atmosphere to cool—battered the Jedi and the Nightsister of the light side, but still they held their own.

As Gethzerion realized her defeat was imminent, she leapt onto a space carrier that was leaving for Zsinj's ship. Han Solo pursued in the *Falcon*, and the carrier fired, but their missiles were ineffective. Rather than let Gethzerion and the other evil Nightsisters loose on the galaxy, Han Solo armed his own missiles and blew up the carrier.

No longer under Gethzerion's control, the witches of Dathomir were free to practice their mystical arts of healing and education. Their uncorrupted exploration of the light side began.

GREEDO

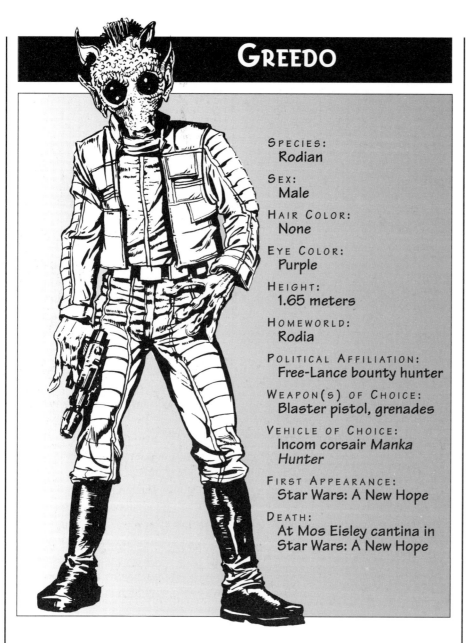

SPECIES:
Rodian

SEX:
Male

HAIR COLOR:
None

EYE COLOR:
Purple

HEIGHT:
1.65 meters

HOMEWORLD:
Rodia

POLITICAL AFFILIATION:
Free-Lance bounty hunter

WEAPON(S) OF CHOICE:
Blaster pistol, grenades

VEHICLE OF CHOICE:
Incom corsair Manka Hunter

FIRST APPEARANCE:
Star Wars: A New Hope

DEATH:
At Mos Eisley cantina in Star Wars: A New Hope

Teeku. Other members of the more peaceful Rodian clan, known as the Tetsus, came as well, and the refugees fled in three large silver spaceships. They relocated to a jungle world and began life anew.

When he was fifteen years old, Greedo and his younger brother, Pqweeduk, discovered the trio of spaceships hidden in a mountain cavern. He asked his mother about them, and she told him of his violent heritage. A month and a day later, the same Rodian who had slaughtered Greedo's father finally tracked the Tetsus down. The invaders began mowing down the settlers.

The two brothers ran to the caves, along with their mother, two uncles, and twenty other clan members. They escaped in two of the ships; the third was destroyed. Nok piloted the *Radion* through hyperspace to the port moon of Nar Shaddaa, where the survivors made their new lives in the Corellian sector.

Greedo grew to be an adult, working with his brother in the bustling districts of Level 88. He had become streetwise, learning petty thievery and black-market tactics. One day, Greedo witnessed two bounty hunters, Spurch "Warhog" Goa and Dyyz Nataz, killing a rogue Imperial spice inspector. When the two hunters were attacked by

A bounty hunter whose dreams far exceeded his grasp, the green-skinned, foul-smelling Greedo managed to rack up more enemies than friends during his short life. But his last mistake was trying to collect the bounty on Corellian smuggler Han Solo. Greedo wasn't very bright, but he wanted to be a hunter in the *worst* way. He succeeded.

Greedo was a Rodian, from the planet Rodia in the Tyrius star system. The Rodians consider bounty hunting an honored profession and a fabulous sport, and

prizes are awarded to the hunter with the most captures or kills. The only dishonorable thing for a Rodian hunter to do is "padding" a catch—driving up a bounty by allowing the prey to commit more crimes, even after they had been located. The Rodian Council of Justice frowned on such activities.

In a more violent time on Rodia, Greedo's bounty-hunter father was murdered and his riches seized. His pregnant wife, Neela, took three-year-old Greedo and left the planet with her older brothers, Nok and

The trio of hunters fled to Tatooine, where Goa and Greedo hooked up with Jabba the Hutt. The obese crime lord was fond of Rodian hunters: they were ruthless, they worked cheaply, and they made great rancor snacks if they fell out of his favor. Working for Jabba would be a perfect way for Greedo to increase his status and his power as a bounty hunter.

When Jabba awarded Greedo the exclusive bounty contract on Han Solo's head, the Rodian saw the galaxy opening to him; the Corellian was a heady prize.

Greedo waited for Solo in Chalmun's cantina. As the Rodian steeled himself, there was a disturbance at the bar; an old man using a lightsaber had attacked an Aqualish and an ugly humanoid. When Chewbacca

a towering cyborg named Gorm, Greedo managed to save their lives by killing Gorm.

When the deadly duo cut the Rodian in on the bounty, he decided to help them, tipping them off to a cluster of Rebels hiding in another part of Level 88. With the Imperial reward, Greedo planned to buy an Incom corsair ship from the mechanic Shug Ninx. He planned to call it the *Manka Hunter*. Every bounty hunter needed a great ship, he had decided.

While he was inspecting his ship-to-be, Greedo couldn't resist stealing a pair of new Dekk-6 power couplings. Unfortunately for him, he was caught by the huge Wookiee known as Chewbacca; the Dekks were for the *Millennium Falcon*. When Han Solo took his rancor-skin jacket as restitution, Greedo threatened him.

Greedo became Warhog Goa's apprentice, learning the bounty-hunting trade from a "master." He was soon to learn the error of his ways. When the Imperials attacked the Rebels on Level 88, the fighting was intense. Greedo barely escaped with Goa and Dyzz in their ship, the *Nova Viper*, before an entire quarter of the Corellian sector exploded in a flash. Greedo realized with a heavy heart that his family was dead, and he was responsible.

escorted the old man and a fresh-faced farm boy back to Solo's table, Greedo grew more nervous. Two stormtroopers walked through the bar, and as they left, Greedo noticed that Solo and Chewbacca were alone. Then Chewbacca got up and left.

Marching up to Solo, blaster drawn, the Rodian demanded the credits Han owed Jabba. If he could get the credits out of Solo, then kill the smuggler, Greedo could be paid twice for the one bounty! Sure of himself, the Rodian kept his blaster trained on Solo, who seemed remarkably unafraid. The Corellian's smug attitude angered Greedo, but before he could threaten Solo

further, the spacer shot a blaster from under the table, killing Greedo instantly.

It was then that Wuher the bartender got a fiendishly clever idea. He recovered Greedo's body and took it below, where he and his new droid, C2-R4, used the Rodian's flesh and blood in their still. The resulting liqueur was the most powerful pheromonal drink Wuher had ever tasted. The bartender was sure that Jabba the Hutt would pay handsomely for the drink.

If he could have withstood the intense flavor, Wuher would have hoisted a second drink to salute Greedo, the greatest tasting Rodian bounty hunter of all time.

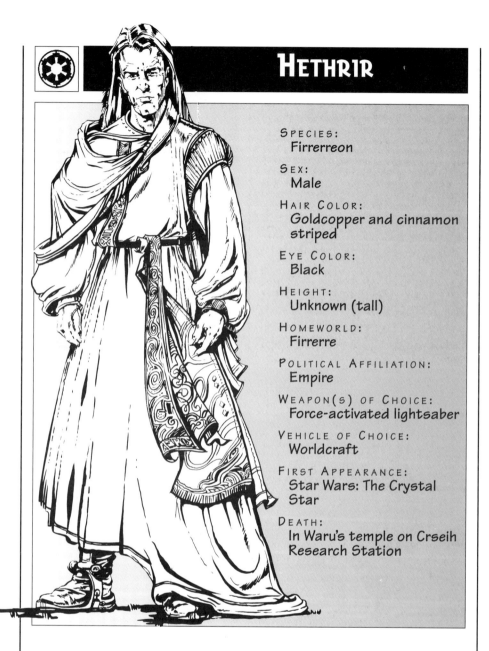

HETHRIR

SPECIES:
Firrerreon

SEX:
Male

HAIR COLOR:
Goldcopper and cinnamon striped

EYE COLOR:
Black

HEIGHT:
Unknown (tall)

HOMEWORLD:
Firrerre

POLITICAL AFFILIATION:
Empire

WEAPON(S) OF CHOICE:
Force-activated lightsaber

VEHICLE OF CHOICE:
Worldcraft

FIRST APPEARANCE:
Star Wars: The Crystal Star

DEATH:
In Waru's temple on Crseih Research Station

Once a student of the dark side, Hethrir became a threat to not only his own son, but also to the children of Han and Leia Organa Solo.

When Hethrir was young, he and his lover, Rillao, trained with Darth Vader. Hethrir was eager to learn the dark side of the Force, but his mate was a disappointment to the Dark Lord. While Hethrir could dampen others' Force abilities, she was a healer and light-side user. When the two conceived a child, Vader had high hopes for turning it to evil.

Rillao spirited herself and her unborn child to a far-distant planet, hiding from her dark mate. The child was a boy, whom she named Tigris, and he had no Force abilities at all. He was also oblivious to his father's identity. Eventually Hethrir found the pair and took his son away, imprisoning Rillao in a torture device on a dead freighter once used by slavers. He kept Tigris as his own personal servant.

Vader appointed Hethrir as one of his agents, the Procurator of Justice, and asked the corrupt Jedi for proof of his loyalty. In

the performance of his duties for the Empire, Hethrir abducted a freighter filled with his own people. He then destroyed his homeworld, killing millions of Firrerreons.

When the Empire fell, Hethrir fled, taking his resources and his followers, drifting out into space on his own small planet, a technological construct called a "worldcraft." The vessel had been one of a precious few that had been dispensed by the Emperor as "treats" to his most cruel and loyal subjects. Aboard the worldcraft, Hethrir planned an "Empire Reborn," with himself as its ruler. To achieve his goals, he needed greater access to the Force, which he could gain through a being called Waru.

Living aboard Crseih Research Station, Waru was a fleshy mass covered in gold scales, who acted as a faith healer for the masses. In reality, Waru robbed some of his victims of their life forces, using the energy to create a portal directly into the Force. Waru wanted to go home through the portal, but to do so he needed to acquire a being of exceptional power.

Hethrir had been kidnapping children from throughout the universe. Those who had Force abilities he would train in the dark side, while those who didn't became slaves. All the while, he sought the one special child whose strength in the Force would appease his "patron saint," Waru.

The Procurator thought he had found the perfect students *and* the solution for Waru when he kidnapped the trio of Solo children: Jacen, Jaina, and three-year-old Anakin. Taking them from the planet of Muntro Codur, Hethrir "enrolled" them in the Dark Jedi school, where the students were rewarded for acts of cruelty or torment.

Hethrir might have succeeded in his mission to deliver Anakin Solo to Waru if he hadn't been confronted by his mate. Rillao, who had been freed by Leia Organa Solo, told the enslaved Tigris that Hethrir was his father. Tigris helped Anakin escape. Deprived of the young, Force-strong child, Waru died, pulling Hethrir into his energy field and destroying them both.

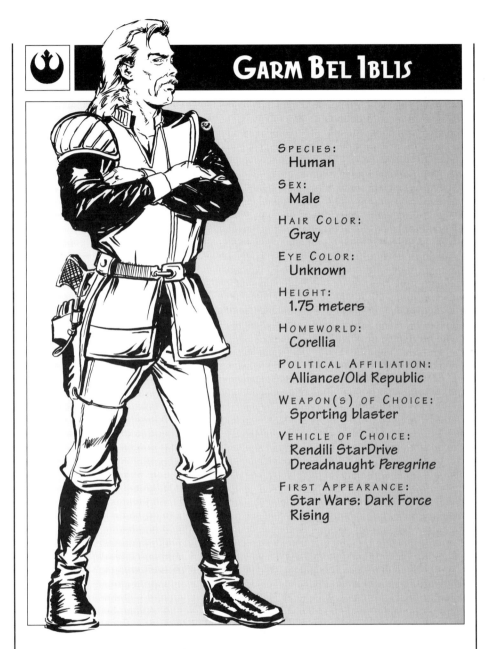

GARM BEL IBLIS

SPECIES:
Human

SEX:
Male

HAIR COLOR:
Gray

EYE COLOR:
Unknown

HEIGHT:
1.75 meters

HOMEWORLD:
Corellia

POLITICAL AFFILIATION:
Alliance/Old Republic

WEAPON(S) OF CHOICE:
Sporting blaster

VEHICLE OF CHOICE:
Rendili StarDrive Dreadnaught *Peregrine*

FIRST APPEARANCE:
Star Wars: Dark Force Rising

One of the founders of the Rebellion against the Empire, Garm Bel Iblis eventually became a rogue agent, striking out on his own against Imperial oppression.

A Corellian senator in the days of the Old Republic, Iblis watched, with growing consternation, the dealings and misdealings of Senator Palpatine. Although he was just as charismatic and popular as Palpatine, Iblis's attempts to undermine the power-hungry senator actually resulted in a loss in influence.

When Palpatine declared himself Emperor, Iblis was one of the first victims of the New Order. The Corellian and his wife and children were rounded up on the planet of Anchoron and arrested. Imperial soldiers executed his family, forcing Garm to watch. Somehow, he escaped and contacted Senator Bail Organa of Alderaan and Mon Mothma of Chandrila, each of whom had contact with anti-Empire underground factions. Iblis suggested a meeting between the two, and the resulting unification of the resistance was called the Corellian Treaty in honor of the former senator.

While Iblis was a brilliant military strategist and tactician, Mon Mothma was a strong inspirational speaker. She used her abilities to bring diverse species and groups to an understanding of their need to work in concert with each other. Bail Organa maintained a strong moderating force on Mothma, but Iblis, having been relegated to a background role in the Rebellion by the two peaceful senators, began to experience conflicts with her.

When Alderaan was destroyed and Bail Organa killed, Iblis was the only leader of the Rebellion with enough status to stand up to Mothma. Their relationship deteriorated significantly as Iblis accused the Chandrilan of wanting to usurp the throne and place herself in control of the galaxy. When Mothma ordered an attack on an Imperial garrison on the planet of Milvayne, in the Gyrica system, Iblis refused to follow her orders, arguing that too many of his men would be slaughtered in her bid for power. Mothma cooly informed him that the Rebel Alliance would have no more need of his services.

Iblis broke away from the Alliance—taking many men with him—and formed his own guerilla cell. He established a hidden mobile base known as Peregrine's Nest, from which he mapped strategies and commanded his private army in strikes against the Empire. He had many successes over the years, though none so major as those enjoyed by Mothma's Rebel Alliance.

Two women served as Iblis's advisors; Sena Leikvoid Midanyl was the chief advisor and unofficial ambassador-at-large, and a pilot named Irenez was the chief of security and intelligence coordinator. Sena had been Iblis's chief aide on Corellia, working beside him on the floors of the senate. She was with him when he helped found the Rebel Alliance, and had left with him when his battles with Mon Mothma had become too severe, only to rejoin him after the split.

Irenez was also a longtime associate of Iblis. Her training at the Old Republic military academy on Corellia—which Iblis had sponsored—left her well prepared for her chosen career as a mercenary and soldier of fortune. Banded together, the three Corellians planned many of the attacks on the Imperials. Their most successful was an assault on an Ubiqtorate Imperial intelligence center on Tangrene that resulted in its complete destruction.

A month after the Tangrene mission, Iblis met a Bothan named Borsk Fey'lya, who was an Alliance Council member. Fey'lya had designs on leading the Alliance, and he knew Iblis disliked Mothma and wanted her removed, so he channeled money into Iblis's accounts and helped protect the Peregrine's Nest from Imperials.

Iblis had taken the name "Peregrine," used for both his ship and his base, from an old Corellian legend about a ghostly man cursed to wander the world forever. At times, the ex-senator felt very much like a ghost. Though quick with jokes or sarcasm in the old days, since the murder of his family and the split from the Rebellion, Iblis had become withdrawn and sullen, even though Sena did her best to keep the commander's spirits high.

Iblis still believed that Mon Mothma would one day seek to turn the New Republic into a dictatorship, with herself as its head, and early on, he was ready to strike with his army if that happened. But the more time that passed after the fall of the Empire, the more he realized Mothma was not power hungry. Fey'lya *was*, although not like Palpatine. Bothans were just naturally power hungry, but Iblis knew Fey'lya also fully supported the aims of the New Republic.

The charismatic senator Iblis was surprised when he was contacted by Alliance hero Han Solo. Iblis had met him many years prior, when as an eleven-year-old youth Solo had asked some precocious questions while the senator spoke at his school. He had followed Solo's progress, and had been disheartened when he was ejected from the Imperial Academy, for Iblis knew that Han could have improve the system from within. Now, Han was changing things for the New Republic.

Iblis was able to assemble his strike force of six Dreadnaught ships from the legendary *Katana* fleet, including his own ship, the *Peregrine,* to aid New Republic forces as they fought to gain control of the remainder of the *Katana* fleet. Although the Alliance managed to salvage fifteen warships, the Imperial forces made off with many more.

Princess Leia Organa Solo asked Iblis to return to the New Republic and work with them again. He did, and discovered his attitude toward Mothma had undergone a metamorphosis. He now understood her fear of entrusting her people's lives to any other leader. Thus, when she asked him to help her defend Coruscant from an Imperial attack, he agreed.

Grand Admiral Thrawn's forces were devastating Alliance ships which had been deployed under the control of the competent but uninspired tactician Admiral Drayson, and Iblis took over from Drayson. When the Imperial admiral released "cloaked" asteroids into the space above Coruscant, invisible to detectors and to the naked eye, Iblis helped develop the Stardust Plan to spot the asteroids using sensor-reflective repolarized dust. Thanks to this strategy and the timely arrival of Talon Karrde, Coruscant's spaceways were soon reopened.

Garm Bel Iblis has stayed on with the New Republic, bringing his personal army and strike-force ships into the Alliance fleet. His input and strategies are valued by the other Alliance leaders, and by his longtime rival, Mon Mothma. A cloud has lifted from the Corellian leader's life, brightening a future once darkened with the birth of the Empire and the death of his family.

IG-88

DROID:
Holowan Mechanicals IG-88 Assassin

SEX:
Inapplicable (Masculine Programming)

HAIR COLOR:
Inapplicable

EYE COLOR:
Red sensors

HEIGHT:
2 meters

HOMEWORLD:
Halowan Laboratories

POLITICAL AFFILIATION:
Free-lance bounty hunter

WEAPON(S) OF CHOICE:
Blaster rifle and other weapons

VEHICLE OF CHOICE:
IG-2000

FIRST APPEARANCE:
Star Wars: The Empire Strikes Back

The most infamous of the semisentient assassin droids is IG-88. Programmers at the high-security Holowan Laboratories had given the IG series the most sophisticated combat programs available, imbuing them with unprecedented levels of autonomy. Upon activation, the five IG prototypes killed twenty-three staff members and escaped Holowan Labs. The first model, IG-72, went into business as a ruthless bounty hunter in the Outer Rim Territories. One of the others, IG-88 was even more daring.

IG-88 worked in and around the Galactic Core, often within the confines of Imperial-controlled worlds on which assassin droids were strictly illegal. It hunted down its designers, executing them for fear they might reveal a flaw in its design. In its time, more than 150 deaths were traced to IG-88, and forty systems had issued "Dismantle on Sight" orders for the tall assassin droid.

The Old Republic and the Empire agreed on few things. One of those things was the fundamental danger of legal assassin droids. No droid exemplified their fears more than the infamous bounty hunter IG-88.

First created in the days of the Old Republic, assassin droids were originally a law-enforcement tool, keeping peace and capturing or killing dangerous criminals. Later versions, called war droids, were used as soldiers in the Outer Rim frontiers and the Corporate Sector. Gradually, the droids began to be misused by warlords, criminal kingpins, and politicians, so in its waning days, the Senate tried to outlaw the droids, but to no avail. Years later, the Empire would have a greater—though still not 100 percent—success rate at outlawing the assassin droids.

To make matters worse, many of the assassin droids gained a kind of pseudosentience and independence from their programmers. To be effective assassins, the droids needed to be designed for autonomy and intelligence.

Ruthless and efficient, IG-88 employs a large arsenal of weaponry, including blaster rifles, grenade launcher, flamethrower, sonic stunner, missile weapons, and various other armaments hidden within its body. An array of sensors on its headpiece allow it to see in all directions at once, sensing movement even at long ranges, and allowing it to laser target its prey. A broadband antenna allows it to intercept and decode most transmissions.

Some ten years before they would come to Tatooine on the mission to find Obi-Wan Kenobi, the droids R2-D2 and C-3PO encountered IG-88 on a droid barge headed for the Hosk Station in the Kalarba system. The assassin had tried to kill Olag Greck by stowing away in his illegal glitterstim spice shipment. Fortunately for Greck, IG-88's batteries had drained, and Greck was able

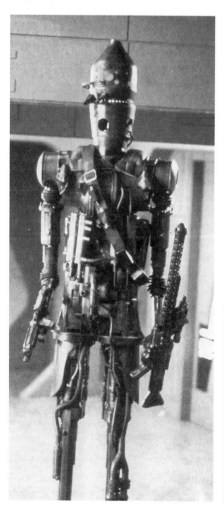

to detain it and have it transferred to his headquarters, Hosk Station. Greck planned to use the assassin in his arena battles. What he didn't know was that IG-88 had set a program trap. When the ship touched down, it broke free, escaping into the station with Artoo at its metal heels.

Greck enlisted the aid of the flustered C-3PO to find the two fugitive droids. After R2-D2 had been forced to help repair the assassin droid, the two attempted to sneak onto a shuttle to Kalarba City. Greck and his Gamorrean guards spotted them and attacked IG-88, pinning it to the wall with a carbonite constrictor net. Ever resourceful, the assassin droid used a gas bomb to mask its exit. It took Threepio hostage, as well, escaping with him and Artoo on Greck's own cruiser.

Greck took another ship, engaging IG-88 in a firefight among the rocky canyons of the Indobok moon. Both ships crashed, but R2-D2 and C-3PO managed to escape in a pod to Kalarba. At this point Greck realized that IG-88 hadn't been sent to kill him—only to *humiliate* him. In that, IG-88 had succeeded.

More than a decade later IG-88, by then considered the second most feared bounty hunter in the galaxy—after Boba Fett—was summoned by Darth Vader to the Super Star Destroyer *Executor*, where the assassin droid was joined by five other bounty hunters: Boba Fett, Dengar, Zuckuss, 4-LOM, and Bossk. Vader wanted them to find Han Solo and the *Millennium Falcon*, a step in his quest to capture Luke Skywalker.

While on Vader's Star Destroyer, IG-88 installed a homing device on Boba Fett's *Slave I*. The assassin droid reasoned that if it couldn't get Solo itself, Fett would. If Fett got him, IG-88 could steal him away. Fett's sensors didn't register the droid's device as he successfully tracked the *Falcon* toward Bespin.

IG-88 was unable to snatch Solo on Bespin before Darth Vader arrived, so the next logical move was to go to Tatooine and wait. Fett was to deliver Solo to Jabba the Hutt, and IG-88, aboard its needle-shaped *IG-2000* ship, would be there first.

As the *Slave I* emerged from hyperspace near Tatooine, Fett was angered to find the *IG-2000* waiting for him. Fett fired, easily destroying the *IG-2000* in one strafing blast. He readied himself; it had to be a decoy. Sure enough, another *IG-2000* roared out of hyperspace, blasting away at the *Slave I*.

Fett sent his ship into a dive toward the planet, ignoring IG-88's monotone threats over the comm. As gravity caught hold of the two bounty ships, Fett used his unique inertial-dampening system to stop the *Slave I*. The *IG-2000* shot past him, propelled by the forces of the planet and its own speed, and Fett grabbed it with his tractor beam. Silently, as always, Fett lined up a concussion missile and blew the *IG-2000* to microscopic bits.

It would appear that IG-88 was destroyed, yet the assassin droid was sighted several more times throughout the galaxy, such as when the body of an IG-88 droid was seen by Chewbacca in the scrap room on Cloud City.

Searching for information to use in the rescue of Han Solo, Luke Skywalker and R2-D2 tracked IG-88 to the planet Stenos, and were surprised to find that Lando Calrissian and Chewbacca had tracked the reptillian bounty hunter Bossk there, as well. In the complications and battles that followed, both bounty hunters escaped. And on the hunter's world of Keyorin, shortly after the Alliance's daring rescue of Han Solo on Tatooine, Bossk and IG-88 tried to collect on a small-time crime boss's bounty on Calrissian's head, but they were beaten yet again.

No one has yet found out how IG-88 has survived certain death, or what happened to the other three IG-series assassin droids. The only people that know the answers—the Holowan scientists—are long dead. But their most deadly creation, IG-88, is still very much "alive" . . . and planning its future.

ROGANDA AND IREK ISMAREN

SPECIES:
Human

SEX:
Female/Male

HAIR COLOR:
Black/Black

EYE COLOR:
Black/Blue

HEIGHT:
Unknown

HOMEWORLD:
Alderaan

POLITICAL AFFILIATION:
Empire

WEAPON(S) OF CHOICE:
Unknown/Lightsaber

VEHICLE OF CHOICE:
Unknown

FIRST APPEARANCE:
Star Wars: Children of the Jedi

Emperor Palpatine left his mark on thousands of worlds, killing and crushing all who stood in the way of his New Order. He also left his mark on several women; it was rumored that Roganda Ismaren bore Palpatine a son, Irek, before the Emperor was killed by the Rebellion.

Two years prior to the Battle of Yavin, at a Senatorial banquet on Alderaan, an eighteen-year-old Princess Leia Organa had seen a beautiful, oval-faced, fragile woman dressed in a beautiful gown with gold and crimson, wearing a jeweled headpiece.

Leia's Aunt Rouge had whispered conspiratorially that she was one of the Emperor's concubines, and later her Aunt Celly had gossiped that the Ismaren woman had borne an illegitimate son by the Emperor.

Later, as a hero of the New Republic, Leia had come to the planet Plawal to investigate rumors of a group of grown-up children of the Jedi. In a marketplace, Leia encountered the Alderaanian woman again, this time dressed in white, and remembered Roganda Ismaren. The woman begged Leia not to reveal her to the New Republic.

Roganda explained that her son had died, and that she was now working as a fruit packer. Leia knew she was lying, but could not figure out why.

Roganda was indeed lying. Her fourteen-year-old son was still alive, and was strong in the dark side of the Force . . . much stronger than his demanding mother. He had begun training in the ways of the dark side at age seven, taught by an Imperial named Nasdra Magrody. Although his lightsaber skills were poor, his Force talents, combined with an implanted computer chip, made him a mechanical prodigy able to influence droids and computers.

Irek had been implanted with a brain chip that enabled him to visualize schematics. By the age of twelve, Irek Ismaren could have qualified for an advanced degree in subelectron physics, or as a droid motivator technician.

Leia eventually found Plett's Well, the hiding place of the Jedi children and their spouses, in underground caverns beneath the legendary Jedi Master Plett's house. Accompanied by R2-D2, Leia was trapped there by Irek and Roganda. Irek challenged Leia to a lightsaber duel, but she realized the best way to save her life was to surrender. Roganda would not allow Leia to be killed; she was too important a hostage.

Irek was already bringing to Plawell the *Eye of Palpatine,* an asteroidlike warship that had been hidden from the Rebellion in space. Unbeknownst to Irek, the light side of the Force was working against him, and the Jedi Nichos Marr destroyed the *Eye of Palpatine* before it reached its destination.

Afraid of Alliance retaliation, Roganda and Irek escaped into the dense, foggy jungles of Plawell, leaving Leia behind. Admiral Ackbar's reports later indicated that the Ismarens had fled to the Atravis sector, where heavy concentrations of Grand Admiral Harrsk's troops had been reported. It's unlikely that the Alliance has heard the last of the mistress and possible heir of Palpatine.

Prince Isolder

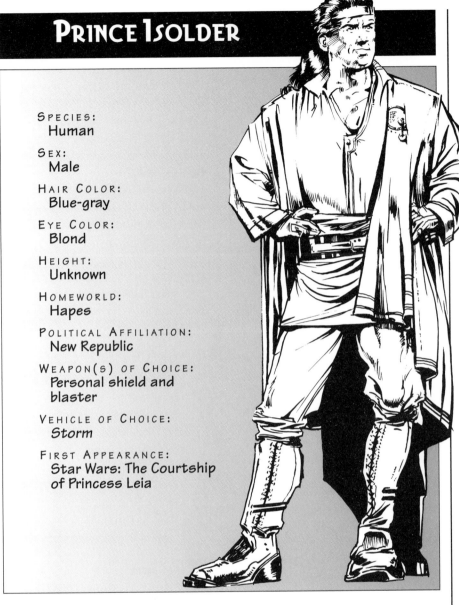

Species:
Human

Sex:
Male

Hair Color:
Blue-gray

Eye Color:
Blond

Height:
Unknown

Homeworld:
Hapes

Political Affiliation:
New Republic

Weapon(s) of Choice:
Personal shield and blaster

Vehicle of Choice:
Storm

First Appearance:
Star Wars: The Courtship of Princess Leia

Prince Isolder is the heir (*Chume'da*) to the royal house of Hapes, next in line to rule the sixty-three worlds of the Hapan cluster. He would have been *second in line* if his older brother hadn't been murdered aboard his royal flagship.

Isolder was in his teens at the time, and was devastated. He disguised himself and worked as a pirateer for two years, looking for the man who shot his sibling. He eventually found the killer—a pirate named Haravan—and arrested him. Haravan was killed in prison before he could tell Isolder who had hired him.

To keep the prince from again roaming off, he was assigned a cadre of statuesque, Amazon-like bodyguards. His personal guard, Captain Astaria, did her best to keep Isolder apprised of the intrigues in the Hapes court. Isolder's first love, Lady Ellian, had drowned in a reflecting pool; more was being plotted behind the scenes than either Astaria or Isolder could imagine.

Isolder's second love was Princess Leia Organa, of the late planet Alderaan. She was an ambassador for the Alliance's New Republic, and struck by her beauty and grace, the prince decided to make her his wife.

Soon thereafter, Alliance monitors on Coruscant were filled with an army of ships from the Hapes cluster, each bearing gifts for Leia. Finally, Prince Isolder himself arrived and asked Leia to be his bride.

Leia was shocked, but she did find the prince handsome and charming, and Hapes reminded her of her long-lost homeworld. But before the couple could make their own decisions, the actions of three other people come into play.

Isolder's mother, Queen Mother Ta'a Chume, did not approve of Leia. Since she had arranged the deaths of her first son and Lady Ellian, she had no compunctions about scheduling an attack on Leia. Only the fast reflexes and weaponry employed by Isolder saved Leia's life.

Han Solo also loved Leia, and he was jealous and desperate enough to spirit her to a planet called Dathomir. The *Millennium Falcon* crashed and they were captured by witches of the Singing Mountain Clan.

One of those witches presented the third major obstacle in Isolder's hunt for Leia. Traveling with Luke Skywalker to Dathomir, Isolder came in contact with the powerful young desert witch, Teneniel Djo. Even while he was facing down the Dathomirian Nightsisters, the rogue Imperial warlord Zsinj, and his own mother, Prince Isolder came to love Teneniel. Leaving Leia and Han to plan their own nuptials, Isolder and his new bride-to-be returned to Hapes. There, they declared the Hapes cluster to be supporters of the New Republic.

Prince Isolder and Teneniel Djo had a daughter, Tenel Ka, whose powers in the Force were strong enough to get her into Luke Skywalker's Jedi academy on the moon of Yavin Four. So the next heir to the Hapes throne may well be a Jedi Knight.

JABBA THE HUTT (JABBA DESILIJIC TIURE)

SPECIES:
Hutt

SEX:
Male

HAIR COLOR:
None

EYE COLOR:
Orange

HEIGHT:
3.9 meters (long)

HOMEWORLD:
Nal Hutta

POLITICAL AFFILIATION:
None

WEAPON(S) OF CHOICE:
Assassins and bounty hunters

VEHICLE OF CHOICE:
Ubrikkian luxury sail barge, repulsor sled

FIRST APPEARANCE:
Star Wars: Return of the Jedi

DEATH:
Aboard his sail barge

One of the most notorious crime lords in the galaxy was also one of the ugliest. Jabba the Hutt could have stayed on top if he hadn't underestimated a Corellian pilot, a lithe princess, and their Jedi friend.

Jabba Desilijic Tiure was a member of a sluglike species more commonly known as Hutts. The species evolved on Varl, a planet in the Ardos system. Hutt genetics are a curious mix of various creatures; they can open their jaws impossibly wide to consume food, and their eyes protrude like rep- tiles', with membranes to keep them wet and safe; like amphibians, their slitlike nostrils seal tightly when underwater; like many land-dwelling vertebrates, their lungs—not gills—bring oxygen to their blood.

Hutts are not vertebrates. Their muscular, sluglike bodies have no skeletons, but do have an interior mantle that shapes the head. A specialized radula, deep in the throat, shreds food on its way to the enormous stomach cavity. Hutt skin is impervious to most weapons, and to all but the harshest chemical corrosion. It constantly secretes mucus and oily sweat, making a Hutt hard to grasp. Underneath the skin, heavy layers of muscle and blubber protect the inner organs.

Hutts have two stubby, swollen arms, which are of little use. On their own, a Hutt can crawl forward using the muscular tail like a foot. In public, most Hutts use hover-sleds or repulsorlift vehicles to ferry themselves around.

One of the longest-living species in the galaxy, Hutts can survive for at least one thousand standard years. The species has involved itself in galaxy crime for quite some time. Great Bogga the Hutt was a crime lord who had his men murder the Jedi Andur Sunrider. Andur's wife, Nomi, and daughter, Vima, would both become great Jedi Knights before Bogga's end.

For thousands of years, the Hutts lived on Varl, but with the increasing number of visitors to their planet, they relocated to the Y'Toub system, which had a yellow star and four habitable planets. They chose Evocar, and moved in with the humanoid Evocaii. Trading technology for real estate, the Hutt clans eventually owned most of the planet. The Evocaii were driven to relocate themselves to Nar Shaddaa, one of the Evocar moons.

The Hutts renamed the planet Nal Hutta, which means "Glorious Jewel" in Huttese. Believing themselves the better of any race or species, Hutt clans used their superior intelligence to build criminal empires. Many clans wiped each other out, but that was the Hutt way. And if anyone other than a Hutt killed a Hutt, there was trouble.

Jabba himself was born to Zorba the Hutt on Nal Hutta. Zorba, one of the top clan leaders, taught his son all about the art of crime; how to deal with smugglers, how to double-cross friends, how to control slaves, how to manipulate the law, how to eliminate enemies.

By the time he was six hundred years old and weighing a hefty one thousand kilograms, Jabba was in charge of his own vast criminal empire. He relocated to Tatooine, setting himself up on that Outer Rim planet, and had a blockhouse at Mos Eisley spaceport converted into Jabba's Town house. Much smaller than the Mos Eisley Inn next door, the town house was nevertheless one of the most heavily guarded buildings in the city. Interior and exterior defenses helped Jabba in secure negotiations with visiting dignitaries, Imperial leaders, or important criminals.

Jabba was most likely found at his palace, far out near the southwestern border of the Western Dune Sea. Made of sandrock and ditanium, the palace was nine stories high and extended underground. Lower levels were mazes and dungeons, while upper levels were living quarters, gaming and conference rooms, and ornate dining halls.

Designed by Derren Flet, the palace was built around the monastery of the B'omarr monks, who wandered the lower corridors or appeared through secret passageways. Many of the monks resided as brains in nutrient jars kept in the catacombs; they would transfer themselves into metallic, spiderlike walking devices when they wished to move out and about. The brain-spiders were unsettling for any who hadn't been warned, and often upsetting even for those who had.

The centerpiece of Jabba's palace was his throne room, located at the base of the main tower. The massive chamber had a dais at one end for Jabba to lie on. The audience chamber allowed many exits and entrances, and a performance area was set up for bands. Jabba kept many slave-girl dancers, from the six-breasted Yarna d'al' Gargan, who reminded Jabba of his mother, to Melina Carniss, whose powerful moves gave her a hungry grace.

Like a queen bee in her hive, Jabba was basically a helpless creature who was catered to and cared for, but exerted an enormous amount of power. His court was a motley collection of aliens and humanoids whose professions ranged from assassin to bounty hunter, dancer to slaver, droid to sycophant.

Jabba's empire included every illegal activity the Empire could outlaw, and many it hadn't yet thought to. Throughout the Outer Rim Territories, Jabba was the top slug when it came to smuggling, glitterstim-spice dealing, slave trading, assassination, loan sharking, protection, piracy, and ship thievery. Every smuggler, pirate, and thief in the Outer Rim eventually took on jobs for him. Those that didn't work out were never heard from again.

Jabba had several lieutenants over time, each helping him control a different facet of his operation. The oldest majordomo was Naroon Cuthus, who had been with Jabba for a long time, but knew too much about Jabba's business to be allowed to retire; Jabba would probably repay him for his service with a quick death. Two who were competing for Cuthus's post were the grubby Corellian smuggler Bidlo Kwerve and the meticulous Twi'lek named Bib Fortuna. Jabba enjoyed pitting Kwerve and Fortuna against each other.

Only one being in the palace—Ephant Mon—was *truly* loyal to Jabba, and the Hutt knew it. Everyone else was a servant, a slave, or a spy.

Jabba and the giant creature known as Ephant Mon had been gunrunners in years long past. Once, when a raid on an Imperial weapons cache went bad, Jabba saved Ephant's life, at considerable risk to his own. Later, on Tatooine, the Hutt gave Ephant a surreptitious job ferreting out conspiracies, thievery, and assassination plans. It was amazing how many palace citizens had plans to kill Jabba or take over his business. Some were spies from the Hutt's main Tatooinian competitor, Lady Valarian, but most were acting on their own. Jabba would often let them play out their plans to a point, and then expose them.

One of Jabba's more unique employees was a fat, grotesque man named Heater. His job was to pose as Jabba for public functions. This allowed Jabba a public face and a surprising trump card when his true identity was revealed. Heater also acted as prey for the stupidest assassins or bounty hunters. Although Heater felt himself important in the organization, Jabba considered him extremely expendable.

The only other seemingly permanent member of Jabba's entourage was Salacious Crumb, a Kowakian lizard-monkey. The bizarre little creature would sit at the edge of Jabba's dais, cackling, muttering, and mimicking visitors. Crumb's job was to make Jabba laugh at least once a day. His longevity proved either his excellent talents, or Jabba's low taste in humor.

Jabba got the majority of his glitterstim spice from Kessel, where mines below the Imperial Correctional Facility contained the powerful drug. Jabba had several associates in positions of power at the mines and the jail. A Rybet named Moruth Doole was Jabba's main source of spice, and Doole's knack for picking competent smugglers made transport much easier. One was a cocky Corellian named Han Solo, who piloted a modified freighter known as the *Millennium Falcon* with his first mate, a Wookiee named Chewbacca.

Doole had no qualms about turning one of his smugglers over to higher authorities if paid the right amount. The right amount came down on one of Solo's spice runs, when Doole provided Imperial tariff ships with Solo's coordinates. The *Falcon* came out of hyperspace, and the law was waiting. Before they could board the *Falcon*, Solo jettisoned the spice. Although he later tried to retrieve it, Solo was unable to regain his cargo—cargo for which Jabba the Hutt had paid in advance. Doole had successfully double-crossed Solo, and had received his money from both the tariff officials and Jabba the Hutt.

Jabba put out word that Solo was to be brought in, little guessing that the Corellian would come to him. The Hutt assigned a new Rodian bounty hunter, Greedo, to bring Solo back, but the smuggler fried the hunter in a Mos Eisley cantina, and was on his way back to his ship when he came upon a humorous sight. Jabba and his men were facing the *Falcon* and ordering Solo to come out.

Solo startled the Hutt, who recovered quickly. The smuggler admitted he had just negotiated a major commission to fly two men and two droids to Alderaan. When he was done, he'd pay Jabba back for the spice lost. Jabba agreed in return for an extra 20 percent on the money owed, but threatened, "If you disappoint me again, I'll put a price on your head so large you won't be able to go near a civilized system for the rest of your short life."

Solo's mission took him farther away from Jabba than he had planned, culminating in his role in helping destroy the first Death Star. On his way back to Tatooine he was attacked and boarded by space pirates. Led by Crimson Jack, the pirates looted Han's ship and left him penniless. Knowing he couldn't pay Jabba back, Han didn't even try to contact the gangster. His path eventually took him back to the Rebellion, where he stayed for several years.

Jabba put out a price on Han's head, but Solo wasn't the only disloyal smuggler to face the Hutt's wrath. Confirming suspicions that Doole was spice skimming, and suspecting Doole's double-cross, Jabba put a contract out on the Rybet. A sadistic bounty hunter made Doole beg for his life, then Skynxnex, Doole's scarecrowlike assistant, killed the hunter.

Doole and those men loyal to him staged a prison revolt. The warden had been one of Jabba's men, but half the guards were still being paid by Doole. With the empire in chaos over the destruction of the first Death Star, Doole's takeover of the Kessel facilities slipped by unnoticed. Jabba let Doole live, deciding that ongoing spice production was better than having to start the mining over again.

Jabba soon had a new pet to take his mind off problematic smugglers or spice slavers. Bidlo Kwerve and Bib Fortuna presented him with a birthday present—a monstrous creature known as a rancor. It came with its own trainer, Malakili, a professional monster handler and beast trainer from the traveling Circus Horrificus.

The rancor was placed in a giant pit below the throne room, with a grating allowing viewers to look down at the beast. A trapdoor was installed, so with a push of a button, Jabba could drop anyone into the pit, for the rancor to devour.

With the demise of Bidlo Kwerve, Bib Fortuna became the new majordomo, and was almost always at Jabba's side, whispering to him through dagger-sharp teeth. Fortuna counseled him on almost every decision, but knew when to back off. And at every opportunity, the Twi'lek made himself both invaluable and worshipful. Jabba knew that even Fortuna schemed against him, but he was the best—and only—majordomo currently in Jabba's employ.

Three years after Solo stiffed him, Jabba received a subspace communication from a space pirate in the Hoth system. Although the pirate only implied he could get Solo, Jabba knew he had more than he was telling. In actuality, Raskar the pirate had already captured the *Millennium Falcon*, Han, Chewbacca, and Luke Skywalker. Displeased with the pirate's coyness, Jabba decided to send Boba Fett, the most dangerous bounty hunter in the galaxy, to get Han.

Fett wasn't immediately successful, and Jabba began to grow impatient. The smuggler had taken a backseat to other priorities. But to have evaded Jabba for three years . . . the Hutt meant to end the matter.

Darth Vader ended it first. He put out a call for bounty hunters to find Solo. Boba Fett responded, as did others who had been or currently were in Jabba's employ. Fett was the victor, tracking the *Falcon* to Bespin's Cloud City and helping Vader set up a devious trap. Solo was frozen in carbonite.

Fett eventually arrived back at the palace, to deliver Jabba's new Han Solo wall sculpture, and to collect his bounty. Arguing that the carbonite piece was art from the hands of Darth Vader himself, Fett was able to talk Jabba into raising Solo's bounty from 100,000 credits to 250,000. Jabba liked the fearless hunter, and kept him steadily employed from that time on.

Almost a year later, the mission to rescue Solo began. The first person to infiltrate Jabba's palace was Lando Calrissian, who took the role of a skiff guard named Tamtel Skreej. Lando sent messages and layouts back to the other members of the team, and sabotaged several droids.

Luke Skywalker sent C-3PO and R2-D2 to Jabba's palace bearing a message. The young man, who claimed to be a Jedi, wanted to bargain with Jabba for the life of Han Solo! Skywalker sought an audience with the Hutt, and left the droids in his employ as a gift. C-3PO became Jabba's new interpreter droid, perched directly to his left on the dais.

Around the same time, Bib Fortuna gave Jabba another gift, a beautiful young Twi'lek dancer named Oola. She refused to dance for Jabba, Fortuna berated her, and the Gamorrean guards beat her. Oola finally did a dance that was graceful and seductive; Jabba pulled her closer as she finished, to give her his special thanks, and she resisted. Tired of this chase, Jabba opened the trap door, and the Twi'lek fell to her death in the rancor pit.

Even as the crowd gathered to watch Oola's death, a laser shot rang out. A smallish bounty hunter came into the throne room, leading Solo's Wookiee copilot in shackles and chains. Jabba agreed to gladly pay a 25,000 credit bounty on Chewbacca, but the bounty hunter, Boushh, balked. He would take no less than 50,000 credits. In a rage, Jabba demanded to know why he should pay the higher amount.

And then he knew. Boushh was holding a thermal detonator, primed and ready. For long moments, Jabba considered his small foe, then began to laugh. "This bounty hunter is my kind of scum," he said. "Fearless and inventive." He offered Boushh 35,000 credits with the proviso that he *really* should settle. The hunter agreed.

Boushh was even more inventive than Jabba had originally thought. For underneath the enclosed helmet and body armor, Boushh was really Princess Leia Organa. Late that evening, Leia crept into the throne room and freed Han Solo from his carbonite crypt. As the lights in the throne room came up, Jabba's bilious laughter filled the air. Leia and Han were trapped.

The next day, despite Jabba's orders that Skywalker be denied entrance, Bib Fortuna led the young man into the chambers. Jabba was angry, yet he knew that the Twi'lek had been pushed by Jedi mind tricks. Jabba himself was aware of, and guarded against, powers of the Force. Although Skywalker appealed to Jabba cleanly and calmly, the Hutt knew he was trying to use Jedi abilities.

"I'm taking Captain Solo and his friends," the youth warned. "You can either profit by this . . . or be destroyed!" Jabba did the predictable thing; he pressed the trapdoor switch, and Luke fell into the rancor pit. A short battle ensued, and Skywalker emerged victorious.

Jabba was *really* enraged, and ordered his guards to fetch Han, Chewbacca and Luke. As Jabba stroked the hair of Solo's woman, now chained to the dais in revealing clothes, he pronounced their sentence. They would be taken out to the Great Pit of Carkoon and fed to the Sarlacc, while Jabba and his courtiers would watch from his luxury sail barge.

As Jabba and his court prepared themselves, Ephant Mon confronted his friend. Jabba refused to listen to his warnings, sure that Ephant was overestimating the Jedi.

In fact, it was Jabba who was underestimating Skywalker. Luke offered Jabba a last chance to free them or die, inspiring a chorus of laughter from almost everyone on the barge. Laughter was replaced by screams and laserblasts as Luke's plan went into effect. In the mêleé Jabba was all but forgotten, but Leia scampered over the top of him, pulling her chain leash tight around his neck.

Unable to pull the chain out from between his fat folds, Jabba choked and died. His body was destroyed a short while later, when the escaping Rebels blew up the sail barge.

Chaos reigned as organizations and crime lords raced to fill the void left by Jabba the Hutt's sudden and unexpected demise. Lady Valarian picked up some of Jabba's business, while a major Hutt clan war ignited throughout the galaxy. Two Hutt leaders, Kumac and Jelasi, emerged with much of the "winnings."

Meanwhile, Jabba's father had long ago been sent to a mudball prison planet known as Kip. Zorba the Hutt was finally released the year after Jabba died, and was stunned to find out his only heir was gone. He made it his mission to retake whatever of Jabba's criminal empire was still left, and to kill Princess Leia. Zorba won Bespin's Cloud City from Lando Calrissian in a sabacc game, and began cooperating with the Imperials.

That collusion eventually got Zorba fed to the Sarlacc on Tatooine—by Trioculus, a pretender to the Imperial throne. But the creature spit him out. Hutts, it seemed, were indigestible because of their tough hides. Zorba is currently at large in the galaxy, but has not been heard from in years. He did put out a bounty on Leia and Solo both. That bounty would haunt them even six years after Jabba's death.

Jabba may be gone, but the slime of the slug has more than gummed up the galaxy for the New Republic leaders. Only the future will tell if Jabba the Hutt's legacy will yet again touch Han Solo's life.

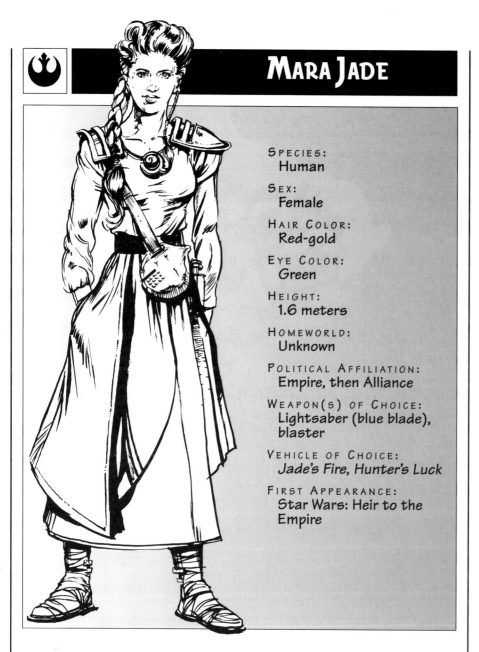

MARA JADE

SPECIES:
Human

SEX:
Female

HAIR COLOR:
Red-gold

EYE COLOR:
Green

HEIGHT:
1.6 meters

HOMEWORLD:
Unknown

POLITICAL AFFILIATION:
Empire, then Alliance

WEAPON(S) OF CHOICE:
Lightsaber (blue blade), blaster

VEHICLE OF CHOICE:
Jade's Fire, Hunter's Luck

FIRST APPEARANCE:
Star Wars: Heir to the Empire

Mara Jade's history is filled with twists and turnabouts, steeped in the battle between the dark side of the Force and the light side.

Nothing is known about her past. It is rumored that Emperor Palpatine took her as a young girl and had her parents killed. He trained Mara as his personal, Force-sensitive assassin, teaching her how to use a lightsaber and how to use rudimentary Force powers. The best of his protectors taught her hand-to-hand combat and marksmanship, and she was trained in spy techniques and political intrigue.

Code-named the "Emperor's Hand," Mara was dispatched to operations that stormtroopers or other troops couldn't handle. She helped expose traitors, eliminated or discredited Palpatine's enemies, and brought down mindless bureaucracies. Most helpful of Mara's Force talents was her ability to hear the Emperor's call from anywhere in the galaxy.

Few in the upper echelons knew that Mara Jade was the Emperor's Hand. Those few who noticed her at all generally thought she was just a beautiful trinket in Palpatine's collection. But even to be seen as the Emperor's consort brought influence, prestige, and respect. The beautiful red-and-golden-haired woman wasn't in love with Palpatine or the Empire, by any means; but she *was* in love with her position and power.

One of Palpatine's more public servants was the Dark Lord of the Sith, Darth Vader. Mara tried to stay out of his way as much as she could, but when Vader lost his son, Luke Skywalker, and captured Han Solo, things began to take a turn for the worse.

Knowing that Luke would eventually return to Tatooine to rescue his friend, Han Solo, Palpatine sent Mara Jade to kill him. Using the name Arica, she auditioned and won a job as a dancer in Jabba the Hutt's palace. While her timing could not have been better, Jade still missed her chance to kill Skywalker when the Hutt took Luke and his friends off to the Great Pit of Carkoon for execution. Mara left Jabba's palace, bitterly tasting defeat and sensing the mind-touch of the Emperor's disappointment. They would discuss the consequences after her next mission, on Svivren.

It was a discussion that was never to occur. Within days, the Emperor was dead, at Darth Vader's hand. The second Death Star was destroyed in orbit above the moon of Endor, and the Empire was in disarray as various warlords wrestled for control. And in the process, the unknown Emperor's Hand lost everything. All Mara Jade had to cling to was the last message the Emperor had sent to her: "You will kill Luke Skywalker."

Mara spent the next four and a half years traveling the galaxy, taking whatever odd jobs she could in order to survive. Without the Emperor around, most of her Force talents disappeared and she wasn't well versed enough to train herself. Over time Mara became Karrinna Janisih, the serving girl in a Phorliss cantina; Marellis, the come-up flector for a Caprioril swoop gang; and Celina Marniss, a hyperdrive mechanic on Tropis-on-Varont.

It was this final job that changed her future.

Two humans landed in the Great Jungle of Varonat, asking to have the hyperdrive fixed on their modified pleasure yacht *Uwana Buyer*. The flashier of the two was Syndic Pandis Hart of the Sif-Uwana Council, while the bulkier "muscle" was Captain Seoul. The two were talked into going on a Morodin safari hunt with associates of the Krish crime lord Gamgalon.

Before they left, Hart verbally sparred with Mara/Celina, and each of them left the conversation knowing the other was not who, or what, they seemed.

"Hart" and "Seoul" were actually top smuggler Talon Karrde and his second in command, Tapper Quelev. They were looking into the profitability of the safaris as a business venture. When they snooped around too much and Tapper got killed, Mara had to rescue Karrde. As they flew off planet, they introduced themselves and Mara asked for a job.

For the next five and a half months, Mara became an indispensable member of Karrde's crew of smugglers and pilots. He didn't ask too many questions about her past—although he wanted to—as he sensed that Mara wore a rock-hard surface on her feelings, designed to keep him and everyone else out. Mara was happy to be useful again, and even enjoyed Karrde's company, but at night, she had nightmares in which Emperor Palpatine came to her again, berating her for her failure.

When Mara and Talon picked up a distress signal from a damaged X-wing, the last person Mara expected to find was Luke Skywalker. Nor did she expect to spare or save his life several times over the coming months, or to have him save *hers*. Mara and Karrde were pulled into the battle against the Imperial forces of Grand Admiral Thrawn and the mad Jedi clone, Joruus C'Baoth. Although she made it brutally clear to everyone she met that she planned to kill Luke Skywalker, Mara gradually became an invaluable resource to the New Republic.

Finally, Mara would face her destiny. During a mission that took them to Wayland to destroy the Emperor's Spaarti cloning cylinders, Luke trained Mara in her slowly returning Force talents. Joruus C'Baoth called both Luke and Mara to him, intending to turn them to the dark side. When it became clear he couldn't turn Luke, he unleashed his own clone of the hero, calling

it Luuke Skywalker. In the battle to follow, Mara killed the Luuke clone, and with help from Luke and Leia Organa Solo, she slew C'Baoth, as well. She had done what the Emperor's compulsion commanded her. She finally felt free.

Back on the New Republic base planet, Coruscant, Luke gave Mara the lightsaber he had lost on Bespin—his father's lightsaber—and urged her to join the New Republic. Although she saw her future with them, she had other duties.

For after the Battle of Bilbringi, Talon Karrde and the smugglers he had gathered

decided to formalize and solidify their support of the New Republic. They formed a guild which, over the following two years, would become the Smugglers' Alliance. Karrde decided to retire, turning the running of his operations completely over to Mara Jade.

When Luke opened a Jedi academy on the moon Yavin Four, Mara visited for a few days. Although she knew Luke had much to teach her, and she considered staying on as a student, she had to run the Smugglers' Alliance, and to help defend a galaxy under attack by Admiral Daala and her fleet.

Following a daring mission with Han Solo and Lando Calrissian, to liberate Kessel's Imperial Correctional Facility, Mara rode in the *Millennium Falcon* as it opposed the Death Star prototype within the black-hole cluster known as the Maw.

After that, a victorious and *very* rich Lando began work on reopening the glitter-stim-spice mines of Kessel. He talked Mara Jade into teaming up with her Smugglers' Alliance to distribute the expensive spice. Lando also had other plans for Mara, but she rejected his romantic overtures. At least at first.

And three years after the defeat of Daala's forces, Mara was contacted on her ship, the *Jade's Fire*, by Leia. Mara was able to help Leia by providing information regarding the original Emperor's plans to wipe out the children of the Jedi.

Mara has proven herself an honest friend and a staunch ally to the New Republic. Luke Skywalker knows that, if she ever comes back and completes her training, Mara Jade may be one of the most formidable Jedi in history.

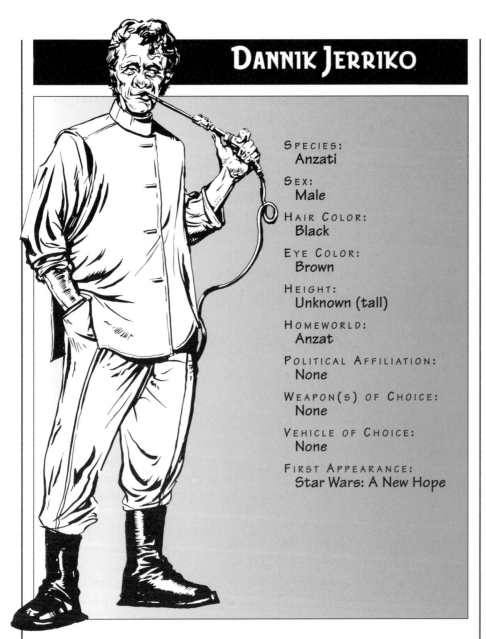

DANNIK JERRIKO

SPECIES:
Anzati

SEX:
Male

HAIR COLOR:
Black

EYE COLOR:
Brown

HEIGHT:
Unknown (tall)

HOMEWORLD:
Anzat

POLITICAL AFFILIATION:
None

WEAPON(S) OF CHOICE:
None

VEHICLE OF CHOICE:
None

FIRST APPEARANCE:
Star Wars: A New Hope

Those who don't sense the menace of Dannik Jerriko before he nears become his prey.

Jerriko is one of the predatorial species known as the Anzati. Tall, gaunt, and largely humanoid in appearance, the Anzati have prehensile proboscises coiled in cheek pockets. When they have captured their prey, Anzat uncoil these proboscises, inserting them in the victim's nostrils and piercing their brains. The Anzati are long-lived; Jerriko himself is 1010 years old.

Unlike the childhood creatures of myth, Jerriko not only drinks the blood of his victims, he eats their Luck, sucking down what he calls the "soup" of their future. Even if they live on—and some do—without Luck, the hapless victims rarely survive long. This is why Jerriko chooses to feed mainly on the Luck of killers and assassins. Who other than their employers would care to miss them?

Jerriko has been a bounty hunter and an assassin for many years, making money doing what most of his hunter race do for free. His work is meticulous, his prices steep. "If you cannot afford to hire me, you do not even know I exist," he has said more than once. Only one employer—his first—complained about the price. The Anzat drank his soup, and the man died. No one ever complained again.

Jerriko has worked for Jabba the Hutt, consuming the failed assassins the slug didn't feed to his rancor. Between assignments, the Anzat returned to Tatooine and its Mos Eisley spaceport, drawn by the incredible mixture of Luck centered in the killers and Rebels. Here would be good eating. Here would be a gourmet feast.

It was while in the Mos Eisley cantina that the Anzat smelled a soup so intoxicating that he was taken aback. When two drunks tried to start a fight with a young farm boy, an older man stepped in, igniting his lightsaber.

The Anzat had not seen a man like this for a hundred years. Here was a Jedi, his aura bright with Luck. And yet, Jerriko knew that this was a Master, knew that he shielded himself from Anzati probing, knew that the soup of this old man would be denied him. The young boy—his student?—would bear some watching, though.

Calmly smoking his pipe, Jerriko watched the Jedi and Jedi-to-be join a tall Wookiee and a Corellian. Then, the scent erupted. The soup of the Corellian was thick and hot and sweeter than any the Anzat had tasted in far too long.

Jerriko watched Han Solo leave, knowing that Jabba the Hutt wanted this man more than any other, and that he had a huge bounty out for him. The crime lord didn't care whether the Corellian was alive or dead. So Jerriko planned to track Solo down for Jabba, but before he delivered him, he would feast on Solo's soup. Unfortunately, Solo escaped the planet.

Angry that he had missed the opportunity, the Anzat put a plan into motion. If he could infiltrate Jabba's palace, perhaps he would be there when Solo was eventually brought in. Dannik Jerriko waited, a nightmare hiding in the darkness.

TENEL KA

SPECIES:
Dathomirian

SEX:
Female

HAIR COLOR:
Rusty brown

EYE COLOR:
Gray

HEIGHT:
Unknown

HOMEWORLD:
Dathomir

POLITICAL AFFILIATION:
Alliance

WEAPON(S) OF CHOICE:
None

VEHICLE OF CHOICE:
None

FIRST APPEARANCE:
Star Wars: Young Jedi Knights #1—Heirs to the Force

Tenel Ka is the young heir of Prince Isolder of Hapes and Teneniel Djo, a Dathomirian witch. Raised a privileged child, Tenel Ka has always longed to make her own way in the universe. Her mother taught her the ways of the Dathomirian witches and allowed her to dress in a warrior woman's scarlet-and-green reptile-skin tunic. Grandma Ta'a Chume didn't approve of her princess granddaughter running about wild, but Tenel Ka has never sought her approval.

Strong in the Force, Tenel Ka chose to train at Luke Skywalker's Jedi academy on Yavin Four. Even so, she used the Force only when it was needed. Muscular and athletic, she preferred the exercises of the body to those of the mind. Though impatient, hard driven, and humorless, she soon made friends with Jacen and Jaina Solo and Lowbacca, the young Wookiee, none of whom knew she was a princess.

Exploring the Massassi jungles of Yavin Four, the quartet found a crashed TIE fighter, apparently incapacitated since the first Battle of Yavin, long before they were born. Jaina began repairing the ship, adding a hyperdrive module to it with her friends' help.

Unfortunately, the TIE pilot, Qoril, was still alive and hiding in the jungles. He managed to capture Jacen and Jaina, but Tenel Ka and Lowbacca both escaped, running headlong into the jungle.

On her way back to the academy to get help, Tenel Ka rescued Em Teedee, Lowie's translator droid. The droid guided her back to the temple just in time for her to show Han Solo and Chewbacca how to save Jacen and Jaina. The children were safe, but before they could stop the TIE fighter, it jumped into hyperspace.

Weeks later, Tenel began to have nightmares about the evil Dalthomirian witches the Nightsisters. Then Lando Calrissian called with dire news: Jacen, Jaina, and Lowie had been kidnapped by Imperial forces.

Luke and Tenel Ka's quest to find the missing young Jedi led them to Borgo Prime, and from there to Dathomir, where the disguised duo offered themselves as candidates for the new generation of Nightsisters. They discovered that the stolen youths were students in the Shadow Academy, a dark Force school run by Nightsister Tamith Kai.

Accepted into the school after demonstrating that they understood the dark side of the Force, they departed for the academy on the *Shadow Chaser*, a fast, quantum-armored ship. Luke tricked the pilot and forced her into an escape pod. The ship proceeded on autopilot.

When Luke and Tenel Ka arrived to rescue the students, they met up with them in the loading bays—the trio was already making their own escape attempt! The four young Jedi and their Master returned to Yavin Four aboard the *Shadow Chaser*.

The return of the Nightsisters at the Shadow Academy worries Luke Skywalker and young Tenel Ka. The Force is with her, but the blood of Dathomir runs in her veins. Could this mean that Tenel Ka could be turned to the dark side?

KABE

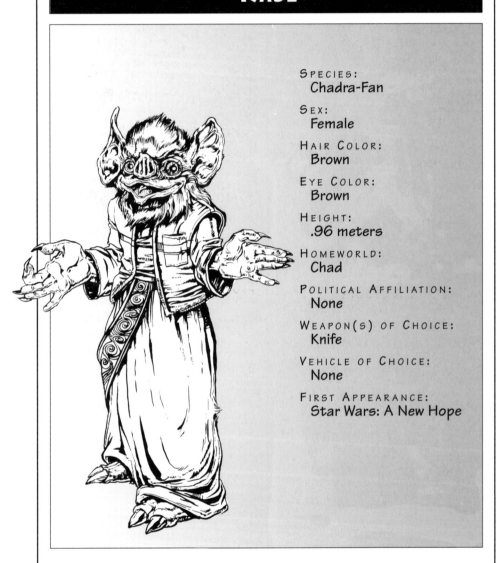

SPECIES:
Chadra-Fan

SEX:
Female

HAIR COLOR:
Brown

EYE COLOR:
Brown

HEIGHT:
.96 meters

HOMEWORLD:
Chad

POLITICAL AFFILIATION:
None

WEAPON(S) OF CHOICE:
Knife

VEHICLE OF CHOICE:
None

FIRST APPEARANCE:
Star Wars: A New Hope

Tatooine could be an unfriendly place, especially for an unlikely pair of aliens. Nevertheless, Kabe and Muftak took care of each other on the streets and in the alleys of Mos Eisley.

Kabe is a young Chadra-Fan, one of the survivors of the quakes that decimated the primitive Chadrian civilization. Taken by slavers to Tatooine, the infant Kabe was left behind when the slave ship's departure had to be rushed. She knows little of her species's heritage, although she does have the Chadra-Fan's instinctive drive to pursue pleasure, the desire to tinker, and the need to avoid solitude.

Due to her small size, keen senses, and quick reflexes, Kabe became a talented thief. To her, thievery and cons were a game, not a crime, yet her skills provided her a reasonable livelihood. Like all Chadra-Fans, Kabe has the extra senses of infrared vision and chemoreceptive smell, both of which came in handy for a thief.

Kabe's favorite scam was dressing up as a Jawa and charging Mos Eisley newcomers "service taxes" for the local—

nonexistent—merchant's guild. This did not sit well with the real Jawas, and the short desert scavengers accosted Kabe many times.

The street-smart Kabe was caught in her thievery often enough that she would have been a blot on the Tatooine ground if not for her giant, fierce-looking, white-furred friend, Muftak.

Born on Tatooine, Muftak knows nothing about his cultural background. He is a Talz, a member of a giant race from Alzoc III. His people were subjugated by the Empire and cut off from the galaxy. Only a handful of Talz exist away from their home planet, and no one knows quite what they are. Because of their great strength, large size, and sharply taloned hands, few but the brave even dare talk to a Talz.

Muftak grew up with no parental figures, living on the streets of Mos Eisley. By watching—with his four eyes—and listening, Muftak learned more about the comings and goings of the spaceport than anyone, with the possible exceptions of bandleader Figrin D'an and the "Long Snoot" spy, Garindan.

Muftak took in the young Kabe and sheltered her for five years in a section of abandoned tunnels beneath Docking Bay 83. The tall, furry creature was very protective of the small Chadra-Fan. Their relationship is platonic, and yet their love for each other is undeniable. Since the Chadra-Fan has an

MUFTAK

SPECIES:
Talz

SEX:
Male

HAIR COLOR:
White and gray

EYE COLOR:
Black

HEIGHT:
2.1 meters

HOMEWORLD:
Tatooine and Alzoc III

POLITICAL AFFILIATION:
None

WEAPON(S) OF CHOICE:
Knife/Beat-up blaster

VEHICLE OF CHOICE:
None

FIRST APPEARANCE:
Star Wars: A New Hope

instinctual need for companionship, Kabe has always been happiest when with her big, furry friend.

With no real goals or responsibilities, Muftak survived on the credits Kabe stole, and the money he made giving out information. Both Kabe and Muftak spent a lot of time in Chalmun the Wookiee's cantina, where Muftak engaged the Ithorian, Momaw Nadon, in semi-intellectual discussions, and Kabe practiced her credit-lifting skills. Kabe couldn't drink much, given that even a small snifter of juri juice would make her pass out.

As Muftak carried the drunken Kabe back to their home one night, he decided to help her on what she considered her most dangerous mission: to rob Jabba the Hutt's Mos Eisley town house! Kabe had found a secret entrance, and the booty from the house could keep them both set for life. So when Kabe sobered up later in the evening, they put their plan into motion.

Once they gained access to the town house through an old vent in the roof, Kabe's acute sense of hearing helped them escape tripping myriad traps and alarms.

Later, as they prepared to leave, Kabe and Muftak stumbled upon the torture chamber, where a Rebel, Barid Mesoriaam, was shackled. He offered the two 30,000 credits if they would deliver a datadot to a Mon Calamari who would be visiting Mos Eisley in a few days. Appealing to them *not* to turn the dot over to the Imperial prefect, he reminded them that the Empire had no place for nonhumans.

During the duo's escape from Jabba's town house, a confrontation with two Gamorrean guards led to a firefight with a dozen others, headed by Bib Fortuna. Kabe found a small exit, but Muftak, knowing he couldn't fit, let his friend escape alone. When she realized Muftak meant to sacrifice himself, the Chadra-Fan returned to the smoky mêleé, and both were able to escape, albeit with little of their stolen loot.

Politically apathetic before, Muftak and Kabe now found themselves involved with the Rebellion—if they wanted to keep their credits and their lives. They met the Mon Calamarian, giving him the datadot. In return, they got 15,000 credits and two stolen travel vouchers signed by Grand Moff Tarkin himself.

The odd couple left Tatooine for the first time, heading toward the Talz home planet of Alzoc III, then onto Chad, striking out in search of their destinies.

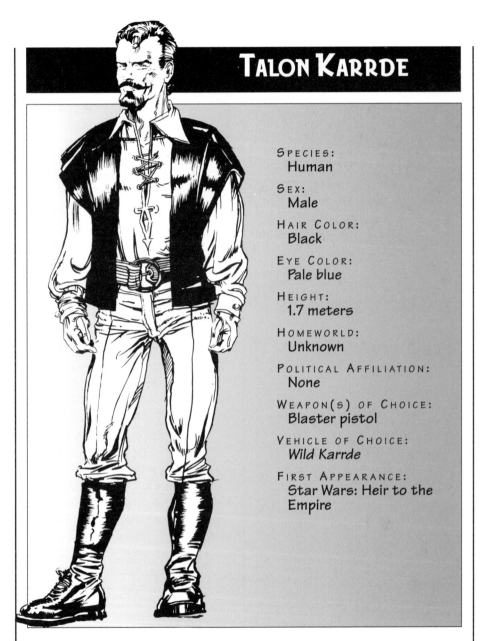

TALON KARRDE

SPECIES:
Human

SEX:
Male

HAIR COLOR:
Black

EYE COLOR:
Pale blue

HEIGHT:
1.7 meters

HOMEWORLD:
Unknown

POLITICAL AFFILIATION:
None

WEAPON(S) OF CHOICE:
Blaster pistol

VEHICLE OF CHOICE:
Wild Karrde

FIRST APPEARANCE:
Star Wars: Heir to the Empire

Mercenaries aren't always known for their honesty, but there are exceptions. Talon Karrde is one of them.

From his original home base on the planet Myrkr, Talon was one of the top operators in the shady fringe of the galaxy—a smuggler *par excellence*, able to get anything in or out of systems without Imperial or Corporate Sector Authority enforcement officials on his trail. Also an information broker, Karrde was considered very honest in his dealings, although his demeanor could be coldly calculating and mercenary.

Two lines Karrde would not cross—or allow his associates to cross—are slave running and kidnapping.

Fortyish and slender, with dark hair and piercing eyes, Karrde wears a roguish mustache, goatee, and flowing cloak. His sense of humor is legendary, as is his preference for picking code names with punnish twists to them. Even his ships have punned names: his attack ships are the *Wild Karrde*, the *Etherway*, and *Starry Ice*, and his space yacht is the *Uwana Buyer*.

Karrde is based on the planet Myrkr,

close to the Borderland Regions. Spread out in the forests, the base contains ten landing pads, a main house, personal and short-term barracks, and four storage sheds. His main crew of smugglers and assistants lives with him.

Aves coordinates Karrde's operatives and offers advice. Chin, a middle-aged Myrkr native, handles and trains Karrde's pet vornskrs, Sturm and Drang. Chin also harvests the mysterious Force dampeners known as ysalamiri. Dankin, Fynn Torve, and Wadewarn are three of Karrde's best freighter pilots. Ghent is a barely-above-teens slicer with tremendous knowledge of computers, droids, and access codes.

For many years, Karrde's most trusted ally was his lieutenant, a human named Tapper Quelev. Karrde had rescued Tapper and some of his smuggling band after the Battle of Endor. The two groups merged, Tapper's men supplementing Karrde's much larger operations. He was with Karrde for four more years until he was killed by the Krish in a mission to infiltrate the Morodin hunting safari on Tropis-on-Varont.

Luckily for Karrde, that was the same mission on which he met a rather bewitching young woman. Although he first met her as a hyperdrive mechanic named Celina Marniss, the redhead was actually named Mara Jade. She helped Karrde escape from the Krish and soon became his loyal sidekick. She was a perfect combination of competence and looks—exactly what Karrde wanted.

As the galaxy restructured itself, Karrde tried to remain neutral in the wars between the Empire and the New Republic. Whoever offered the most credits would win Karrde's job. Meanwhile, he had a greater shot at the smuggling trade, and absorbed much of the late Jabba the Hutt's empire into his own. He didn't crow about his standing in the smuggling community; as flashy as he was to look at, Karrde preferred to keep his business low-ley and unobtrusive.

When Grand Admiral Thrawn contacted Karrde to provide him with the Force-dampening ysalamiri, Karrde was more than happy to comply. On his way to deliver the creatures to Thrawn, he found Luke Skywalker in a damaged X-wing, floating in space. Knowing that Thrawn had a 30,000 credit bounty out for Skywalker, Karrde agreed to take Luke to Myrkr. The young Jedi's Force powers were useless while near the ysalamiri, and the smugglers locked him in a storage shed. Perhaps the New Republic would pay a higher bounty for Skywalker.

Coincidentally, an old buddy of Karrde's, Lando Calrissian, showed up with the Corellian smuggler Han Solo. They were looking for a slicer to help aid the Alliance in cracking diplomatic codes. While they were being led around Karrde's operation center, Luke escaped from the storage shed. Mara Jade quickly went to retrieve him.

Han and Lando soon found evidence that Luke had been a captive of Karrde's, and the smuggler boss explained that he had only kept Luke for the bounty. Promising to get Luke back, he contacted Mara Jade, who was taking Luke toward Hyllyard City, where a garrison of Imperial troops was stationed. A set of complications ensued, during which Luke, Lando, and Han were reunited and escaped on the *Millennium Falcon*. Mara and Karrde had bigger concerns.

Thrawn was coming to Myrkr to retrieve Skywalker, and Karrde didn't have him anymore. The smuggler chief and his crews packed up their base as quickly as they could and fled into space. None of them wanted to face a severely disappointed Imperial Grand Admiral. But Karrde had grown to love the planet, and vowed to one day return.

Karrde knew the location of the lost *Katana* fleet of Dreadnaught ships, and planned to auction that information as his next business venture. But on the planet of Rishi, Mara found out that there was a 20,000 credit bounty on Karrde's head, compliments of Thrawn. Unfortunately for Mara, she was captured by Thrawn, and her

past as the "Emperor's Hand" did little to help her situation. After she offered Thrawn her aid in locating the *Katana* fleet, Mara was allowed to leave to meet Karrde. But the Imperials had planted a homing beacon on her ship and she led them right to her boss. The Imperials captured Karrde, and told Mara where to find—and kill—Luke Skywalker. Instead, Mara teamed up with Luke to rescue Karrde from the Star Destroyer *Chimaera*.

Karrde and Mara felt they owed Luke and the New Republic for saving them, and so they helped support the Rebel fleet in the battle for the Sluis Van shipyards. Mara was hurt in the mission and was shuttled off to Coruscant to recover. And a month later, hiding out on Calius with his crew, Karrde ran into Luke, who was searching for the empire's Spaarti cloning cylinders.

The smuggler boss helped track the trail to Chazwa, where the clone cylinders had been transported long ago before being moved to another planet. Thrawn's *Lancer* frigate found and attacked the *Wild Karrde*—and smuggler Samuel Tomas Gillespee's ship, *Kern's Pride*—but the battle was short. Karrde and Gillespee escaped to

Trogan, where they hoped to find information about cloning at that planet's infamous cantina, the *Whistler's Whirlpool*. Unknown to the group of high-profile smugglers who were meeting with Karrde, one of their group, Niles Ferrier, was Thrawn's spy.

Despite harassment from Imperials and Ferrier's attempt to discredit Karrde, the smugglers all eventually reconvened at Hijarna. They agreed with Karrde that the smugglers would do better throwing their lot—and their firepower—in with the New Republic. After aiding Princess Leia Organa Solo in getting to Wayland and helping to destroy Mount Tantiss and the Spaarti cloning cylinders, Karrde flew to Bilbringi. There, in a heated space battle, he was joined by the other smugglers. The cluster of new spaceships helped him turn the tide for the New Republic, and the Imperials fled, defeated.

Following the Battle of Bilbringi, the smugglers decided to formalize and solidify their support of the New Republic. They formed a smugglers' guild, which, over the next two years, would become the Smugglers' Alliance. Karrde decided to retire, turning his operations over completely to Mara Jade.

While Jake and the Smugglers' Alliance aided the New Republic when they could, Karrde basically disappeared. He called Mara at prearranged times to talk to her, but his home base was mobile. Karrde said it was because he feared a bounty on his head. Mara knew better. She knew that Talon Karrde, the most dashing smuggler baron in the galaxy, just wanted to escape from the bother and fuss of his old life. He would live as a private citizen for a time, but Mara knew that one day, Talon Karrde would be back in business.

KEN

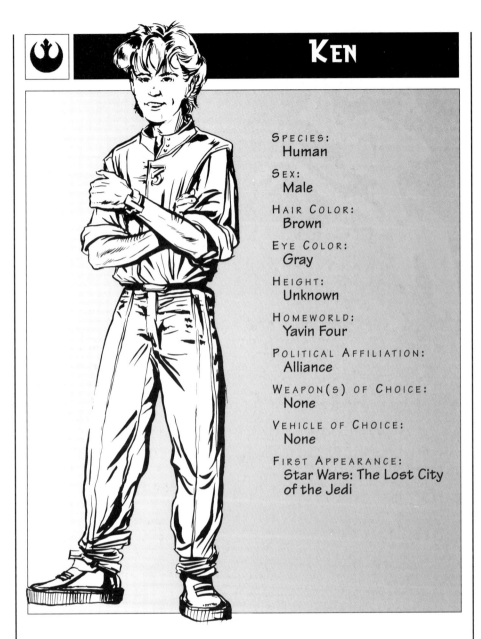

SPECIES:
Human

SEX:
Male

HAIR COLOR:
Brown

EYE COLOR:
Gray

HEIGHT:
Unknown

HOMEWORLD:
Yavin Four

POLITICAL AFFILIATION:
Alliance

WEAPON(S) OF CHOICE:
None

VEHICLE OF CHOICE:
None

FIRST APPEARANCE:
Star Wars: The Lost City of the Jedi

The grandson of Emperor Palpatine, the young Jedi named Ken lived sheltered deep in the bowels of the Lost City of the Jedi, until a brush with the Alliance unraveled his past *and* his future.

Ken was the son of Palpatine's three-eyed mutant offspring, Triclops, and a Jedi Princess, Kendalina. Triclops had been imprisoned in the Imperial asylum of Kessel, where Kendalina had been forced into servitude. The two fell in love, and conceived a child.

Sometime after Ken's birth, Kendalina was killed. A brown-robed Jedi Master took the child to the Lost City deep underground on Yavin Four. There, he was to be trained to reject his heritage, and to embrace the light side of the Force. The only reminder Ken had of his father was half of a silver birth crystal he wore about his neck. The other half was on a silver chain around Triclops's neck.

The droid DJ-88 was the caretaker of the Jedi Library and Ken's teacher, while HC-100 was in charge of Ken's homework. A small droid named Microchip—nicknamed "Chip"—was created to be Ken's friend, and a small feathered Mooka named Zeebo was his pet. The more Ken heard about the war against the Empire, the more he wanted to meet the Alliance heroes, especially Luke Skywalker. Ken learned to use some of his Force talents, including the abilities to cloud minds and to levitate small objects.

A year following the Battle of Endor, when Ken was twelve, he made his way "top-world," to the planet's surface. Taking Chip with him, Ken set out into the forests of the Yavin moon, and was quickly discovered by Luke Skywalker and a Ho'Din healer named Baji. Before he could reveal the location of the Lost City, Ken was taken away by DJ-88, who had followed his errant student.

Meanwhile Kadann, the Supreme Prophet of the Dark Side, had predicted that a young Jedi Prince would destroy prospective emperor Trioculus, so the ruthless Imperial leader came to Yavin Four, intent on killing Ken. With the help of Skywalker, Han Solo, and Chewbacca, Ken and the droids foiled Trioculus's plans. Ken left the Lost City to join the Alliance and train with Skywalker.

Ken had several adventures alongside the heroes of the Alliance, but was destined to collide with his unknown past. On the planet Duro, near the Valley of Royalty, the Imperials kept Triclops in the Imperial Reprogramming Institute. The son of Palpatine rewired an assassin droid, and escaped his confinement. In the mazelike walls of the Valley of Royalty, Triclops met the Alliance leaders and recognized the pendant around Ken's neck.

Later, when Kadann fed Ken a truth serum, Ken betrayed the location of the Lost City. When the two reached the city, Kadann told Ken about his father, Triclops, his mother, Kendalina, and his grandfather, Palpatine.

Luke Skywalker, also a prisoner, escaped and rescued Ken, trapping the prophet and his troopers in the shut-down city.

Ken planned to confront his father, but Triclops had escaped into the jungles of Yavin Four. Nothing is known of the whereabouts of Ken *or* his father. It is unlikely, however, that the son and grandson of the evil Emperor have disappeared for all time.

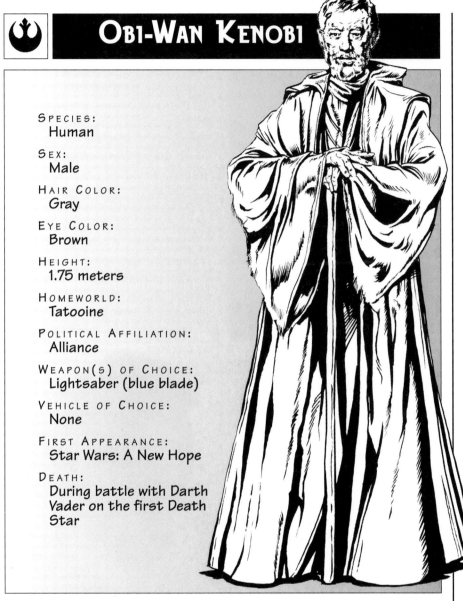

OBI-WAN KENOBI

SPECIES:
Human

SEX:
Male

HAIR COLOR:
Gray

EYE COLOR:
Brown

HEIGHT:
1.75 meters

HOMEWORLD:
Tatooine

POLITICAL AFFILIATION:
Alliance

WEAPON(S) OF CHOICE:
Lightsaber (blue blade)

VEHICLE OF CHOICE:
None

FIRST APPEARANCE:
Star Wars: A New Hope

DEATH:
During battle with Darth Vader on the first Death Star

One of the most prominent Jedi Knights of the Old Republic was also one of the last survivors of the Clone Wars. And in his old age, Obi-Wan "Ben" Kenobi sacrificed his life for the future of the Alliance and the hope of a new league of Jedi Knights.

Records of Kenobi's youth are spotty. It is not known where he grew up, but he does have at least one brother, Owen Lars, who died on Tatooine. It is not known when or at what age Obi-Wan became a trainee in the use of the Force; he eventually wound up under the tutelage of the centuries-old Jedi Master named Yoda, who taught him the ways of the Force, the energy field that surrounds the galaxy and binds every living thing together. Yoda was on constant guard with Obi-Wan, warning him of the dangers of the dark side of the Force.

Obi-Wan learned many of the Jedi Force skills, including control over mind and body, extra senses, and the power to alter the Force lines in nature and life. He also became adept at using the lightsaber, the elegant weapon of the Jedi Knights.

The Jedi Knights served as the protectors of the universe, and of the Old Republic, for nearly a thousand generations. It was during the Clone Wars—approximately thirty-five years before the Battle of Yavin—that Obi-Wan Kenobi became a general of the Republic as well. In the Clone Wars, he served under Prince Bail Organa of Alderaan, and the two became lifelong friends. Organa later became the Viceroy and First Chairman of the Alderaan system.

During the wars, Kenobi met a hotshot young star pilot named Anakin Skywalker. Obi-Wan saw in him great potential toward the Force, so he made Anakin his first Jedi pupil.

Unfortunately, in his zeal to train Anakin, Obi-Wan failed to notice that his pupil was exploring the dark side of the Force. By the time Kenobi clearly understood how deeply Anakin had fallen into sync with the dark side, it was too late. He tried to bring his friend and pupil back from the brink, but Skywalker refused, and he and Obi-Wan engaged in a vicious lightsaber battle that ended when Anakin fell into a molten pit. What emerged from the fiery pool was a burnt husk of a man carrying in him hatred for Kenobi, and the power of the dark side. In that black moment, Anakin Skywalker became Darth Vader.

As Darth Vader aligned himself with the self-proclaimed Emperor Palpatine and his New Order, Obi-Wan feared for the future of the Republic. He changed his name to Ben Kenobi, and moved from the forefront of the Jedi into hidden retirement. He kept in contact with Anakin's estranged wife, who, unbeknownst to Vader, was pregnant with twins. Obi-Wan knew the children had tremendous potential as future Jedi.

On the day the twins, Luke and Leia, were born, Kenobi and the Skywalker mother separated them. Leia lived on Alderaan, where she was adopted by Bail Organa. Obi-Wan took the infant Luke Skywalker to his brother's home on Tatooine, where Owen and Beru Lars promised to raise the child as if they were his aunt and uncle. Though the Larses raised Luke well, they lied to Luke about his father, telling him only that his father had been a great pilot, and later, a navigator on a spice freighter.

Ben stayed on Tatooine and watched over Anakin's son. He made a home for himself in the barren and treacherous Jundland Wastes, at the southwestern edge of the First Quadrant, near the Western Dune Sea. He became known as a crazy wizard and a hermit, appearing infrequently in nearby towns, and disappearing almost as quickly as he had come. Ben knew of the swift destruction of the Jedi Knights at the hands of Vader and Palpatine's Imperial soldiers. He brooded on his great failure with Vader and the havoc the fallen Jedi now wreaked within the Republic, and upon the threads of the Force. And yet Ben stayed in hiding, knowing of Luke's great capacity for the Force, and fearing that somehow Vader would find the children. He envisioned Luke as the new hope for the Alliance.

Once, when Luke was a teenager, Kenobi saved the youngster and his friend, Windy, when Luke crashed his T-16 sky-hopper in Beggar's Canyon. Ben then tried to give Luke his father's lightsaber, but Owen ran Kenobi off the property, telling him never to return.

When Princess Leia Organa was captured by Darth Vader's troops, she programmed a message—and the stolen plans for the Death Star—into R2-D2's memory banks. Artoo was to find Obi-Wan Kenobi on Tatooine, and deliver the message. Before Artoo could find the Jedi, the little astrodroid was captured by Jawas and sold to Owen Lars along with the protocol droid C-3PO. When Luke found the recording from Leia, he mentioned the name "Obi-Wan Kenobi" to Owen, opining that it could be Ben Kenobi. Owen warned Luke never to go near the "crazy old hermit," and told him to flush Artoo's memory.

Luke was too late, though, as R2-D2 had already set off on a quest to find

Kenobi. The next morning, when Luke and C-3PO caught up to Artoo, they were attacked by Tusken Raiders, but the desert nomads were scared off by the hunting cry of a krayt dragon, a large and fearsome beast that roamed the Jundland Wastes.

It was no dragon however, for Ben Kenobi had used his powers to mimic the call. Kenobi took Luke and the droids back to his home, where he viewed the message. Leia implored him to take R2-D2 to Alderaan and to aid the Alliance and her father in reestablishing the Republic.

Presenting Luke with his father's lightsaber, Kenobi asked him to come along, and to learn the ways of the Force. Initially, the young man refused, but upon returning to the Lars homestead, he discovered it had been destroyed and his "aunt" and "uncle" were dead. With no reason to stay on Tatooine, Luke decided to accompany Ben.

Luke and Ben took the droids to Mos Eisley space-port, where they hoped to hook up with a freighter pilot. In a cantina, Ben began nego-

tiating with the Wookiee copilot, Chewbacca, when Luke got into a bar fight and Ben had to step in, lightsaber flashing, to save the young man once again.

Shortly thereafter, Ben made a deal with Han Solo to provide passage on the *Millennium Falcon*. En route to Alderaan, Ben explained aspects of the Force to the novice Luke and the disbelieving Han, and he had Luke practice with a lightsaber against a remote "seeker" target.

By the time the *Falcon* reached the Alderaan system, the Death Star satellite had already destroyed the planet. Ben felt the psychic pain from the destruction, noting that it was "as if millions of voices suddenly cried out in terror and were suddenly silenced." Pursuing a TIE fighter, the *Falcon* was trapped in a tractor beam from the orbiting Death Star, and pulled inside.

Han hid the crew in smuggling compartments on the *Falcon*, enabling them to escape into the space station. While Ben went to disable the tractor beam, Luke and Han engaged in their reckless rescue of Princess Leia. On his way back to the *Falcon* to join the rest, Kenobi was not surprised when Darth Vader emerged from the shadows.

Teacher and pupil engaged in a savage but evenly matched lightsaber battle. As Vader taunted him for being weak, Kenobi warned him, "If you strike me down, I shall become more powerful than you can possibly imagine." Suddenly, Ben glimpsed Luke and Leia making their escape; he had to distract Vader and the Imperial troops, to ensure the future of the Jedi.

Ben deactivated his lightsaber, and stood, waiting. Vader swung his own weapon, cleaving through Kenobi's robes, but the noble Jedi Master himself disappeared, becoming one with the Force.

Moments after Ben's sacrifice, Luke heard Ben's voice in his mind, warning him to escape quickly. Later he heard his teacher again, when the Alliance attacked the Death Star near Yavin Four. As

Skywalker's fighter neared the target that would destroy the battle station, Luke heard Ben's voice calmly telling him to "use the Force." Closing his eyes and feeling the pull of the Force, Luke let the missiles fly. The Death Star exploded into billions of tiny fragments.

Obi-Wan's life force appeared several times over the next four years, first on Hoth, as Luke crawled away from an attack by the wampa. Ben told him to go to the Dagobah system to learn from Yoda, "the Jedi Master who instructed me." Later, on Dagobah, a frustrated Yoda complained that Luke was unteachable and full of anger and recklessness. "Was I any different when you taught me?" the ghostly Ben asked.

When Luke sensed that his friends were in danger on Bespin, he packed to leave Dagobah, despite pleas by Yoda and Ben to stay and complete his training. "If you choose to face Vader, you will do it alone," Ben told him. "I cannot interfere." As Luke left, Ben cautioned, "Don't give in to hate. That leads to the dark side." After Luke left, Yoda and Ben discussed the hope of the Jedi, with Yoda cryptically reminding Ben that there was one "other."

Shortly after the siege on Tatooine, Luke returned to Dagobah to complete his training, only to find that Yoda was dying. After Yoda passed away, the spirit of Ben appeared to Luke. The young Jedi confronted his teacher about his true parentage, so Kenobi told him a little of the tale of Anakin Skywalker, and informed him about his twin sister, Leia Organa. Ben added that Luke must face Vader, or the cause of the Rebellion would be lost.

When Luke and the Alliance were victorious in the Battle of Endor, a celebration was

held. There, for a few moments, he saw Obi-Wan Kenobi, Yoda, and Anakin Skywalker, all smiling to him.

Shortly thereafter, Kenobi appeared to Luke on Endor to warn him of the impending invasion of the Ssi-ruuk, and to tell him of the importance of the battle for Bakura. The final time Luke saw his mentor was in the Imperial Palace on Coruscant—once the throne of the Empire. Ben appeared to him as he slept, though Kenobi assured Luke he was not a dream. "The distances separating us have become too great for me to appear to you in any other way. Now, even that path is closed to me," he added. Obi-Wan bid the young Jedi good-bye, adding, "I loved you as a son, and as a student, and as a friend. Until we meet again, may the Force be with you."

And then, as he disappeared forever, he told Luke to think of himself not as the last of the Jedi, but "the first of the new."

KHABARAKH

SPECIES:
Noghri

SEX:
Male

HAIR COLOR:
None

EYE COLOR:
Black

HEIGHT:
1.3 meters

HOMEWORLD:
Honoghr

POLITICAL AFFILIATION:
Empire

WEAPON(S) OF CHOICE:
Blaster, claws, teeth

VEHICLE OF CHOICE:
Fast-attack patrol ship

FIRST APPEARANCE:
Star Wars: Heir to the Empire

Khabarakh is one of the Noghri, a species of compact, deadly, killing machines. He is of the clan Kihm'bar. Like others of his predatorial people, he has gray skin, large eyes, and a mouthful of piranhalike teeth.

The Noghri had been indebted to Darth Vader since the Clone Wars. Vader had come to them after a massive starship battle above their planet had left their world devastated. One ship had even crashed onto the world, setting off cataclysmic groundquakes and releasing toxic chemicals into the air.

The Dark Lord had explained that the destruction had been caused by the Rebellion, and that if the Noghri swore loyalty to the Empire, he would help them rebuild. They agreed, and the Dark Lord was somewhat true to his word. The Emperor and Vader dispatched medical supplies, droids, and cleanup crews to Honoghr, and used them to make certain the Noghri came to depend on Imperial aid.

The Noghri had been indebted to Darth Vader for many, many years. They became a space-faring race of assassins—Death Squad Commandos for Vader, and later for Grand Admiral Thrawn.

On a mission to capture Leia Organa on the Wookiee world Kashyyyk, a group of Noghri died, except for one. Khabarakh survived and used his uncanny sense of smell to identify Leia as the Mal'ary'ush, the daughter of Vader. He knew she was to be revered, not hunted.

Leia promised the young commando that she would accompany him back to his people, to present to them the cause of the Alliance. Khabarakh agreed to rendezvous with her over the planet of Endor, the site where Vader had been killed.

Leia eventually traveled to Honoghr with Khabarakh, and did her best to convince the Noghri that Vader had deceived them. Khabarakh was chastised by Grand Admiral Thrawn, who called him a traitor to his people. The young commando was punished and imprisoned.

But the other Noghri soon came to realize the truth of "Lady Vader's" words, and rose up against the Imperials. Khabarakh was freed, and became part of Leia's ten-person Noghri honor guard. The guard's commander was Cakhmaim, of the clan Eikh'mir; his lieutenant, Mobvekhar, of the clan Hakh'khar, protected Leia, her assistant Winter, and her twins, Jacen and Jaina. The Noghri aided the Alliance in their attack on Mount Tantiss, where one Noghri, Rukh, slew Thrawn.

With the true help of the New Republic, the Noghri now concentrate on rebuilding their ravaged planet. It will be a long time before the clans can live in any areas besides a few uncontaminated valleys, but they are patient. Khabarakh now serves as the caretaker of the lush hidden valley known as the Future of the Noghri. He knows that it will probably not be in his future that Honoghr is healed, but that he will have contributed to that healing perhaps more than any other Noghri.

PRINCESS KNEESAA

SPECIES:
Ewok

SEX:
Female

HAIR COLOR:
Gray

EYE COLOR:
Black

HEIGHT:
.75 meters

HOMEWORLD:
Endor

POLITICAL
AFFILIATION:
Unknown

WEAPON(S)
OF CHOICE:
Bow and arrowl

VEHICLE OF CHOICE:
Glider

FIRST APPEARANCE:
The Ewoks and
Star Wars Droids
Adventure Hour

Life on the uncivilized forest moon of Endor can be an adventure. For the young Ewok, Princess Kneesaa, adventures are a welcome part of her life . . . as long as they are shared with her best friend, Wicket W. Warrick.

Kneesaa is the daughter of Chief Chirpa, the Ewok leader of Bright Tree Village built fifty meters off the ground among the boughs of the three-hundred-meter trees that forest the moon. Her mother was the late Ra-Lee, while her long-lost older sister was Asha. Later in life, her father remarried, and Kneesaa's new stepmother bore two new woklings, Nippet and Wiley. Kneesaa was often asked to babysit the woklings.

Kneesaa was always more trusting than many of the Ewoks, though she was still cautious of the many dangers lurking in the forests. And she encountered many of those dangers, from skirmishing with the warlike Duloks, to fighting the evil Morag, the Tulgah witch, and her giant pterodactyl-like mantigrue. Standing beside her for most of these conflicts were Wicket, Kneesaa's male friends Teebo and Paploo, and her female friends Latara and Malani.

Kneesaa and Wicket became the heroes of the village while in their youth, when they helped save the ancient trees of the forest from the giant green Phlogs that had come from a land called Simoom. The Phlogs planned to chop down the ancient trees to build their ruler a new castle. With help, Kneesaa and Wicket drove them away. As a reward for their actions, the village Council of Elders made Wicket and Kneesaa honorary council members. Although this title held no privileges, the young Ewoks were nevertheless happy.

One winter, Wicket came in contact with a savage female Ewok called the Red Ghost. He described the crimson-furred female to Kneesaa, and she felt sure it was her long-lost older sister. When Kneesaa was little older than a wokling, Asha had been caught by a terrifying hanadak, and their mother, Ra-Lee, had tried to save her child. By the time Kneesaa had run to the village and come back with help, Ra-Lee was dead, and Asha was missing.

Kneesaa and Wicket embarked on a quest to find the female Ewok, eventually coming upon her in the snowy night. As Kneesaa had guessed, the savage was her sister. The red-furred Ewok explained that the tigerlike Corrinas had found her and raised her as their child. Asha agreed to return to the village only if she first could get rid of the hunting party of Duloks. She did, then returned home to her grateful father's arms.

Nothing is known of Princess Kneesaa's life beyond her adolescence, nor of her siblings. Her father, Chief Chirpa, is still chief after forty-two seasons, but he is getting old and senile. Perhaps she will begin courting her longtime friend, Wicket, whose bachelorhood is acting as a magnet to the eligible Ewok females. Or perhaps Kneesaa is traveling Endor, searching out her own new adventures.

EXAR KUN

SPECIES:
Human

SEX:
Male

HAIR COLOR:
Black

EYE COLOR:
Gray

HEIGHT:
Unknown (tall)

HOMEWORLD:
Unknown

POLITICAL AFFILIATION:
Dark Lords of the Sith

WEAPON(S) OF CHOICE:
Lightsaber (blue blade)

VEHICLE OF CHOICE:
Starstorm One

FIRST APPEARANCE:
Star Wars: Dark Apprentice

DEATH:
seven Years after the Battle of Endor

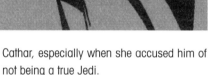

Four thousand years prior to Anakin Skywalker's conversion to the dark side, a Jedi named Exar Kun became one of the early Dark Lords of the Sith, launching one of the greatest wars in the history of the galaxy.

On Dantooine, Exar Kun was tutored in the ways of the Force by Master Vodo-Siosk Baas. He pushed himself hard, but felt he was excellent Jedi material. He prided himself in his ability to wield a lightsaber and in the other Force skills he had gained.

Kun used his Master's Holocron to learn about the past of the Dark Lords of the Sith. Vodo-Siosk Baas was not amused to find his student studying the Sith history. Too much knowledge about the dark side was not a good thing for young Jedi.

Kun didn't like his fellow students Crado and Sylvar, catlike lovers from Cathar. He didn't believe that animals—even sentient ones—made good Jedi. In a particularly brutal lightsaber exercise, Kun goaded Sylvar too much, and she clawed him, raking furrows deep into his right cheek. It was all Kun could do to keep from killing the

Cathar, especially when she accused him of not being a true Jedi.

Master Vodo-Siosk stopped Kun from killing Sylvar, challenging him to a duel of walking stick versus lightsaber. The young Jedi was defeated at first, but when he snatched a second lightsaber, he was able to angrily press his attack against the Master. The stick broke, and Kun felt he had proved himself. The rage passed, but Master Vodo-Siosk began to see just how close his student was to the dark side.

More than a month went by, and Kun left Dantooine. He traveled to Onderon, posing as a Jedi archaeologist who needed to see Freedon Nadd's Sith artifacts. With the aid of two Nadd followers, Kun visited the Dxun moon, where he forced his way into Nadd's tomb. Hesitating for just a moment—the light side of the Force barely whispering to him to turn away—Kun entered the tomb. Confronted by the spirit of Nadd, he was led to two scrolls, which contained the secret of the Sith resting place. Exiting the tomb, he found Nadd's followers and killed them in anger. The dark side was already beginning to eat away at his spirit.

He translated the scrolls and soon arrived on Korribun, a desolate planet. With Nadd's spirit's help, Kun gained access to the planet's tombs, but he had second thoughts and wanted to back out. When a convenient rock slide trapped him in the tombs, and an attack by Nadd left him broken and dying, the haughty Jedi called for Master Vodo-Siosk. Attempting to help his student through the light side of the Force, Vodo-Siosk was turned away by the immense blackness that surrounded Kun's body and spirit.

Nadd offered Kun a way to live, and to repair his broken body: if he embraced the dark side, he would be healed. The betrayal of light was not an easy one for Kun, but the desire to live was stronger still. He accepted the dark side, his screams reaching out across the galaxy and creating ripples in the Force.

Whole again, Kun walked the tombs while Nadd's spirit told him of the alchemical experiments that an ancient Sith Lord, Naga Sadow, had performed on Yavin Four. The experiments gave flesh to the spirits of the dead. Nadd told Kun to travel there to complete Sadow's work—and give him a new body. The ex-Jedi assured Nadd he would go to Yavin Four to research, but that he would never give in to the dark side. "Oh, but you already have," Nadd's spirit said, laughing.

On Yavin Four, Kun renounced the dark side, telling Nadd's spirit to trouble him no more. He was attacked by the Massassi, mutated descendants of Sadow's alchemy. Refusing to use the dark side, and cut off from the light side, Kun was stunned by the creatures. Their

leader and temple priest, Zyhtmnr, knew that Kun was the one for whom they had waited. The Massassi took him to the massive Temple of Fire, where he was staked out for death in a Massassi blood sacrifice. He could feel the dark side calling him, especially from an amulet the priest placed on the broken statue of Naga Sadow. And then a huge and horrible monster appeared to hold Kun in its death grip and Nadd's spirit taunted him, telling him to use the power of the Sith amulet.

Once again, Kun used the dark side to save his life, pulling the amulet to him. It grafted to his arm, and he felt immense power and energy coursing through him. He unleashed the strength of the Sith and the power of the dark side on the

monster and the Massassi, obliterating all who dared oppose him . . . including the spirit of Freedon Nadd. But as he died for the second time, Nadd called out to Aleema

and Satal Keto, two of the Krath to whom he had given Sith secrets. He told them that Exar Kun was a pretender to the Sith, and that the real power of the Sith belonged to the two of them and the soon-to-be-fallen Jedi, Ulic Qel-Droma.

Over the following months, Kun was accepted by the Massassi as their leader. He cared little for their devotion, except to use it to have them build temples of an ancient Sith design. The temples would focus great dark-side energies onto Yavin Four, giving him more power. One of the smaller temples even had a statue of him atop it, carved from black stone. This temple became his private retreat.

In a subterranean cavern deep below the lush jungles, Kun found the alchemical instruments of Naga Sadow, as well as a spaceship. Now he would not be trapped on Yavin Four. Kun used the instruments to begin changing the Massassi, making them into monstrous creatures of death. Then he departed on the spaceship with two Massassi, headed for the Empress Teta system to destroy Nadd's final Sith followers.

Kun arrived at Cinnager mere minutes

before the Jedi Knights mounted an attack on the Krath stronghold. Waiting until the Jedi left the city, Kun confronted Ulic Qel-Droma and Aleema. Qel-Droma had already killed Satal Keto, saving Kun the trouble. The dark Jedi ignited his lightsaber to face Ulic. As they battled, equally matched, their Sith amulets began to glow. Crackling energy filled the air, and then they saw the Sith Lords, speaking to the future from the past like a Dark Holocron.

The foremost creature in the vision bestowed the title of Dark Lord of the Sith on Exar Kun, and the title of Sith Apprentice on Ulic Qel-Droma. Each of them was branded with tattoos on their foreheads, dark symbols from an evil power. "The ancient Sith have spoken,"

Exar Kun said. "Together we will bring down the galaxy."

Exar Kun and Ulic Qel-Droma disappeared for several years, gaining tremendous powers of the dark side.

Kun created a distorted version of the Jedi Code for his dark-side followers, establishing a powerful Brotherhood of the Sith. Qel-Droma reappeared, commanding his own militaristic and bloodthirsty Krath sect. Eventually, Kun, Qel-Droma, and Aleema joined forces against the Galactic Republic and the Order of the Jedi Knights.

The Great Council of Jedi convened on Deneba to discuss how to proceed. Master Vodo-Siosk Baas volunteered to go to his onetime student and attempt to help him away from the dark side, but Kun slew his Master, forever severing his ties to the light side of the Force.

The conflict that resulted would become known through the ages as the Sith War, one of the largest and bloodiest wars the galaxy ever witnessed. The armies of the Sith and the Krath were responsible for millions of deaths. In the end, Ulic Qel-Droma betrayed Exar Kun by telling the Jedi about the Sith Lord's base of power on Yavin Four.

The Jedi banded together and came to the jungle moon. Combining their power in the Force, they should have defeated Kun. The battle leveled most of the temples Kun had had erected and razed many of the rain forests. Faced with total destruction, Kun drained the life force from every Massassi on the planet. This bolstered his own powers only enough to keep his spirit trapped in the Yavin temples when the Jedi destroyed his physical body. The Jedi thought they had won, but Kun still existed, albeit with no corporeal form.

Four thousand years after the Sith War, the Rebels established a base on Yavin Four. Eleven years after the Death Star was destroyed and the Rebel base on Yavin Four was abandoned, the last Jedi, Luke Skywalker, returned to Yavin Four to open a training academy for a new generation of Jedi. He based it in the Great Temple, which had been the focus of Kun's battles in the Sith War. Unaware of the presence of Exar Kun's spirit, Luke didn't guard himself or his students against the Sith Lord until it was too late.

Skywalker's mistake would allow Exar Kun to tempt the young Jedi students. When Kun showed a student named Gantoris the deaths of his Eol Sha friends in an Imperial massacre, the Jedi initiate charged Kun's dark spirit, lightsaber blazing. But when the other Jedi students went to Gantoris's room the next morning, all they found was his body, incinerated from the inside out, and his newly constructed lightsaber lying near him on the floor.

Then Kun appeared to the powerful young Kyp Durron, promising forbidden secrets of the Force. Like Anakin Skywalker, Ulic Qel-Droma, and others over the millennia, Kyp felt he could control himself and his contact with the Force enough that he wouldn't be sucked into the dark side. Like the others, he was wrong.

Eventually, Kyp requested Kun's aid to pull the superweapon known as the Sun Crusher from the gaseous heart of Yavin. All was going as planned until Luke confronted Kyp. The young man attacked the Jedi Master with the help of Exar Kun, using dark-side Force lightning to separate Luke's spirit from his body.

In the morning, Tionne found Luke's body on the top of the temple, still alive, but deathly still. She summoned the other trainees, who realized they were now on their own in the fight against Exar Kun. The Sith Lord intended to lure the Jedi trainees to him. Either they would turn to the dark side or he would consume their power and their life.

Luke's spirit survived in the same netherworld that Exar Kun's shade inhabited. Luke soon found that Kun had become adept at using the dark side of the Force to influence the living world. Over the following weeks, Kun used his powers to try to destroy Luke's body, but it was protected by the twelve Jedi initiates, Luke's sister, Leia Organa Solo, and her two Force-strong children.

Even worse for the Sith Lord, the dozen Jedi students were now aware of him, and guarded themselves against his enticements and advances. In the abandoned war room of the Rebel Alliance, they planned their trap for Exar Kun. Tionne explained how the combined power of many Jedi had trapped and defeated Kun. Now, the new generation of Jedi must also use its powers in concert to destroy the Sith Lord's lingering spirit.

The initiates used Streen as bait, luring Kun to appear in the grand audience chamber where Luke's body lay in repose. As they focused their will into a single entity of the Force, the spirits of Luke and Vodo-Siosk Baas appeared to aid them.

Kun mocked the students and their minor Force talents; yet this time, he had no Massassi to feed his waning power. The combined powers and energies of the Jedi extinguished the dark light of Kun's spirit. Screaming into the black void, the Dark Lord of the Sith was no more.

LABRIA

SPECIES:
Devaronian

SEX:
Male

HAIR COLOR:
None

EYE COLOR:
Brown

HEIGHT:
1.8 meters

HOMEWORLD:
Devaron

POLITICAL AFFILIATION:
None

WEAPON(S) OF CHOICE:
Unknown

VEHICLE OF CHOICE:
None

FIRST APPEARANCE:
Star Wars: A New Hope

T he devilish-looking Labria fancied himself an important information broker at the Mos Eisley spaceport on Tatooine. In reality, the creature was the city's biggest drunk and *worst* spy. That didn't stop him from pulling a triple cross that's still discussed in terms of wonder and awe.

Labria is a typical Devaronian male, filled with wanderlust and a desire to experience the full range of life in the galaxy. Like all males of his species, he has pointed ears and a pair of dark horns on his head. Unlike most of the males of his pack, Labria

has two sets of teeth, marking him as a genetic throwback to older Devaronian tribes. His skin is hairless and red tinted.

On his home planet, he had been a ruthless captain in the Devaronian army. His name was Kardue'sai'Malloc, and he was the third in his line to bear the name. Army life suited him, as it had for sixteen generations of his family. When the Rebellion broke out on the planet, Kardue'sai'Malloc and his men aligned themselves with the Empire, and at the Battle of Montellian Serat, the Devaronian oversaw the execution

of seven hundred captive men, women, and children.

At the end of the war, Kardue'sai'Malloc resigned from the army and left the planet, taking with him only his extensive music collection. The Rebels put a five-million-credit bounty on the head of the "Butcher of Montellian Serat," but knew it was unlikely they'd ever collect. A passionate music aficionado, Kardue'sai'Malloc followed the great musical artist Maxa Jandovar to the remote desert planet of Tatooine, but missed seeing her. He decided to settle on the twin-sunned world, renting a small underground apartment in Mos Eisley, home of a busy and bizarre intergalactic spaceport. Changing his name to Labria—a word in the Devaronian tongue meaning "cold food"—the Devaronian deposited a secret stash of 5,000 credits in a local bank under the name "Airbal"—his name spelled backward—and set himself up as a source of secrets.

Though he called himself an information broker, Labria's information was always suspect; he didn't often check the accuracy or validity of the rumors and conversations he overheard. He was often very drunk, although sometimes he faked drunkenness to wheedle information from others at the bar. Locals knew to feed Labria only those "facts" they wanted him to know, and newcomers were sometimes too frightened by his appearance to speak with him.

The one cache of valuable information Labria did appear to possess was his knowledge about Jabba the Hutt's criminal empire. He often provided secrets about the

Hutt to the master spy Garindan, but more often than not, even that information was false or only partially usable.

A regular at all the Mos Eisley cantinas, Labria was always the first in the door at Chalmun's cantina, visiting with his friend, the bartender Wuher. One day Labria learned that Figrin D'an and the Modal Nodes had arrived on Tatooine, and were going to play for Jabba the Hutt. Labria tried to wrangle a way into Jabba's grace in order to hear the band, and arranged to sell Jabba the services of a Moorin bounty hunter named Obron Mettlo. The plan backfired; the hunter angered Jabba and was fed to the rancor.

Depressed, Labria went on a drunken binge and was mugged behind the cantina on the fifth day. Retreating into his apartment, he recuperated. By the time he returned to the cantina to see Wuher, he had come up with a new plot.

Lady Valarian was getting married, and Max Rebo and his band were to play the reception. Labria visited the Whiphid female—who was Jabba's biggest competition on the planet—and told her about Figrin D'an's band, assuring her *this* was the band she really wanted. The Devaronian knew that if D'an took Valarian's offer, Jabba would be angry. To atone for his mistake with the Moorin bounty hunter, Labria informed Jabba of Figrin D'an's musical engagement at the wedding reception.

Labria orchestrated the day expertly. Jabba arranged for Valarian's reception to be raided; she always had illegal gambling devices on hand. After the raid, the angry Valarian wouldn't pay the band, and Wuher would offer them a job at the cantina.

The plan went without a hitch. D'an and his band agreed to sign a two-year contract at Chalmun's cantina. After signing the contract, Figrin accepted Labria's challenge to a

game of sabacc. By the time they were finished playing, Labria owned all of the musicians' instruments, except Doikk Na'ts's Fizzz. The band wouldn't be able to leave the planet until Figrin D'an bought the instruments back from the Devaronian. So Labria would have a concert from his favorite band every day.

Prior to the fall of the Empire, Labria had toyed with the idea of offering his services to them as a commissioned spy. However, after the death of Jabba the Hutt and the destruction of the second Death Star, Labria's two best hopes for the future were gone.

Remaining on Tatooine, Labria weathered the changes in power, though the fate of the drunken information broker is unknown.

OWEN AND BERU LARS

SPECIES:
Human

SEX:
Male/Female

HAIR COLOR:
Gray/Brownish gray

EYE COLOR:
Blue/Blue

HEIGHT:
1.7 meters/1.5 meters

HOMEWORLD:
Tatooine

POLITICAL AFFILIATION:
None

WEAPON(S) OF CHOICE:
Blaster carbine

VEHICLE OF CHOICE:
Landspeeder

FIRST APPEARANCE:
Star Wars: A New Hope

DEATH:
During stormtrooper raid on Tatooine

Moisture farmers on Tatooine, Owen and Beru Lars never dreamed that the child they raised as their own would become the hope of the Rebel Alliance.

Owen Lars was never as flashy as his brother, Obi-Wan Kenobi, one of the strongest of the Jedi Knights, nor as daring as Kenobi's friend, Anakin Skywalker. He was content to marry Beru and live a practical life in the arid wastes of Tatooine, moisture farming in order to irrigate his underground produce gardens. Lars used

vaporators to distill water from the air, a difficult task on a planet with two suns and many seasons each year. He made some money selling excess water to those who maintained hydroponic gardens, such as the nearby family with an infant daughter named Camie.

When Obi-Wan brought the infant Luke Skywalker to the Lars, they promised to raise the child as if they were his aunt and uncle. Luke was taught strong values such as loyalty and commitment, and from his aunt he learned compassion. What he was-

n't taught was anything about his father, who he was told had died before Luke's birth. All Luke knew was that his father had been a great pilot, and later a navigator on a spice freighter. The Larses were trying to protect Luke from ever finding out that Darth Vader was his father.

When Luke became a teenager and began racing skyhoppers with Biggs Darklighter and his other friends from the nearby town of Anchorhead, Lars began to fear the boy was slipping away. Luke had dreams of a galaxy of adventure, but Owen attempted to keep him grounded in reality on Tatooine. Although Luke petitioned his uncle to allow him to enter the Academy with Biggs, Owen stalled him repeatedly, telling him he could go "next season." Beru could only offer sympathy.

As moisture farming was intensive work, Owen, by this time in his mid-fifties, needed many droids to aid himself and Luke. Two of the many droids he pur-

chased from the scavenger Jawas were C-3PO and R2-D2. When Luke found a recording from Princess Leia within the memory systems of R2-D2, he mentioned the name "Obi-Wan Kenobi" to Owen and Beru over dinner, opining that it might refer to Ben Kenobi. Owen warned Luke never to

go near the "crazy old hermit" and told him to flush the R2's memory.

The following day, Luke and the droids both disappeared. Owen assumed they had gone to work early, and he and Beru were surprised when Imperial stormtroopers showed up demanding information about the droids. Neither Owen

nor Beru would give the troopers the information they sought, and the Imperials killed them, burning their homestead.

Luke returned to the homestead at dusk, to find the charred bodies of the only parents he had ever known. He had come home to keep his commitments, and had discovered a horror that would propel him to the destiny that was his birthright.

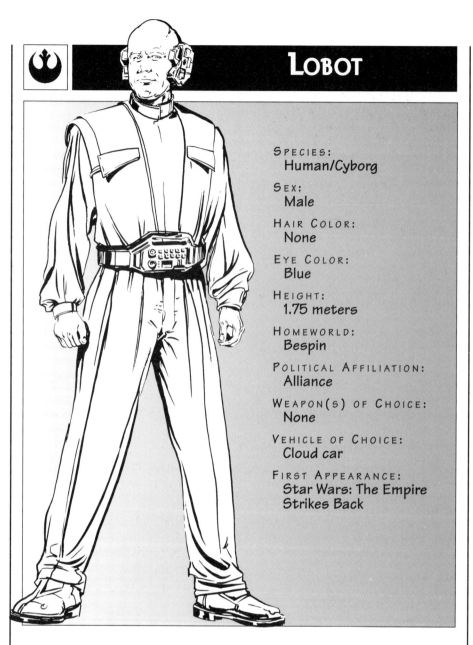

LOBOT

SPECIES:
Human/Cyborg

SEX:
Male

HAIR COLOR:
None

EYE COLOR:
Blue

HEIGHT:
1.75 meters

HOMEWORLD:
Bespin

POLITICAL AFFILIATION:
Alliance

WEAPON(S) OF CHOICE:
None

VEHICLE OF CHOICE:
Cloud car

FIRST APPEARANCE:
Star Wars: The Empire Strikes Back

The real power behind the running of Bespin's famous Cloud City is not the Baron Administrators. Rather, it is the city's computer-liaison officer, connected directly into the central computer core. The first and only known person to hold that job is a thirty-eight-year-old cyborg named Lobot.

The title of Baron Administrator has passed from hand to hand many times in Cloud City's history, sometimes through appointment, other times through assassination, and even through a losing gamble.

Since the city had always been run entirely by its computer core, and maintenance of the core required dozens of specialists, Baronness Administrator Ellisa Shallence decided a more centralized control needed to be established.

A young man named Lobot had recently arrived on Cloud City. He had been born a slaver's son, learning the "trade" as he grew, and had accompanied his father on raids to primitive systems. When he was fifteen, Lobot was taken into slavery by a band of space pirates who killed his father.

Lobot was in slavery to the pirates for two years, until he managed to escape to Cloud City.

Although he had come to Bespin as a free man, Lobot had no money, no job, and no home. He was forced to steal to survive, and was eventually caught and convicted. Baroness Shallence saw potential in the young vagabond and proposed that rather than serve a lengthy prison term, Lobot could indenture himself to the city by becoming the first cyborg computer-liaison officer.

He agreed, and was fitted with advanced cyborg enhancements. The visible implants were a computer bracket that wrapped around the back of Lobot's skull, and the devices increased his intelligence dramatically, allowing him to communicate directly with the city's central computer. Lobot could control issues of bureaucracy, law enforcement, computer programming and repair, and security, as well as the comm systems, repulsorlifts, and life-support systems.

The only negative side effect was that the neural connections wore away at Lobot's speech centers, reducing his speech to minimal—and infrequent—sentences. He felt less need to speak with the implants any-

how; his observations of the world came to focus on numbers and formulas. His gradual loss of humanity was eerie and jarring only to those who had just met him.

Lobot proved adept at his job, keeping the managerial networks running efficiently even as Cloud City expanded in population and commerce; for fifteen Standard years, Lobot worked, fulfilling his "sentence." Shortly after the fall of the Old Republic, he was freed from his service, but chose to remain connected to Cloud City's management. He was rewarded by being made chief administrative aide to the Baron Administrator.

Lobot worked with several Baron and Baroness Administrators in his years of service, some of them good for the city, some of them bad. It was while working for the inept Baron Administrator Raynor that Lobot saw a chance to better the struggling hierarchy of the floating city. A roguish gambler named Lando Calrissian had arrived.

Lobot inconspicuously aided Lando when Calrissian challenged Raynor to a game of all-or-nothing sabacc. When Calrissian won Cloud City in the high-stakes game, he became its new Baron Administrator. He kept Lobot as his chief aide, utilizing the cyborg in many ways he had never been used before. Lobot proved equally adept at handling Calrissian's more clandestine operations, as well.

Due perhaps to his upbringing and slavehood, Lobot held no great affection for the Empire. He didn't object when Lando would surreptitiously aid the Rebellion, assisted Calrissian when prominent scientist Dr. Len was murdered and Rebels were accused, and saved Lando's life when the rogue robot EV-9D9 planted bombs that rocked Cloud City.

When Calrissian made the deal to turn Han Solo over to Darth Vader and Boba Fett, Lobot didn't question his administrator's

orders. He did, however, urge Lando to help the Rebels if at all possible. When it became clear Vader was not to be trusted, Lando asked Lobot to assemble a dozen of Calrissian's personal guardsmen to rescue Princess Leia, Chewbacca, and a dismembered C-3PO.

As the troopers and prisoners neared the phalanx of Cloud City guards, Lando gave the command "Code Force Seven," and Lobot had the men draw their weapons on the surprised Imperials. Lobot handed off trooper weapons to Leia and Chewbacca as the Imperials surrendered them.

Lando utilized the public-address systems of Cloud City to announce that Imperial takeover was imminent. He urged the citizens to evacuate, then escaped on the *Millennium Falcon* moments later. Lobot stayed behind in the city as it eventually came under Imperial control. But the Imperials hadn't counted on a revolt of the Ugnaughts, who hated the Empire.

Months after his hasty departure, Lando Calrissian returned to Cloud City on Bespin. It appeared deserted, but Lando soon found Lobot. The cyborg's motivational-programming capsule had been damaged by the rebellious Ugnaughts. Although Lobot initially attacked Lando as an intruder, Calrissian managed to remove the damaged capsule and repair it. Lobot was then able to use his computer interfaces to disarm eleven bombs

the Ugnaughts had strategically placed throughout the city.

When Lando was hurled off Cloud City by Imperial Navy Captain Treece, Lobot used lifejets to save him. Teaming with the rebellious Ugnaughts, who now hid on the surface of Bespin, Lando and Lobot staged a raid on Cloud City, joining Luke Skywalker and Lieutenant Shira Brei, who were already engaging the Imperial troops. In the ensuing battle, Lobot's headpiece was shot by Captain Treece. Once the Imperials were defeated, Lando sent out a call that Cloud City was no longer under the Empire's control.

Lando had Lobot completely repaired, and the cyborg served as his aide whenever Lando wasn't off flying missions for the Rebellion. Then Lobot disappeared when Lando lost ownership of Cloud City to Zorba the Hutt, in the year following the battle against the second Death Star.

Fifteen years later, Lando Calrissian opened GemDiver Station, a sprawling corusca-gem-mining industrial station in orbit around Yavin's gaseous surface. Once again, Lobot returned as his assistant. Lando allowed Jacen and Jaina Solo to come to the station on a field trip from Luke's Jedi academy, accompanied by Lowbacca and his droid, Em Teedee. Imperial ships struck while the children were on board. Tamith Kai, a woman from the new order of Dathomir Nightsisters, wanted the young Jedi children, and she would stop at nothing to get them.

Despite Lobot and Lando's best efforts, GemDiver Station was boarded, and the children and Lowbacca were captured. Lando offered to help find the children, but Luke Skywalker and Tenel Ka were already tracking them. So Lando and Lobot focused their energies on finding the best ways to protect the station so that an invasion or pirate attack could never succeed again.

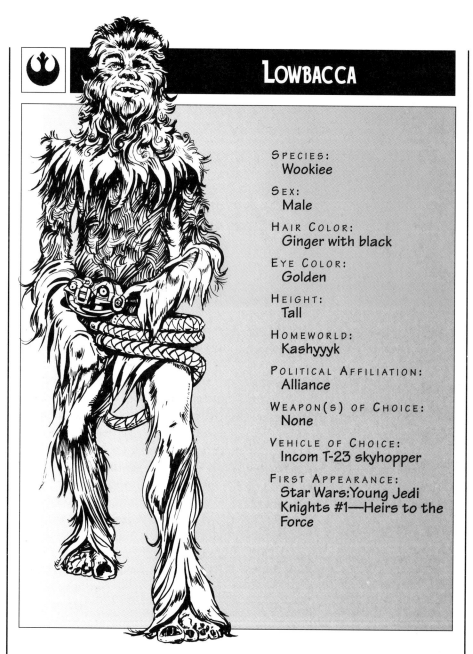

LOWBACCA

SPECIES:
Wookiee

SEX:
Male

HAIR COLOR:
Ginger with black

EYE COLOR:
Golden

HEIGHT:
Tall

HOMEWORLD:
Kashyyyk

POLITICAL AFFILIATION:
Alliance

WEAPON(S) OF CHOICE:
None

VEHICLE OF CHOICE:
Incom T-23 skyhopper

FIRST APPEARANCE:
Star Wars: Young Jedi Knights #1—Heirs to the Force

The tall, furry Wookiees have always had an affinity for the Force, so it was no surprise to Luke Skywalker when Chewbacca's nephew, Lowbacca, became an initiate at the Jedi academy.

The nineteen year old—barely an adolescent by Wookiee standards—would train there with other students, including Han and Leia's own twins, Jacen and Jaina Solo. The twins quickly befriended the tall, lanky Wookiee. Lowbacca didn't wear any kind of training clothes. In fact, all he wore was a glossy, syren-fiber belt, which held a strange little egg-shaped electronic device: a Miniaturized Translator Droid known as Em Teedee. It translated Lowie's growls, barks, and snuffles for the other students and the Jedi instructors at the academy. Em Teedee had been programmed by C-3PO, the prissy, golden protocol droid, and had the same speech pattern and basic personality that Threepio does.

Lowie, as he likes his friends to call him, soon became friends with the humorless Dathomirian girl named Tenel Ka. Together, the quartet of youngsters explored the jun-

gles of Yavin Four, and on a solo flight of his T-23 skyhopper, Lowie saw a crashed TIE fighter, apparently incapacitated since the first Battle of Yavin. Utilizing Jaina's mechanical talents, they began repairing the ship, even adding a hyperdrive module.

But the TIE pilot, Qorl, was still alive, and more than a little crazy. He managed to capture Jacen and Jaina; Tenel and Lowie escaped, but in the excitement Em Teedee was knocked off Lowie's belt.

Lowie was unable to communicate with anyone at the Great Temple that housed the academy, as none of them spoke Wookiee. Finally, using the communication equipment to call the *Falcon,* he told Chewbacca what was going on. His uncle and Han returned just in time to save Jacen and Jaina, but not in time to stop the TIE fighter from escaping.

Weeks later, Lowie and the twins accompanied Lando to his corusca-mining GemDiver Station. A fleet of Imperial Skipray blastboats and an assault shuttle attacked the station. Raiding it, the stormtroopers and a mysterious Dathomirian Nightsister captured the trio of young Jedi.

The Nightsister, Tamith Kai, planned to train them at the Shadow Academy in the Core systems. The three were separated, and Em Teedee was taken away from Lowbacca.

Tamith kept Lowie in seclusion, pelting him with high-pitched sonics and cold-water blasts. Little by little, the witch brought out the Wookiee's anger. When he destroyed the sonic generator, she returned Em Teedee to him. But the translator module had been reprogrammed. "The Empire is your friend," the little droid chirped. Lowbacca switched it off, knowing that he could not afford to give in to the dark side.

Eventually, the Solo twins and Lowie did manage to escape, arriving in the shuttle bays just as Luke and Tenel Ka were arriving to rescue them. The Jedi Master and his students returned to Yavin Four, where Lowbacca reprogrammed Em Teedee and returned to his studies.

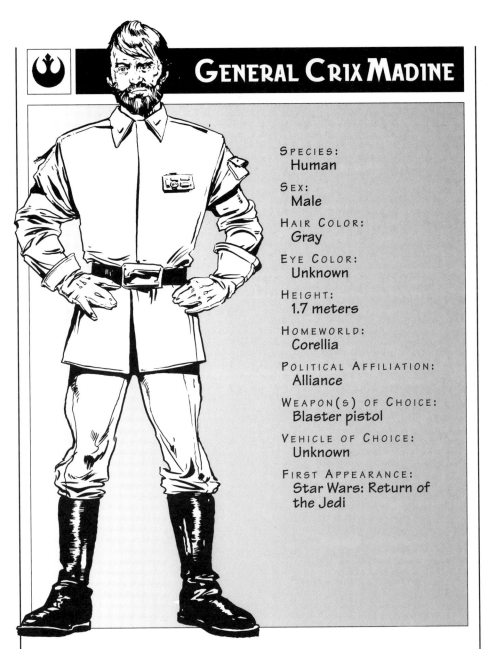

GENERAL CRIX MADINE

SPECIES:
Human

SEX:
Male

HAIR COLOR:
Gray

EYE COLOR:
Unknown

HEIGHT:
1.7 meters

HOMEWORLD:
Corellia

POLITICAL AFFILIATION:
Alliance

WEAPON(S) OF CHOICE:
Blaster pistol

VEHICLE OF CHOICE:
Unknown

FIRST APPEARANCE:
Star Wars: Return of the Jedi

No one can fight the Empire better than one of their own, as General Crix Madine of Corellia proved.

Madine had been a top-notch commander in the Imperial Army during the days of Palpatine's New Order. His men were exceedingly well trained, and he himself was confident and assured—some would even say "cocky." Madine treated his soldiers fairly and equally; one's background did not matter as much as one's future.

He earned an admirable record, winning many commendations and gaining command of an elite army commando unit. His troops suffered few casualties, experienced no major defeats, and—most importantly in his mind—committed no atrocities of war. Madine had a conscience, and would rather change someone's mind than eliminate them. This conscience eventually drove him to join the Rebellion.

It is rumored that Madine's final mission for the Empire was left uncompleted. He had apparently received orders so vile—directly from Emperor Palpatine—that he defected in the midst of the mission. The cocky, beard-ed Corellian made contact with friends whom he knew to be Imperial defectors, then switched sides.

Although they initially thought him a possible double agent, the High Command Advisory Council accepted him in on the recommendations of General Rieekan. Madine was assigned to the Alliance Council, working as a chief military advisor to Mon Mothma. She wanted a fresh perspective on Imperial methods, and Madine, having recently been on the other side of the fence, could offer them. He introduced many new and innovative concepts, working on ground tactics as Admiral Ackbar developed space combat tactics.

When the Alliance learned that the Empire was building a second Death Star above the moon of Endor, Madine helped to devise a plan. The partially complete space station was protected by an energy shield generated from the moon. Madine's troops would need to deactivate it before Ackbar's fleet could attack in space.

Madine's commandos stole a small Imperial shuttle and disguised it as a cargo ship. Using a stolen Imperial code, the shuttle was to land on the forest moon of Endor, and a strike team, led by General Han Solo, would deactivate the energy shield. The team was successful, and the Death Star was destroyed, but at a great loss of life.

Staying on as a valued Alliance leader, Madine refused a post on the Provisional Council, telling Mon Mothma, "I'm a warrior, not a politician. Leave that work to those with more knowledge and experience." Instead, he took the position of field commander, and delivered many victories.

Five years after the destruction of the second Death Star, he was involved in the battle against Grand Admiral Thrawn. The following year, he was instrumental in devising the attacks on the new Imperial World Devastators from Pinnacle Base on the Fifth Moon of Da Soocha. He continues to serve the New Republic, knowing that one day peace will be fully restored.

NICHOS MARR

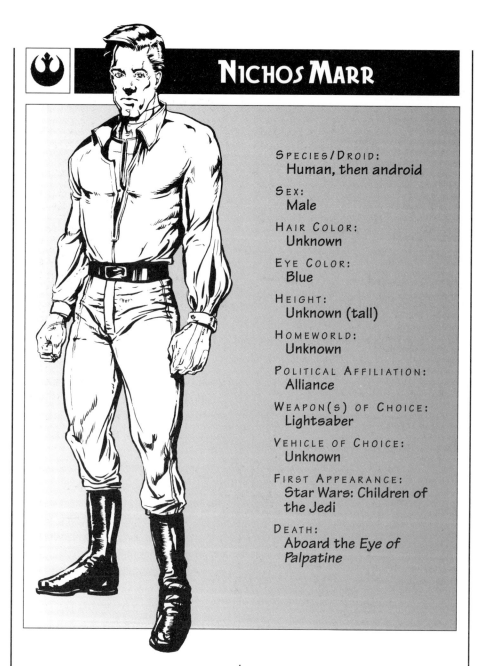

SPECIES/DROID:
Human, then android

SEX:
Male

HAIR COLOR:
Unknown

EYE COLOR:
Blue

HEIGHT:
Unknown (tall)

HOMEWORLD:
Unknown

POLITICAL AFFILIATION:
Alliance

WEAPON(S) OF CHOICE:
Lightsaber

VEHICLE OF CHOICE:
Unknown

FIRST APPEARANCE:
Star Wars: Children of
the Jedi

DEATH:
Aboard the Eye of
Palpatine

E ven for those strong in the Force, tragedy can strike. Jedi student Nichos Marr knew tragedy, first losing his body, and then his life.

When a young Marr came to the moon of Yavin Four to be trained in the skills of the Force, his goals were to perfect his Jedi training and to marry his fiancée, the beautiful blond scientist, Cray Mingla, who was also gifted in the Force. But Nichos was only able to study with Master Luke Skywalker for a year before he was stricken with the deadly Quannot's Syndrome.

Cray was a leading expert in artificial-intelligence programming, and had studied earlier research through which Stinna Draesinge Sha had proved that it was possible to transfer an entire persona into a mechanical construct. Rather than let her lover die, Cray and the technicians of the biomedical institute on Coruscant created a synthetic body for Marr.

Nichos's droid body was encased in a smooth, form-fitted armor of brushed, pewter-gray steel, and was exquisitely articulated to mimic human functions and mus-

culature. The technicians even duplicated a small scar on his little finger to provide him continuity. Nichos Marr appeared relatively human, but he had lost the ability to feel emotions, along with his connection to the Force.

Six months after the operation/transfer, Nichos accompanied Luke and Dr. Mingla on Jedi tasks to the lush paradise of Ithor. He was trying hard to adjust to the process of programming his mind like a computer, of thinking in binary and random numbers rather than using human thought processes.

When the Rebels learned of the existence of something called Plett's Well, and heard rumors of children of the Jedi, it led Nichos to voice his partially remembered past. He had been one of the children of the Jedi Knights, who with their families had been hidden away from the Imperial forces by Plett, a Jedi Master. So Nichos was able to assist Skywalker and Leia Organa Solo in finding both Plett's Well and the Eye of Palpatine, an early prototype Imperial battle station orbiting within the Moonflower Nebula.

Cray and Nichos accompanied Luke and Threepio to destroy the battle station. There, they were surprised to discover that the essence of a Jedi woman called Callista was trapped inside the computer core. She had kept the weapons systems incapacitated for thirty years.

On board the Eye, Nichos realized that, since he could no longer have any feelings for Cray, she would be cheated if she stayed with him. So when Callista revealed she had a way to detonate the Eye, but that it required the death of whomever implemented the plan, Nichos volunteered, allowing the others to escape.

Feeling she couldn't live without Nichos, Cray also stayed behind. Together, Cray and Callista used their Force powers to transfer Callista's essence into Cray's body, and ejected her in an escape pod. Nichos Marr and Cray died in the violent explosion that ripped apart the Eye of Palpatine. In their shared death, they were together once again, alive in the Force.

EPHANT MON

SPECIES:
Chevin

SEX:
Male

HAIR COLOR:
Dark golden

EYE COLOR:
Unknown

HEIGHT:
2.5 meters

HOMEWORLD:
Vinsoth

POLITICAL
AFFILIATION:
Loyal to
Jabba the Hutt

WEAPON(S)
OF CHOICE:
Vibroblade

VEHICLE OF CHOICE:
Unknown

FIRST APPEARANCE:
Star Wars: Return of
the Jedi

The oddest-looking creature to frequent Jabba's palace was Ephant Mon, the Chevin. For his species, Ephant Mon was a decent specimen, but most creatures found him repulsive.

The Chevins lived on the planet Vinsoth, hunting and building nomadically on its wide plains. But Ephant was unhappy with this simple life, and pined to reach the stars. Eventually, he did.

Ephant worked as a mercenary for much of his early adult life, and began running guns. He sold to any military organization, from petty guerilla groups to the Rebel Alliance. Eventually he came in contact with Jabba the Hutt, and the two began gunrunning together. They were going to liberate an Imperial weapons cache on the icy moon of Glakka when fate intervened.

Jabba had been betrayed to the Imperials by one of his own people, and the snowtroopers arrived. Ephant and Jabba managed to protect each other and save their own lives, but were trapped on the icy moon. As heat stole away, Jabba gathered the freezing Ephant to him, forcing his oily fat folds around him.

The rescue kept Ephant alive, although Jabba was nearly frozen by the time some of Jabba's associates returned to the planet the next day. Feeling he owed a life debt, Ephant Mon became completely loyal to Jabba.

Back on Tatooine, Jabba gave Ephant a surreptitious job—to hang around Jabba's court, and root out conspiracies, thievery, and assassination plans. Sometimes Ephant's information came from the B'ommar monks in their spiderlike brain cases; other times through a show of force. Most often, just keeping his senses attuned let him know when something was up. Jabba's main competitor, Lady Valarian, kept trying to buy Ephant's services, but she already had half a dozen spies in the palace, and he was loyal to Jabba.

Ephant saw the potential for trouble clearly when a bounty hunter showed up with Han Solo's Wookiee, and was soon unmasked. Then a young Jedi appeared, and was taken captive—or allowed himself to be taken. Ephant tried to warn Jabba, but the Hutt didn't believe him.

When the Rebels were loaded onto the gigantic sail barge, Ephant Mon stayed behind. His path would lead elsewhere.

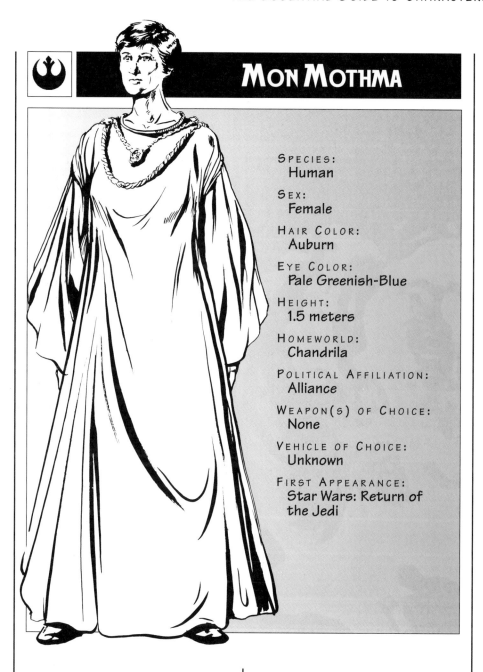

MON MOTHMA

SPECIES:
Human

SEX:
Female

HAIR COLOR:
Auburn

EYE COLOR:
Pale Greenish-Blue

HEIGHT:
1.5 meters

HOMEWORLD:
Chandrila

POLITICAL AFFILIATION:
Alliance

WEAPON(S) OF CHOICE:
None

VEHICLE OF CHOICE:
Unknown

FIRST APPEARANCE:
Star Wars: Return of the Jedi

A s leader of the Rebel Alliance, the stately Mon Mothma is in control of the reshaping of a galaxy. Unlike other leaders, she has not let her power corrupt her.

Mon Mothma was the daughter of an arbiter-general of the Old Republic. As she watched her father settle disputes, she learned diplomacy, tact, and the strong need for compromise. Mothma's mother was the governor on her home planet of Chandrila; she taught her daughter organization and leadership skills. Together, her parents were intelligent, fair, and compas-sionate, but unyielding when it came to principles they believed in.

Those same principles helped Mon Mothma gain senatorship when she was barely an adult. Although the Old Republic was already being eroded, Mothma fought hard for the things she believed important, even when she was challenged by the ambitious Senator Palpatine, whom she didn't trust. Despite Palpatine's opposition, Mothma was elected to the post of senior senator of the Republic—and was the last to hold that title.

Senator Bail Organa of Alderaan recognized the importance of the principled Chandrilan woman, and lent her his support. The two plotted to stop Palpatine from achieving senatorial presidency, but their plans failed. All too soon, Palpatine was not only president, but he had declared himself "Emperor" of the Republic. His allies in the Senate blocked all counter-efforts from the horrified senators such as Mothma, Organa, and the Corellian, Garm Bel Iblis.

Mothma began organizing cells of resistance, diverting funds into groups that were at first political in nature. Mothma's involvement with the growing Rebellion was discovered by Imperial secret police, and only a tip from Organa allowed her to escape Coruscant with her life.

A hunted woman, Mothma journeyed to a secret meeting in the Corellian system. Garm Bel Iblis had called on her and Organa to help bring about a unified leadership for a stronger Rebellion. So three main resistance groups came together, with many smaller ones being absorbed, as well. The resulting unification was called the Corellian Treaty. Mothma drafted a strongly worded Declaration of Rebellion that directly addressed the Emperor and his policies, and announced the formation of the Rebel Alliance. Palpatine was unimpressed and formally disbanded the Senate: the galaxy's last vestige of political freedom.

Bail Organa's involvement with the Rebellion remained miraculously undetected, and he retired to Alderaan, serving as its viceroy and chairman. Alderaan, a planet of peaceful people, became a planet of secrets, as Organa maintained his close ties to the freedom fighters now led by his close friend.

Mon Mothma proved inspirational, and was soon elected chief of state of the Rebel Alliance. She used her abilities to help diverse groups understand the need to work in concert in order to defeat the corrupt Empire. The central leadership she put in place brought about improved communications, rapid decision making, strong lines of authority and responsibility, and greater accounting and access to critical funds, supplies, vessels, and weaponry. Mothma delegated power to others, teaching them to inspire their own people and take initiative.

Rebel spies managed to steal plans for the Empire's new superweapon, a battle station known as the Death Star. On her way to deliver those plans, Princess Leia Organa and her crew were captured by Darth Vader. When Leia refused to give the Death Star's commander, Grand Moff Tarkin, the location of the main Rebel base, he decided to show her that the station was fully operational, firing on the planet of Alderaan and destroying it completely.

With Alderaan gone and Bail Organa killed, only one leader of the Rebellion had power equal to Mothma: Garm Bel Iblis. Their relationship deteriorated, and this began to affect the Alliance. Iblis accused the Chandrilan of wanting to usurp the throne of the Emperor and place herself in control of the galaxy. Mothma could not convince him otherwise.

When Mothma ordered an attack on an Imperial garrison on the planet Milvayne, in the Gyrica system, Iblis refused to follow her orders and broke away from the Alliance—taking many of his men with him. He formed his own guerrilla cell of fighters, and through the years, his group made many of their own successful attacks on the Empire. Though nowhere near as effective as the Rebellion, Iblis's group was a welcome aid to the Alliance. What Mothma didn't know was that Iblis still believed that she would one day turn the New Republic into a dictatorship, with herself as its head, and he was ready to strike if that happened.

Following the Battle of Yavin and the destruction of the first Death Star the Rebellion picked up many supporters. The Empire had been exposed in its tyranny, and galaxywide dissent bubbled just under the surface. Mothma was a tremendous delegate, spreading her beliefs in the freedom and the rights of all beings to inspire others to action. As the Rebellion engaged the Empire with hit-and-run tactics, the Rebels

gained both weaponry and prestige. They also proved that the Empire was *not* all-powerful, thus giving hope to those who had thought the situation hopeless.

The day following the destruction of the Death Star and the death of Palpatine, Wedge Antillies intercepted an Imperial drone ship carrying news from Bakura. The planet was under attack by an alien invading force, and the Imperials had been overrun and signaled for help from Palpatine's forces. Since Bakura had repulsorlift production facilities, Mothma cleared a strike team to proceed to the planet, including General Han Solo and, as ambassador, Princess Leia Organa, whom Mothma had begun to groom for political duties. Reluctantly, Mothma included a weakened Luke Skywalker in the team, as well.

The Bakuran mission was a success, and it further inspired the Rebel leaders. With the Empire in shambles and leaderless, Mothma stepped up the Alliance's plans to reestablish a New Republic. She began sending ambassadors to planets that had been under Imperial rule. Many immediately joined the Alliance, while some held back to see what the fallout of the galactic war would yield. Others were hostile, but Mothma wished to keep the Alliance clear of aggression unless action was absolutely needed. She and her Provisional Council were well aware how fragile and tenuous the balance of power was.

The Alliance maintained a number of new headquarters prior to settling on a permanent residence. These included bases on the moon of Endor and the forest planet of Arbra. Meanwhile, Mothma established a short-lived private strike team of the Alliance's most daring heroes, calling it the Senate Interplanetary Intelligence Network (SPIN). The team consisted of Leia, Luke Skywalker, Han Solo, Chewbacca, Lando Calrissian, R2-D2, and C-3PO. Ackbar and Mothma assigned them missions personally, though Mon Mothma eventually disbanded the special group in order to redirect her resources.

Finally, the Alliance High Command convened a Constitutional Convention to establish a second Galactic Republic. Months dragged on as politics were played and replayed, and even Mon Mothma's famous patience was tested. Finally, a provisional government was created to handle the running of the New Republic while formal details were discussed and ratified. This Provisional Council consisted of many of the same beings who had led the Alliance in the past, including Chief Councilor Mon Mothma, Commander-in-Chief Admiral Ackbar, Bothan Councilor Borsk Fey'lya, Alderaan Councilor Leia Organa Solo, Sullust Councilor Sian Tevv, Corellian Councilor Doman Beruss, Kashyyyk's Wookiee Councilor Kerrithrarr, and Elom Councilor Verrinefra B'thog Indriummsegh. Mothma expressed their main task as "To become the New Republic in fact as well as name."

While the Provisional Council was trying to deal with its political issues and struggles, the war against the Empire was continuing as skirmishes on the outer edges of the galaxy—and sometimes in the heart of it. A smaller group, the Inner Council, was formed, consisting of Mothma, Ackbar, Fey'lya, and Leia Organa Solo. The Inner Council helped serve the immediate day-to-day decisions facing the New Republic.

Eventually the New Republic decided to move its headquarters to Coruscant, once the seat of Emperor Palpatine. Luke Skywalker argued vehemently against the plan, especially moving into the Imperial City which had once caused so much trouble, but for Mon Mothma and the others who had once sat in the Senate on Coruscant, it seemed the correct message to send to the galaxy. The Empire was dead and conquered, and the New Republic sat benevolently in its place.

One of the greatest challenges that faced the Council came with the appearance of Grand Admiral Thrawn and his fleet. Mothma and Ackbar oversaw the battle at Sluis Van shipyards, and the resulting battle for control of the *Katana* Dreadnaught fleet, then faced an attack on Coruscant as Thrawn released invisible "cloaked" asteroids into orbit, stopping all ships from leaving the planet.

This led to the reuniting of Garm Bel Iblis and his forces with the New Republic. Princess Leia Organa Solo made the initial overtures, and Iblis discovered that his attitude toward Mothma had undergone a metamorphosis. He had come to understand Mothma's reluctance to entrust her people's lives to any other leaders. So Iblis stayed on, and his input and strategies came to be valued by the other Alliance leaders, including his longtime rival.

Within days of Thrawn's defeat, six Starfleet commanders joined with survivors of the Emperor's Ruling Circle to stage an assault on Coruscant. They succeeded in driving the New Republic away, and the New Republic placed their headquarters on the fifth moon of Da Soocha in the Syax system. From there, Mothma and the other Inner Council leaders dealt with attacks orchestrated by a "resurrected" clone of the Emperor, and in the midst of the battles, Mon Mothma and Luke both realized that, for the future of the New Republic to be certain, they needed a New Order of Jedi Knights.

In short order, the Republic launched a successful attack on Byss, and narrowly avoided disaster when the Da Soocha Pinnacle Base was destroyed by the Emperor-clone's Galaxy Gun. The Republic had abandoned the base shortly before the attack, and all the leaders survived to relocate to the abandoned floating space city of Nespis VIII.

Within months, they attacked the Imperial City on Coruscant yet again and succeeded

in driving the remnants of the Empire away. The New Republic Council resumed their attempts at restructuring an intergalactic government, and one of their first decisions was to approve Luke Skywalker's petition to build a new Jedi academy.

Mon Mothma, now chief of state, became busier and busier. For example, the efforts that went into one single day included working with Jedi trainee Gantoris to approve Dantooine as a relocation site for the settlers of Eol Sha, negotiating with Ugnaughts over salvage rights to destroyed spaceships in Coruscant's orbit, and meeting with Leia Organa about an upcoming ambassadorial reception.

That reception would prove to be a deadly one for Mon Mothma. Ambassador Furgan of Carida—the planet of the Imperial Academy—was attending the reception to negotiate conditions under which Carida would join the Alliance. Minister of State Leia Organa tried her best to be pleasant to the exceptionally irritating man, but when he threw a drink in Mon Mothma's face and denounced the New Republic, Leia could barely contain herself.

Over the following weeks, Mon Mothma's health began to deteriorate rapidly, her skin becoming gray and sunken. She passed more of her duties on to Leia, with-

drawing into her private chambers. When she was supposed to be on a four-day conference on Cloud City, she was really floating in bacta tanks, with medical droids and technicians trying desperately to halt a wasting disease that was consuming her body.

Finally, Mothma told Leia that she was dying. Seeking someone who could provide a moderate voice on the Council should Mothma succumb, Leia journeyed to Calamari to ask the estranged Ackbar to return to active duty with the New Republic, and eventually Ackbar did return, with distressing news. The Mon Calamari traitor Terpfen had revealed that Ambassador Furgan had poisoned Mothma with the drink he had thrown in her face. No known medicines would stop the progressive disease. With only a few days left to live, Mothma tendered her resignation but helped choose her replacement. Leia would be the new chief of state.

Luke Skywalker was training a Jedi student, Cilghal, who had Force talents in healing, and she was brought to Mon Mothma's side. After many hours of careful work, Cilghal was able to extract the poison from Mothma's system; the Republic's onceleader would survive.

But Mothma refused to take back her Council position. Knowing that the illness had made her weak—not only in body, but in the eyes of the New Republic—she felt that Leia was needed to lead the Republic forward strongly into the future.

For the galaxy was changing, and Mon Mothma had been through the changes and emerged older and wiser, but definitely more tired. As she looked to the future, decades of hard work and a legacy of tireless, selfless sacrifice behind her, Mon Mothma was confident that tomorrow would be glorious.

MOMAW NADON

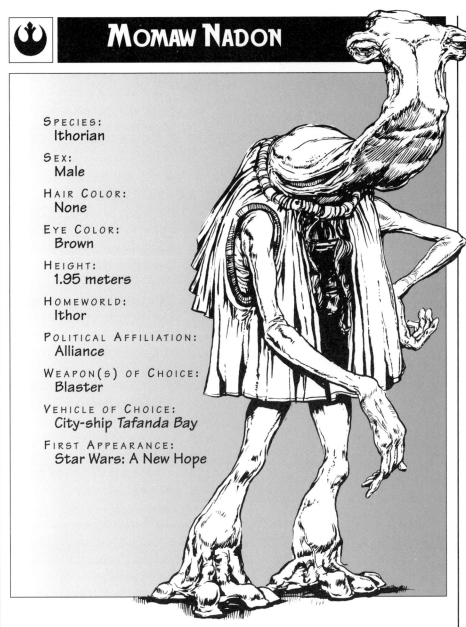

SPECIES:
Ithorian

SEX:
Male

HAIR COLOR:
None

EYE COLOR:
Brown

HEIGHT:
1.95 meters

HOMEWORLD:
Ithor

POLITICAL AFFILIATION:
Alliance

WEAPON(S) OF CHOICE:
Blaster

VEHICLE OF CHOICE:
City-ship Tafanda Bay

FIRST APPEARANCE:
Star Wars: A New Hope

A peaceful gardener on a paradise planet, Momaw Nadon never expected to be exiled to Tatooine or to ally himself with the Alliance.

Nadon is an Ithorian, a species called Hammerheads throughout the galaxy. Their heads are shaped like an "S," with long, curved necks topped by a T-shaped cranium. Ithorians have mouths on both sides of their curved necks, giving them an odd stereo sound when they speak. Their feet are spread out, and resemble thin tree trunks.

Ithor is an isolated paradise, almost completely undeveloped. Many of the Ithorians live in Herds, floating cities that migrate about the planet's three civilized continents. Still others travel throughout the galaxy in space-going Herds, selling unusual merchandise. The gentle, optimistic, peace-loving Ithorians prefer work in agricultural, artistic, diplomatic, mercantile, or space-faring fields. A select number choose to take on the mantle of ecological priests, keeping the "Mother Jungle" preserved and unharmed.

Momaw was once the high priest Herd Leader of the Grand Herd Ship *Tafanda Bay*, a grand planetary visitor's center full of beautiful vegetation and graceful plastisteel towers. Although initially oblivious to the evil spread of the Empire, he soon awoke to the evil growing outside Ithor. He was stunned when the Star Destroyer *Conquest* began orbiting the planet. The Imperials began scrutinizing and interrogating Ithorians, quietly at first, but more brazenly as months went by. The Herd leaders knew that something was amiss in the galaxy.

Aboard the *Tafanda Bay,* biospheres replicated every type of terrain and weather pattern known on Ithor and many other planets of the galaxy. The Empire wanted the agricultural secrets of the Ithorians, but for religious reasons, the Ithorians protected them strongly. The Imperials initially tried to entice several Hammerheads to spy for them, but none would. Tired of delays, the Imperials sent six people to raid the files in the *Tafanda Bay's* computer network.

When the spies were banished and the Herd ships closed to off worlders, the *Conquest* captain Alima became enraged. His men trained the Destroyer's turbolasers on the sentient forests of Cathor Hills, killing thousands of Bafforr trees. Alima then issued an ultimatum: either the Ithorians turn over their agricultural secrets, or he would begin to destroy the *Tafanda Bay*. It befell Momaw Nadon to reply to the Imperials. Seeing no way to avoid destruction of Ithor's nature, Nadon gave the Imperials the data they requested.

The Ithorians were angry, and Momaw was stripped of his power and put on trial. Although he gave an impassioned—and controversial—speech, Nadon was exiled from Ithor until the next Meet of the Herds, three Standard years later.

Wandering from spaceport to spaceport, Momaw eventually ended up on Tatooine, where he stayed for several years. There was little vegetation on the planet, and he felt he was doing penance by tending the sand and by using his agricultural knowledge to create new forms of plant life that would thrive on arid Tatooine.

With money from the investments he made, Nadon lived in an opulent, plant-filled villa in the midst of Mos Eisley. He had seven black-leaved Bafforr trees brought in, as well as a poisonous Arool cactus, a phosphorescent Gorsa tree, and a hungry Alleth plant. An underground, secret shelter for six beings was hidden underneath a large semi-intelligent carnivorous plant known as the Vesuvague Hanging Tree. He used the space to aid the Rebellion on missions to Tatooine, providing information and sheltering fugitives.

Before he left Tatooine, Nadon was able to exact his vengeance against the Empire. The recently demoted Lieutenant Alima had been stationed on Tatooine as punishment. When stormtroopers began questioning natives about two missing droids, Nadon had his Talz friend Muftak sell news of his aid to the Rebels to Alima.

Lieutenant Alima came to his house alone, sure that Momaw didn't have enough violence in him to be a threat. The Imperial killed a Bafforr, threatening Nadon that if he didn't find the missing droids through his Rebel contacts, his whole garden would be destroyed in front of him.

Angry enough to kill, Momaw purchased a blaster rifle and confronted Alima in an alley. The Hammerhead was tricked by the Imperial and stunned. With

less than a day left on Alima's deadline, Momaw planned how he would finally, irrevocably, kill the lieutenant. He went to the Mos Eisley cantina, where he sat with Muftak and Kabe, his spirits dark.

Momaw didn't pay attention when a fight broke out near the bar, but he was shocked at what he witnessed next. The old man, Ben Kenobi, used a Jedi lightsaber, fighting off an obnoxious human and an equally foul Aqualish. Nauseated by the bloodshed, Momaw left the cantina, but not before he had intuited that the droids Kenobi had brought into the bar were the same ones Alima was seeking.

As he returned home, Momaw prepared for his destiny. Then, laser shots rang out at a near-

by docking bay, and stormtroopers rushed from all over. As the *Millennium Falcon* blasted skyward, Momaw watched, knowing the droids were on board. Then, as Alima tried to find someone to blame, Momaw Nadon stepped forward.

The Ithorian called out to the captain, telling him that he had told Alima the previous evening that Solo would be escaping with the droids. In a rage at the traitor's actions, the captain shot Alima three times; Momaw watched in shock as the Imperials left the man's body cooling on the street. To atone for the death he had caused, Momaw took two genetic samples from Alima. He would use the cloning facilities on Ithor to create two lives from one death.

Following the death of Emperor Palpatine, Momaw departed Tatooine and returned to Ithor for the Meet. There, he was able to convince the convened elders to support the Alliance. Momaw was reinstated as Herd leader of *Tafanda Bay* and reunited with his wife and son. He continued to work hard to make amends for his perceived misdeeds. The twin Alima clones grew in peace and wisdom. When the Alliance asked for his help, Nadon was also quick to aid them.

When Wedge Antilles took the brilliant scientist Qwi Xux to Ithor for a vacation, Mon Mothma asked Nadon to be their guide—and protector, if need be. Nadon arranged for luxurious staterooms for the two Alliance members, then got them an open-air skimmer to allow them to sightsee above the pristine Ithorian landscape. But the Ithorian was not able to prevent Kyp Durron from sneaking into Qwi Xux's stateroom and erasing her memories with his dark-side Force talents. Whether this "failure" will drive Momaw Nadon back into depression and penance has yet to be seen.

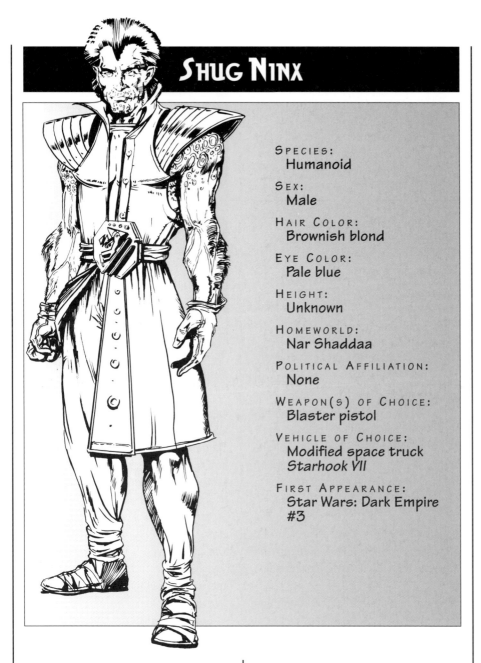

SHUG NINX

SPECIES:
Humanoid

SEX:
Male

HAIR COLOR:
Brownish blond

EYE COLOR:
Pale blue

HEIGHT:
Unknown

HOMEWORLD:
Nar Shaddaa

POLITICAL AFFILIATION:
None

WEAPON(S) OF CHOICE:
Blaster pistol

VEHICLE OF CHOICE:
Modified space truck
Starhook VII

FIRST APPEARANCE:
Star Wars: Dark Empire
#3

If the Empire hadn't hated half-breeds, Shug Ninx might have been one of their top pilots and mechanics. Instead, he wound up working against them.

With a Corellian father and a mother from the extinct Threelin race, Shug Ninx experienced the prejudice the Empire had fostered for half-breed human-alien mixes. The only visible signs of his alien parentage are mottled spots around his mouth and chin, and his strange two-fingered, one-thumbed hands. Shug's future was limited by his genes: he'd never be accepted into the Imperial Academy, or get work as a scout. If he were going to fulfill his dreams as a space-soaring free man, he'd have to build the opportunity himself.

Shug Ninx had an aptitude for fixing machinery and spaceships, and soon got jobs as a mechanic. He saved his credits, and when he had enough money to set up his own shop, he went to the smuggler's moon of Nar Shaddaa, where the crazy-quilt city and towers afforded a wealth of opportunity. He created his own spacebarn deep in the vertical city, quickly gaining a reputation as a miracle worker for damaged ships.

Shug was friendly with the up-and-coming smugglers and blockade runners, most of whom worked for the Hutt gangs. He became a father figure to many of them, including a cocky young Corellian named Han Solo. It was Solo who introduced him to the gambler pilot Lando Calrissian, a Wookiee named Chewbacca, and the stunning and capable Salla Zend. They and other spacers would often hang around the barn, talking, joking, drinking, and challenging Shug to races, or helping with repairs or modifications on the ships.

Sometimes there were problems, but Ninx or his main assistant, an ambidextrous Corellian named Warb, would handle them. A young Rodian named Greedo once tried to steal a pair of Dekk-6 power couplings meant for Solo's *Millennium Falcon*. Ninx caught the young thief, but Solo didn't want him killed. Instead, the Corellian humiliated the Rodian, and eventually took his rancor-skin jacket as a gift for Warb.

Eventually, Solo and Lando stopped coming around as much. After an accident in space lost Salla Zend her ship, she wanted to settle down with Han, but he wasn't ready. A rejected Salla showed up at Shug's spacebarn, looking for work. He brought her on board and eventually made her his business partner.

Over the next decade, Shug amassed a small fortune and a great reputation. He worked for wealthy crime lords as well as pirates and smugglers. Due to security problems, Ninx "acquired" a chute from the second Death Star, which he installed as the mile-long, well-guarded entrance to his spacebarn. Lateral-firing turbolasers destroyed any unauthorized ship that entered the chute. The space in front of the opening was rented out to a local fizzyglug drink company as a hologram billboard.

Six years after the second Death Star was destroyed, Shug's barn received some familiar visitors: Han Solo and Chewbacca, accompanied by Leia Organa Solo and the droid C-3PO. Han offered Shug and Salla 100,000 credits in cash for legal transport into the Deep Galactic Core, to the Emperor's homeworld of Byss. As Solo and Leia left to get replacement power couplings, Salla, Chewbacca, and Shug worked to finish installing the hyperdrive on Salla's *Starlight Intruder*. When word reached them that Han had been betrayed to bounty hunters, Shug and Salla took off with the *Intruder*, magnetically adhering the *Falcon* to its hull. Han and Leia rendezvoused with the *Intruder* astride a Hutt floater, and the ship left Nar Shaddaa.

The *Intruder* arrived at Byss and was allowed through the planet's security shields, docking at the Imperial freight complex at the outskirts of Emperor Palpatine's ruling city. Shug and Salla stowed away in the *Falcon* for the trip to Palpatine's Imperial Citadel. When Han and Leia allowed themselves to be captured, Salla took off with the *Falcon*, using the blasters to help take out the guards escorting the Alliance heros. They hid Solo's freighter inside a fellow smuggler's ship, the *Hyperspace Marauder*.

When trouble arose, Shug and Salla hotwired the circuits of a giant Arakyd Hunter-Killer droid, then used it to free Solo and Chewbacca.

Soon, Leia,

Luke, C-3PO, and R2-D2 joined them. Reboarding the *Falcon*, they fled through the atmosphere, jumping into hyperspace moments before the ship would have collided with the planetary shields. They fled toward Mon Calamari with security codes provided by Luke. Stored in R2-D2's memory circuits, the codes were transmitted to the destructive World Devastators, allowing the Alliance to disable and destroy them.

Weeks later, Shug and Salla accompanied Han, Chewie, and Leia back to Nar Shaddaa. When they finally arrived at Shug's repair facility, they found Darktrooper soldiers interrogating Warb and his repair droids. A firefight followed, in which Shug's prize starfighter was blown up by the *Falcon*'s lasers. Shug and the smugglers managed to shoot all of the Imperials, but the destruction had put out of commission all but the beat-up space truck *Starhook VII*.

While Leia and Han hunted for Vima-Da-Boda, Shug and Salla were attacked again by the Imperial Dark Siders. They left the smuggler's moon, taking the *Starhook VII* on a return trip to Byss in an attempt to recover the *Starlight Intruder*. They left Han and Leia a final message with one of the damaged droids in the mostly destroyed spacebarn: they should give up the Rebellion and think about making some money.

Shug bluffed his way through the Imperial gauntlet on Byss by posing as a maintenance worker with an order of obsolete parts for the *Hyperspace Marauder*. Shug and Salla met the *Marauder*'s captains, Lo Khan and Luwingo, in the Byss Bistro to discuss the best way to get the *Starlight* back. While lunching, they were surprised when the Alliance made an attack on the Emperor's citadel on Byss, using hijacked Viper Automadon war droids.

Salla decided that she and Shug should aid the Rebels, and gathered a team of smugglers to help. Using Shug's *Starhook VII*, Lo Khan's *Hyperspace Marauder*, and another

smuggler's ship, the *Bespin Bandit*, the ragtag crew joined the attack on the Emperor's citadel. Shug rescued several Alliance heroes, including Lando Calrissian, Wedge Antilles, R2-D2, and C-3PO. Surviving an attack by a Warbeast, the *Starhook VII* escaped into the skies, flying perilously close to the orbiting Galaxy Gun—the Emperor's fearful new superweapon. The smugglers and Rebels escaped into hyperspace, surprised to find they hadn't been fired upon.

Soon after, Shug and the gang of smugglers joined with the *Falcon* and three Alliance X-wings to defend New Alderaan from the Dark Siders and their AT-ATs. Shug and Salla touched down in the carnage to rescue Leia and her children, Luke and his Jedi initiates, Winter, and Vima-Da-Boda. The squadron of ships evacuated to the distant Auril system and the abandoned floating space city Nespis VIII, where the Alliance had formed a new base.

Shug doesn't see much money to be made by staying with the Alliance, but the *Starlight Intruder* is still in the hands of the Empire. Besides, Shug Ninx has more than a few frustrations to work out on the Imperials.

HET NKIK

SPECIES:
Jawa

SEX:
Male

HAIR COLOR:
Unknown

EYE COLOR:
Yellow

HEIGHT:
.96 meters

HOMEWORLD:
Tatooine

POLITICAL AFFILIATION:
None

WEAPON(S) OF CHOICE:
Jawa blaster

VEHICLE OF CHOICE:
Sandcrawler

FIRST APPEARANCE:
Star Wars: A New Hope

DEATH:
On Tatooine shortly before
Millennium Falcon's
escape

and at analyzing mechanical devices.

Tatooine's moisture farmers are prime targets for the Jawas' technological recycling sales. The scavengers also have a lot in Mos Eisley known as Jawa Traders, run by a female Jawa named Aguilae. Traders specializes in vehicle- and starship-repair droids, making it the perfect marketplace for a spaceport full of pilots and smugglers.

When he was young, Het Nkik and his best friend and clan-mate, Jek Nkik, stumbled upon a crashed fighter. Though most of it was unusable, they recovered a severely damaged E522-model assassin droid from the wreckage. Their clan leader, Wimateeka, watched the boys' progress even though they attempted to keep their work secret. When the youngsters unveiled the droid, fully repaired but without weaponry and reprogrammed for peaceful intentions, Wimateeka outwardly scolded them. Inside, though, Wimateeka admired their brashness. The two later sold the droid to the Whiphid, Lady Valarian.

Generally cowards, the Jawas have been known to fight, but only in defense. Their sandcrawlers have been attacked by Tusken Raiders, and by the monstrous krayt dragons that roam the Jundland Wastes. Their weapons are usually cobbled together from various technologies.

A member of Tatooine's scavenger species of Jawas, Het Nkik rebelled against his clan mentality, daring to challenge old ideas with new.

The Jawas are intelligent, rodentlike natives who scavenge the deserts and city alleys, looking for outmoded and abandoned hardware. The meter-high creatures wear rough-woven, homespun cloaks and hoods, protecting themselves from the fierce double suns. While their glowing eyes are visible under the hoods, and the smell of a Jawa is unmistakably nasty, few sentient beings have ever seen what a Jawa looks like without its hood. The diminutive scavengers understand Basic, but prefer to speak in their own language.

The Jawas roam Tatooine in giant, treaded fortress-homes known as sandcrawlers. Each crawler holds a Jawa community of about three hundred members. By repairing or rewiring droids and machinery that they pick up, Jawas can often make tidy profits on the desert throwaways. Despite their appearance and smelly living conditions, Jawas are excellent at repairs

The same summer that the Death Star was to be destroyed by a farm boy from Tatooine, Het Nkik traveled to the annual gathering of the clans. It was his third year to attend the event as an adult. He was still awed by the phalanx of sandcrawlers among the sand dunes, and by the hundreds of Jawas who set up a swap meet below, scurrying around like sand ants. Het looked forward to seeing his friend, Jek, who had been sent to another clan two years prior.

As he searched for his friend, Het smelled fear and concern from his clan leader, Wimateeka, who was talking with another clan's leader. The Tusken Raiders had attacked one Jawa fortress, and it was feared that Jek's clan's sandcrawler may have met a similar fate. Het argued with the elders, asking them why the Jawas hadn't fought the Sand People rather than fleeing them. Wimateeka could only apologize for the brash young Jawa.

As he rushed away, angry, Het was hailed by a Jawa trader from the Kkak clan. Expressing admiration for the young clansman's ideas, the Kkak Jawa produced a BlasTech DL-44 rifle. The weapon was for-bidden to Jawas, but Het bargained for it anyhow, coming away from the transaction with few credits left, but holding a powerful weapon in his hands.

Jek's sandcrawler never showed up, nor was any word received. When the meet ended, Het persuaded the sandcrawler pilot to move along the routes that Jek's clan might have taken. They came upon the smoking, burned-out wreckage of the crawler, and all but Het hurried to scavenge usable scrap. An elderly human and two droids stood near the crawler, disposing of the Jawa bodies in a crackling funeral pyre.

The man spoke to the new arrivals in the Jawa tongue, expressing his sorrow for the clan loss. Het studied the tracks and blaster marks made by the attackers. Though they appeared to be bantha tracks, and there were gaffi sticks all around, he could only smell the scents of plastisteel and lubricants. The smell of stormtroopers, not of Sand People.

The old man confirmed what Het told his clan leaders. He warned them that the Imperials would continue their attacks on both the Jawas and the Tusken Raiders, fomenting violence between the desert natives. "The Jawas are not powerless," the human told them, "if they do not wish to be."

As the old man stared at him, Het knew he had bought the blaster for a reason. He forfeited his share of the salvage from Jek's crawler in return for a small personal transport that would carry him to Mos Eisley . . . and the Imperials.

By the time he reached the spaceport, Het knew he needed a target for his anger . . . and his blaster. While he formulated a plan, he went into a cantina and ordered a drink. When he saw the old man and a young farm boy enter the cantina, he envisioned it as an omen of strength. Even more empowering was seeing the man's grace with the most dazzling weapon Het had ever seen—a lightsaber.

Before the Jawa could leave, a Ranat named Reegesk cornered him. The short trader offered him a bantha-horn, Tusken battle talisman. Het took it as another sign, and bargained for the charm, showing the Ranat his blaster. Grasping the blaster and the talisman, he went to make his dreams a reality.

Climbing the wreckage of the crashed ship *Dowager Queen*, the Jawa took a bead on a contingent of eight stormtroopers—a small contingent, but representing a larger blow for vengeance. Het knew he would probably die soon, but he would become Tatooine's most famous Jawa . . . the one who fought back.

With a close approximation of the Tusken war cry, Het Nkik rose from the wreckage and fired at the troopers, again and again. Unfortunately, nothing issued from the blaster—the brave young Jawa hadn't noticed that the Ranat had stolen its power pack. One of the troopers aimed and fired, blasting Het back into the wreckage. The Jawa was dead before he hit the sand.

The inspirational legend that Het Nkik sought for himself never came true; the Jawas remain as cowardly as ever, even after the fall of the Empire.

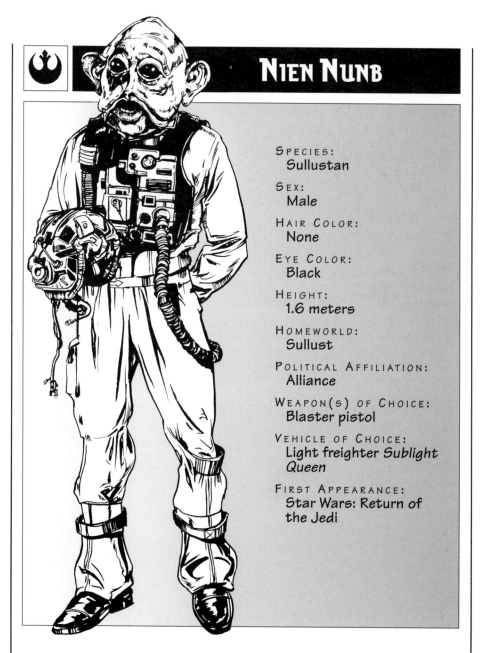

NIEN NUNB

SPECIES:
Sullustan

SEX:
Male

HAIR COLOR:
None

EYE COLOR:
Black

HEIGHT:
1.6 meters

HOMEWORLD:
Sullust

POLITICAL AFFILIATION:
Alliance

WEAPON(S) OF CHOICE:
Blaster pistol

VEHICLE OF CHOICE:
Light freighter *Sublight Queen*

FIRST APPEARANCE:
Star Wars: Return of the Jedi

A brilliant navigator and pilot, the Sullustan known as Nien Nunb played an integral part in the Battle of Endor and the destruction of the Empire's second Death Star.

Nien Nunb was a native of Sullust, a dark, volcanic planet. Like his fellow Sullustans, he grew up in the cool but humid cities that generations of Sullustans had built underground. Many of his people worked for the giant SoroSuub Corporation, a leading mineral-processing company that had energy, space-mining, food-packaging, and techno-production divisions throughout the galaxy.

SoroSuub had set itself up as the supreme authority on Sullust, issuing sweeping proclamations supporting the Empire's policies and dictates. Despite this, many Sullustans, including Nien Nunb, supported the Rebellion.

Tall for a Sullustan, Nien Nunb nevertheless carries many of the characteristics of his species; he is jowled, with large ears and round black eyes. The ears make him sensitive to the slightest sounds, while his large eyes allow him to adapt his vision for nocturnal activities and darkened caves. As with most Sullustans, Nien Nunb also has an enhanced sense of direction, giving him advantages in memorizing maps, pathways, star charts, or coordinates. As such, he makes an excellent navigator and pilot.

Nunb's ship was an older stock light freighter he had named the *Sublight Queen*. He used it as a trade runner for SoroSuub, carrying minerals and raw materials to outlying systems. It was during several of these runs that he met and became friends with the roguish gambler Lando Calrissian. When the corporation decided to support the Empire and take over the government of Sullust, Nien Nunb felt he could no longer work with them. He quit his job immediately, exiting in a hail of blaster fire and pursued by company starfighters. SoroSuub was sorry to see the dependable—and fast—pilot go.

They were even sorrier when Nunb utilized his smuggling skills against them. He publicly robbed SoroSuub consignments and shipped them to the Rebellion. As his notoriety grew, several other Sullustans decided to follow his example. Soon, SoroSuub was besieged by pirates supporting the Rebellion, and by low worker morale from the people who supported their "folk heroes."

SoroSuub officials called in the Empire to help, and a full complement of Star Destroyers was dispatched. In the ensuing battle, and in a later one against an Imperial blockade, most of the "outlaws" lost their ships. Nien Nunb and others escaped, deciding to join the Rebellion full time.

Lando Calrissian picked Nien Nunb to copilot the *Millennium Falcon* in the assault against the second Death Star. General Calrissian was Gold Leader, in charge of the attack, working under Admiral Ackbar. The Rebel ships needed a static starting point from which to coordinate their mass jump into hyperspace; they chose a location in orbit around the planet Sullust to amass

their forces. By this time, even the SoroSuub leaders had decided to surreptitiously support the Alliance.

Above the moon of Endor, the Rebel fleet attacked the Imperials, even though the Death Star's shields were still up. When the Rebel operatives on the surface of Endor blew up the shield generators, it freed Lando and the others to make their attack runs. Lando and Nien Nunb piloted the *Falcon* down the main reactor shaft, followed by several X-wings and TIE fighters.

The *Falcon* and Wedge Antilles's X-wing fighter made it to the reactor core. Wedge targeted the power regulator and Lando torpedoed the main reactor. Then the two ships had to retrace their perilous flight through the Death Star superstructure, even as it collapsed and exploded around them. With milliseconds to spare, Wedge and the *Falcon* escaped into open space. Behind them, the Death Star blew up.

Shortly after the destruction of the second Death Star, Nien Nunb copiloted the *Falcon* once again, this time with Han Solo, on a mission to a former Imperial prison planet. There they were supposed to pick up two of the Venerated Ones from the Metalsmiths Guild of Vandelheim but when they arrived, they discovered that the passengers-to-be were a teenage girl and a toddler boy.

Unfortunately, as they neared their final destination on Vandelheim, they flew the *Falcon* into an Imperial asteroid trap. Piloting through the space rocks, Han touched down on Vandelheim, delivering the children to the proper authorities.

Then when the guildmaster turned out to

be an Imperial sympathizer, Han was forced back to the *Falcon*, where Nien Nunb had been taken prisoner by a stormtrooper. Using quick action, Han, the two children, and Nien Nunb managed to free themselves, killing the trooper and dropping the traitorous guildmaster to his death. When more troopers attacked, Han and the kids were saved by Nien Nunb, wielding one of Chewbacca's blasters.

In space, Nien Nunb and Han defeated Imperial Admiral Mordur aboard his command barge above Vandelheim, thus saving a line of drone barges containing valuable ores and metals destined for the Alliance starship yards.

Nien later put his career on the line by helping Solo bluff the Godoans when they refused to heal an ailing Lando Calrissian. Lando had contracted an affliction while helping the Godoans, and Han threatened to start a military strike on their main city. Nien, Wedge, and other Alliance pilots backed Han up, even though Admiral Ackbar objected. Luckily, the Godoans agreed to treat Lando before they had to find out if Han was

bluffing.

When the Alliance leaders decided to abandon their temporary headquarters on the moon of Endor, they expected an attack by the aggressive N'Gai. Han was unable to fly at that time, so Chewbacca and Nien Nunb manned the *Falcon* in the space battle high in orbit. The Alliance fighters were able to successfully aide the handful of vacating New Republic diplomatic ships.

Finally, seven years after the Battle of Endor, Lando planned on reopening the spice mines of Kessel, teaming with Mara Jade and her Smugglers' Alliance to distribute the spice. Rather than use the slave labor that the Empire and Moruth Doole had used in the pitch-black mines, Lando planned to hire Nien Nunb to run the installation, with droids working the mines. The Sullustan agreed, and now works as administrator of Calrissian's profitable spice mines. But should the Alliance need his help again, Nien Nunb is only a holo away.

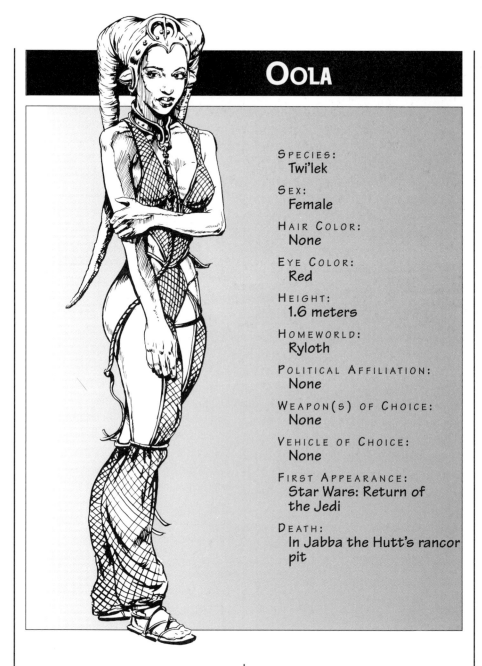

OOLA

SPECIES:
Twi'lek

SEX:
Female

HAIR COLOR:
None

EYE COLOR:
Red

HEIGHT:
1.6 meters

HOMEWORLD:
Ryloth

POLITICAL AFFILIATION:
None

WEAPON(S) OF CHOICE:
None

VEHICLE OF CHOICE:
None

FIRST APPEARANCE:
Star Wars: Return of the Jedi

DEATH:
In Jabba the Hutt's rancor pit

Thinking she would live a life of sensual luxury, the beautiful Twi'lek girl Oola allowed herself to become the property of Jabba the Hutt. It would prove to be a fatal misjudgment.

Oola had grown up on the harsh, windy planet of Ryloth, in a Twi'lek city on the dark side of the planet. Like all her people, she had twin tentacular appendages coming from the back of her skull, used for cognitive functions as well as sensual pleasures. The Twi'lek called these appendages *lekku*, although every-one else called them "head-tails" or "worms."

Slavers often scoured Ryloth, taking the Twi'leks into their ships for harsh service on other worlds. Often, the heads of the clan would sell their own people off to gain wealth or protection.

Oola, the daughter of a clan head, caught the eye of Jabba the Hutt's majordomo, Bib Fortuna. The beautiful young Twi'lek was a seductive dancer, her head-tails caressing and accentuating her ceremonial moves. Fortuna kidnapped Oola, taking her to his smuggling complex along with another tiny young girl, Sienn. There, they were trained by other slave dancers in even more seductive dances. Four months later, Fortuna felt the girls were ready. His assistant, Jerris Rudd, took them to Tatooine, where Oola dreamed of her luxurious life-to-be, relaxing on cushions and dancing for her handsome new master. After all, Fortuna was to present the two dancers as gifts to Jabba the Hutt, the most powerful and rich being on Tatooine.

At Mos Eisley, Rudd put Sienn and Oola into hiding. Something strange was going on at the spaceport. The dancers were surprised when a dark-cloaked young human approached them, telling them his name was Luke Skywalker. He offered to help them escape their slavery; he would take them off planet when his business with Jabba the Hutt was done. Sienn escaped with Luke, but Oola would not give up her dreams of her good life in Jabba's desert palace.

The dreams were shattered as soon as she arrived. Jabba was grotesque, his court filled with horrible creatures and a particularly bad band. The gang lord was smitten with the beautiful girl, and despite her refusal to dance for him, he added her to his harem. She would dance soon enough.

Two days later, Oola spoke conspiratorially with the protocol droid, C-3PO. He told her that Luke Skywalker was going to come to Jabba's palace to rescue his friends. Once again, Oola had hope. And then as the band struck up a jazzy version of "Lapti Nek," Jabba told her to dance. Buoyed by her thoughts of the young Jedi, Oola danced better than she ever had in the past, ending her performance with a supremely sensual pose. It was her best dance, and she had decided that it would be the last one Jabba would ever see her do.

Jabba pulled her closer, to caress and molest her. Protesting, she hung back, pulling on her neck collar and chain. And then Jabba released her, tired of the game. He pressed the button that opened the trapdoor to the rancor's pit, and Oola fell to her death.

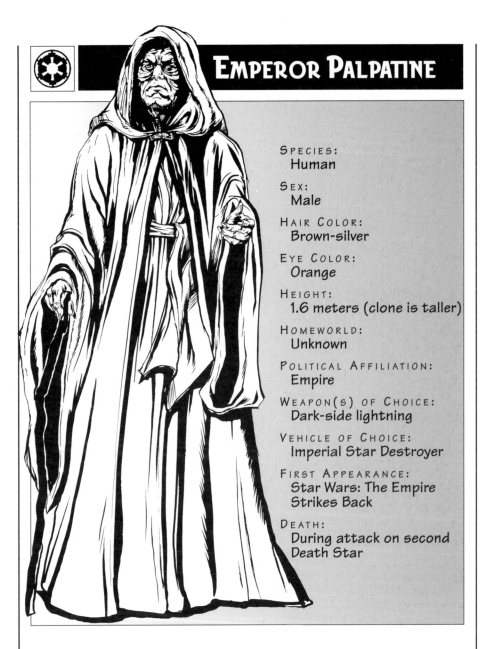

EMPEROR PALPATINE

SPECIES:
Human

SEX:
Male

HAIR COLOR:
Brown-silver

EYE COLOR:
Orange

HEIGHT:
1.6 meters (clone is taller)

HOMEWORLD:
Unknown

POLITICAL AFFILIATION:
Empire

WEAPON(S) OF CHOICE:
Dark-side lightning

VEHICLE OF CHOICE:
Imperial Star Destroyer

FIRST APPEARANCE:
Star Wars: The Empire
Strikes Back

DEATH:
During attack on second
Death Star

The dark side of the Force manifested itself in one man who was so malevolently evil that he would almost destroy the entire galaxy in his search for power. The name of Emperor Palpatine would resonate through the rivers of galactic history, a deep current of darkness and despair.

Palpatine's rise to power was a long one. The galaxy was ruled by the Old Republic for thousands of years, protected by a benevolent order of Jedi Knights. In time, the Old Republic grew too large, too heavily burdened with its own bureaucracy. It began to become corrupt from within.

Little by little, Old Republic senators began to be seduced by illegitimate power and wealth. Some allied themselves with huge corporate interests, others turned on their fellow senators, undermining, blaming, and corrupting. The Old Republic was falling, and the honest senators did not seem strong enough to shore it up.

Senator Palpatine, an unassuming man whose record was largely unimpressive, began his bid for power. Over the years, he had turned down placement on important advisory boards and powerful committees. He had been a quiet observer, and had gained very few enemies. He *seemed* to have a lack of ambition, which worked in his favor.

As the Old Republic and the Senate rotted and disintegrated, Palpatine moved forward, calling in favors and gaining support. A few in the Senate—Senior Senator Mon Mothma, Senator Bail Organa of Alderaan, and Garm Bel Iblis of Corellia—recognized Palpatine's machinations for what they were, and did their best to stop him.

Their best wasn't good enough. Republic worlds were tired of the corruption and social injustices. They wanted a strong leader to pull them out of the quagmire. Supported by big businesses and the other power-hungry senators, Palpatine ascended to the head of the Senatorial Council, then was elected president of the Republic.

Many Republic loyalists were taken in by Palpatine's astute political maneuverings, believing they would be able to use him to bring back the glory days of the galaxy. Those who wanted the power thought they could use Palpatine as a figurehead while they themselves continued to plunder in the background. The constituent worlds of the galaxy, on the other hand, saw a new leader whom they hoped would start the wheels of government turning again. None of them had any clue as to what was to come.

Once he was secure in his office and had established enough contacts, Palpatine introduced his New Order, and declared himself Emperor of the galaxy. He evoked almost mythic images of past empires and dynasties, promising to lead what was once the Old Republic to heights unparalleled in galactic history. The Empire was born.

The New Order caught on very quickly, often by force of arms. Senators who were too vocal or considered too dangerous were blackmailed or eliminated; termination orders were issued for Mon Mothma and Garm Bel Iblis. Mothma escaped, as did

Iblis, but his family was murdered.

It is unclear when the Emperor began using the dark side of the Force, or when he was finally consumed by it. Palpatine was opposed by the Jedi Knights, whose precepts decried his New Order. But the Jedi were few in number compared to the support he was amassing. His Imperial Army and Navy were growing, the young humans of the galaxy were volunteering or being forced into service in Palpatine's war machine.

But the Jedi weren't the only threats to the Emperor's rule. Many of the senatorial dissidents who had opposed him started a Rebel Alliance designed to bring back the Old Republic. Mon Mothma even dared send a Formal Declaration of Rebellion to Palpatine and the hypermedia. The Emperor wasn't terribly concerned with the underfunded and undermanned rebellion; in fact, he rather welcomed it. The threat of a rebellion would give him the excuse to wipe away most of the last remnants of the Old Republic.

Palpatine eventually grew tired of the battles with the Jedi, who, with their light side Force powers, might actually somehow turn the tide against him. So he and the newest Dark Lord of the Sith, Darth Vader, instigated a great Jedi purge. The men, women, and aliens who wielded the light side of the Force soon found that their lightsabers were no match for those who could turn the Force against them. The Jedi were all hunted down and killed, as were the majority of the children of the Jedi.

Palpatine set up a group of Force-sensitive candidates for training in different areas of the dark side. Some became the warrior-like Dark Siders, while others, such as Roganda Ismaren, became his companions. The beautiful young Mara Jade was shaped into an assassin and the perfect spy; as the mysterious "Emperor's Hand," Jade could travel the galaxy doing her Master's bidding. Palpatine could call to

Jade anywhere in the known systems, and she could communicate with him using the dark side.

Although he generally hated aliens, Palpatine did recognize that many of them had Force talents. He collected some of these Force adepts and took them to his citadel on Byss, where he initiated them in the powers of the dark side. All of those he taught, human or alien, were only taught enough to fulfill Palpatine's wishes. He did-

n't want any of them rising up against him. Bad enough that Vader was as powerful as he was, though Palpatine *was* certain of Vader's loyalty to the dark side.

The Empire continued to grow as each new planet was subjugated and enslaved. High-ranking officers soon found that new, *higher* ranks were instituted, giving them new incentive. Admirals could become one of the twelve Grand Admirals. World governors could become moffs of entire sectors of the galaxy, ruling many planets instead of one. Eventually, Palpatine instituted the rank of Grand Moff, granting control over a number of sectors, including priority sectors, to

one person. That one person would report directly to Palpatine.

The first Grand Moff was the ruthless and ambitious Grand Moff Tarkin, who was put in charge of Oversector Outer, which included almost all of the Outer Rim Territories. Tarkin crafted a brilliant document, extrapolating on the theories and practices of the Emperor. That document was implemented through the ranks of the Empire, and was officially known as the Tarkin Doctrine.

The Tarkin Doctrine offered two important elements. The first was a cogent and important plan for the Empire's future: "Rule through the fear of force, rather than the force itself." The second was to establish an invulnerable and powerful superweapon, part dramatic symbol, part real threat. Tarkin himself was developing plans for the weapon and he had established a hidden think tank of designers and scientists in a black-hole cluster known as the Maw. The Grand Moff didn't think the Emperor yet knew of his secrets, and intended to present the plans for any weapons developed himself, taking all the credit. Palpatine *did* know though, as he knew of Tarkin's ambitions.

Palpatine effectively set up a system whereby the Empire couldn't function without him. Once that system was in place, he became more distant and reclusive, seen only by those who needed to see him. His leaders and commanders would present the public face for him, while Darth Vader would present a public threat.

Along with the dark-side arcana that Palpatine continued to master, he studied much of the old knowledge put aside with the conquest of the Old Republic. Palpatine was fascinated with the Spaarti cloning cylinders, and hoped they might be used to clone his own bodies; he was old and frail already, and using the dark side was consuming him faster. Perhaps he could use the Force to transfer his spirit and mind into a younger, stronger clone, effectively giving him a fully sentient rebirth.

He experimented, creating a clone of the Jedi Master Jorus C'Baoth, who had once been Palpatine's Jedi advisor in the Old Republic Senate. He soon found that clones that were brought to maturity too fast had mental instabilities. At the same time, C'Baoth's clone had proven that clones did inherit sensitivity to the Force. The Emperor established a top-secret cloning

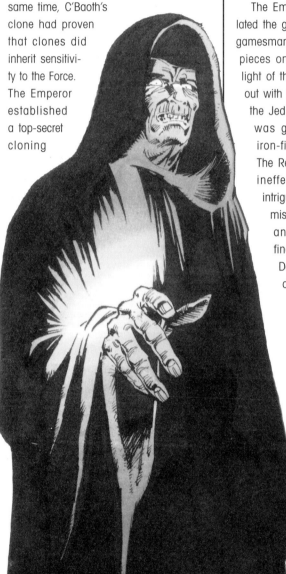

facility on Byss, growing dozens of clones of his own body—slowly, so as not to corrupt them. He placed some of the remaining Spaarti cloning cylinders in a weapons depot called Mount Tantiss, on the hidden planet of Wayland.

The Emperor had manipulated the galaxy like a master gamesman would manipulate pieces on a holoboard. The light of the galaxy had gone out with the extermination of the Jedi. The Old Republic was gone, replaced by iron-fisted Imperial rule. The Rebellion was largely ineffective, its petty intrigues and hit-and-run missions no more than an annoyance. And finally, Tarkin's superweapon, the Death Star, was ready to unleash on the galaxy.

All hope seemed lost.

Then hope erupted again, flashing brightly with the hiss of an ignited lightsaber. From the swirling desert of Tatooine, Jedi Master Obi-Wan Kenobi appeared, leading the son of Vader, Luke Skywalker, to his destiny. Darth Vader struck down Kenobi on board the Death Star, but the Jedi's spirit only strengthened the burgeoning Force powers in young Luke. Indeed, the youth almost single-handedly destroyed the Death Star.

The Rebellion suddenly had a major success to its credit and uprisings began on worlds throughout the galaxy. The Emperor kept track of progress, sure that his servants would triumph, but several years passed, and the Rebellion grew.

Both the Emperor and Vader knew Luke would be an important and powerful ally if he could be turned to the dark side. He could also be a powerful enemy if he became a Jedi himself. After Vader's failure to corrupt Luke on Bespin's Cloud City, the Emperor dispatched Mara Jade with instructions to kill Skywalker, but she, too, failed.

The Emperor had a backup plan, though. A trap was set in the Endor system, where a second Death Star was being built. Luke and other Rebellion heroes were lured to the forest moon where they would attempt to destroy an energy shield that protected the new battle station. Luke had not come for the shield, though. He turned himself over to Darth Vader, who took him to the Emperor.

Pitiably, Luke tried to impress Palpatine with his strength in the Force. He could never be turned to the dark side, or so he thought. When he was confronted not only with the destruction of the attacking Rebel fleet, but also with a prolonged lightsaber

attack by Darth Vader, Luke was weakened, but stood fast. He even offered Vader absolution if Vader reverted to the light side.

Then, Vader and Palpatine both gained access to Luke's innermost thoughts, those that protected his sister, Princess Leia Organa. "If you will not turn to the dark side, then perhaps she will," Vader threatened. It was the catalyst that broke Luke's Jedi calm. He ferociously attacked Vader, chopping at him with dazzling lightsaber attacks. And then, when Vader's hand was cut off and the Dark Lord was helpless, Luke confronted the Emperor, announcing, "You've failed, Your Highness. I am a Jedi, like my father before me."

Palpatine knew then that the younger Skywalker would join him, so he called on the dark side, throwing blue Force lightning into Luke. It crippled and incapacitated the young man, reducing him to writhing agony in minutes, but as Palpatine prepared to deliver the

killing bolts, Vader betrayed him.

The Dark Lord lifted his master into the air and threw him into the burning shaft of the power core. As Palpatine disappeared into the abyss below, Force lightning crackled around and through his body, and then the Emperor was gone. Minutes later, Darth Vader also died, Luke escaped, and the Death Star was destroyed.

The leadership of the Empire was dead, leaving turmoil and disarray. Palpatine's inner circle of ministers and governors attempted to take control, as did dozens of rogue Imperial warlords. The Empire dwindled in size and power, even as the New Republic was born out of the rise of the Rebel Alliance. Pretenders to the throne, like Trioculus and the dark-side prophet Kadann, appeared and were defeated.

The Dark Side Adepts at the Emperor's citadel on Byss stayed out of most of the battles, biding their time. A very few of them knew what was to come. The Emperor's clones were still alive, and were young, strong, and vital, secure inside their cloning

cylinders. And one of them had achieved sentience a year after the destruction of the second Death Star, claiming to be the embodiment of Palpatine's essence that was released upon his death.

The clone rested and gathered its strength for six years, training seven of his best adepts to be Dark Jedi. Meanwhile, the New Republic gained power, and fought against Grand Admiral Thrawn. As time went on, Luke Skywalker became a Jedi Master, with his own students. Leia, too, was training in the Force, and her twin children and unborn child showed tremendous potential in the Force.

For a short time, Luke Skywalker accepted training under the Palpatine clone, intending to destroy the dark side from within. Palpatine guarded against that destruction, and actually succeeded in bringing Luke over to the dark side, for a time. Finally though, Luke and Leia's combined strength helped defeat the reborn Emperor.

Later that year, the Emperor reappeared in another clone body. With the aid of Military Executor Sedriss and his elite dark-side warriors, he intended to have Leia captured so that he could turn her unborn child to the dark side. The new Palpatine ordered an attack on the Alliance headquarters on the moon of Da Soocha, to be carried out using his superweapon, the Galaxy Gun.

That attack was only partially successful, as the Alliance had abandoned the base, and likewise the Emperor clone's strike force of Dark Siders was unsuccessful at capturing Leia and her children, or at killing Luke.

Luke Skywalker knows that the Emperor has a limited supply of clones, but the capacity to create more. Palpatine himself is terrified of a "final" death, which will lead to his perpetual madness as a disembodied spirit, adrift in the dark side of the Force.

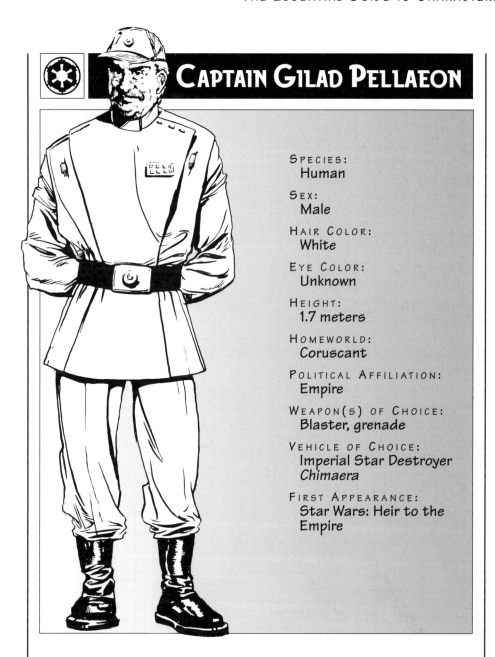

CAPTAIN GILAD PELLAEON

SPECIES:
Human

SEX:
Male

HAIR COLOR:
White

EYE COLOR:
Unknown

HEIGHT:
1.7 meters

HOMEWORLD:
Coruscant

POLITICAL AFFILIATION:
Empire

WEAPON(S) OF CHOICE:
Blaster, grenade

VEHICLE OF CHOICE:
Imperial Star Destroyer
Chimaera

FIRST APPEARANCE:
Star Wars: Heir to the
Empire

With over fifty years of service to the Imperial fleet, Captain Gilad Pellaeon has seen the rise of the Empire and the fatal blows struck it at the Battle of Endor. With the rise of Grand Admiral Thrawn, Pellaeon found hope.

Fifty years prior to the destruction of the first Death Star, Pellaeon was a young Corellian who lied about his age to get into the Imperial Academy. He graduated in the top third of his class.

Ensign Pellaeon's first command assignment was to take a squadron of transport vessels to the planet Garvyn. They were stopped by pirates, but Pellaeon managed to trick and destroy the pirate vessel. For his quick thinking, he was promoted to the command crew of the Star Destroyer *Chimaera*, and worked his way up to second in command. Among the ship's missions were several slaving runs to Kashyyyk, where the Empire captured Wookiees to use as slaves.

During the Battle of Endor, when the second Death Star was attacked by Rebels, Pellaeon took command of the *Chimaera* after the captain was killed. Reluctantly, he ordered the few other surviving ships to withdraw as the hopes of the Empire exploded before their eyes. Emperor Palpatine was dead, as was his right-hand man, Lord Darth Vader.

Five years passed, and Pellaeon worked with others to bring the remnants of the Empire back to power. Finally, Pellaeon got a new commander—Grand Admiral Thrawn—who chose the *Chimaera* as his new base ship. Unlike Pellaeon's previous commanders, Thrawn actually welcomed his opinions, even if they were dissenting.

Pellaeon commanded the *Chimaera* in the Battle of Sluis Van. Acting on Thrawn's orders, he hired Niles Ferrier and Mara Jade to find the long-missing *Katana* Dreadnaught fleet.

The Dark Jedi Joruus C'Baoth caused major problems for Pellaeon when, in a show of power, he seized control of the officers aboard the *Chimaera,* using his darkside powers. Then, when Pellaeon was preparing to lead the Imperial fleet in an attack on Coruscant, the Dark Master decided to go to Wayland to take charge of its facilities. C'Baoth was completely unstable, but Thrawn seemed to think that he had all the cards in his favor, and that C'Baoth would not be an impediment to the return of the Empire.

Pellaeon knew better; Thrawn was overestimating everyone's loyalty and abilities. The attack on Coruscant failed. On Wayland, C'Baoth was killed by Luke Skywalker and Mara Jade. The Battle of Bilbringi that involved the *Chimaera* and the Imperial fleet was not going well. And then, almost as if insult and injury were not enough, Rukh, Thrawn's Noghri bodyguard, killed his master.

Thrawn would have somehow snatched victory from the Rebels at Bilbringi. But Pellaeon was not Thrawn. He knew that, if the Imperials regrouped in the Core systems, they would live to fight another battle. If they stayed, they would be defeated. Pellaeon called a retreat, and his armada vanished into the realms of hyperspace.

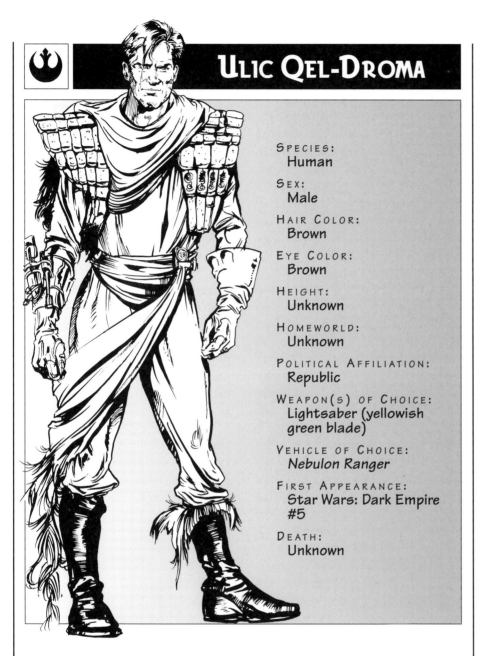

ULIC QEL-DROMA

SPECIES:
Human

SEX:
Male

HAIR COLOR:
Brown

EYE COLOR:
Brown

HEIGHT:
Unknown

HOMEWORLD:
Unknown

POLITICAL AFFILIATION:
Republic

WEAPON(S) OF CHOICE:
Lightsaber (yellowish green blade)

VEHICLE OF CHOICE:
Nebulon Ranger

FIRST APPEARANCE:
Star Wars: Dark Empire #5

DEATH:
Unknown

Four thousand years prior to the Jedi awakening of Luke Skywalker, another young Jedi, Ulic Qel-Droma, began his own path with the Force. Unfortunately for the galaxy, Qel-Droma eventually turned to the dark side, and the results were catastrophic.

Force talents ran in the Qel-Droma family. Both Ulic and his younger brother, Cay, had great potential to learn the ways of the Force. The brothers began their training on the mining world of Arkadia, home to Jedi Master Arca Jeth and his other Jedi student,

the Twi'lek Tott Doneeta. Ulic learned quickly, mastering the art of lightsaber dueling. Those who watched him thought he was arrogant; those who knew him recognized that he was brash, adventurous, and confident.

After years of training, Master Arca felt the Jedi trio was strong enough to go on its first mission: travel to the planet Onderon to help quell the centuries-old civil war between city dwellers and outland lawbreakers.

Maneuvering their ship, the *Nebulon*

Ranger, through the attack of the outland Beast Riders did little to give the Jedi hope. They landed at a docking tower atop the royal citadel in Iziz, and soon met the haughty Queen Amanoa and her daughter, Galia. The Jedi soon got to show their talents; the Beast Riders had discovered a breach in the perimeter and attacked the citadel. In the ensuing battle, Beast Riders made off with Galia. Ulic vowed to save the queen's heir, despite Cay and Tott's misgivings that something seemed out of place among the Onderonian city dwellers.

Their *Nebulon Ranger* had been shot down by the outlanders, so the Jedi utilized Tott's Force talent in talking to beasts to provide themselves transportation. They arrived in Modon Kira's forest stronghold just in time to save Galia from a forced marriage to Modon's son, Oron. What they found surprised them, though: Galia wanted to marry the Beast Lord, and the outlanders were the ones who wanted peace!

Even more shocking was the history of Iziz. The city was full of dark-side Force power, brought to it four hundred years earlier by a Sith Lord named Freedon Nadd. Both Galia's ailing father, King Ommin, and

her mother were one with the dark side. The king was dying, kept alive only by machinery, but the queen had managed to make trouble.

Ulic felt he could still negotiate peace—as was his mission there—and asked Galia and Oron to come with him to speak to the queen. If they couldn't find grounds for a truce between the Onderonians, the Jedi would join the Beast Warriors in their attack in Iziz. Not surprisingly, the enraged Queen Amanoa launched a dark-side attack on them, disowning her "traitorous" daughter. Grudgingly, the Jedi signaled the Beast Warriors to begin their massive attack on Iziz. In the ensuing battle, Cay's left arm was cut off.

The battle was won by the Beast Warriors with the help of Master Arca, who had arrived on his ship and used his Jedi powers to influence the tide of the war. Arca was disappointed in his students, but realized that the dark side of the Force was so strong on Onderon that they would have almost surely failed anyhow.

Investigating the source of the dark-side power, Arca and his students found the crypt of Freedon Nadd. Opening it killed Queen Amanoa, but freed Galia of her own dark-side destiny. She and Oron were married soon after, and their union brought peace to the planet for the first time in centuries. Afterward, as Cay tinkered with his new robotic arm, Ulic questioned Arca. How could Freedon Nadd, a Jedi, have fallen to the dark side? "It has happened more than

once," his Master warned. "Pray that it never happens to you."

The peace did not last long. Followers of Freedon Nadd and the dark side were fomenting insurrection against Queen Galia. Arca and his Jedi returned to the planet to keep peace, and were soon joined by a fourth Jedi, Oss Willum. At Arca's suggestion, Nadd and Queen Amanoa's sarcophagi were to be transported to the moon of Dxun. Before the funeral ships could take off, the Nadd followers attacked, stole the sarcophagi, and escaped.

Galia led Master Arca and his Jedi to her father, who introduced them to the spirit of Freedon Nadd, not resting in the Force, but held to Onderon by his Sith magic. King Ommin revealed his strength in the dark side, attacking and defeating Arca with dark lightning. No longer invalid, he captured Arca, stealing him away as Ulic defended his daughter against Nadd's followers. Ulic put out a call to Ossus, a Jedi stronghold world, and to Coruscant, home of the Galactic Republic. More Jedi and the Republic warriors were needed on Onderon to stop the Freedon Nadd uprising. The team of Jedi chosen for the task included Dace Diath, Shoaneb Culu, Grrrl Toq, Kith Kark, and Nomi Sunrider.

The Jedi ship arrived at the ruling city of Iziz as Galactic Republic forces stormed its walls to fight the followers of Freedon Nadd. Meanwhile, the Jedi responded to Ulic Qel-Droma's distress beacon coming from inside Modon Kira's forest citadel. With the help of the five other Jedi, Ulic and his forest warriors were able to turn the tide of the battle.

The united Jedi soon tracked their way to King Ommin's subterranean lair. In a righteous rage, Ulic used his lightsaber to cut through the iron exoskeleton that allowed Ommin to walk, causing the old man to collapse. The evil spirit of Freedon Nadd appeared, pulling Ommin's dying spirit into the dark side, and bid the Jedi farewell, promising that though they thought they had won the battle, in the future they would find that they had lost.

As the Onderonians repaired their cities and their lives, the Jedi stayed, protecting and exploring. Ulic and Nomi grew fond of each other, but tragedy was to strike. Freedon Nadd had given Sith teachings to Satal Keto and Aleema, two spoiled heirs to the throne of the Empress Teta system. Now, using their Sith magic as part of a group of dark-side magic users known as the Krath, Satal and Aleema were spreading the ways of the Sith.

Most of the Jedi returned to Ossus to deal with the problem, leaving Master Arca, Ulic, Cay, Nomi, and Tott behind on Onderon. Cleaning up Freedon Nadd's Sith materials, Ulic found a talisman . . . and the spirit of Freedon Nadd, still able to take form. Nadd told Ulic he would become one of the greatest of the Sith Lords, but that another would be greater still. Confident as always, Ulic knew that Nadd was trying to goad him.

Master Arca soon assigned Ulic and Nomi to lead the joint peacekeeping fleet of the Galactic Republic and the Jedi Knights. As the fleet emerged from hyperspace to protect the planet Koros Major, the Krath ruler Aleema attacked. In the battle that followed, Ulic was hit in the side by a piece of shrapnel. Nomi pulled it out, willing the Force to heal him. Overwhelmed by the Krath ships, the Republic commander ordered his fleet to retreat. A show of force hadn't worked. A new attack strategy was needed.

Ulic Qel-Droma was made watchman of the Empress Teta system, but his job soon became more complicated. The Krath let it be known that they had declared war on the Jedi Knights. Most of the Jedi in the galaxy converged on the red planet of Deneba, meeting atop Mount Meru to discuss their plans. Addressing the gathering, Ulic argued that to engage the Krath in war would do no good and would lose thousands of lives. He proposed instead to allow one person—himself—to infiltrate the Krath and find the secrets of their growing power in the Sith ways.

Much discussion followed, but before a decision could be made, the Krath unleashed a set of war droids upon the Jedi. In the battle, Master Arca was cut down, his spirit joining with the light side of the Force even as his student held him. Ulic would conquer the dark side and destroy it from within. He would avenge his fallen Jedi Master.

Despite the warnings of many Jedi Masters, Ulic stood firm. Boarding a smuggler's freighter, the *Kestrel Nova*, he departed for the Empress Teta system.

His arrival in Cinnagar, the ruling city of the system, did not go unnoticed by Aleema and Satal Keto, but Aleema wanted Ulic kept alive. She arranged a staged assassination attempt for the following day, and Ulic fell right into her trap.

Satal didn't trust Ulic, and injected him with a Sith poison. If he was loyal, he would live. He lived, but the poison also lived within him. Another test followed months later. The Krath guards had captured Nomi Sunrider, who had come to see how Ulic was doing. Satal asked Ulic to execute the Jedi woman to prove his allegiance to the Krath. Unable to avoid Nomi's accusing eyes, Ulic agreed to kill her at dawn. But Satal discovered Ulic still felt allegiance to the Jedi, and tried to have him assassinated. Ulic survived.

Nomi escaped before

morning, and she called Ulic's brother, Cay, and Tott Doneeta to the citadel from their planetary orbit in the *Nebulon Ranger*. Although the trio of Jedi valiantly attempted to save Ulic, the Sith poison within his system lowered his defenses and shields. Roiling anger exploded inside him. Striking down Satal in revenge, Ulic was consumed by the dark side. As Nomi, Cay, and Tott escaped from the planet, Ulic knew that his path had no return. He was no longer one of them.

Aleema gave Ulic a Sith amulet that the late Satal had gotten from Freedon Nadd's spirit. She teased him for a moment, and then the city erupted in the screams of fighter ships. Nomi had led the Jedi back to Cinnagar in one more attempt to rescue Ulic from the dark side. Attacking the Krath stronghold, Nomi faced down Aleema, destroying her Sith illusions. Then Cay and Nomi tried to make Ulic confront how deeply he had become enmeshed in the dark side, but their arguments only made him angrier. He lashed out, striking Nomi with a bolt of dark-side lightning. The Jedi woman finally knew then that Ulic was lost. Sadly, Nomi and the other Jedi turned their backs and left. Cay was the last to leave, silently promising himself he'd be back at the earliest opportunity.

Watching the Jedi leave the city, Ulic Qel-Droma and Aleema were surprised to be confronted again, this time by Exar Kun, main inheritor of the Sith powers. The Dark Jedi blasted Aleema with his power and ignited his lightsaber to face Ulic. As they battled, equally matched, their Sith amulets began to glow. Crackling energy filled the air, and then they saw a Sith Lord speaking to the future from the past like a Dark Holocron.

The creature in the vision bestowed the title of Dark Lord of the Sith on Exar Kun, and the title of Sith Apprentice on Ulic Qel-Droma. Each of them was branded with tattoos on their foreheads, dark symbols from an evil power. "The ancient Sith have spoken," Exar

Kun said. "Together we will bring down the galaxy."

For several years, nothing was heard of Ulic Qel-Droma, though Aleema survived and led the Krath. Then, Ulic reappeared with tremendous powers of the dark-side and the Sith. He served alongside the Sith Lord, Exar Kun, but commanded his own Krath sects. Ulic's followers were extremely militaristic and bloodthirsty. Ulic cut a galaxywide swath of conquest, pillage, and destruction, amassing a great armada of warships as he went.

The Republic declared Qel-Droma an enemy even as the Krath Lord declared himself an enemy of the Jedi. Aleema joined forces with Ulic and Kun, using her dark-side talents in connection with their own, and her followers with theirs.

The resulting conflict between the Krath and the Jedi was—as Ulic himself had once predicted when he was a Jedi—one of the largest and bloodiest wars the galaxy ever witnessed. It was the Sith War, the first war in which dark-side powers were used on such a massive scale, and the armies of the Sith and the Krath were responsible for millions of deaths.

In the end, Ulic Qel-Droma betrayed Exar Kun, leading the assembled Jedi to the Sith Lord's base of power on the moon of Yavin Four.

THE MAX REBO BAND : SY SNOOTLES/MAX REBO/DROOPY McCOOL

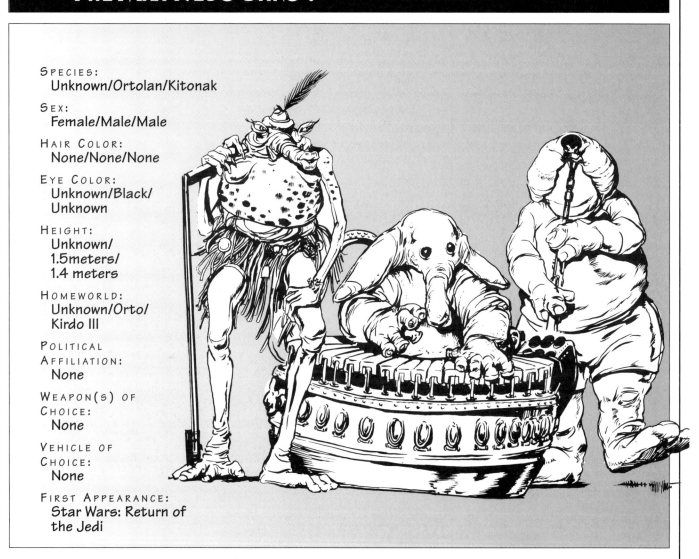

SPECIES:
Unknown/Ortolan/Kitonak

SEX:
Female/Male/Male

HAIR COLOR:
None/None/None

EYE COLOR:
Unknown/Black/
Unknown

HEIGHT:
Unknown/
1.5meters/
1.4 meters

HOMEWORLD:
Unknown/Orto/
Kirdo III

POLITICAL
AFFILIATION:
None

WEAPON(S) OF
CHOICE:
None

VEHICLE OF
CHOICE:
None

FIRST APPEARANCE:
Star Wars: Return of
the Jedi

A multispecies jizz band is no surprise in the galaxy, but the Max Rebo Band is unusual enough to draw stares from any crowd. The leader of the group is Max Rebo, a squat Ortolan with floppy ears, a snout, and bright blue, velvety fur. Originally from the planet Orto, in the Orto system, Rebo has very acute senses. His people's main priority in life is food and the consumption thereof.

Because of their highly developed sense of hearing, the Ortolans love music. Besides leading the band, Max Rebo plays keyboard on his Red Ball Organ.

Droopy McCool—born with the name of Snit—is a member of the Kitonak species, a lumpy, pudgy people with almost inpervious leathery skin. His home planet, Kirdo III, is a white-desert world, prone to tremendous windstorms. The Kitonak are an extraordinarily patient nomadic race, following their main food, Chooba slugs. The Kitonak often hollow chidinka plants to create flutelike instruments and play songs of love. Unfortunately for some of the better musicians, slavers with an ear for music have been known to capture them and bring them into the galaxy to work as jizz wailers in seedy saloons, cabarets, and cantinas.

The third member of the group is Sy Snootles, the reedy-voiced lead singer. Standing on spindly legs, with a bulbous body and lips that jut out at the end of a proboscis, Snootles looks like a gourd on stilts. Her yellowish green skin with its blue blotches completes the bizarre look.

The trio had originally been in a band named Evar Orbus and His Galactic Jizz

Wailers. The lead singer, Evar Orbus, was an eight-tentacled Letaki, puffed with pride until a gang of Bith musicians mugged the quartet. Orbus had a hidden flamethrower in a fake tentacle, but all that succeeded in doing was causing the repulsorlift airbus carrying the Bith and the band to crash. As the quartet escaped, Orbus was shot and killed.

Soon, the renamed band made contact with Jabba the Hutt. The gang lord liked them and offered a lifetime contract, paying

with all the food they could eat. Rebo agreed, thinking it was the finest contract he had ever heard of. Sy just glared. So did Droopy, who had enough slugs in a crated stasis field to last for years.

Looking for additional ways to make money, Sy was pleased when the droid M3-D2 approached her to spy for Lady Valarian. And then sixteen others arrived, one after the other, all asking her to spy for them or their masters or mistresses. Sy was also contacted by Jabba's Twi'lek lieu-

tenant, who told her to take the commissions but report to him. He would give her the information to leak out, and Jabba would also pay her.

Meanwhile, Max made friends with the cook, and Droopy learned something interesting from one of the Gamorrean guards: the pig had seen a group of Kitonaks in the deep desert of Tatooine!

The band continued to play, watching the ever-changing menagerie of Jabba's court room and the internal politics and per-

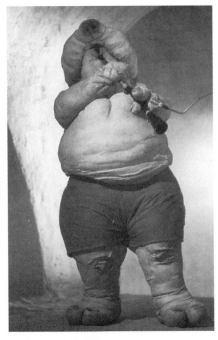

sonalities that appeared and disappeared as credits were exchanged or lives ended. Eventually a woman whom Max recognized as being from the Royal Family of Alderaan was taken captive, and then a Jedi. The band was called on to play in the lower levels on Jabba's sail barge at an execution of the Jedi and a pair of smugglers.

Max looks back on that day with mixed memories. The princess had killed Jabba, ending the band's bountiful contract, and her friends had caused the destruction of the sail barge. The band members had barely escaped with their lives, jumping into the sand, leaving their instruments behind.

But Max Rebo knows that his band will play again.

REE-YEES

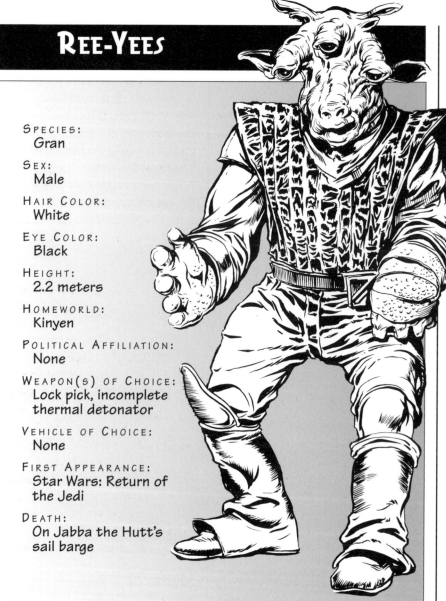

SPECIES:
Gran

SEX:
Male

HAIR COLOR:
White

EYE COLOR:
Black

HEIGHT:
2.2 meters

HOMEWORLD:
Kinyen

POLITICAL AFFILIATION:
None

WEAPON(S) OF CHOICE:
Lock pick, incomplete thermal detonator

VEHICLE OF CHOICE:
None

FIRST APPEARANCE:
Star Wars: Return of the Jedi

DEATH:
On Jabba the Hutt's sail barge

almost destroyed by loneliness until he got off planet. He survived by imbibing copious amounts of liquor—especially Sullustan gin—and by becoming surly, unpleasant, self-centered, and a credit-ante thief. Of course, were he ever sober, Ree-Yees might have noticed that those very traits were ostracizing him more than the Gran decree ever had.

Somehow, Ree-Yees ended up in the court of Jabba the Hutt. Although everyone there grew to despise him, Ree-Yees wasn't killed by the gang lord. Perhaps Jabba was amused at the reaction to the foul creature or at the fights the Gran often had with the much tougher Ephant Mon, or Tessek, the Quarren lieutenant.

Ree-Yees tended Bubo, the grotesque watchdog the Jawa had brought into the palace. What no one knew was that Ree-Yees was using a transmitter hidden among Bubo's boils and skin flaps. The Empire had provided him with a detonator with which to kill Jabba, shipping the components in packages of Gran goatgrass. In return, they would wipe out Ree-Yee's murder record and he would be able to return to Kinyen.

When Jabba and his court went to the Pit of Carkoon to feed a group of Rebels to the Sarlacc, Ree-Yees accompanied them. The humans escaped, and Ree-Yees discovered that it was not his destiny to kill Jabba. The Rebel woman killed the Hutt in front of him while he did nothing.

And then, as the sail barge exploded, Ree-Yees knew that he was to die in the fire. It was a sobering thought. His last.

The three-eyed, goat-faced Gran thief known as Ree-Yees was not liked by anyone at Jabba the Hutt's palace. How he ever escaped being murdered is a mystery lost to the ages.

Ree-Yees was one of the Gran species of the peaceful planet Kinyen. All the Gran had three eyestalks, and the women also had three breasts. They roamed the planet, eating sweet goatgrass and mating.

When Ree-Yees murdered another Gran, he was outcast from his people. Highly social, as were all the Gran, Ree-Yees was

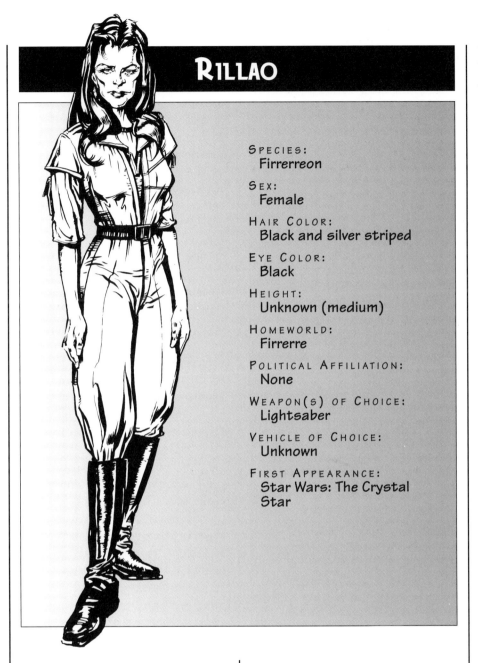

RILLAO

SPECIES:
Firrerreon

SEX:
Female

HAIR COLOR:
Black and silver striped

EYE COLOR:
Black

HEIGHT:
Unknown (medium)

HOMEWORLD:
Firrerre

POLITICAL AFFILIATION:
None

WEAPON(S) OF CHOICE:
Lightsaber

VEHICLE OF CHOICE:
Unknown

FIRST APPEARANCE:
Star Wars: The Crystal Star

Once tutored by Darth Vader, and later imprisoned by her husband, Rillao was all that stood between destruction and the Alliance's Jedi children.

The beautiful, golden-skinned woman comes from a proud race of Firrerreons. People of her race are not allowed to have their names spoken aloud, for they believe that gives the speaker power over them.

As a young woman, Rillao had strong Force abilities, which brought her to the attention of Darth Vader. She began training with him, and met another student, a Firrerreon named Hethrir. Unfortunately for Vader, Rillao would not embrace the dark side; she was a healer and a light-side user, but when she became pregnant, Vader had high hopes for turning the child.

The Dark Lord of the Sith appointed Hethrir as his Procurator of Justice, and asked the corrupt Jedi for proof of his loyalty. Hethrir abducted freighters full of his own people, exiling them from their home planet of Firrerre, then destroyed his homeworld, killing millions, most of them children.

Horrified at her mate's actions, Rillao took herself and her unborn child into hiding. The child was a boy, whom she named Tigris. He had no Force abilities at all, and she raised him in peace and solitude.

With the fall of the Empire, Hethrir refused to free the hundreds he had exiled. He sold many as slaves, and kidnapped children from other planets, as well. They would either be sold as slaves, or, if they had Force talents, they would be trained in the dark side.

Eventually Hethrir found his mate, took his son away, and imprisoned Rillao in a weblike torture device on a dead slave freighter abandoned deep in hyperspace. Hethrir kept Tigris as his personal servant, not revealing that he was his father, and convinced the boy his mother was a traitor.

Rillao might have died had not Princess Leia Organa Solo and Chewbacca arrived. They were searching for Leia's children, who had been kidnapped by Hethrir. Although Rillao didn't like accepting any offer of help, she allowed Leia and Chewbacca to free her. After five years as a prisoner, she wanted to know the fate of her son, Tigris . . . and wished to bring about the fate of her ex-mate.

Tracking Hethrir to the Crseih Research Station, Rillao confronted him, and Tigris learned the truth. News of his father's deceptions allowed him to break through the layers of lies; Tigris took the young Anakin Solo from Hethrir, who planned to feed the boy's Force powers to the creature known as the Waru. In place of the child, the Waru consumed Hethrir.

Mother and son returned to Coruscant, where they planned to join the New Republic. Rillao had high hopes for her son; he could be a scientist, an artist, or an explorer-diplomat, but he would never be consumed by the Force. And what of her own future?

Rillao has considered going back to studying the Force, with Luke Skywalker as her Jedi teacher. A healer could do so much good in the New Republic. And in the light side of the Force, perhaps Rillao could heal herself.

ELDER SH'TK'ITH (BLUESCALE)

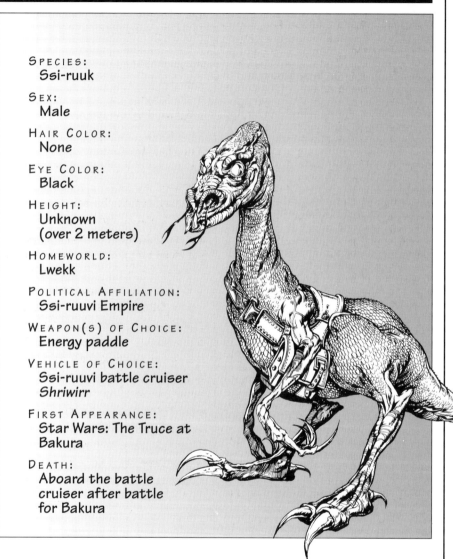

SPECIES:
Ssi-ruuk

SEX:
Male

HAIR COLOR:
None

EYE COLOR:
Black

HEIGHT:
Unknown
(over 2 meters)

HOMEWORLD:
Lwekk

POLITICAL AFFILIATION:
Ssi-ruuvi Empire

WEAPON(S) OF CHOICE:
Energy paddle

VEHICLE OF CHOICE:
Ssi-ruuvi battle cruiser
Shriwirr

FIRST APPEARANCE:
Star Wars: The Truce at
Bakura

DEATH:
Aboard the battle
cruiser after battle
for Bakura

From beyond the Outer Rim, the reptilian Ssi-ruuk came, seeking human souls to fuel their death machines. Led by the blue-scaled Elder Sh'tk'ith, the Ssi-ruuki might have succeeded in their mission had it not been for the powers of the Jedi.

Elder Sh'tk'ith was one of the species of massive, bipedal lizards who populated Lwekk. Two Sssi-ruuk species dominated the planet, warring not with each other, but with other inhabitants of the galaxy. Ruled by His Potency the Shreeftut, the Ssi-ruuvi races had long faces, tongues in their beaklike noses, eyes with nictitating triple eyelids, and long muscular tails.

Sh'tk'ith's species—which dominated the planet—had narrower faces and tiny blue scales. The other species dominated the military, and was sleek and russet scaled, with prominent black Vs on their foreheads. A third species, perhaps a throwback, were the P'wecks, whose drooping eyes and skin, short tails, and dull wits made them a perfect servant race.

Elder Sh'tk'ith, or "Bluescale," led an expedition into the Outer Rim. The Ssi-ruuk had developed a process called "entechment," whereby souls and electrical brain impulses were placed in the casings of metallic battle droids. The Ssi-ruuk had discovered that humans made the best subjects for entechment, and had already raided several human colonies, capturing and killing the populace. On G'rho they found a ten-year-old boy named Dev Sibwarra, whose Force talents greatly assisted the entechment process.

Sh'tk'ith used a hypnotic eye, and a combination of drugs and torture to turn Dev against his own kind. Occasionally he would renew the brainwashing process in order to wipe out any vestige of rebellion that might hide in the boy's spirit. He deployed Dev as a scout for raids on human systems; his Force powers could locate subjects, then calm them when they were enteched. Dev was aided by Firwirrung, a younger member of the V-marked Ssi-ruuk.

Traveling in the battle cruiser Shriwirr, under the command of Admiral Iupikkis, Sh'tk'ith was leading the attack on an outpost world known as Bakura when Dev Sibwarra located another Force user, one so powerful that he might facilitate major entechment without the need to imprison human subjects. That "other" was Luke Skywalker, weak from the attacks of the Emperor aboard the second Death Star only a few days before.

Although Sh'tk'ith was able to use Dev to lure Skywalker to the Shriwirr, he was unable to break the bond that humans—and Jedi—have for one another. The boy turned on his masters, killing Firwirrung and others, but he was cut down before he and Luke escaped.

Luke did escape with the mortally wounded Dev, as the Imperial patrol cruiser Dominant destroyed Sh'tk'ith's ship, killing everyone aboard.

The Ssi-ruuk have not launched another attack in the known galaxy since, although it may only be a matter of time.

DEV SIBWARRA

SPECIES:
Human

SEX:
Male

HAIR COLOR:
Black

EYE COLOR:
White

HEIGHT:
Unknown (short)

HOMEWORLD:
Chandrila

POLITICAL AFFILIATION:
Ssi-ruuvi Empire (brain washed)

WEAPON(S) OF CHOICE:
None

VEHICLE OF CHOICE:
Ssi-ruuvi battle cruiser Shriwirr

FIRST APPEARANCE:
Star Wars: The Truce at Bakura

DEATH:
After the battle for Bakura

Slave of the reptilian species known as the Ssi-ruuvi, Dev Sibwarra had been brainwashed to use the Force for their insidious purposes. The shining spirit of Luke Skywalker helped the young boy save himself . . . but at a high cost.

Dev was raised on Chandrila, the son of a female Jedi apprentice and an unknown father. Although she had not completed her own Jedi training, his mother still trained Dev in the ways of the Force, teaching him awareness and communication. Then the Empire began its great Jedi purge, and his family was forced to flee to the isolated planet of G'rho.

The Empire wasn't the only threat the Sibwarra family faced. The reptilian Ssi-ruuk came to G'rho, capturing and killing the populace. Barely ten years old and small for his age, Dev hid in a ravine, and soon felt his mother's Force essence disappear. The invaders found him shortly thereafter, but didn't kill him.

Dev was shipped back to the Ssi-ruuvi home planet of Lwekk, where the lizards discovered his Force abilities. They kept him for five years, training him in their languages and culture—and brainwashing him with their beliefs. In turn, he taught them about humans. They planned to use Dev as a scout for their raids on human systems in the galaxy; his Force powers could both locate subjects and calm them during "entenchment."

The Ssi-ruuk had been experimenting for years in the transfer of brain patterns and memories into huge battle droids, and had discovered that the best subjects for the entenchment process were human minds. Dev helped the lizards take several human outposts, aiding the Ssi-ruuk master Firwirrung with the entenchments. Dev longed for the privilege of entenchment himself so that he would have no more pain, and no more fear. Firwirrung had promised to entech the boy personally someday.

Dev Sibwarra was with the Ssi-ruuk when they invaded Bakura, shortly after the destruction of the Empire's second Death Star. And then, clearly and distinctly, the young man felt another person with Force powers . . . a stronger person, perhaps a full Jedi. The touch of the other Force user awakened feelings and thoughts long buried in Dev, memories that even the calming, hypnotic "renewals" that Elder Sh'tk'ith gave him couldn't erase or beat down.

Those feelings erupted completely when Dev met the Jedi, Luke Skywalker. Although he helped his Ssi-ruuk masters capture Luke, Dev later helped him escape. Overcoming his programming by using the Force, Dev eventually slew many of his masters, but was cut down before he and Luke could get off the Ssi-ruuvi battle cruiser *Shriwirr*.

Though Dev instinctively went into a Jedi healing trance, and received support from Luke and Alliance medical technicians, his wounds were too grievous. As Luke linked with him, Dev said good-bye to his past and his future, becoming one with the light side of the Force.

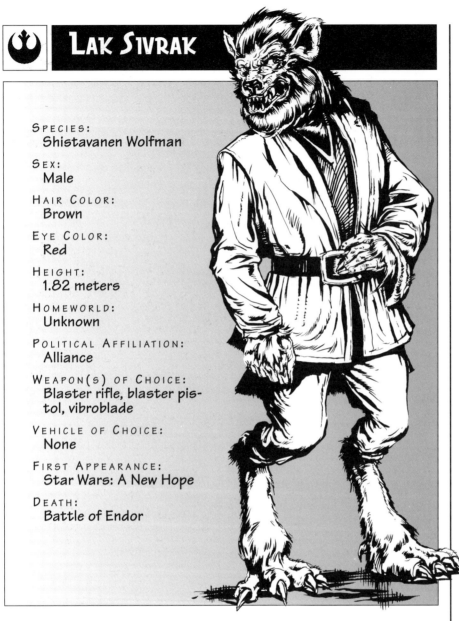

LAK SIVRAK

SPECIES:
Shistavanen Wolfman

SEX:
Male

HAIR COLOR:
Brown

EYE COLOR:
Red

HEIGHT:
1.82 meters

HOMEWORLD:
Unknown

POLITICAL AFFILIATION:
Alliance

WEAPON(S) OF CHOICE:
Blaster rifle, blaster pistol, vibroblade

VEHICLE OF CHOICE:
None

FIRST APPEARANCE:
Star Wars: A New Hope

DEATH:
Battle of Endor

A hunter and a scout, the furry wolfman Lak Sivrak was a prime example of the ways in which the galactic Rebellion caught individuals up in its principles.

Sivrak was a Shistavanen Wolfman, part of the species that ruled a group of planets in the Uvena system. They were excellent hunters, and the Empire used them as scouts and explorers of new and untamed worlds until shortly before the destruction of the first Death Star, when it decided to cut off exploration in the Outer Rim Territories and closed them off from scouts.

One of the Empire's best and most famous scouts was Sivrak, an ambitious and productive explorer of dangerous territories. Out of touch with civilization, Sivrak wasn't even aware of the Rebellion against the Empire until he stumbled onto a Rebel safe colony secluded deep in a rocky moon.

From the refugees, Sivrak learned about the atrocities and tyrannies of the Empire. He aided them, promising not to betray the location of the Rebel camp. His report to the Empire noted no life on the moon. But another scout happened upon the settlement and reported it to the Imperial Navy.

Sivrak's cover-up effort was revealed by a tortured Rebel, and the Empire sent stormtroopers after the wolfman. He killed them and dropped his forename, fleeing to Tatooine's Mos Eisley spaceport.

On the desert planet, Sivrak revealed little about himself or his past, wary of the many information brokers who would happily turn him in to the Empire. He entertained thoughts of aiding the Alliance as a guide, in exchange for big credits, but he didn't know how to contact them.

Sivrak finally made contact with a Rebel in a popular Mos Eisley cantina, when he met the seductive Florn lamproid, Dice Ibegon. The two were soon wrapped in a romantic embrace, Dice's muscular coils wrapped around the wolfman. But their hormonal discharges were derailed when a fight broke out between two humans and a pair of ruffians. With a flash of some kind of static laser weapon, the older human dispatched the pair.

Not wanting to be spotted by authorities he knew might show up, Sivrak ducked out, taking the Florn female with him. That night, and many thereafter, they discussed the Rebellion, and grew to love each other. Sivrak's desire to support the Alliance grew stronger and stronger.

They joined the Alliance about a year before the Battle of Hoth. The snow-covered planet would become a place of tragedy for Sivrak when Dice was killed in the evacuation of Echo Base. As she lay dying, the lamproid told her lover to believe in the Force and to continue against the Empire. He was the hunter; they were his prey.

The following year, Sivrak piloted an X-wing fighter when the Alliance made their surprise attack on the second Death Star. His ship was fatally damaged and Sivrak crashed on the moon of Endor, taking several TIE fighters with him. In the end, Lak Sivrak and Dice Ibegon were together again, their spirits shining as a part of the Force.

LUKE SKYWALKER

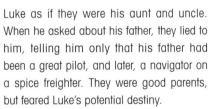

SPECIES:
Human

SEX:
Male

HAIR COLOR:
Blond

EYE COLOR:
Blue

HEIGHT:
1.72 meters

HOMEWORLD:
Tatooine (by adoption)

POLITICAL AFFILIATION:
Alliance

WEAPON(S) OF CHOICE:
Lightsaber (blue blade in Star Wars, green blade in ROTJ forward)

VEHICLE OF CHOICE:
Incom T-65B X-wing fighter

FIRST APPEARANCE:
Star Wars: A New Hope

Galactic history is full of heroic Jedi Knights, but perhaps none have been as influential as Luke Skywalker, a young Tatooine farm boy heir to a legacy of darkness and light.

In the time after the Clone Wars, the Jedi Knight Obi-Wan Kenobi asked his brother and sister-in-law, Owen and Beru Lars of Tatooine, to raise Luke, the son of Kenobi's Jedi student who had been seduced by the dark side of the Force.

Moisture farmers in the barren deserts of a twin-sunned world, Owen and Beru raised

Luke as if they were his aunt and uncle. When he asked about his father, they lied to him, telling him only that his father had been a great pilot, and later, a navigator on a spice freighter. They were good parents, but feared Luke's potential destiny.

Ben watched over Luke from afar, hiding his own home in the barren and treacherous Jundland Wastes. Growing up, Luke only saw the "crazy hermit"—as his uncle called Ben Kenobi—a few times, including once when Luke and a friend crashed a skyhopper in Beggar's Canyon. Ben helped save

them, but Owen ran him off the property, telling him never to return.

Luke had a tremendous aptitude for flying repulsorlift vehicles such as skyhoppers and landspeeders. He became good friends with another hotshot, Biggs Darklighter, as well as a crowd of kids at the nearby Anchorhead settlement: the jealous Fixer, sexy Camie, and tag alongs Deak and Windy. Sometimes they were joined by Tank, another hopeful pilot. Fixer and his friends nicknamed Luke "Wormy."

Luke and Biggs developed a fast friendship. They raced their landspeeders and skyhoppers through Beggar's Canyon in the Jundland Wastes, "tagging" womp rats. They both planned to enter the Imperial Space Academy together and fight great space battles. They also planned to buy a spaceship after their graduation. Neither of them envisioned the galaxy of turmoil that existed beyond Tatooine.

While Luke saw his future in the stars, his uncle kept him firmly at work at the farm. Season after season, he turned down Luke's request to apply to the Academy. Meanwhile, Biggs and Tank applied and were both accepted into the Academy.

Out working with the moisture vaporators one day, Luke saw what he was sure was a space battle above the planet. He quickly went to Fixer's shop in Tosche power station to tell his friends, and was surprised to see Biggs there. He was about to embark on his first mission aboard the merchant ship *Rand Ecliptic*, as its first mate, and had returned to Tatooine to see Luke and his family. In private, Biggs told Luke that he was going to join the Rebellion.

Luke was right about the space battle. When Uncle Owen bought two droids, R2-D2 and C-3PO, from the Jawas, Luke couldn't imagine the adventures he was about to tumble into. Artoo carried a hologram of a beautiful princess, which eventually led Luke to Ben Kenobi. At Ben's house, Luke learned that his father had been a Jedi Knight, who had been betrayed and murdered by Darth

Vader. Ben gave Luke his father's lightsaber.

After Imperials murdered his aunt and uncle in their search for the droids, Luke agreed to go with Ben to Alderaan and to learn the ways of the Jedi like his father before him. Luke, Ben, and the droids booked passage on the *Millennium Falcon*, a modified freighter piloted by Han Solo and his Wookiee first mate, Chewbacca. As they headed toward Alderaan, Ben began teaching Luke the ways of the Force. But the training would not last long. The *Falcon* emerged from hyperspace where Alderaan should have been, only to find the planet destroyed and a massive space station— the Death Star—nearby. When the *Falcon* was sucked inside the station, the passengers stowed away in smuggling holds. Ben soon left the ship to disable the tractor beam and allow their escape. Although he warned Luke and Han to stay behind, they were soon engaged in an ill-planned attempt to rescue Princess Leia.

Amazingly, the plan worked—but Ben was killed on the Death Star. The *Falcon* went to the Rebel base on Yavin Four, where the technical readouts of the Death Star were analyzed. Fighter pilots for X-wings and Y-wings were chosen from the ranks. Luke passed flight-simulator

tests and was awarded a T-65B X-wing fighter, with Artoo-Detoo to fly as his onboard astromech droid.

Luke was reunited with his friend Biggs, also flying in the mission against the Death Star. Both were flying with the X-wing Red Squadron. Unfortunately, Han decided not to join the mission, calling it a suicide run. Luke was sorry to see the Corellian gambler go; he had grown to like him.

When Red Leader's first strike team was killed on their approach down the Death Star trench, Luke, Biggs, and a young man named Wedge Antilles started their run of destruction. Luke led, with the other two pilots as backup. Unfortunately, Darth Vader and two TIE fighters dogged the trio. First Wedge's ship was hit and he had to abort, and then Biggs's X-wing was destroyed in a blast from Vader's ship. Luke choked back his remorse over the loss of his friend and completed his run alone. With the timely arrival of the *Millennium Falcon*, Luke's pursuers were scattered. He heard Ben's voice, telling him to use the Force. Shutting off his targeting computer and calmly reaching out with the Force, Luke fired his proton torpedo into the targeted thermal-exhaust port. His missile destroyed the Death Star.

As he zoomed away from the exploding space station, Luke heard Ben's voice again. "Remember, the Force will be with you . . . always."

Over the following three years, Luke would become an integral part of the Rebel Alliance, flying on many missions, both solo and with many others. He found traces of Jedi and Force-strong individuals, but Luke was still largely untrained himself. Meanwhile, Luke began to construct a new family. Artoo-Detoo was almost constantly at his side. He grew to love Han, Chewbacca, Threepio, and especially Leia.

Luke went with Leia and the droids on a diplomatic mission to Circarpous, but they were forced to make an unscheduled landing on the jungle planet Mimban, where they were caught up in a search for the

Force-powerful Kaiburr Crystal at the Temple of Pomojema. At the temple, Luke and Leia faced Darth Vader, who had arrived to get the crystal as well. Luke used his lightsaber to drive Vader back into a pit, then used the power of the crystal to heal the wounds Leia had received from Vader's attack.

Luke was instrumental in the discovery of the ice planet of Hoth, which would become the Rebel base after the evacuation of Yavin Four. He was promoted to commander by General Jan Dodonna, and later given leadership of the elite X-wing Rogue Squadron. On the icy planet of Hoth, Luke and Rogue Squadron learned how to handle combat snowspeeders, custom-modified Incom T-47 repulsorlift speeders. The training proved very useful when Imperials attacked Hoth, launching All Terrain Armored Transports—AT-ATs—toward the Rebels' Echo Base. Luke helped repel the attack, but the base was overrun. Most of the Rebel forces had evacuated, but rather than meeting them at their secret rendezvous point, Luke had another mission.

Ben's spirit had appeared to Luke on Hoth, telling him to go to the Dagobah system, where he could train to be a Jedi under Yoda, the Master who had taught Kenobi. Luke and Artoo went to the dense swamp planet, crashing the X-wing into a watery bog. Shortly thereafter, Luke met a strange little green creature who talked in disjointed sentences. The creature promised to take him to Yoda, but Luke became impatient.

It was then that he found out the diminutive being was Yoda. The Jedi Master discussed Luke's future with the spirit of Kenobi, then commenced training Luke immediately. He lectured him about the Force while Luke performed rigorous physical and psychological exercises, warning him against the easy path of anger and the lure of the dark side. One of Luke's most difficult tests was when Yoda told him to go into a tree suffused with dark-side energy. When Luke asked what was inside, the enigmatic Master said, "Only what you take with you."

Inside the tree, Luke dueled with an apparition that resembled Darth Vader—until the helmet cracked and Luke saw his own face. He too could become part of the dark side.

Luke learned other valuable lessons when Yoda had him practice levitation using the Force. Luke despaired when he spotted his X-wing sinking in the bog. Yoda ordered him to use the same powers to raise his ship as he had on rocks and supplies. Luke said he'd try, but was cut off curtly by Yoda. "No! Try not. Do. Or do not. There is no try."

Finally, Yoda instructed Luke to open his mind to memories of old friends, and the possibilities of the future. Jarred by visions of Han Solo and Leia in pain on Cloud City, Luke decided to leave to rescue his friends. Yoda and the spirit of Kenobi both warned Luke that the decision could destroy everything his friends had fought for, and that he was much too susceptible to the dark side of the Force. Torn between his knowledge that Yoda and Ben were right, and the visions of his friends in danger, Luke left Dagobah, promising to return to complete his training.

Bespin's Cloud City was a trap; instead

of his friends, Luke found Darth Vader. The two engaged in a tremendous lightsaber duel, and Vader finally drove Luke out onto a gantry above a reactor shaft. The Dark Lord distracted Luke long enough to lop off his right hand. Still clutching the lightsaber, Luke's hand fell into the warm winds below.

But the worst was yet to come, as Vader told him the truth of his past that Ben Kenobi had hidden from him: "I am your father," he said solemnly. "Search your feelings. You know it to be true."

Vader told Luke that they could overthrow the Emperor and rule the galaxy together as father and son. Luke didn't even reply. Looking sadly at the monster his father had become, he calmly stepped off the platform and fell.

He was sucked into an exhaust pipe and emerged on the underside of the floating city, where he barely caught an electronic weather vane to stop his fall. Using the Force, he called out weakly to Leia, who was escaping the city aboard the *Millennium Falcon*. They turned back and rescued Luke as he was about to fall to his death. But as they flew away, Luke could feel the presence of Vader in his mind.

Back with the Rebel fleet, Luke received a new bionic hand, but while it and his lightsaber were replaceable, his innocence

was not. Ben had lied to him, Vader had tempted him . . . Luke faced an uncertain future.

Soon afterward, Luke was back at work with the Alliance, planning with Leia, Chewie, and Lando Calrissian the best way to rescue Han Solo from Jabba the Hutt. By the end of the rescue, Luke had helped destroy Jabba the Hutt and save Han. Upon leaving Tatooine, Luke returned to Dagobah to finish his training, only to discover that Yoda was dying. The Jedi Master confirmed Luke's fears about Vader, and told him that to complete his own Jedi training, Luke must face Vader one final time. Luke then confronted the spirit of Ben Kenobi, and learned an even more shocking element of his past: Leia was his twin sister!

Torn by his feelings, Luke became moody and withdrawn. When the Alliance planned a mission to destroy the second Death Star above Yavin's moon, Luke did not choose to fly with Rogue Squadron. Instead, he accompanied a strike force to the moon's surface, where they planned to destroy the electronic shield generator that protected the battle station.

On Endor, Luke finally faced up to his destiny. Quietly, in the Ewok village, he told Leia about his father . . . about their father. Luke could feel him nearby, waiting. He

needed to go to Vader, not to destroy him, but to save him from the dark side. Luke surrendered himself to Vader's Imperial troops and met his father. He tried to reach the goodness that was Anakin Skywalker, hidden deep below the dark-side powers and black armor, but the power of the dark side was too great.

On board the Death Star, Emperor Palpatine goaded Luke about the fate of his friends until Luke attacked; Vader defended his Master. Father and son were soon locked in deadly combat, but then Luke regained control of his anger and refused to fight.

Probing his son's feelings, Vader sensed something he had never seen before: the secret of Luke's twin sister, Princess Leia. "If you will not turn to the dark side, then perhaps she will," Vader threatened. It was the catalyst that broke Luke's Jedi calm. He attacked his father again, hacking and stabbing with the lightsaber. He finally beat his father down, chopping off his right hand.

Turning his back on the crippled Dark Lord, Luke confronted the Emperor, "You've failed, Your Highness. I am a Jedi, like my father before me." Palpatine attacked Luke with blue Force lightning, knowing that the younger Skywalker would never join him. But as Palpatine prepared to deliver the killing bolts, Vader rose up from behind, lifted his Master into the air, and threw him into the burning shaft of the power core. Vader tried to follow him into oblivion, but Luke stopped him.

Vader was dying, and he asked Luke to take his helmet off so he could look at his son with his own eyes for the first time. As he struggled to breathe, he told Luke that he was right. He did have goodness left in him. And then, repentant, he died.

Luke took Vader's armor to the moon of Endor and burned it in a funeral pyre. Later that night, as he slipped away from a joint Rebel and Ewok celebration, he was surprised at a vision. For a few moments, he saw Obi-Wan Kenobi, Yoda, and Anakin Skywalker, all smiling to him. Kenobi and

Yoda's pupil—and Skywalker's son—was, now and forever, a Jedi. And his father, Anakin, was part of the light side of the Force once again.

The day after the destruction of the second Death Star, Luke was part of the strike force that freed the planet Bakura from an invasion by the reptilian Ssi-ruuk. The following year, Luke was involved in Mon Mothma's short-lived private strike team, called the Senate Interplanetary Intelligence Network—SPIN. While on a mission with them, Luke met a young Jedi Prince named Ken, as well as the crazed son of Emperor Palpatine, Triclops. He also gained access to the Lost City of the Jedi below the surface of Yavin Four, but the city was destroyed.

Luke's relationships with feisty women would strike again—literally—when he accompanied Hapan Prince Isolder to Dathomir, where they hoped to talk some sense into Han Solo. Whacked with a club by a Dathomirian witch named Teneniel Djo, Luke was amused to find out he was supposed to be her betrothed. Once he helped her and her Singing Mountain Clan defeat the evil Gethzerion and her Nightsisters, Luke was freed of his "obliga-

tion." Djo and Isolder would marry, and years later, their Force-strong daughter would enter Luke's life.

Luke saw his earlier mentor for the final time in the Imperial Palace on Coruscant. Ben appeared to him as he slept, warning him that the pathways were closing for the fading Jedi. He assured Luke that he was a powerful Jedi, and a hope for the future. Obi-Wan then bid him good-bye, adding, "I loved you as a son, and as a student, and as a friend. Until we meet again, may the Force be with you." Then, as he disappeared forever, he told Luke to think of himself not as the last of the Jedi, but "the first of the new."

Shortly thereafter, Luke was caught up in the battle against Imperial Grand Admiral Thrawn and his forces. He was also stalked by Mara Jade, a beautiful woman whose compulsion to kill him came from the long-dead Emperor. And finally, he began to train with—and then reject the teachings of—the mad Jedi clone Joruus C'Baoth.

Using tissue from the hand Luke had lost on Bespin, Joruus had grown a clone of his own. Luke faced his clone, Luuke, in the throne room of the Emperor's Mount Tantiss facility on Wayland. When Mara killed Luuke, Luke joined with her and Leia to defeat and destroy C'Baoth.

Surviving Imperial forces drove the New Republic off Coruscant; its temporary headquarters were established on the Fifth Moon of Da Soocha in the Cyax system. Lando, Wedge, and Luke attacked Coruscant, but their ship crashed. Although the others escaped in the *Falcon*, Luke allowed himself and Artoo to be sucked up into a crackling blue Force storm. It transported him to an Imperial dungeon ship, which, in turn, took him to Byss. There, he was surprised to find the

clone of Emperor Palpatine, alive and willing to teach him.

Like a few others in the history of the Jedi, Luke felt he could learn about—and destroy—the dark side of the Force from within. As the training went on, Luke was sure he was staying with the light, but he was becoming corrupted. It wasn't until Leia confronted him, her lightsaber flashing, that he realized how much he had almost lost. Working together, Luke and Leia helped destroy the clone.

Later, Luke found a fallen Jedi named Kam Solusar and freed him from the dark side. Following the advice of the Jedi Holocron, Luke and Kam searched for other lost Jedi on Ossus, the ancient center of Jedi culture. Luke found new students, Jem and Rayf Ysanna, as well as the ruins of a Jedi library. Later, on New Alderaan, Jem was killed when Imperial Dark Siders attacked an Alliance settlement.

Realizing that the training he was giving Leia and a few of the other Force-powerful people he found was not enough, Luke petitioned the Provisional Council for permission to begin a Jedi academy. He founded it in the Great Temple of Massassi on the jungle moon of Yavin Four. Luke's first class had twelve Jedi initiates, including the exotic-looking Tionne, the generational clone Dorsk 81, the Bespin gas prospector Streen, the angry Gantoris, the Dathomirian witch Kirani Ti, and Kam Solusar. Later, Kyp Durron, Nichos Marr, and the Mon Calamari Ambassador Cilghal would join the trainees.

Skywalker taught his students all aspects of the Force, as he had been taught by his Masters Obi-Wan Kenobi and Yoda: levitation, visualization of battles, sensing other living creatures, calming and healing, and many other Force exercises. He also allowed them access to Vodo-Siosk Baas's Jedi Holocron.

But the evil spirit of Dark Lord of the Sith Exar Kun was trapped on Yavin Four. Kun first tempted Gantoris, but the student turned on him and was killed. Later, Kyp Durron would be seduced by Kun's promises of power. The boy helped the Dark Lord attack Luke, leaving the Jedi Master's body comatose.

Luke's spirit survived in the same netherworld Exar Kun's shade inhabited. Luke soon found out that Kun had become adept at using the dark side of the Force to influence the living world. Over the following

weeks, Kun used his powers to try to destroy Luke's body, but it was protected by the Jedi initiates, Leia, and her two Force-strong twin children, Jacen and Jaina.

Finally, the initiates lured Exar Kun to appear in the grand audience chamber where Luke's body lay in repose. Joined by Jacen and Jaina, they focused their will into a single entity of the Force, and Luke's spirit appeared to aid them, as did Vodo-Siosk Baas's spirit. Their combined powers and energies of the Jedi extinguished Kun's dark light.

Shortly thereafter, a penitent Kyp Durron returned to face his punishment for the crime he had committed while in the thrall of the dark side. Luke was forgiving; he accepted Kyp back into Jedi training, and later traveled with him to the black-hole cluster known as the Maw to help destroy the deadly Sun Crusher ship and the threats of Imperial Admiral Daala.

Peace was restored to the galaxy for a brief, shining moment. Luke knew that he had set out on the correct path; the Jedi he trained would be the hope of the future. But even though he had an academy to run, Luke didn't stay on Yavin Four. One of his adventures found him taking Nichos Marr and scientist Cray Mingla to check out an inoperative spaceship called the *Eye of Palpatine*. On the ship, Luke was surprised to discover that the essence of a Jedi woman named Callista, trapped inside the computer core, had kept the weapons systems incapacitated for thirty years.

In order to destroy the *Eye*, Nichos and Cray stayed behind, sacrificing themselves. Luke mourned not only their loss, but that of

Callista, whose dream presence and computer conversations he had fallen in love with. To his surprise, Cray reappeared in an escape pod, but he soon discovered it was not really Cray; Callista and Cray's essences had been exchanged before the *Eye* blew up. Callista accompanied him to Yavin Four, where they began to plan a future together.

Two years later, Luke was caught up in a search to find Han and Leia's missing children. They had been kidnapped by the dark Force user Hethrir, who planned to use them to revitalize the dark side. Luke was tempted by the doorways to the Force guarded by Hethrir's ally, Waru, but the calls of his sister and her children helped return him from the brink of destruction.

Luke's twin nephew and niece, Jacen and Jaina, eventually arrived to train at his Jedi academy. By then, many cycles of students had come to train, and many more were yet to come. Luke Skywalker has faced a destiny that was his before he was even born. In bringing back the ancient order of the Jedi, he has provided hope for the future, and a shining beacon for the light side of the Force.

ANAKIN SOLO

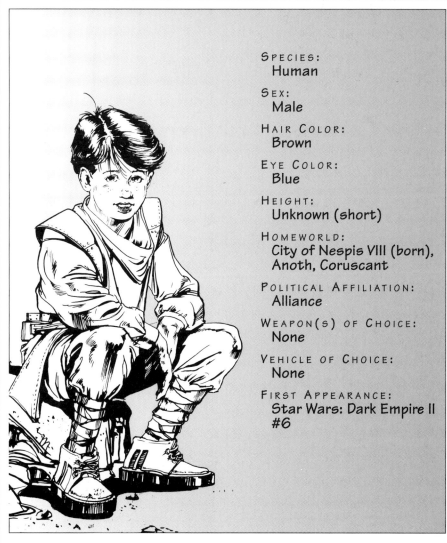

SPECIES:
Human

SEX:
Male

HAIR COLOR:
Brown

EYE COLOR:
Blue

HEIGHT:
Unknown (short)

HOMEWORLD:
City of Nespis VIII (born),
Anoth, Coruscant

POLITICAL AFFILIATION:
Alliance

WEAPON(S) OF CHOICE:
None

VEHICLE OF CHOICE:
None

FIRST APPEARANCE:
Star Wars: Dark Empire II
#6

The youngest child of Han Solo and Princess Leia Organa Solo, Anakin Solo was born six years after the death of his grandfather, Anakin Skywalker, whose life as Darth Vader had been renounced as he died.

Anakin was born in trying circumstances. His parents and siblings had just been rescued from New Alderaan, arriving at the temporary Alliance base in the abandoned floating space city of Nespis VIII just as Leia went into labor.

When their parents relocated with the New Republic back to Coruscant, the infant Anakin and his twin brother and sister Jaina and Jacen lived on a faraway world called Anoth in a heavily guarded facility. Leia's assistant, Winter, took care of them.

When the twins were two, Winter returned them to Coruscant to live with their parents. Anakin, at six months, was still much too young, so Winter kept him on Anoth. No one knew Anoth's location except Luke Skywalker, Admiral Ackbar, and Winter, but an Alliance traitor did manage to track Ackbar there, and gave the coordi-

nates to Imperial Caridian Ambassador Furgan.

The bloated Imperial led an attack force to Anoth to capture the young Jedi child. He was foiled by the quick-thinking and resourceful Winter, Ackbar, Leia, and a Mon Calamari named Terpfen. Following the incident, Leia and Han decided that Anakin would be just as safe on Coruscant with them.

So Anakin grew up happily playing in the corridors of New Republic power at the Imperial palace. If Winter wasn't around, the fussy droid C-3PO or the giant Wookiee Chewbacca watched Anakin and his siblings. They attended many important diplomatic functions—such as the Time of Meeting on Ithor—often being introduced in a formal manner.

When he was three and a half years old, Anakin was kidnapped, along with Jacen and Jaina, by the Firrerreon lord Hethrir. A trainee of Darth Vader, Hethrir was intent on teaching the ways of the dark side to Force-sensitive children, and the Solo kids certainly qualified. On Hethrir's worldcraft, Anakin made friends with a youth named Tigris. It was this friendship that saved Anakin's life when Hethrir tried to feed his spirit to Waru on the Crseih Research Station.

As Anakin grows older, his Force powers are more evident. Although he's likable, his demeanor is at times intense and quiet. He is even more gifted in mechanics than Jaina, having taken apart and reassembled computers at the age of five. His ice-blue eyes are full of curiosity, while his unruly brown hair betrays his youth, his genes, and his distractedness. He seems able to alter and control some of his surroundings, and with his power to sense emotions, he may grow toward figuring out the complex puzzles of people.

Anakin, jealous of his brother and sister, looks forward to attending the Jedi academy on Yavin Four. His uncle, Luke Skywalker, who leads the academy, has already been impressed by the strength of his nephew's Force talents. Anakin dreams of the day he, too, will be a Jedi hero.

HAN SOLO

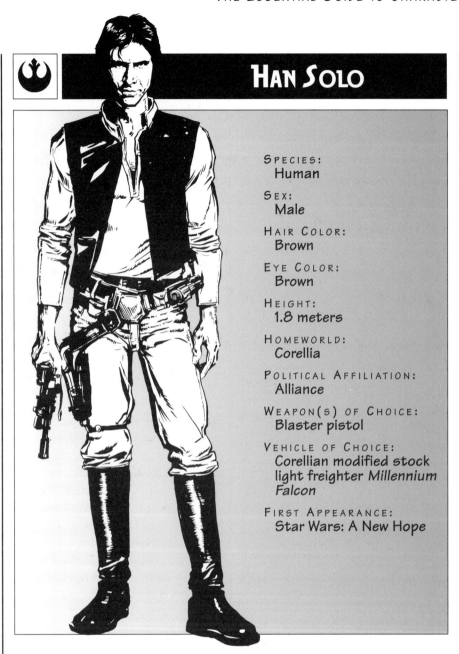

SPECIES:
Human

SEX:
Male

HAIR COLOR:
Brown

EYE COLOR:
Brown

HEIGHT:
1.8 meters

HOMEWORLD:
Corellia

POLITICAL AFFILIATION:
Alliance

WEAPON(S) OF CHOICE:
Blaster pistol

VEHICLE OF CHOICE:
Corellian modified stock light freighter *Millennium Falcon*

FIRST APPEARANCE:
Star Wars: A New Hope

Notorious throughout the galaxy, Han Solo has been a starship pilot, smuggler, pirate, and target for bounty hunters. He's also been a Rebel hero, a general for the Alliance, and even a husband and father.

Han has revealed very little of his past, even to his allies and friends in the New Republic. Most of what they've found out has been gleaned through conversational asides, public records, bounty posters, or old friends. Solo is a Corellian, and may be part of an illustrious yet controversial line;

Berethron e Solo introduced democracy into the Corellian empire, but Dalla Solo—also known as Dalla Suul or Dalla the Black—was a notorious kingpin of organized crime. It isn't known whether or not Han is actually related to either.

Han was a talented swoop and speeder pilot by the time he entered the Imperial Space Academy. There he made friends with the older Mako Spince, and "Trooper" Badure. Han soon earned the nickname "Slick," due to a particularly slick maneuver he performed in a malfunctioning U-33

loadlifter during class exercises.

Mako and Han became the best of friends, breaking rules and engaging in horseplay and practical jokes. Spince went a little too far when he used a gram of anti-matter from the physics lab to blow up the Academy's "mascot moon." He was expelled two years before Solo graduated.

Han did graduate, with honors, and accepted a commission in the Imperial Starfleet. He might have had a brilliant career in the Imperial Navy, if not for an encounter with a large, hairy Wookiee. Wookiees were a species enslaved under Imperial law, but Han felt he couldn't stand by and watch a slaver badly mistreat one particular Wookiee. For his interference, Solo was court-martialed, stripped of his commission and rank, and ejected from the Navy. At the time, he considered himself lucky not to have been shot by a firing squad.

Han soon found out that the Wookiee, Chewbacca, had established a "life debt" to him. This Wookiee custom was an oath of allegiance to a person or persons who had saved a Wookiee's life. Once a life debt was undertaken, a Wookiee would follow his rescuer from one end of the galaxy to

another, serving at their side. At first, Han was annoyed, but he eventually came to appreciate Chewbacca's company and life-saving gestures, and to consider him a friend.

Solo eventually hooked up with Mako, who had used the Spince family money to buy a ship and become a disreputable smuggler. Mako taught his old friend the adrenalin-pumping pleasures and profits of the smuggling trade, keeping the Corellian around as a sidekick. Spince and Solo made their headquarters on the smuggler's moon of Nar Shaddaa, where modern cities were built upon cities of the past, creating an underworld maze of hideaways and headquarters for illicit business. Nar Shaddaa orbited Nal Hutta, home to the notorious species of sluglike creatures known as the Hutts.

Han and Mako worked with Roa's gang, smuggling water to the polluted industrial world of Rampa. Roa taught Han about the huge trade in spice smuggling from Kessel. Han also met the half-breed Corellian master mechanic Shug Ninx, the beautiful and exotic Salla Zend, and the dashing con-man gambler Lando Calrissian. Han set up a small home in the city-maze of the Corellian sector of Nar Shaddaa, with a droid named ZZ-4Z, "lost" to Han by Mako in a game of sabacc, set up as the housekeeper for his scruffy home.

Solo was a canny gambler and terrific sabacc player. His cocky attitude hid his thoughts; unless they were mind readers, his foes were stymied. He was also incredibly lucky—all the other gamblers had noticed that. Han was in his share of fire-fights—both in ships and on foot—and he always seemed to come out on top. Han developed a healthy ego, and the beginnings of a healthier reputation. All he needed was his own ship.

Lando was the answer to that problem. Han played him a game of sabacc, walking away with Lando's modified Corellian stock light freighter, the *Millennium Falcon*. Smuggling became easier with the fast *Falcon*, and "captain" Han and "first mate" Chewie modified it constantly, usually in the spacebarn of Shug Ninx. The Corellian and the Wookiee were becoming tighter as a team, and they were now inseparable *friends* rather than life-debt partners. Han even learned to understand the Wookiee's language, although he himself sounded stupid when he tried to speak it.

Han and Salla were also growing closer. They had a friendly rapport, trading techno-jargon and smuggler's tales; both of them ran spice to the Stenness system, a friendly rivalry keeping them competing as to who could make the Kessel Run the fastest or who could cut the tightfisted 'Nessies the best deal. Three years passed, and the two enjoyed each other's company, though neither wanted to make any commitments.

Then Salla had an accident that destroyed her ship and forced her to face her own mortality. Badly shaken by the experience, she debated her future, and saw it in the arms of Han Solo. She wanted to retire from smuggling, and wanted Han to retire with her. Solo didn't want to be tied down so early in his adventurous life, and bid good-bye to Salla through a holomessage.

Tired of the Empire, Han and Chewie departed for the more lawless Corporate Sector, where they did runs for crime lords and smuggler barons like Big Bunji and Ploovo Two-For-One, as well as for the Corporate Sector Authority. They were joined on their adventures by the droid Bollux and his miniature supercomputer companion, Blue Max.

The *Falcon* needed repairs, and an old friend, Jessa, agreed to do the work if Solo promised to rescue her father. Han did rescue Doc, destroying the prison asteroid's Stars' End Tower in the process. Soon after, Han was forced into a slaving run and was required to work with Fiolla, the beautiful assistant auditor general of the CSA, in order to catch the ring of slavers. In the process, Han made enemies of Gallandro, an old-style gunslinger.

Han and Gallandro faced off on the planet of Dellalt, where the Corellian was helping an old friend, Badure, track down the treasure ship called the *Queen Of Ranroon*. Gallandro was faster on the blaster draw than Han, leaving the smuggler with a laser scar on his shoulder and forearm. Before Han could be killed, though, hidden security lasers in the *Queen* killed Gallandro. Shortly thereafter, Han and Chewie decided

to take a break from the Corporate Sector and returned to Imperial space.

Han Solo's reputation as one of the best smugglers—and pilots—grew proportionately as his more daring exploits made the rounds of the cantinas and the crime lords, and Han began taking on spice-smuggling jobs from Jabba the Hutt and others. Chewbacca's reputation grew, as well; his strength, head-sized fists, loaded bowcaster, and reputedly violent temper enhanced his ability to watch Han's back.

Moruth Doole was one of Han's spice suppliers, acquiring his contraband by skimming the drug from miners on Kessel. On one of Han's spice-smuggling runs to Jabba the Hutt, Imperials stopped the *Falcon*, and in order to avoid arrest, Han jettisoned his spice shipment, intending to pick it up later. Unfortunately, by the time he was able to return, the spice was gone. Solo and Chewbacca both knew Jabba was not going to be happy. What they didn't know—until years later—was that Doole had set them up, getting paid a fee by the authorities, and keeping the price Jabba had paid in advance for the spice.

Han and Chewie eventually went to Tatooine to face Jabba, landing at Docking Bay 94 at the Mos Eisley spaceport. Before heading to see the Hutt crime lord, they stopped in at Chalmun's cantina. There, they picked up a job that would change their lives forever. An old man, Ben Kenobi, wanted a fast ship to Alderaan, carrying only himself, a smart-alecky young kid named Luke Skywalker, and two droids, C-3PO and R2-D2. Han negotiated a 17,000 credit fee, for which Han wouldn't ask any questions. That would be enough to pay Jabba off and get back to business.

Before they could leave, Han was stopped by a Rodian bounty hunter named Greedo. Han had humiliated him years earlier on Nar Shaddaa, but now he was working for Jabba. Han distracted him long enough to shoot him, using a blaster hidden under the table. Even with Greedo dead, Han still had to face Jabba outside the docking bay.

The smuggler promised the Hutt he would return soon with the money; Jabba warned Solo that if he disappointed him again, he'd "put a price on your head so large you won't be able to go near a civilized system for the rest of your short life."

Han and Chewie were rapidly swept up in much more than they bargained for. The two droids were wanted by the Empire, and their destination—the entire planet of Alderaan—had been destroyed by a huge battle station known as the Death Star. The

Falcon was pulled into the station, but Han and Chewie managed to hide themselves and their passengers in smuggling compartments. When the old man left to disable the tractor beams, things turned even *more* complicated.

Lured by the promise of rewards from a rich princess named Leia—who was being held captive on the station—Han and Chewie joined Luke on a crazy rescue mission that almost got them shot, drowned, and crushed in a garbage compactor. Amazingly, the rescue worked . . . after a fashion. The *Falcon* got off the station and escaped into hyperspace, with the princess on board. Han soon found he liked the spunky aristocrat; he suspected she would

like him, too, if she'd only admit to his brilliance.

Dropping Luke and Leia at the Rebel base on Yavin Four, Han would have been content to leave with his reward, but Chewbacca played to his conscience. So Solo brought the *Falcon* into the battle against the Death Star battle station, just in time to save Luke's X-wing from certain disintegration. Luke's proton torpedo found its mark and destroyed the Death Star. Back on the moon of Yavin, Han, Chewie, and Luke were all feted as heroes.

Han didn't plan to stay with the Rebellion, although events would soon transpire that would lead him back to his new friends. On the way back to Tatooine to pay Jabba, the *Falcon* was attacked and boarded by space pirates. Led by Crimson Jack, they looted the ship and left Han penniless. Solo didn't even try to contact the gangster; with the Hutt's bounty on his head, the Rebellion suddenly seemed a safer place than the smuggling underworld.

He stayed with the Alliance for several years, adventuring, piloting, smuggling, and racking up an impressive rap sheet and bounty not only from Jabba, but also from the Empire. Han helped the Alliance scout out new locations for their base, and helped establish Echo Base on Hoth. Soon thereafter, Han had to aid in evacuating the base when an Imperial probe droid found them. Taking Leia, Threepio, and Chewie, Han loaded the *Falcon* and barely escaped as the Imperials invaded.

Han used the *Falcon* for an incredible evasive run against several Star Destroyers and TIE fighters. He then traveled to Bespin, where his old ally Lando Calrissian was set up as Baron Administrator on Cloud City. Wanting Lando's people to repair the *Falcon*, Han didn't realize he had been betrayed. Darth Vader and the bounty hunter Boba Fett were waiting for Han, intending to use him as bait to lure Luke Skywalker to Cloud City.

Vader soon used Han for another insidious purpose: testing a carbonite-freezing chamber on a living person. Before he was lowered into the carbonite pit, Han and Leia said their good-byes. "I love you," she told him, tears in her eyes.

"I know," he replied. And then the intense, incredible cold came, and Han couldn't scream, couldn't move, couldn't see. Conscious but not conscious, Han almost went mad in the dark prison of carbonite, his mind playing the memories of his life.

And then he was freed, blind and sick from "hibernation," his own body betraying him. He had spent almost a year as a wall decoration in Jabba the Hutt's palace on Tatooine, until a bizarre rescue mission enabled Luke, Leia, Lando, Threepio, and Artoo to rescue Han, killing Jabba in the process.

Han himself—still blinded from the carbonite ordeal—had hit Boba Fett in the hunter's rocket pack, causing the armor-clad man to hurtle into the mouth of the carnivorous Sarlacc. Han knew that even the Pit of Carkoon would probably not be a match for Fett; they had met before, and would doubtless meet again.

After his rescue, Solo had changed. While he still had no use for government or authority figures of any kind, Han had a personal stake in the battle for freedom. Luke was like a kid brother, and Leia was . . . well, he wasn't sure what he wanted Leia to be, just yet. Along with

Chewie, they were an extended family, though, and maybe that was what the Corellian finally needed.

Han accepted a general's commission from Mon Mothma and her Advisory Council. Leia was surprised with the news when she heard it while planning a mission; General Solo would lead a strike team to Endor to destroy the energy-shield generator that protected the second Death Star.

On Endor, Han and Leia came to understand just what they meant to each other. With the help of the fuzzy little Ewoks, the team managed to destroy the bunker. Above them, in orbit, Lando Calrissian—flying the borrowed *Falcon*—and Wedge Antilles succeeded in destroying the Death Star. Emperor Palpatine and Darth Vader were both dead, and the Empire was in shambles.

If he was entertaining thoughts of leaving then, Han never showed them. Days after the Battle of Endor, he was off with Leia, Luke, and other Alliance heroes to Bakura, where he helped fight the reptilian Ssi-ruuk invaders and the Imperials who turned on them afterward.

For a short time, Mothma established a private strike team of the Alliance's most daring heroes. Called the Senate Interplanetary Intelligence Network—SPIN—the team consisted of Leia, Luke, Han, Chewie, Lando, Artoo, and Threepio. The SPIN strike force went on a variety of adventures, fighting Jabba's father, Zorba the Hutt, and causing the death of a pretender to the throne of Palpatine, Trioculus. Mon Mothma eventually disbanded the special group as different sorts of missions began to present themselves.

Eight years after the rescue attempt aboard the first Death Star, Han finally had to make a choice about his relationship with Leia. Hapan Prince Isolder had arrived on Coruscant—now the seat of the New Republic—and asked for Princess Leia's hand in marriage.

Challenged by a rival who could offer her more than he ever could, Han kidnapped Leia and took her to Dathomir, trying to convince her to marry him. Pursued by Isolder and Luke, as well as by the rogue Imperial warlord Zsinj, Han eventually saved the day and won Leia's heart. He and Leia were married soon thereafter, while Isolder married a Dathomirian witch, Teneniel Djo.

Five years after the Battle of Endor, the Alliance faced the return of the brilliant and ruthless Grand Admiral Thrawn and his Imperial forces. Han and Chewie were instrumental in bringing Talon Karrde, Mara Jade, and the other smugglers to aid the Alliance in that and many battles that followed. Han fought in the assault for the Sluis Van shipyards and in the battles for control of the long-lost *Katana* Dreadnaught fleet, and got to once again meet his early childhood idol, Garm Bel Iblis. He also led the strike-force attack to destroy the weapons depot and cloning facilities in Mount Tantiss, on Wayland.

In the midst of the battles, Leia had twins. Han was present to help deliver his children, marveling at the lives he had helped bring into being. They named them Jacen and Jaina Solo, and the pair never lacked for attention; if their parents weren't

with them, Leia's assistant, Winter, was taking care of them.

The following year, Han and Chewie went on various missions against the reborn Emperor Palpatine, first rescuing Lando and Wedge Antilles's strike teams on Coruscant. Then, Han revisited Nar Shaddaa, with Leia in tow, and ran into Mako Spince, Shug Ninx, and Salla Zend. Pursued by hunters seeking the bounty for the long-ago death of Jabba the Hutt, Han and Leia fled the spaceport moon, riding aboard Shug and Salla's *Starlight Intruder*. They went to Byss, making a run to save Luke Skywalker from the dark Force clutches of the Emperor.

Shortly thereafter, when Han and Leia returned to Nar Shaddaa, they had another run-in with both Mako and Boba Fett. Mako betrayed Han to the Empire, but unlike Lando Calrissian, who had lived to regret his similar act, Mako didn't survive long; Han decoyed the Star Destroyer *Invincible* into grabbing Spince's control tower—where Mako was situated—in its tractor beam. The resulting explosion was spectacular.

Han was still pursued by Fett's *Slave I*, so he and Leia entered an interstellar gas cloud. Inside it they found the archaic battleship *Robida Colossus*, home of the paraplegic Jedi, King Empatojayos Brand. They enlisted his help in fighting Palpatine's revitalized forces, and allowed him to put a lightning gun on the front of the *Falcon*. The gun was instrumental in fighting Fett's ship when they emerged into real space, and against the dark-side troops that attacked New Alderaan days later.

Han and Leia arrived back at the New Republic's temporary base on the abandoned floating space city of Nespis VIII, and just in time—Leia went into labor, and hours later, delivered a baby boy. The proud parents named him Anakin Solo, after his great Jedi grandfather.

Within months, the Alliance attacked the Imperial City on Coruscant yet again, and succeeded in driving the remnants of the Empire away. Han and Leia allowed their three children to be sequestered away on the hidden planet of Anoth, protected and tutored by Winter.

The following year, Han agreed to act as New Republic ambassador to Kessel. The planet had once been home of the Imperial Correctional Facility, as well as the main supply line of the addictive glitterstim spice. Once there, Han and Chewie were taken captive by Moruth Doole, who thought Solo had returned to kill him. He put the two in the spice mines, intending to kill them.

With the help of a young Force-powerful prisoner, Kyp Durron, Han and Chewie escaped, only to be taken captive by Imperials from the black-hole cluster known as the Maw. The secrets they uncovered there would require a great deal of attention from the New Alliance: a deadly weapon called the Sun Crusher, a brilliant scientist named Qwi Xux, and a scheming Imperial Admiral Daala and her long-forgotten Star Destroyer fleet.

Along the way, Han grew very fond of Kyp, and risked his life to stop the boy when Durron was consumed by the dark side of the Force. Han also finally got to participate in payback for Doole when Lando and Mara raided Kessel; Doole was eaten by the giant, glassy, carnivorous spiders that actually produced the glitterstim. And, as if to add a coda onto his past, Han and Lando finally settled the ownership of the *Falcon* once and for all. Han lost it to Lando in a game of sabacc, then won it back, then lost it again. Lando presented it to his friend as a gift, never to be gambled for again.

The Solo kids were brought back to Coruscant to live, and Han tried his best to be a good father, and a good husband for an important politician, but even on vacation, Han couldn't seem to put down his blaster. With Leia and the kids on Plawell, Han got caught up in the search for Plett's Well, a legendary refuge of the children of the Jedi. Ever the skeptic, Han also helped expose Roganda Ismaren's plan to establish a new Imperial regime.

On a mission to help Luke find a lost Jedi, Han discovered the secret of a strange alien named Waru. On Crseih Research Station, he was able to help save his own son, Anakin, from the Force-consuming Waru, and in the course of events Anakin's kidnapper Hethrir, died instead.

As the children grew older, and their father headed toward middle age, Han never quit adventuring. Twenty-three years after he had first met Luke Skywalker, he was delivering not only his own twins, but also Chewbacca's nephew, Lowbacca, to Luke's Jedi academy on the Fourth Moon of Yavin. Anakin would attend later.

Han had once laughed as Ben Kenobi described the Force to a younger Luke. Han may not have believed in the Force at that time, but something certainly believed in Han. Now, as he grows older, Han has realized how lucky he has been. The galaxy has been one tough sabacc game, and Han Solo is still holding the winning hand.

JACEN AND JAINA SOLO

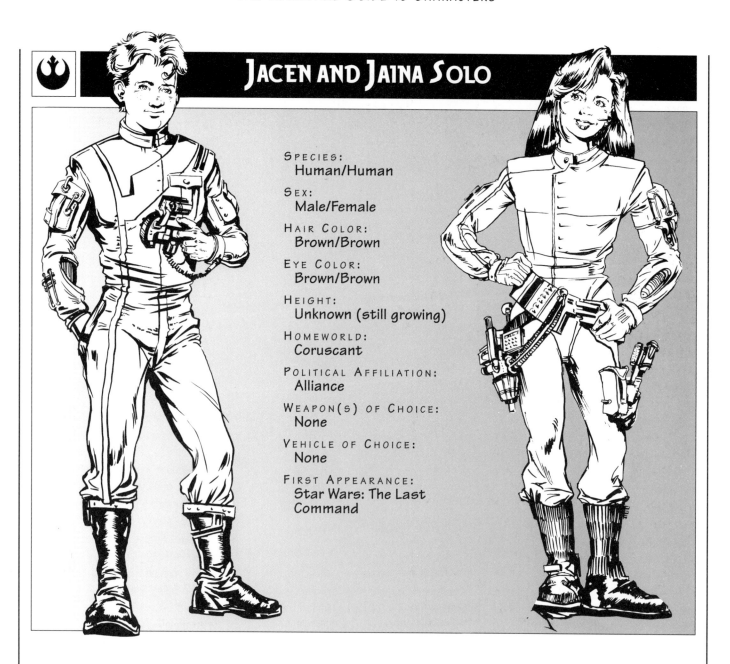

SPECIES:
Human/Human

SEX:
Male/Female

HAIR COLOR:
Brown/Brown

EYE COLOR:
Brown/Brown

HEIGHT:
Unknown (still growing)

HOMEWORLD:
Coruscant

POLITICAL AFFILIATION:
Alliance

WEAPON(S) OF CHOICE:
None

VEHICLE OF CHOICE:
None

FIRST APPEARANCE:
Star Wars: The Last
Command

The fraternal twins Jacen and Jaina Solo have a lineage of power and luck. Power in the Force comes from their grandfather, Anakin Skywalker, and from their mother, Princess Leia Organa Solo. The power of luck comes from their Corellian father, Han Solo.

Leia had sent her thoughts through the Force down into her unborn children's minds as they grew inside her, but they had been too undeveloped to respond. Shortly before their birth, though, one of the minds had responded, using the Force to clutch at

Leia as a child would hold its parent's finger. When the one mind calmed the other mind, Leia knew that the twins were strongly attuned to each other, and strong in the Force.

After ten hours of labor with a nervous Han at Leia's side, Jaina was born first, and Jacen arrived soon after. Leia didn't have much time to be a mother, though, as duties called and battles against Thrawn's forces and the mad Jedi clone Joruus C'Baoth commenced. Luckily, Leia had a trio of Noghri assassins for her children's

bodyguards, and a very capable assistant, the woman called Winter.

After the battle against C'Baoth, and another against the equally mad clones of Emperor Palpatine, Leia and Han realized the danger their children could be exposed to if they stayed with their parents at any of the Rebel bases. For, if someone using the dark side of the Force got near the children, they could be harmed or stolen. And since Leia was pregnant again, she was even less able to adequately protect the twins.

Mon Mothma found an exotic world,

New Alderaan, on which Winter could sequester and raise the children. All went well until a group of the Emperor-clone's Dark Siders attacked. With the aid of Salla Zend and the *Millennium Falcon,* Winter, the twins, and the other settlers of the planet escaped. They evacuated to the distant Auril system and the abandoned floating space city Nespis VIII, where the Alliance had formed a new base. It was there that their new brother, Anakin, was born.

While their parents relocated along with the New Republic back to Coruscant, the twins and the infant Anakin were taken to a distant world called Anoth, which had been scouted by Admiral Ackbar and Luke Skywalker. A heavily guarded facility was constructed in which Winter could raise and teach the Solo children. No one knew Anoth's location except Luke, Ackbar, and Winter. Several times a year, Winter would bring a long-distance shuttle to Coruscant, allow Leia and/or Han to board, and then take multiple hyperspace jumps to cover its path. Thus, even the two parents were protected from knowing where Anoth was.

When Jacen and Jaina were two years old, Winter brought them back to live on Coruscant, keeping the infant Anakin back on Anoth. Although Leia did her best to take care of the mischievous twins, most of the time the duty was relegated to the fussy C-3PO, or to their giant hairy Wookiee "uncle," Chewbacca. When he was home, Han would read stories to them at bedtime; their favorite was *The Little Lost Bantha Cub.* They always preferred Han's stories to C-3PO's, even though the droid was a masterful storyteller.

Life in the Imperial Palace on Coruscant was more of an adventure for the twins than their parents ever thought possible. Driving C-3PO out of his circuits was the most fun. In the Skydome Botanical Gardens, during

an important reception for Caridian Ambassador Furgan, the twins managed to entangle Threepio in a giant tentacle cactus. And when their father took Kyp Durron skiing, they packed the droid in snow on the hover-ski slopes of the polar regions.

Perhaps nothing was as exciting, or scary, as when they lost Threepio and Chewbacca in the Holographic Zoo of Extinct Animals, and took an unused turbolift to the depths of the ruins below Imperial City. There, they met the feral ex–civil servants of the Emperor, and their king Daykin. Daykin took the twins back topside, to return them to their parents.

Jacen and Jaina eventually went to Yavin Four, where their uncle Luke Skywalker was in grave danger. While in the chamber where Luke's comatose body lay,

the twins discovered they could see Luke's spirit calling to them from another plane of the Force. He had them relay warnings about Exar Kun to his Jedi students. When Kun sent flying beasts to attack Luke's body, Jacen and Jaina helped defeat them. Not even three years old, Jacen used Luke's own lightsaber as if he had been practicing for years. Eventually, the combined Force powers of the Jedi students, the spirits of Vodo-Siosk Baas and Luke, and Leia and her twins defeated and destroyed Kun's spirit.

Shortly after the incident on Yavin Four, Ambassador Furgan attacked Anoth in an attempt to steal Anakin. He was repelled by Winter, Leia, Ackbar, and a Mon Calamari named Terpfen. Afterward, Leia and Han decided that Anakin would be just as safe on Coruscant with them and the twins.

Because their mother was a chief of state and their father was an inveterate adventurer, the children grew up happily playing in the corridors of the Imperial Palace on Coruscant. They attended many important diplomatic functions—such as the Time of Meeting on Ithor—often being introduced in a very formal manner.

When they were five years old, Jacen and Jaina were kidnapped, along with Anakin, by the Firrerreon lord Hethrir. Having trained under Darth Vader, Hethrir was intent on teaching Force-sensitive children the ways of the dark side, and the Solo kids certainly qualified. On Hethrir's worldcraft, Jacen and Jaina were insolent and rude to their "Master," keeping their spirits whole and clean by using the strength of the Force bond they shared. They helped the other children escape when Hethrir was consumed by Waru on the Crseih Research Station.

As they grew older, the twins began to resemble their dark-haired, dark-eyed parents, although Jacen had curly hair, and Jaina had straight hair. Their Force talents began manifesting themselves more clearly, finally giving them some individuality in their twin-ness. Jacen was skilled at working with animals, his Force talents allowing him to communicate with dozens of pets, some of a very odd nature. Jaina's talents were mechanical in nature. By the time she was nine, she was helping Han fix parts on the *Falcon*. She could invent just about anything mechanical if given enough time.

Uncle Luke kept a close watch on the children and their constantly increasing ties to the Force, and they often visited him on Yavin Four when their mother or father went to see him. Jacen and Jaina wanted to attend the Jedi academy, and finally got the opportunity to do so when in their early teens.

They were fourteen when they met two exciting new students: the athletic Tenel Ka and the giant Wookiee, Lowbacca. Jacen and Jaina called the Wookiee "Lowie," and communicated to him through the Miniaturized Translator Droid, Em Teedee, on his belt. The four soon became fast friends, exploring the Massassi jungles of Yavin Four.

One afternoon, the quartet found a crashed TIE fighter, apparently incapacitated since the first Battle of Yavin, long before any of them were born. They returned several days in a row, and Jaina began repairing the ship. She even added a hyperdrive module that her father had given her as a gift.

Unfortunately, the TIE pilot, Qorl, was still alive and hiding in the jungles. Surprising the children, he managed to capture Jacen and Jaina, but Tenel and Lowbacca both escaped, running for help. When his ship was fixed, Qorl took off, leaving the twins to die in the jungles. They were soon rescued by Han, Chewie, Tenel, and Lowie, though the *Millennium Falcon* wasn't fast enough to

stop the TIE fighter before it jumped into hyperspace, using Jaina's module.

A few weeks later, the twins and Lowie accompanied Lando to his corusca-mining GemDiver Station. Suddenly, a fleet of Imperial Skipray blastboats and an assault shuttle attacked the station. Raiding it, the stormtroopers and a mysterious Dathomirian Nightsister captured the trio of young Jedi, stunning them and spiriting them away.

The Nightsister, Tamith Kai, had learned about the students from the TIE pilot, Qorl. She planned to train the kids in the dark side of the Force at her Shadow Academy in the Core systems. At the Academy the three were separated, and only allowed to see each other during their lessons.

Although they resisted the dark-side teachings, Jacen and Jaina were almost caught in an angry web of evil woven by the academy headmaster, Brakiss. He was an ex-student of Luke's who had gone to the dark side. In class one day, Jacen confronted him, and Brakiss attacked the young boy with blue Force lightning. Shortly thereafter, using a combination of holograms and trickery, "Master" Brakiss pitted the twins against each other in an almost-deadly lightsaber duel. When they discovered who they were fighting, they refused to continue.

Jaina used the Force to open the door to her cell, and quickly freed Jacen and Lowie. They found their way to the landing bays, where, by fortunate coincidence, Luke and Tenel Ka had just landed, staging their own rescue attempt! After struggling with the bay doors, the four young Jedi and their Master escaped back to Yavin Four aboard the *Shadow Chaser*.

As the children grew in their Jedi knowledge, they also began to understand the dangers they—and their Force-strong younger brother Anakin—would be facing in their lives, by virtue of their birthright. Meanwhile, they are living the reckless lives of youth. Jacen is eager to continue lessons in using a lightsaber, while Jaina can't wait to pilot her own ship. There is little doubt, however, that the tales of the Jedi children Jacen and Jaina Solo will one day be famous throughout the galaxy.

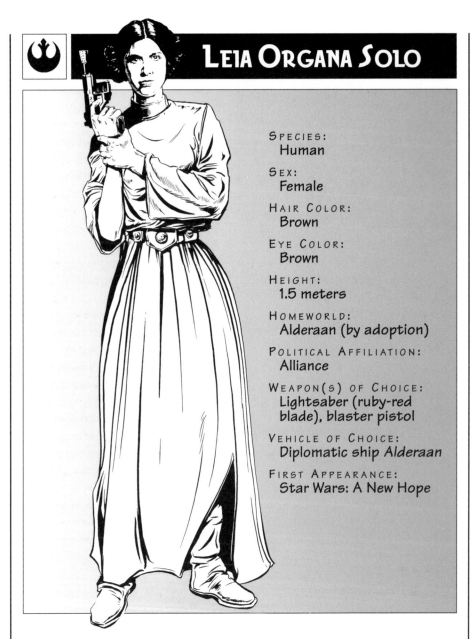

LEIA ORGANA SOLO

SPECIES:
Human

SEX:
Female

HAIR COLOR:
Brown

EYE COLOR:
Brown

HEIGHT:
1.5 meters

HOMEWORLD:
Alderaan (by adoption)

POLITICAL AFFILIATION:
Alliance

WEAPON(S) OF CHOICE:
Lightsaber (ruby-red blade), blaster pistol

VEHICLE OF CHOICE:
Diplomatic ship Alderaan

FIRST APPEARANCE:
Star Wars: A New Hope

Once one of the firebrands of the Imperial Senate, Princess Leia Organa of Alderaan would become many other things as her life progressed: councilor, diplomat, leader, wife, mother, and Jedi-Knight-in-training. Along the way, the tragedies of her hidden past blossomed into triumphs of her future.

In the time after the Clone Wars, the Jedi Knight Obi-Wan Kenobi arrived at the home of his old friend, Viceroy and First Chairman of Alderaan, Bail Organa. Kenobi's Jedi student, a hotshot young star pilot named Anakin Skywalker, had been seduced by the dark side of the Force and had become the Dark Lord of the Sith, Darth Vader. Kenobi brought with him Skywalker's wife and her young newborn twins, Luke and Leia. Bail sheltered the woman and her daughter in the Royal House while Obi-Wan brought the infant Luke to Tatooine to be raised by Kenobi's brother, Owen Lars.

Leia was adopted into Bail's family and made a princess. She lived in the Royal House in the capital city of Aldera, where the environment was peaceful and serene; weapons and violence had been banned.

Leia has very few memories of her mother, but she grew up with a trio of gossipy aunts—Tia, Rouge, and Celly—and a playmate named Winter. While Leia was rough-and-tumble, Winter was regal and beautiful; people often thought Winter was the princess, which amused the two girls to no end.

Watching her father work as a senator in the Old Republic, Leia learned the principles of justice and honor. She soon became the youngest senator in galactic history, even as Emperor Palpatine made his ascent to power. Behind the scenes, Bail was working with Mon Mothma and Garm Bel Iblis to formalize a Rebel Alliance against the Emperor. Meanwhile, in the Imperial Senate, Leia became a voice of dissent, constantly challenging Palpatine's new Imperial policies.

Although Bail objected, Leia used her status as a senator to aid the growing Rebellion. She regularly transported food and medical supplies, delivered funds, and recruited new members into the Alliance. On the planet Ralltiir, she had a close scrape when the Imperial lord Tion and Darth Vader almost caught her with a Rebel spy. The injured man told her of a terrifying new

weapon that the Empire was building, the battle station Death Star.

Leia and Bail attempted to gain more information about the Death Star from Lord Tion, but at a private dinner with the Imperial, Leia let slip what she knew. Tion threatened her with his blaster, but she wrestled with him. The blaster went off, and Tion was killed. His body was taken to a game preserve, where a suitable accident could be arranged.

When Rebels on Toprawa captured the technical readouts for the Death Star, Leia left aboard her consulate ship, the *Tantive IV*, to retrieve the plans from restricted space. But the Imperial Star Destroyer *Devastator* challenged them and they fled into hyperspace, the *Devastator* fast on their heels.

The *Tantive IV* had a second mission to complete: Bail Organa had told Leia to find Obi-Wan Kenobi and return with him to Alderaan. Coming out of hyperspace near Tatooine, the *Tantive IV* was fired upon by the *Devastator*. Although it made a second desperate run for freedom, the smaller ship was caught in a tractor beam. Knowing the Imperials would board the ship, Leia hurriedly placed the stolen data inside an astromech droid named R2-D2, ordering him to find Kenobi in the Tatooine deserts and show him a holomessage she recorded on the spot. Moments later, Leia was stunned by invading stormtroopers, but Artoo and his counterpart droid, C-3PO, got away in an escape pod.

Darth Vader took Leia prisoner personally. Her diplomatic immunity could not help her now; not only was she caught red-handed in an attempt to help the Rebellion, but the Emperor had just dissolved the Imperial Senate. Aboard the Death Star, Vader used an Imperial interrogator droid to find the location of the main Rebel base from Leia, but it too was ineffective. He used his own powers of the Force as well, but it did no good, so more drastic measures were called into play. Leia felt her defiance melt away when Grand Moff Tarkin threatened to destroy her home planet of Alderaan unless she told them what they wanted. Quietly, she admitted that the base was on Dantooine.

And then, when Tarkin ordered Alderaan destroyed anyway, Vader forced Leia to watch. Later, when Tarkin found she had lied about Dantooine, she was scheduled for termination. In shock, Leia barely noticed.

When her cell door in Detention Block AA-23 opened, Leia was surprised to find a short stormtrooper ogling her. She soon found out it was Luke Skywalker, there with

Ben Kenobi to rescue her. Unfortunately, Kenobi was elsewhere, and the rescue attempt was being made by Luke, a grating Corellian named Han Solo, and his giant Wookiee companion Chewbacca. Still, for all its bumps and starts, the rescue worked. Though Kenobi was killed by Darth Vader, in death he allowed a way for the others to escape on Solo's *Millennium Falcon*.

Using the plans still stored in R2-D2, the Rebellion quickly mobilized an attack plan and against all odds destroyed the Death Star.

In a special ceremony, Leia presented medals to Han and Luke for their bravery in the battle. She smiled at the Corellian, who had the audacity to wink at her in front of the entire assembled throng of the Alliance.

Leia had now been exposed as a member of the Rebel Alliance, so she was drafted to work as a diplomat to get new worlds to join the Alliance. But on the way to one of her first direct diplomatic missions, Leia was forced to make an unscheduled landing on the jungle planet of Mimban. With Luke, Artoo, and Threepio, she was caught up in a race to find the Force-powerful Kaiburr Crystal in the Temple of Pomojema.

At the temple, Leia faced the source of her nightmares: Darth Vader, who had come for the crystal as well. Luke was trapped by a fallen stone, so Leia clumsily used his lightsaber to help defend herself against Vader. Untrained and undisciplined, Leia was wounded badly by the Dark Lord before Luke finally freed himself and drove Vader to fall into a pit. He then used the power of the crystal to heal Leia's wounds.

Over the following three years, Leia would become more of an important force in the leadership of the Rebel Alliance. With Alderaan gone, she took on Luke, Han, and Chewbacca as her new family. Leia had numerous adventures, both with and without her fellow Alliance heroes. She was a little confused, though, by her feelings for Luke and Han. As difficult and coarse as Han could be, he ignited a fire inside her, a siren call to adventure and passion. She also had strong feelings for Luke, but they weren't romantic. Something else was there, some connection she was unable to fathom.

When the Alliance moved its headquarters to the frozen world of Hoth, Leia went with them. Han came along, and the sparks of their relationship grew more frequent. All too soon, though, the Empire found them, and the base had to be evacuated. Cut off from their transport ship, Leia and Threepio were forced to board the *Millennium Falcon*.

Leia would have found Han's problematic escape attempt humorous if her life hadn't been on the line. Still, he did get them away from the Imperials, even if he did get a little too close to her in the process. Cornering her as she helped make repairs on his ship, Han moved through her defenses. Protesting that he was a scoundrel, Leia had to face his answer that she might just like scoundrels. They had just kissed—the most incredible kiss in Leia's life—when Threepio interrupted. The moment was gone, but the feelings weren't.

Shortly thereafter, they landed on

Bespin's Cloud City, where Han's old buddy, Lando Calrissian, flirted with Leia. Unfortunately, he also betrayed them to Darth Vader. Leia finally admitted her love to Han as he was forced into a carbonite-freezing chamber. His last words to her were "I know."

Han's body, frozen in a block of carbonite, was given to the bounty hunter Boba Fett to take to Jabba the Hutt. Despite Lando's change of heart and rescue of Leia, Chewie, and Threepio from the Imperials, it

was too late to save Han. Rocketing away from Cloud City aboard the *Millennium Falcon*, Leia felt a familiar presence in her mind: Luke. Lando and Chewie piloted back, using Luke's connection to Leia to guide them to a weather vane underneath the city. They rescued Luke and returned to the Rebel fleet.

Leia, Lando, Chewie, and Luke all went on various missions to support the Alliance and find information that would help them mount their rescue of Han. Each of the core Alliance heroes was to infiltrate Jabba the Hutt's desert palace on Tatooine. Leia gained entrance while masquerading as the Ubese bounty hunter Boushh, who was bringing Chewbacca the Wookiee to Jabba for the reward.

Leia did free Han from his carbonite prison, but her identity was discovered and

she had to endure the humiliation of being Jabba's slave for a time. She got revenge for these indignities during Luke's escape, strangling the sluglike crime lord with the very chain that held her captive.

Returning to the Alliance, Leia got involved in the plot to destroy the second Death Star. She was surprised and pleased to find that Han Solo had accepted the rank of general in the Alliance forces, and volunteered to accompany him on his strike team. They traveled to the forest moon of Endor, where Leia's diplomatic skills helped gain the favor of the furry little Ewoks that lived in the forests. With their help, the Rebels were able to destroy the energy-shield generator that protected the orbiting Death Star, allowing the Rebel starfighters to destroy it.

On Endor, Leia found that she was truly in love with Han. She also learned news that she would have difficulty coming to grips with in the future: she and Luke were the twin heirs of Anakin Skywalker, the man she knew as Darth Vader. She too had the power and potential to become a Jedi Knight. She came to understand, though, that as an ambassador for peace, perhaps she was more important than she would be as a Jedi.

The day after the Battle of Endor, the New Republic received a plea for help from Bakura, a planet whose main export was repulsorlifts. Leia accompanied a strike team to the planet, which was fighting an invasion force of reptilian Ssi-ruuk, and won a permanent truce with the Bakurans, who united with the Alliance soon after the Ssi-ruuk were defeated.

The truce wasn't the most important part of the trip for Leia's mental health; Anakin Skywalker's spirit appeared to her in her suite on Bakura. The man who had once been Darth Vader begged her forgiveness,

trying to take away her anger. "Anger is the dark side," he cautioned, adding, "I do not ask for absolution. Only your forgiveness." But Leia refused to forgive the man who had tortured her, helped destroy her world, and frozen Han in carbonite.

Eventually, in the heat of the Bakuran battle, she did come to at least forgive her father. Even if she would never forget, every world she took from the Empire would help ease the pain of her memories.

The Bakuran mission was a success, and Leia was assigned more and more missions as an ambassador to planets of the galaxy that had been under Imperial rule. Leia used all of her diplomatic courtesies, often aided by C-3PO, to keep any hostility at a low level. She and the other members of the Provisional Council knew how fragile and tenuous was the balance of power.

For a short time, Mothma established a private strike team of the Alliance's most daring heroes. Called the Senate Interplanetary Intelligence Network—SPIN—the team consisted of Leia, Luke, Han, Chewie, Lando, Artoo, and Threepio. When Jabba's father, Zorba the Hutt, took out a bounty on Leia for the death of his son, the SPIN strike-force team helped rescue her. Mon Mothma eventually disbanded the special group as missions of more importance came into place.

The Alliance High Command finally convened a Constitutional Convention to establish a second Galactic Republic, and a pro-

visional government was created. This Provisional Council included Chief Councilor Mon Mothma, Commander in Chief Admiral Ackbar, Bothan Councilor Borsk Fey'lya, Alderaan Councilor Leia Organa, and others. Mon Mothma saw their main task "to become the New Republic in fact as well as name."

A smaller group, the Inner Council, consisted of no one but Mothma, Ackbar, Fey'lya, and Leia. While the Provisional Council was trying to deal with its political issues and struggles, the war against the Empire was still skirmishing on the outer edges of the galaxy—and sometimes in the heart of it. The Inner Council helped make the immediate, day-to-day decisions facing the New Republic.

Eventually the New Republic Council decided to move its headquarters to Imperial City on Coruscant, once the seat of

Emperor Palpatine. There, Leia and Han finally had to reconcile their feelings for each other when Hapan Prince Isolder arrived on Coruscant, bearing gifts from the sixty-three worlds of the Hapes cluster. The dashing and handsome prince asked for Leia's hand in marriage, and she considered the request; an earlier visit to Hapes had reminded her very much of Alderaan, and Isolder was stable and charming.

Of course, Han wasn't about to give up without a fight, and he kidnapped Leia and took her to Dathomir, a planet he had won in a card game. But Han's schemes always took wrong turns. His romantic overture was interrupted by a war between two clans of Force-wielding Nightsisters. However, by the time Luke and Isolder joined the battle and helped win it, Leia had decided she was better off with the roguish scoundrel. Han and Leia were married six weeks later, in

the White Room in Imperial City.

One of the most pressing issues to face the Council was the appearance of Grand Admiral Thrawn and his fleet. Pregnant with twins, Leia tried to help as best she could. Leia was instrumental in bringing the Noghri out of service to the Empire and into the New Republic, and in inviting Garm Bel Iblis and his forces to rejoin the Alliance. She also helped Luke and Mara Jade destroy the mad Jedi clone Joruus C'Baoth.

In the midst of the battles, Leia birthed her twins, Jacen and Jaina Solo. Between dealing with her dozens of Council meetings and assignments and taking care of the twins, Leia tried to train her Jedi powers with Luke. She had little time for Jedi training, though. Luckily, she had Winter to help her with the children.

After surviving Imperial forces drove the New Republic off Coruscant, Winter took the twins to New Alderaan, where they would be protected from Imperials and the forces of the dark side. The New Republic placed their temporary headquarters on the Fifth Moon of Da Soocha in the Cyax system.

Pregnant again, Leia had to deal with the clone of the Emperor, and his seeming

corruption of Luke. On the way to help her brother, Leia and Han visited Nar Shaddaa, where Leia was recognized as a Jedi by Vima-Da-Boda and given an ancient lightsaber.

The clone tried to corrupt Leia as well, knowing that her Force powers, and those of her children, were strong indeed. Her will was stronger, though, and she escaped, taking Palpatine's Jedi Holocron with her. Later, she returned to Luke's side, and joined her will with his to defeat the cloned Emperor.

Soon after, Leia and Han returned to Nar Shaddaa to find Vima-Da-Boda. Later, on New Alderaan, she helped defend her children from another Dark Sider attack before returning to the Republic's temporary base on the abandoned floating space city of Nespis VIII. They arrived just in time. Leia went into labor, and hours later delivered a baby boy. The proud parents named him Anakin Solo, after his great Jedi grandfather.

Within months, the Alliance won back the Imperial City on Coruscant, and the New Republic Council resumed their attempts at restructuring a galactic government. Han and Leia allowed their three children to be sequestered away on the hidden planet of Anoth, protected by Winter.

As time progressed, Leia accepted more and more responsibilities in the provisional government. She remained the voice of reason, often supporting the decisions of Mon Mothma or Admiral Ackbar above others. Luke eventually went off to Yavin Four to build a new Jedi academy, while his sister became the minister of state, the most important diplomat in the New Republic.

Over the following year, Leia had many crises to deal with. Mon Mothma was dying of a mysterious wasting disease, and her protégée gained even more duties. While Anakin stayed with Winter on Anoth, the twins were returned to Coruscant to live with their parents . . . except that Han was missing on his diplomatic mission to Kessel.

Disasters continued to strike. Leia and Ackbar traveled to Vortex for an important

diplomatic meeting; the Mon Calamari ended up crashing his B-wing fighter into the Vors' crystalline Cathedral of the Winds. Disgraced, he resigned. Without Mothma or Ackbar, Leia was the sole voice of reason when Imperial Admiral Daala and her forces emerged from the black-hole cluster known as the Maw. As if things weren't bad enough, Luke was comatose on Yavin Four, his spirit gone from his body.

Things began to turn around as Leia brought disparate elements of the galaxy together. She helped clear Ackbar of blame in the Vortex incident, and arrived with him on Anoth in time to help save her son from invading Imperial forces. She was with Luke's Jedi trainees as they used their combined Force powers to destroy the spirit of Dark Lord of the Sith Exar Kun. Finally, she brought the Jedi initiate Cilghal to Coruscant, where she was able to heal Mon Mothma.

But Mon Mothma had already tendered her resignation to the Council, and had chosen Leia as her replacement as chief of state. Even as the Republic's leader, though, Leia refused to compromise her time with her family. A vacation on Ithor became a search for the lost children of the Jedi on Plawell and a battle against Roganda Ismaren and her son Irek, who planned to use Leia as a valuable pawn in their plans to build a new Empire. Then a diplomatic visit to tour the forests and castles of Muntro Codur led to terror when the rogue Dark Jedi slaver Hethrir kidnapped Jacen, Jaina, and Anakin. Leia helped rescue her children with the aid of Chewbacca, Artoo, and Hethrir's ex-mate, Rillao.

Twenty-three years after she had launched a mission to find the final Jedi, Obi-Wan Kenobi, Leia enrolled her own children in Luke's Jedi academy. Until the galaxy is whole again, and happy under the leadership of the New Republic and the protection of the reborn Jedi Knights, Princess Leia Organa Solo will continue to be leader, mother, and Jedi. Her fathers—both of them—would be proud.

MAKO SPINCE

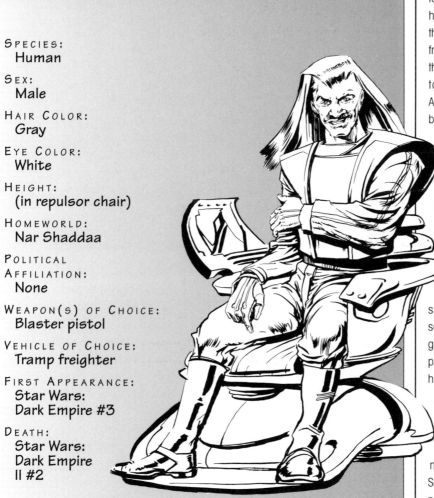

SPECIES:
Human

SEX:
Male

HAIR COLOR:
Gray

EYE COLOR:
White

HEIGHT:
(in repulsor chair)

HOMEWORLD:
Nar Shaddaa

POLITICAL
AFFILIATION:
None

WEAPON(S) OF CHOICE:
Blaster pistol

VEHICLE OF CHOICE:
Tramp freighter

FIRST APPEARANCE:
Star Wars:
Dark Empire #3

DEATH:
Star Wars:
Dark Empire
II #2

Spince's later pranks at the Academy included programming the food dispensers with gene-lab samples and broadcasting a fake holo of Dean Wyrmyr's death during a homecoming function. He went too far, though, when he stole a gram of antimatter from the physics lab and used it to blow up the Academy's "mascot moon." The actual target for the antimatter had been the Academy's official seal, emblazoned on the barren rocky planetoid that orbited high above the Academy.

Needless to say, Mako's superiors were not amused by what he called a "silly prank." He was expelled two years before his friend Han graduated. His final act as he left the Academy was to droidnap ZZ-4Z from the recycling plant. After that, Mako disappeared for a while, using his parent's money to buy himself a ship and reemerge as a smuggler who was renowned for making some of the riskiest smuggling runs in the galaxy. He seemed willing to take any risk, provided he was well paid. His family cut him off from the Spince Trust.

Rebellion against authority was a character trait Spince shared with Han Solo, who was banished from military service when he helped a Wookiee slave named Chewbacca escape. Mako taught Solo the adrenalin-pumping pleasures and profits of the smuggling trade, keeping the no longer innocent Corellian around as a sidekick. The Wookiee also made an excel-

The son of an influential and important senator in the days of the Old Republic, Mako Spince lived an aimless life. Although he was healthy and had a sharp mind, he had no clear goals, preferring to fritter away his time and his father's money.

Shortly after the Clone Wars brought unrest in the galaxy, he finally decided to pursue a military career. Although he was in his late twenties, and thus considered old for an entrant into the Imperial Space Academy, Mako's father gained him admission. Advisors were hopeful that Spince would show the type of leadership his father had shown.

Unfortunately for the Academy, Mako proved less than officer material. He broke rules and disobeyed orders, sure that his father's influence could help him out of any trouble. He became friends with a young Corellian named Han Solo. Besides Solo, Spince made friends with ZZ-4Z, the outmoded housekeeping droid of Dean Horace Wyrmyr, who unwittingly gave him many secrets of the dean's past.

lent bodyguard. Tired of ZZ-4Z's endless banter, Mako wagered him to Solo in a game of sabacc and lost. Solo set ZZ up as the housekeeper of his scruffy home.

Spince and Solo made their headquarters on the smuggler's moon of Nar Shaddaa, where cities were built upon cities of the past, creating an underworld maze of hideaways and headquarters of illicit businesses. Nar Shaddaa orbited Nal Hutta, home to the notorious species of sluglike creatures known as the Hutts. The Hutts, including Jabba the Hutt, were galaxywide gangsters who ruled the smuggling trade, employing the Nar Shaddaa smugglers for their own ends.

On a smuggling run in the Ottega system, Mako's ship was caught by the NaQuoit Bandits, who crippled him, forcing him into semiretirement. Confined to a repulsor chair, he became a traffic controller on Nar Shaddaa. The last time he saw Han Solo was shortly before the doomed spice run on which Solo had to dump a valuable

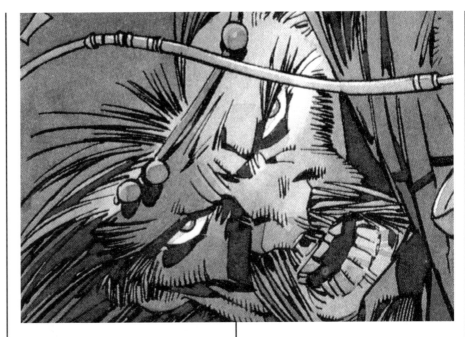

shipment of Jabba the Hutt's to avoid an arrest.

A decade later, Solo returned to Nar Shaddaa to seek the help of Shug Ninx and Salla Zend. Mako was surprised to hear from his longtime friend, especially since the Hutts had quadrupled the bounty for Solo and Leia after the death of Jabba the Hutt on Tatooine. Although he allowed the *Millennium Falcon* to find safety in the twisting constructed canyons of the Corellian sector, Mako contacted Boba Fett and Dengar, offering them Han and Leia in exchange for enough money to allow him to retire.

When Han returned to his lodging deep in the city, he found that Mako had let Fett and Dengar enter first. Spince apologized to Solo, but the last he saw of his once-friend was his blaster fire as Solo and Leia made their escape. Still, Mako had been pre-paid by the bounty hunters, and it was their mistakes that allowed

Solo to escape. The credits from the reward could make his life easy again.

Despite the bounties, Spince didn't leave his job as overseer of sector space traffic after all. Thus, weeks later, when Han and the *Falcon* returned to Nar Shaddaa on a mission to find Vima-Da-Boda, Spince tracked them for the Star Destroyer *Invincible*. As the Imperial ship attempted to catch the *Falcon* in its tractor beam, Han piloted his freighter behind Spince's traffic-control pylon.

The pylon was pulled up in the tractor beam, spearing the core of the *Invincible*. The Star Destroyer and pylon crashed into floating structures above Nar Shaddaa and were destroyed. Spince's final double-cross on Han Solo had been his ultimate undoing.

NOMI SUNRIDER

SPECIES:
Human

SEX:
Female

HAIR COLOR:
Rusty brown

EYE COLOR:
Blue-green

HEIGHT:
Unknown

HOMEWORLD:
Unknown

POLITICAL AFFILIATION:
Republic

WEAPON(S) OF CHOICE:
Lightsaber (green blade)

VEHICLE OF CHOICE:
Lightside Explorer

FIRST APPEARANCE:
Dark Horse Comics #7

DEATH:
Unknown

third approached from behind, carrying a poisonous gorm worm. The creature bit Andur, killing him instantly.

Nomi rushed to her husband, but he had already become one with the Force. His glowing form appeared to her, telling her to pick up his lightsaber and defend herself. In life, Andur had always known Nomi was capable of becoming a great Jedi, but she was too timid to train in the Force. With Andur's death, Nomi was transformed, and killed two of the thugs.

Honoring her husband's wishes, Nomi continued, with her daughter and Threedee, on the trip to see Master Thon. She landed the *Lightside Explorer* on the ringed world of Ambria. There, in the desolate wastes, Nomi met the Jedi Oss Willum and the armor-plated creature known as Master Thon. The two Jedi and Nomi defended Thon's homestead when Bogga the Hutt and his thugs—having followed Nomi's ship—attacked in search of the crystals.

Nomi agreed to stay on Ambria and train to be a Jedi, but in the months that followed, Thon ignored her. Nomi raised her daughter, protecting her from dangers with her nascent Force talent, which seemed to be the ability to alter events with her mind. She did not yet know, but this talent was a part of the Jedi battle meditation.

Knowing a battle with the dark

Four thousand years prior to the Empire's great Jedi Purge, the Jedi Knights faced major battles against an uprising of evil and the coming of the Dark Lords of the Sith. One of the most illustrious of the Jedi was Nomi Sunrider, whose powers would pass down through her lineage to generations of future Jedi.

Nomi was the wife of the Jedi Andur Sunrider, and the mother of the newborn Vima. They lived on a craggy world, assisted by their personal droid A-3DO. From his Master, Chamma, Andur had received a

parcel of Adegan crystals—the best gems for constructing lightsabers. Since Nomi always worried about his safety, Andur decided to take his family with him to deliver the crystals. They departed for the Stenness system, where the legendary Jedi Master Thon was watchman.

Unfortunately, Great Bogga the Hutt found out about their precious cargo when they docked at the Stenness Hyperspace Terminal. Two thugs arranged a diversion while a side was imminent on the other side of the galaxy, Thon finally decided to begin training Nomi. Her grief for her husband had lessened, and she could train now without her emotions becoming a problem. Oss Willum was leaving Ambria with Master Arca, to fight the Freedon Nadd uprising with the apprentices Ulic and Cay Qel-Droma and the Twi'lek, Tott Doneeta.

Still angry at his defeat on Ambria, Bogga ordered the space pirate Finhead Stonebone to attack Master Thon and steal the Adegan crystals. Thon had begun training Nomi, but the now Jedi-to-be refused to build or even use a lightsaber. Taking Nomi and Vima through the exotic terrain of his planet, Thon stressed that a lightsaber was more than a tool of defense; it focused the mind, assisting a Jedi's connection to the Force.

Nomi still refused, so Thon taught her, using a Jedi Holocron, about the millennia-old battle between the light side and the dark side of the Force. The Holocron gatekeeper, Master Ood Bnar, prophesized that Nomi would play a large role in the coming battle against the dark side. Conflicting emotions ran through Nomi. She didn't want to kill to defend the galaxy. She wanted to take her daughter and leave Thon and begin her life anew.

Events forced her to decide otherwise. Finhead Stonebone and his pirates arrived, attacking Thon. Nomi still refused to fight, and took her daughter to safety among the rocks. Before he had allowed himself to be captured by the pirates, Thon had told her to use her special Force talents. Nomi used her connection to the Force to intensify the pirates' aggressions, causing them to fight one another, as well as Bogga's men.

Finally, Nomi realized she could not turn away. Taking Thon's ancient lightsaber, she charged the group, wielding the blade as if she had done so for years. Between her skills and Thon's Force shields and waves of energy, the pirates were defeated. Few survived to return to Bogga, and in the aftermath of the battle, Nomi knew she must continue her training.

Nomi's training eventually took her and her daughter to Ossus, the third planet in the Adegan system. Ossus was a thriving center of Jedi learning, and Thon brought her there to apprentice to Master Vodo-Siosk Baas. Baas trained her in the making of her own lightsaber, using one of the crystals her husband had given her.

Nomi trained in many Jedi ways on Ossus, but one day a fateful assembly was called. The Jedi Master Arca had fallen to Sith sorcery on Onderon, and a team of Jedi was needed to rescue him. Nomi was one of those chosen for the task. Leaving her daughter to the care of the other Jedi, Nomi traveled to Onderon for the coming battle against the Dark Siders.

The Jedi ship arrived at the ruling city of Iziz, as Galactic Republic forces stormed its walls to fight the followers of Freedon Nadd. The Jedi touched down their ship, charging to rescue Arca and his students. In the fortress walls, Nomi could feel the dark side, and she confronted it, ignoring the savage battle around her.

Nomi was struck down by a blast thrown by King Ommin. She was kept safe by Ulic Qel-Droma, whom the other Jedi had rescued. The surviving Jedi, their numbers cut to seven, stormed the citadel, intent on rescuing Master Arca from Ommin. The king himself attacked them, driving them back with the power of the ancient Sith, but Ulic prevailed. The evil spirit of Freedon

Nadd appeared, pulling Ommin's dying spirit into the dark side, and bid the Jedi farewell, promising that though they *thought* they had won the battle, in the future they would find that they had lost.

Over the following weeks, the Jedi stayed on Onderon, protecting and exploring it. Nomi and Ulic grew fond of each other, but tragedy was to strike. Arca knew that a Sith uprising was shaping in the Empress Teta system. The Ossus Jedi were to return to their planet to prepare, but Nomi stayed behind to train with Arca in the Jedi battle meditation that shaped her unique Force talents. Just as she had become an expert in the use of a lightsaber, and had become a confident leader rather than a timid follower, so too would Nomi gain strength in her other talents.

Arca soon assigned Nomi and Ulic to lead the joint peacekeeping fleet of the Galactic Republic and the Jedi Knights. As the fleet emerged from hyperspace to protect the planet Koros Major, the Krath ruler Aleema used her Sith magic to create illusions of powerful space monsters. Nomi used her powers to defeat Aleema, but the Krath mobilized a counterattack.

Aboard the command ship *Reliance*, Ulic was hit by a piece of shrapnel, but Nomi pulled it out, willing the Force to heal him. Meanwhile, the Republic commander ordered his fleet to retreat and plan a new attack strategy.

With the threat of the Sith growing stronger, most of the Jedi in the galaxy converged on the red planet of Deneba to discuss their plans. Ulic Qel-Droma proposed allowing one person to infiltrate the Krath and find the secrets of their growing power in the dark side. But before a decision could be made, the Krath unleashed upon them a set of war droids. One of the droids snatched Vima, but another Jedi, Sylvar, cut the droid down.

In the battle, Master Arca was killed. Later, in the victorious aftermath, Nomi confronted Ulic, who planned to infiltrate the Krath to learn the dark side and how to destroy it from within. She cautioned him, having been taught that the dark side could tear him apart. Ulic would not reconsider, though; the need to conquer the dark side and avenge the fallen Jedi burned within him.

Ulic departed for the Empress Teta system aboard a smuggler's freighter, *Kestrel Nova*, kissing Nomi good-bye. She knew that when she next saw Ulic, he would be a greatly changed man.

Time passed, and with no word from Ulic, Nomi took his brother, Cay, and Tott Doneeta with her to the Empress Teta system. She traveled to the city of Cinnagar

alone so that Ulic's secrets would be safe. A visit from one might not arouse suspicions, but a visit from three would. In the city, Nomi discovered that Ulic was held within the dark citadel of the Krath. To gain entrance, she revealed herself as a Jedi and allowed her capture.

Unfortunately, Nomi's plan backfired. The Krath leaders, Satal Keto and Aleema, asked Ulic to execute the Jedi woman in order to prove his allegiance to the Krath. But Nomi broke free

and used her Force powers to turn the guards against each other. Then she called Cay and Tott to the citadel from their planetary orbit.

The trio of Jedi valiantly attempted to save Ulic, but he had been injected with Sith poison. Nomi, Cay, and Tott escaped from the planet, knowing that Ulic was no longer one of them.

Back on Ossus, Nomi led an attack on Cinnagar, accompanied by Cay Qel-Droma, Tott Doneeta, Dace Diath, Oss Willum, Shoaneb Culu, Qrrrl Toq, and Oron Kira. Although they knew they couldn't win against the Krath, Nomi and Cay hoped they could at least rescue Ulic from the dark side.

After a successful run into Cinnagar, the transport disgorged Warbeasts, ridden by Nomi and three others. In the Krath stronghold, Nomi faced down Aleema, destroying her Sith illusions. Aleema hid behind her lover, Ulic, who berated Nomi for her rescue attempt. Nomi finally admitted she had risked all because she loved him.

Working with Cay, Nomi tried to make Ulic confront how deeply he had become enmeshed in the dark side. In his anger, Ulic lashed out, striking Nomi with a bolt of dark-side lightning from his Sith amulet. The Jedi woman knew then that it was as the Jedi Masters had forewarned. Ulic must choose to leave the dark side on his own, or be lost in its evil. Sadly, Nomi and the other Jedi turned their backs and left.

Nomi Sunrider's ultimate fate is unknown, but her descendants brought honor to both her name and to the Jedi. Thousands of years after Nomi first picked up her lightsaber, her multigreat-granddaughter, Vima-Da-Boda, became a prominent and illustrious Jedi Knight. Vima served the Force for over 100 years, but fell in disgrace. She began the path to redemption when she encountered Princess Leia Organa Solo, one of the new breed of Jedi. Mother to daughter, and to daughter again, the example of Nomi Sunrider would forever be legend in the annals of Jedi history.

GRAND MOFF TARKIN

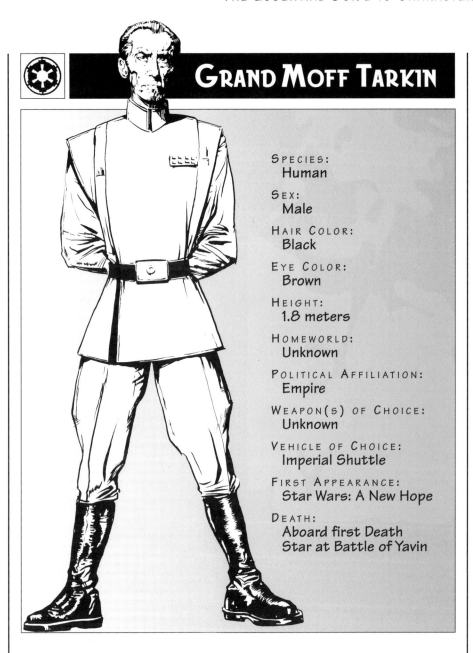

SPECIES:
Human

SEX:
Male

HAIR COLOR:
Black

EYE COLOR:
Brown

HEIGHT:
1.8 meters

HOMEWORLD:
Unknown

POLITICAL AFFILIATION:
Empire

WEAPON(S) OF CHOICE:
Unknown

VEHICLE OF CHOICE:
Imperial Shuttle

FIRST APPEARANCE:
Star Wars: A New Hope

DEATH:
Aboard first Death Star at Battle of Yavin

In the days of the Old Republic, those with ambition learned to mask themselves. They gained their political power through the electoral process, careful whose support they bought, bargained, or blackmailed for along the way. That changed when Senator Palpatine was elected president of the Republic and introduced his sweeping New Order.

One of the greedy, power-hungry governors who supported Palpatine was the young Tarkin, then a governor of the Seswenna Sector, deep in the wild frontiers of space known as the Outland Regions. Governor Tarkin was a gaunt, tall man, with sunken cheeks and piercing eyes. His intense demeanor brought him respect tinged with fear. His ruthless Tarkin Doctrine, taught in the Imperial Navy, was "Rule through the fear of force, rather than the force itself."

From his outpost on the planet Eriadu in the Seswenna sector, Tarkin rose in the ranks from governor, in charge of sectors, to moff, in charge of governors in numerous sectors. He established a strategically important Navy refueling station on Ryloth, where he met a young Twi'lek named Tol Sivron. He also experimented with Omwat children, knowing that the race had a genetic capability toward breeding brilliant designers. He took ten ten-year-old Omwats to tutor and test in a pursuit for the galaxy's best engineers. Among them were Qwi Xux, who would prove to be the top pupil.

Eventually Tarkin became the first Grand Moff, with unlimited decision-making power in priority sectors. As Grand Moff, he reported only to the Emperor. He was put in charge of Oversector Outer, which included almost all of the Outer Rim Territories.

Despite the fact that he had a stately wife on Phelarion, Tarkin took as his lover a beautiful Navy woman named Daala. He had her in mind to take charge of a secret project deep in the black-hole fields outside Kessel, an area known as the Maw. At the start of the project, Tarkin made her the Navy's first female admiral.

The Maw Installation was intended as a super thinktank where the most brilliant scientists and theoreticians could convene and create new weapons. Tarkin kept the installation a secret from Emperor Palpatine so that he could take credit for any destructive devices created. It was there that administrator Tol Sivron, top Imperial designer Chief Bevel Lemelisk, and Omwat designer/engineer Qwi Xux created the plans for the Death Star. They built a prototype of the space station, which orbited the installation. When Tarkin saw the skeletal structure of the station, he gave the trio medals on the spot.

Seeing the plans for Tarkin's dream project, Emperor Palpatine approved the Death

Star to support his Imperial space fleet. Tarkin took Lemelisk from the Maw Installation to supervise creation of the space station with destructive power far beyond any vessel known in the galaxy. The engine of destruction was constructed in orbit around the planet Despayre in the Outer Rim's Horuz system. Workers in a planetary penal colony—many of them Wookiees—performed much of the construction.

Tarkin returned to the Maw Installation to see his lover, Daala, several times. The final time, he gave the scientists a challenge to create a weapon that far surpassed the Death Star. He gave them nine years to complete the task. He said good-bye to Daala, fully intending to see her again.

As Tarkin was en route to the completed Death Star from the Governor's Palace on Eriadu, his ship was attacked by Rebels. Following a firefight with Admiral Motti's Star Destroyer, the Rebels escaped with Tarkin's servant, a Mon Calamari named Ackbar. Meanwhile, another group of Rebels had secretly stolen the plans for the battle station. Undaunted, Tarkin performed his first act as commander of the Death Star, and had the penal colony of Horuz destroyed

with the superlaser cannon.

Tarkin proved to be a brilliant strategist and excellent supervisor. He was supported by Imperial Navy Admiral Motti, and Imperial Army General Tagge, a grand tactician. The crew of the Death Star grew to 1,206,293 human personnel and 400,000 droids.

Knowing he was in control of the most powerful weapon in space, Tarkin had dreams of deposing Palpatine when the time was right. Tarkin hid those dreams from most everyone, but could not hide them from Darth Vader, whom the Emperor had assigned to aid Tarkin on the station. Vader kept silent about Tarkin's ambitions. General Tagge, however, barely hid his contempt for Tarkin, his ambitions, and Darth Vader. Motti plotted in secret, making himself indispensable as Tarkin's second in command. He also impressed upon Tarkin that he knew the Grand Moff's power would be equal to the Emperor's once the Death Star was at full power.

When it became known that the technical readouts for the Death Star had been stolen by Alliance spies, Darth Vader was dispatched to intercept them. He captured Princess Leia Organa and brought her to Tarkin and the Death Star. Tarkin was elated by the news that the Emperor had just dissolved the Imperial Senate, but the Rebellion's capture of the readouts gnawed at him. At first, Tarkin ordered Leia interrogated, first by humans, then by a needle-wielding interrogation droid. Meanwhile, he had the station moved to orbit Alderaan, Leia's home planet.

When the interrogations failed, Tarkin had Leia brought to one of the viewing bridges aboard the station. He coldly informed her of the destructive power of the space station, and threatened her with Alderaan's destruction. "You would prefer another target? A military target? Then name the system," he ordered. Although Leia finally seemed to have told him the location of the Rebel base, he still ruthlessly ordered the destruction of Alderaan.

Later, Imperial ships found the remains of the Rebel base on Dantooine, but it was deserted. Knowing Leia had lied to him even under the most dire of circumstances, Tarkin ordered her execution. Shortly thereafter, when the *Millennium Falcon* was captured, Tarkin was shocked to hear Vader's pronouncement that Obi-Wan Kenobi was aboard the station. Still, he deferred to Vader's advice to let Leia and her rescuers escape. A tracking device had been placed aboard the *Falcon*, allowing the Death Star to follow the Rebels back to their real base, on the Fourth Moon of Yavin.

When the Rebels mounted their attack on his ultimate weapon, Tarkin was incredulous. Even when his advisors informed him that there was a chance the station could be destroyed, Tarkin would not be

moved. "Evacuate? In our moment of triumph? I think you overestimate their chances," he snapped at a chief officer.

Tarkin was soon to find out how wrong he was. Only moments before the Death Star was to destroy the moon, Luke Skywalker's missiles found their mark. The Death Star exploded into billions of fragments, killing Tarkin and everyone aboard.

Tarkin's legacy caught up with the Rebellion several times more. Shortly after the Battle of Yavin, Leia

Organa and a fellow Rebel, Hume, were caught in Empire-controlled space by Darth Vader's Star Destroyer. Hume knocked Leia out and placed her aboard an escape shuttle, ejecting it into the atmosphere of Phelarion, an Imperial labor colony run by Lady Tarkin, the widow of the late Grand Moff. The slaves in the colony were mining the heat-sensitive Megonite moss, used by the Empire as a source of fuel.

Leia was picked from a crowd by Lady Tarkin and forced to be her servant at the Thirteenth Imperial Diplomatic enclave. There, Leia barely escaped notice by Darth Vader. Lady Tarkin was incensed when Vader accused her of allowing Megonite to be smuggled out, not knowing that Leia had helped the

smugglers and had used Lady Tarkin's transponder to call for help. Leia escaped; Lady Tarkin's fate is unknown.

A short time after the Battle of Bespin, a Rebel spy discovered an Imperial project in the Patriim system. Code-named the *Tarkin*, the giant weapon combined the Death Star's main offensive battery and ionic cannon with a set of engines and defensive field generators. Not yet operational, the *Tarkin* was targeted for destruction by an elite team of Rebels: Luke Skywalker, Leia Organa, Chewbacca, C-3PO, and R2-D2. The quintet infiltrated the construction crew, gaining access to the interior of the station.

On board, Chewbacca and the droids destroyed the tractor-beam generator, while Luke narrowly escaped another battle with Darth Vader. Luckily, Leia used the schematics of the ion cannon to reverse its polarity modes. As the Rebels escaped in the *Millennium Falcon*, gunners tried to fire the *Tarkin's* cannon, and the station exploded.

Tarkin's legacy struck yet again four years after the Battle of Yavin, when a second Death Star was constructed. As before, the Rebellion destroyed the station. The remnants of the Empire have not made an attempt to realize Tarkin's dreams a third time.

TESSEK

SPECIES:
Quarren

SEX:
Male

HAIR COLOR:
None

EYE COLOR:
Turquoise

HEIGHT:
1.8 meters

HOMEWORLD:
Mon Calamari

POLITICAL
AFFILIATION:
None

WEAPON(S)
OF CHOICE:
Vibroblade, sonic
grenade,
holdout blaster

VEHICLE OF
CHOICE:
Repulsor swoop

FIRST
APPEARANCE:
Star Wars:
Return
of the Jedi

tant for Jabba the Hutt.

Tessek's conscience bothered him, and he plotted how to get out of his job with his life—and some fortune—intact. He had diverted Jabba's funds for years, setting up clean businesses that he would control when the Hutt was gone. Those closest to Jabba knew Tessek planned betrayal, and told the Hutt not to trust him.

When a young Jedi came to entreat Jabba to release Han Solo, Tessek was horrified to learn that Jabba knew of his betrayals. Jabba planned to kill the Jedi, Solo, and the smuggler's Wookiee companion at the Pit of Carkoon, and he insisted Tessek accompany him.

Tessek knew his days were numbered. Observing defiance in the eyes of Leia, Tessek knew that the Alliance would attack and there would be some kind of rescue attempt. With great care, he addressed Jabba, his eyes communicating his support to Leia. He wanted to be taken to freedom; he could come back for his hidden fortunes later.

When the Jedi and his friends rescued themselves, Tessek escaped, flying away from the exploding sail barge on a repulsor swoop. Returning to Jabba's palace at nightfall, Tessek tried to take control, but chaos ensued. Tessek was elated, though; he was finally rid of Jabba. He was free.

T essek is a native of watery Calamari. His people share the world with the Mon Calamari, highly intelligent, salmon-colored amphibian bipeds. Long ago, the species agreed to work together, the Quarren providing materials and the Mon Calamari shaping them into huge floating cities. Although the Quarren can breathe air, they prefer water, and live in the lowest underwater levels of the cities.

The gray-skinned Quarren are often called "squid heads" because of their mushroom-shaped heads and four facial tenta-cles. The leathery skin and suction-cupped fingers only enhance the image.

The Empire had once enslaved the species of Calamari, but the Quarren and the Mon Calamari worked together to drive the Empire away. Many cities were destroyed, and many members of the two species fled their home planet.

Tessek escaped, and found his way to the desert planet of Tatooine. It wasn't the best place for a creature who needed regular water baths to survive, but the Quarren found a good job: He became an accoun-

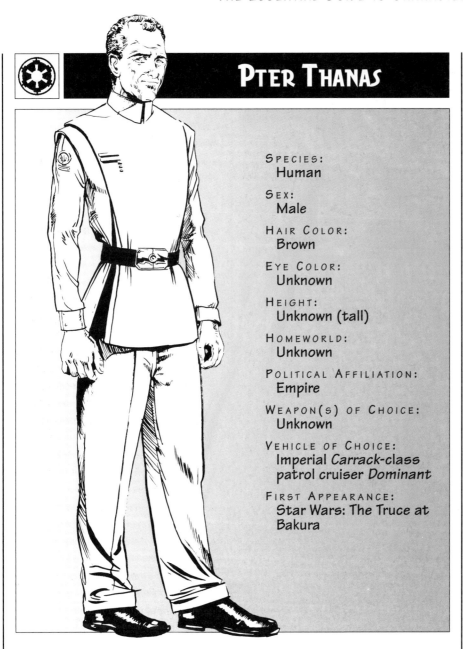

PTER THANAS

SPECIES:
Human

SEX:
Male

HAIR COLOR:
Brown

EYE COLOR:
Unknown

HEIGHT:
Unknown (tall)

HOMEWORLD:
Unknown

POLITICAL AFFILIATION:
Empire

WEAPON(S) OF CHOICE:
Unknown

VEHICLE OF CHOICE:
Imperial *Carrack*-class patrol cruiser *Dominant*

FIRST APPEARANCE:
Star Wars: The Truce at Bakura

In his fifties, Commander Pter Thanas had been a loyal and hardworking officer of the Empire. But an inner revolution began in him when he met the Jedi Master Luke Skywalker.

Thanas had been in charge of a colony of furry Talz miners on Alzoc III. He knew that if the Talz were treated better, they worked harder, so he had their food rations increased. The Talz learned of his kindness, and repaid him by saving his life when he stepped too close to a mine shaft.

But an Imperial colonel arrived six months later and lowered the food rations to save credits. The Talz complained, and the colonel ordered their village wiped out. Thanas refused and was ordered aboard his own ship, "pending reassignment." Stormtroopers destroyed the Talz village, and Thanas was sent to the dead-end Outer Rim planet of Bakura. The planet's only tactical advantage for the Empire was its repulsorlift production capacity.

Thanas was in charge of the defense of Bakura, second only to Imperial Governor Wilek Nereus. When the Ssi-ruuk attacked

Bakura and destroyed most of their defense fleet, Nereus sent a distress call to Emperor Palpatine. But unknown to the isolated Imperials on Bakura, the Empire had just fallen, the Death Star had been destroyed, and Palpatine had been killed.

On the forest moon of Endor, members of the Rebel Alliance intercepted the message and gathered a strike force to aid Bakura. When they arrived, Thanas immediately accepted their help. The Alliance leaders, including Leia Organa, Luke Skywalker, and Han Solo, met with Nereus, Thanas, and others, working out a truce for their battle against the Ssi-ruuk.

Thanas was awed by Skywalker—his bearing, his calm, and his lightsaber. With Solo and the others, Thanas mapped an attack. After a tremendous battle, the Ssi-ruuk began to withdraw. Then Thanas ordered his men to turn on the Rebels.

The Imperial commander didn't know how close he came to being rammed by the *Millennium Falcon* as he pursued attacking the lead Ssi-ruuk ship. Finally though, his ship, the *Dominant*, blew out its lateral thrusters, and was unable to move. Faced with destruction or surrender, Thanas was forced to consider the possibilities.

He had been used and abused by the Empire, and would be punished or killed if he returned to it. He could destroy the ship and everyone on it, perhaps taking out the Rebels as he did so. Or he could surrender. Thanas knew the final option was the best; Skywalker and his friends had been nothing but honorable.

Thanas remanded himself into the custody of the Alliance command. The Rebels gained control of the planet, and Senator Gaeriel Captison declared a permanent truce and a joining with the Alliance.

As he watched the last of his troops leave the planet, Pter Thanas removed a knife from his pocket. With a swift slice, he removed his rank insignia, then announced his defection to the Alliance, and walked toward his own freedom.

GRAND ADMIRAL THRAWN

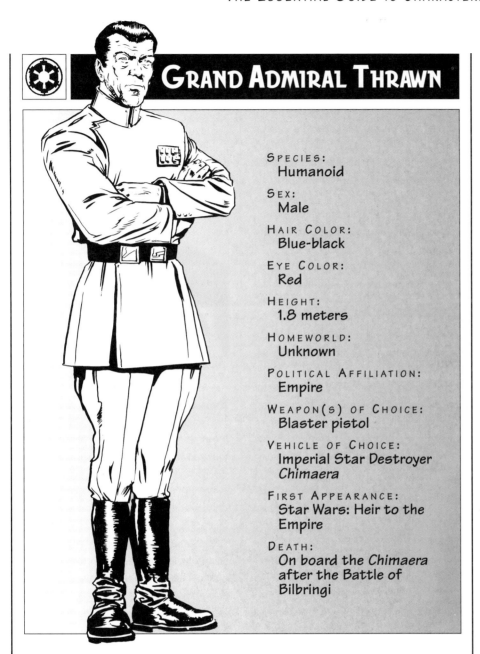

SPECIES:
Humanoid

SEX:
Male

HAIR COLOR:
Blue-black

EYE COLOR:
Red

HEIGHT:
1.8 meters

HOMEWORLD:
Unknown

POLITICAL AFFILIATION:
Empire

WEAPON(S) OF CHOICE:
Blaster pistol

VEHICLE OF CHOICE:
Imperial Star Destroyer Chimaera

FIRST APPEARANCE:
Star Wars: Heir to the Empire

DEATH:
On board the Chimaera after the Battle of Bilbringi

The highest-ranking nonhuman in the Empire's history was the regal, blue-skinned Thrawn. He would also become one of the New Republic's greatest threats.

Thrawn's origins are unknown. His blue skin, blue-black hair, and glowing red eyes marked him as an alien, but his species and home planet remained a mystery to all save the Emperor. Following Palpatine's ascendency to power, Thrawn had been placed in charge of the barbaric Unknown Regions. He was so successful in bringing the worlds to Imperial control that the Emperor bestowed an unheard-of honor on him: Thrawn became one of the twelve Grand Admirals of Empire, and the only nonhuman among them.

Thrawn continued his subjugation of the Unknown Regions, utilizing his incredible military and tactical genius for the Empire's greater glory. Analyzing and correlating threads of disparate information, he was able to pull stunning victories from certain defeat. His men came to respect and support him. Even those whose careers and military stations his own had surpassed considered Thrawn a remarkable leader.

Five years after the destruction of the second Death Star, Thrawn returned to the Empire's galaxy, only to discover it was no longer controlled by them. Palpatine was dead, and a New Republic had arisen to lead the planets to a peaceful future. Grand Admiral Thrawn quickly took control over the ships in the Imperial fleet, rallying the remnants and inspiring them to pull together for a carefully crafted attack on the Rebellion.

Thrawn's plans for the defeat of the Rebels had several parts. From his seat on the Star Destroyer *Chimaera*, supported by the competent Captain Pellaeon, Thrawn orchestrated these pieces in a way that almost brought the New Republic down.

On the planet Myrkr, he gained control of a species of creatures known as ysalamiri. These tiny rodents had the ability to push away the Force, making Jedi—and any minor Force user—powerless. Then, on the forgotten planet of Wayland, inside the Emperor's storehouse Mount Tantiss, Thrawn gained three more elements of his plan: a cloaking device, the Spaarti cloning cylinders, and the services of the Dark Jedi Joruus C'Baoth.

The legacy of Darth Vader had left Thrawn the services of the ruthless Noghri. One of them, Rukh, served as his ever-present and ever-deadly bodyguard. Other Noghri became his personal Death Commando squadron, and he dispatched them to capture Leia Organa Solo so that C'Baoth could train her and her unborn children in the ways of the dark side. C'Baoth himself was attempting to lure Luke Skywalker into his clutches.

Using his spies and surveillance devices on Coruscant, Thrawn was able to track and dissect the Rebellion's movements. He refused to refer to the group as the "New Republic." They were traitors and rebels, undeserving of the legitimacy the other title bestowed on them.

Thrawn used his private chambers on

board the *Chimaera* to meditate and to plan his strikes on the Rebellion. His spacious quarters were a museum of sorts, containing holograms of the galaxy's greatest art treasures from hundreds of worlds. He believed that by understanding a species' art, he could understand their thinking and defeat them.

Besides the *Chimaera*, Thrawn's main fleet consisted of several other ships: the four other Star Destroyers, twelve *Strike*-class cruisers, twenty-two *Carrack*-class light cruisers, and thirty full squadrons of TIE fighters—in addition to the TIE squadrons already aboard the Star Destroyers.

To test the readiness of his fleet, Thrawn launched an attack on Bpfassh and two other planets in the Sluis system, ordering a hit-and-run attack. It was not meant to obliterate the Bpfasshi, but to frighten them into calling for New Republic reinforcements. The New Republic ships—if captured—could be used to enhance Thrawn's own fleet.

The Grand Admiral also stole a complement of mole miners from Lando Calrissian's mining operation on Nkllon, intent on using them for his next move. His first main strike

against the Rebellion was in the Sluis Van shipyards, but his takeover attempt was thwarted, and he withdrew. Later, he blackmailed smuggler Niles Ferrier into providing the location of the long-missing *Katana* Dreadnaught fleet. Thrawn and his ships swooped in to steal the fleet from under the Rebels' noses, and escaped with 180 of the two hundred ships. The first gauntlet was thrown down, and only the arrival of Han Solo and Luke Skywalker kept complete victory from Thrawn's grasp.

Although Thrawn had no one to crew the stolen fleet, his scientists had found a way to use Spaarti cloning to provide an unlimited supply of soldiers.

The ysalamiri proved effective when the mad Jedi Joruus C'Baoth became difficult, unpredictable, and uncontrollable. Thrawn had special shoulder harnesses created for himself that allowed him to wear an ysalamiri at all times, protecting himself and those in close range from C'Baoth's powers. This was never more important than when—in a mad show of power—C'Baoth took control over everyone on the *Chimaera* except for Captain Pellaeon and Thrawn.

Before any clones could be grown, Thrawn made several other strikes on the Rebellion. His cloaked fleet attacked the food-production planet Ukio and the metal-production planet Woostri. Finally, in a move designed to trap the Republic leaders on their own planet, Thrawn's ships

released cloaked asteroids into orbit above Coruscant. Only twenty-two asteroids were cloaked and deadly, but Thrawn had released three hundred sensor images to confuse the New Republic scanners.

While C'Baoth practiced making clones on Wayland, Thrawn was planning his next move. He wanted the final twenty *Katana* ships, which were docked at the Bilbringi shipyards. During the attack on Bilbringi, he was surprised by the appearance of smuggler ships helping the Rebels. Thrawn's forces were defeated yet again, despite his expert tactical moves.

And then the randomness of the universe struck. Thrawn, who overestimated the loyalty of his people, was killed by the one closest to him. The Noghri assassin Rukh had learned that Thrawn had betrayed his people. Rukh killed him and escaped.

The Empire had suffered much since the death of the Emperor, and Thrawn had represented hope. But that hope was based on fear, betrayal, and wild schemes. The death of Grand Admiral Thrawn represented a crippling end to the stranglehold of the Empire.

TIGRIS

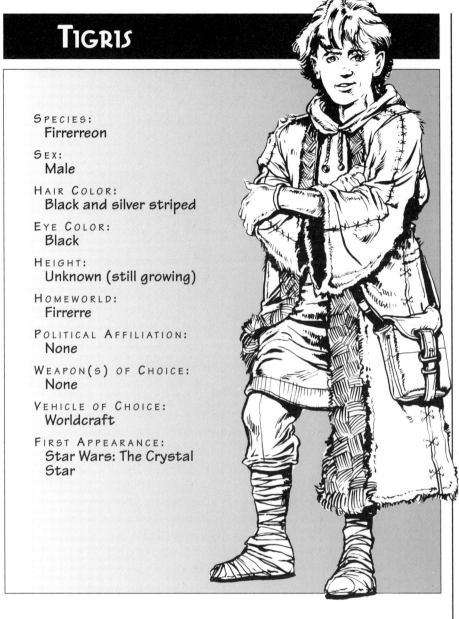

SPECIES:
Firrerreon

SEX:
Male

HAIR COLOR:
Black and silver striped

EYE COLOR:
Black

HEIGHT:
Unknown (still growing)

HOMEWORLD:
Firrerre

POLITICAL AFFILIATION:
None

WEAPON(S) OF CHOICE:
None

VEHICLE OF CHOICE:
Worldcraft

FIRST APPEARANCE:
Star Wars: The Crystal Star

The son of two parents strong in the Force, the powerless Tigris was trapped in a tug-of-war between the dark side and the light side, until his delivery by the heroes of the New Republic.

Tigris was the son of two Firrerreons: Hethrir and Rillao. The two had been students of Darth Vader, but Rillao's powers came from the light side of the Force, and she rejected Vader's teachings. Hethrir *embraced* those teachings, so the gap between the two widened, and when Vader asked for proof of his loyalty to the Empire, Hethrir helped destroy his own world.

Rillao fled to a distant planet with her unborn child. Her baby boy was born and she named him Tigris. Growing up on a remote, boring, pastoral planet, Tigris knew nothing of the fate of his father.

Even when the Empire fell, his mother felt alone and frightened, fearing for her son's life. Eventually, Hethrir found them, overpowered his ex-mate, and imprisoned her in an abandoned Imperial slaving vessel, taking the boy.

Hethrir inspired the young Tigris, who still was unaware that the man was his father. Seeking his approval for every action, Tigris served him as a personal servant. Hethrir was disappointed in his son for not having Force powers, but there was little he could do. He had planned to one day make Tigris his heir in the "Empire Reborn," but abandoned his hopes.

Tigris came to have a twisted opinion of his mother, seeing her as Hethrir portrayed her: a traitor, a weakling, and a fool. Once, Hethrir took Tigris to the slave ship to denounce Rillao. Even seeing his mother's body in the silvery webs of a torture device, the boy cruelly turned his back on her. She was to remain imprisoned for five years, until her rescue by Leia Organa Solo.

Tigris assisted his master in the running of his worldcraft, aboard which he stored dozens of kidnapped children from throughout the galaxy. If the children showed Force talents, Hethrir would turn them to the dark side. If they did not, he sold them to slaving rings. The children's cries led Tigris to sneak them food and comfort.

When Hethrir kidnapped the three Solo children from Muntro Codur, the plight of Jacen, Jaina, and young Anakin profoundly affected Tigris. Especially fond of Anakin, he became excited when Hethrir revealed that he planned to take Tigris to Anakin's "purification" in the temple of the Waru on Crseih Research Station.

But Rillao was waiting for them at Crseih Station. In the temple of the Waru, Tigris was stunned to learn that his beloved Master was really his father. He also found out that Hethrir intended for Anakin's Force powers to be absorbed into the Waru.

Snatching Anakin from Hethrir's arms, Tigris ferried him to safety, as his father was swallowed whole by the imploding Waru. With the influence of the dark side gone, Tigris accompanied his mother to Coruscant, where they joined the New Republic. Rillao had high hopes for her son; he could be a scientist, an artist, or an explorer-diplomat, but he would never be consumed by the Force.

TIONNE

SPECIES:
Human

SEX:
Female

HAIR COLOR:
Silver

EYE COLOR:
Pearly white

HEIGHT:
Unknown

HOMEWORLD:
Unknown

POLITICAL AFFILIATION:
Alliance

WEAPON(S) OF CHOICE:
Lightsaber (unknown blade color)

VEHICLE OF CHOICE:
Unknown

FIRST APPEARANCE:
Star Wars: Dark Apprentice

Tionne was one of Luke Skywalker's earliest trainees at his Jedi academy on the moon of Yavin Four, eleven years after the first Death Star was destroyed in orbit above that very world. Luke's *praxeum*—a place for the learning of action—was housed in the ancient Massassi temple that had once housed the Rebel base.

The exotic-looking Tionne was one of twelve Jedi initiates to wear the dark-brown Jedi robes. Others included the generational clone Dorsk 81, the Bespin gas prospector Streen, the angry Gantoris, the Dathomirian witch Kirani Ti, and son-of-a-Jedi Kam Solusar. Later, Kyp Durron, Nichos Marr, Cray Mingla, and the Mon Calamari ambassador Cilghal would join them.

Skywalker taught his students all aspects of the Force. He also allowed them access to Vodo-Siosk Baas's Jedi Holocron. This was important for Tionne's Force talents; Luke knew she wasn't nearly as strong in the Force as the others, but her devotion and enthusiasm were absolute.

Tionne was fascinated with the Holocron, which was filled with thousands of years of Jedi history. She wove the legends of the Jedi into ballads, using the Force to create her haunting music. She accompanied herself with a stringed instrument she had created: two hollow, resonating boxes affixed to a shaft strung with cords.

Tionne also began researching the evil Dark Lord of the Sith, Exar Kun.

His spirit still resided in the Massassi temples, and he intended to lure the Jedi trainees to him. So when the dark spirit made his move, Tionne provided her fellow students as much information as she could about Kun's past, and how the combined power of many Jedi had trapped and defeated him.

They put a plan into motion, luring Kun to appear in a grand audience chamber, then surrounding him. Kun mocked the gathered students, singling out Tionne for her lack of strong Force powers. "Someday the songs will tell of our great victory over Exar Kun," she replied with a smile, "and I will sing them." The Jedi combined their might, and extinguished the dark light of Kun's essence.

Shortly thereafter, Luke Skywalker addressed his students. "You are the first of the new Jedi Knights. You are the core of what will become a great order to protect the New Republic. You are champions of the Force."

Nine years later, when Luke was away on a mission, he left the training of a newer crop of students to Tionne. She taught the initiates every bit as well as Luke had, only with a different touch. By using parables, fables, and music, she communicated the core of the lessons more effectively.

Tionne helped instruct the youngest students at the academy, teaching them to find their own special skills in the Force. Through her teachings and her musical cultivation of the Jedi legends, Tionne was inspiring untold numbers of prospective Jedi to reach for the future . . . a future of peace and prosperity for a galaxy protected by a strong new generation of Jedi Knights.

BREA AND SENNI TONNIKA

SPECIES:
Kiffu

SEX:
Female

HAIR COLOR:
Black

EYE COLOR:
Unknown

HEIGHT:
1.6 meters

HOMEWORLD:
Kiffex

POLITICAL AFFILIATION:
None

WEAPON(S) OF CHOICE:
None

VEHICLE OF CHOICE:
None

FIRST APPEARANCE:
Star Wars: A New Hope

Had the Tonnika twins been anything but gorgeous women, they would have long ago been frozen in carbonite, or thrown to a hungry rancor. But they are beautiful, and have swindled some of the richest men in the galaxy.

Abandoned as children, Brea and Senni were taken into a trusting Kiffex colony. Running with the wild crowds, they manipulated Kiffex colonists into giving them what they wanted most: *money.*

The twins "escaped" from the colony with a gullible young scout who had set down on Kiffex for fuel and supplies. In a galaxy full of wealthy and powerful aliens, the two quickly learned bigger and better con games. Often, because both twins used the combined name "Bresenni," their victims didn't know there were *two* Tonnika sisters. Only after Brea and Senni had picked them clean did the men learn that their credit vouchers and valuables were missing.

One of their victims was Imperial Grand Moff Argon, whom they conned out of 25,000 credits. The Grand Moff was not forgiving, though, and had his men scour the Outer Rim Territories for the sisters. The Tonnikas had made a deadly enemy.

On smuggling missions for Jabba the Hutt, Han Solo met the sisters, and was intrigued—but cautious. Whenever he was around them, he kept one hand on his credit belt. And while the two traded gambling stories with him, he thought up a perfect scam. Could they con a con man by the name of Lando Calrissian?

With Han's help, "Bresenni" quite literally fell in Lando's lap while he was gambling at the High Stakes Casino on Balfron. For several weeks, Lando and Bresenni were almost inseparable, dancing at zero-g clubs, dining, and gambling. The pair fairly oozed charm. Lando began to think he was in love with the beautiful woman.

Then, the mood swings started. Bresenni would go from happy and cheerful to angry and antisocial in very brief spaces of time. Despite the crazy shifts, Lando nevertheless decided to propose to Bresenni. As he knelt to ask her hand in marriage, the other sister came from another room, bearing a holoprojector. On the disk was a message from Han, having a good laugh at Lando's gullibility. Although he chuckled on the outside, Lando promised himself he'd get Han back.

Years later, the Tonnikas managed to wrangle an invitation to Jabba the Hutt's seven-week party on Tatooine, hoping to case dozens more potential victims.

Meanwhile, unbeknownst to Brea and Senni, a pair of women were masquerading as the Tonnika sisters, and were looking for a pilot at a popular Mos Eisley cantina. Before the imposters could find their target, Imperials entered the cantina, and several were agents of Grand Moff Argon. The "Tonnika twins" were arrested, but escaped with help from a Rebel spy and quickly left Tatooine.

Oblivious to the goings-on at Mos Eisley, the *real* twins worked Jabba's party. And after that, another party. And another. After all, there were still thousands of planets in the galaxy where they would be welcomed with open arms . . . and open wallets.

CINDEL TOWANI

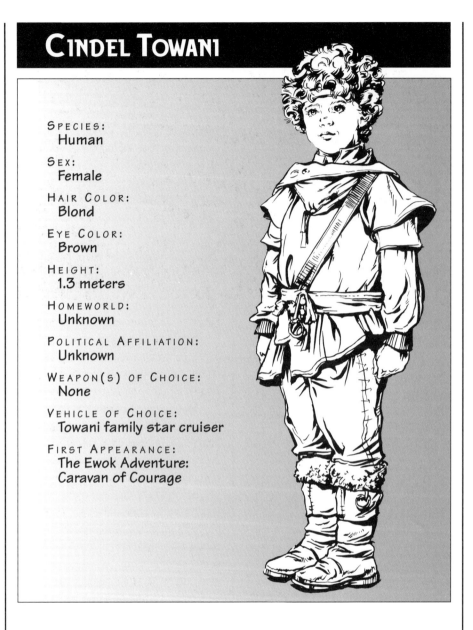

SPECIES:
Human

SEX:
Female

HAIR COLOR:
Blond

EYE COLOR:
Brown

HEIGHT:
1.3 meters

HOMEWORLD:
Unknown

POLITICAL AFFILIATION:
Unknown

WEAPON(S) OF CHOICE:
None

VEHICLE OF CHOICE:
Towani family star cruiser

FIRST APPEARANCE:
The Ewok Adventure:
Caravan of Courage

Cindel was the youngest child in the Towani family. Her father and mother, Jeremitt and Catarine, were piloting their family star cruiser home when they crashed on the forest moon of Endor.

Leaving Cindel and her older brother, Mace, with the crashed ship, the Towani parents struck out to try to find civilization. Unfortunately, they ran into the Borra, a hideous beast controlled by the monstrous giant, Gorax. The Borra took the parents back to Gorax's cliffside lair, where the giant imprisoned them.

Without their parents, the children foraged for food on their own. They knew their mother and father were alive, because they sported safety devices known as life monitors around their wrists. All four lights were blinking, indicating that all four family members were alive. Despite Mace's best efforts though, Cindel became sick and feverish from exposure to something in the new environment.

One evening, the Ewok named Deej was out looking for his sons, Weechee and Widdle, when he spotted the crashed cruis-

er. Inside the ship, Deej found the young Cindel, and he and his children comforted her. Although Mace was suspicious of them at first, the Ewoks took the children back to their village, where Deej's wife helped make an herbal medicine that nursed the little girl back to health. Cindel soon became friends with Deej's adventurous and playful son, Wicket W. Warrick.

Impatient and wanting to find his parents, Mace woke Cindel one night and escaped with her through the forest. Unfortunately, they were cornered by the Borra, and spent the night in a hollow tree. Deej's family rescued the children, killing the Borra, and Mace found one of his parent's life monitors on a collar around the Borra's neck.

With the help of the Ewok medicine man, Logray, the children learned that their missing parents were captives of the giant Gorax. They asked the Ewoks to help them rescue their mother and father. Deej and his three sons struck off with the Towani children, and their caravan was soon joined by the stocky Ewok lumberjack Chukha and an Ewok priestess named Kaink.

The eight adventurers found many obstacles and new experiences in their way: Cindel clung for her life to a stampeding Pulga horse, while Mace had to be rescued from a deadly pool of magic water. Cindel herself used a magic candle given to her by Logray to help the fairylike Wisties get home.

At the entrance to Gorax's stronghold, Deej made Wicket and Widdle stay just inside the cave entrance to protect Cindel. The rest of the group ventured into the dark cliffs, where they faced a giant spider, and the giant Gorax itself. Down below, Wicket himself killed another giant spider that had attacked.

In the battle against Gorax, Chukha was killed, but the Towani parents were freed. Cindel, who had come into the caverns herself, almost became a victim of Gorax, but with a well-aimed hatchet throw, Mace caused the creature to fall to his death.

Wicket's family took the reunited Towani family back to the village, where they celebrated their good fortunes. Logray presented all of the heroic Ewoks—plus Mace and Cindel—with white ear-wing headdresses of hope. Jeremitt expressed hope that Deej and Logray could help him rebuild the star cruiser's transmitter, for he didn't yet know that the Ewoks had absolutely no knowledge of technology.

Several months later, Jeremitt had managed to repair the ship enough that the family could leave Endor. By this time, Cindel and Wicket had become the best of friends, and she had even taught Wicket the rudiments of Basic language. They often spent days together, having imaginary adventures in the forest; Cindel couldn't remember when she had been happier.

That joy ended one day as Wicket and Cindel returned to the Ewok village, only to find it under attack by seven-foot-tall Marauders. Cindel witnessed the death of her mother and brother, but escaped to find her father. When she and Wicket returned to the star cruiser to find Jeremitt, they found that Marauder King Terak and the witch Queen Charal had found him first. Warning his daughter away and trying to escape himself, Jeremitt was mortally wounded.

While fleeing, Cindel and Wicket were captured by the shape-changing Charal. Locked in a caged wagon with other captive Ewoks, only Wicket and Cindel were small enough to escape through a pried-up floorboard, and they ran into a cave as Marauders shot at them. Trapped, Wicket and Cindel slipped out the other side, only to face a sheer cliff and a hungry condor dragon. Wicket rescued

Cindel from the dragon's claws, and the two spent the night in a hollow tree trunk.

The next morning, Cindel and Wicket were woken by a superfast alien creature named Teek. The odd little creature took them to the cottage of his human master, a hermit named Noa. Although he initially chased the girl and the Ewok out of his house, Noa eventually took pity on them and allowed them to stay. He found himself bonding to the orphan Cindel in an almost grandfatherly way.

One morning, Wicket and Cindel followed Noa in his travels, where they were surprised to find another spaceship. The old man's own star cruiser had crashed on the planet many years earlier, and he needed a crystal oscillator power unit to leave Endor. Cindel herself hoped that one day she and Noa could leave the forest moon and return home.

In the morning, Cindel was trapped by the shape-changing witch, Charal, who took her to the castle of Marauder King Terak. Thinking the crystal oscillator, taken

from the Towani cruiser, was a source of personal power, he demanded that she bring the power back to the crystal unit. When she couldn't, Terak had Cindel thrown in the dungeons with the captive Ewoks.

Sneaking into Terak's stronghold, Noa, Wicket, and Teek rescued Cindel and the other Ewoks, taking the power unit with them. Unfortunately, Charal overheard their plans to use it for Noa's star cruiser. Charal led Terak and his soldiers to Noa's cruiser, where they engaged the Ewoks in a bitter battle, during which the spunky Cindel helped Deej and the Ewoks save Wicket from the Marauders.

In the midst of the fighting, Terak was again able to capture Cindel. He proposed to trade the child to Noa for the crystal oscillator. Although Noa tried to duel the dark Terak, it was Wicket's sharp aim with his slingshot that broke an enchanted ring around Terak's neck. The king turned to stone, and Charal was trapped in the form of a raven, forever. The Marauders fled into the woods, disorganized.

Later, after all the other Ewoks had been freed, Cindel decided to accompany Noa off planet in his star cruiser, while Teek stayed behind with his new Ewok friends. Cindel saved her fondest farewell for the brave Wicket, promising him that she would one day return to the forest moon of Endor.

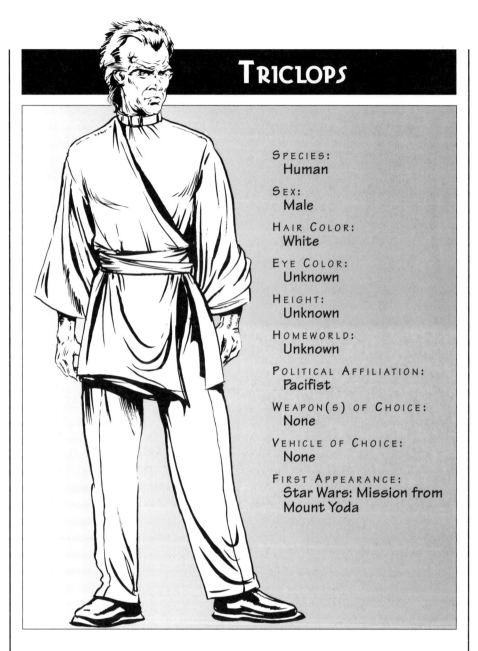

TRICLOPS

SPECIES:
Human

SEX:
Male

HAIR COLOR:
White

EYE COLOR:
Unknown

HEIGHT:
Unknown

HOMEWORLD:
Unknown

POLITICAL AFFILIATION:
Pacifist

WEAPON(S) OF CHOICE:
None

VEHICLE OF CHOICE:
None

FIRST APPEARANCE:
Star Wars: Mission from Mount Yoda

The son of Emperor Palpatine, the three-eyed mutant known as Triclops was banished the day he was born. The Emperor sensed the boy could be more powerful in the dark side of the Force than he was, but missed an essential truth about his son; Triclops was a *pacifist*.

The Empire began to administer shock-therapy that drove Triclops into madness, scarring his face and temples. He was eventually sent to the Imperial insane asylum on Kessel. There, he met a nurse named Kendalina, a Jedi Princess. The two fell in love, and conceived a child.

When Kendalina was killed, a brown-robed Jedi Master took the child, Ken, to the Lost City of the Jedi on Yavin Four, where he was to be trained to embrace the light side of the Force. The only reminder Triclops had of his son was half of a silver birth crystal, which he wore about his neck.

Triclops was sent to work in the Kessel spice mines. He came under the control of an ambitious slave lord who also had three eyes, the mutant Trioculus. The ruthless Trioculus became the Lord Overseer and Supreme Slavelord, and conceived a plan to take Triclops's place as the son of Palpatine.

The Imperial Central Committee labored to make sure Triclops's true nature was kept secret. When Triclops became unstable, he was transferred to a succession of asylums, and the Empire realized that his Force powers were becoming active. In his dreams, Triclops conceptualized numerous weapons and technological breakthroughs, and the Imperials learned how to use his ideas.

Very few of the Imperial hierarchy knew what had happened to the son of Palpatine. One of those was the Supreme Prophet of the Dark Side, Kadann, so when Grand Moff Hissa and Trioculus sought his blessing in having Trioculus declared the new Emperor, Kadann confronted them. Hissa revealed that Palpatine's insane offspring was still alive on the planet Duro, in the Imperial Reprogramming Institute.

Doing some reprogramming of his own—on an Imperial assassin droid—Triclops was able to escape. Among the mazelike walls of the Valley of Royalty, Triclops met the Alliance leaders.

Pledging pacifism and a desire to see an end to the Empire, Triclops accompanied them to the Alliance's Defense Research and Planetary Assistance Center. There, the Alliance was alarmed to discover that Triclops experienced weapon-producing dreams, and was concerned to find that Triclops was sleepwalking, and studying old defense files. They also discovered that Triclops had an Imperial implant that transmitted his thoughts to Imperial probe droids.

They deliberately planted misinformation in a file, and allowed the sleeping Triclops to transmit it to a probe droid. Scientists found that the rare macaab mushrooms could destroy the implant without damaging Triclops's mind, so Luke Skywalker led a mission to find the mushrooms on the planet Arzid, but the operation was never performed.

On Yavin Four, Triclops wrote an impassioned letter to Ken. When he finished, he escaped the Rebel headquarters and disappeared into the jungles of Yavin Four.

TUSKEN RAIDERS

SPECIES:
Humanoid

SEX:
Male & Female

HAIR COLOR:
Unknown

EYE COLOR:
Unknown

HEIGHT:
1.9 meters

HOMEWORLD:
Tatooine

POLITICAL AFFILIATION:
None

WEAPON(S) OF CHOICE:
Gaderffii "gaffi" sticks

VEHICLE OF CHOICE:
Banthas

FIRST APPEARANCE:
Star Wars: A New Hope

The vicious desert bandits known as Sand People or Tusken Raiders are feared throughout the wastes of Tatooine.

The nomadic Raiders wear strips of cloth, swaths, and bandages covering their bodies, protecting themselves from the rays of Tatooine's double suns. A breathing apparatus helps filter out the sand particles constantly in the arid air, as well as adding moisture as they breathe. Eye filters protrude from their bandaged faces, allowing them to see in the shifting winds of the Dune Sea.

The Sand People's bodies are covered from the time they are small children, and no discernable secondary sex characteristics are visible. Only in the privacy of their tents may Raider mates see each other's faces beneath the wrappings.

Clans of twenty to thirty Raiders wander the more desolate regions of the deserts. Their language seems like an unintelligible combination of snorts, growls, laughs, and repetitive conso-

nants. Raider legends are passed down through meticulously worded chants from the clan storyteller.

Tusken Raiders are known for their fearlessness and for their fierce attacks. Few things can scare off an advancing sand person, although krayt dragons and Sarlacc tentacles do get wide berths. The Raiders sometimes attack moisture-farmer homesteads or Jawa scavenging parties, although they are more likely to wait until an individual or small group is isolated before attacking.

Raiders distrust technology and do not generally use mechanical devices. They are sometimes seen with older-model blaster carbine rifles, but their more common weapon is the gaderffii stick, a double-edged ax made from freighter plating.

For transportation or heavy burdens, Sand People ride banthas, huge, four-legged, spiral-tusked beasts. These two- to three-meter-high herbivores are treated as equal members of the tribe, and the banthas share an empathic bond with the Sand People that they share with no other creature on any other planet. The Raiders ride their banthas in single file, allowing them to hide their numbers from the unlucky parties they are approaching.

DARTH VADER

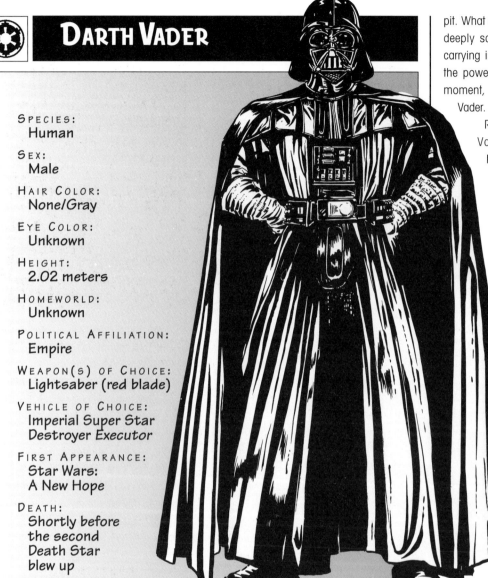

SPECIES:
Human

SEX:
Male

HAIR COLOR:
None/Gray

EYE COLOR:
Unknown

HEIGHT:
2.02 meters

HOMEWORLD:
Unknown

POLITICAL AFFILIATION:
Empire

WEAPON(S) OF CHOICE:
Lightsaber (red blade)

VEHICLE OF CHOICE:
Imperial Super Star
Destroyer Executor

FIRST APPEARANCE:
Star Wars:
A New Hope

DEATH:
Shortly before
the second
Death Star
blew up

Once he was a Jedi Knight named Anakin Skywalker, waging the battles of the light side of the Force. Corrupted and seduced by the dark side, he would soon come to be known as the dread black-garbed Darth Vader.

Almost nothing is known about Anakin Skywalker's early years. As a youth, he was infamous as a hotshot pilot, but it was his hidden and untapped talents that would lead him to his destiny. A great Jedi Knight named Obi-Wan "Ben" Kenobi saw in Skywalker great potential in the Force.

Amazed at how strong the Force was within him, he made Anakin his first Jedi pupil. But in his zeal, Obi-Wan failed to notice that his pupil was being seduced by the dark side of the Force. The dark side was easier to master, and it held faster promise.

By the time Kenobi clearly understood how deeply Anakin had fallen into sync with the dark side, it was too late. He tried to bring his friend and pupil back from the brink, but Skywalker refused. He and Obi-Wan engaged in a vicious lightsaber battle, which ended when Anakin fell into a molten

pit. What emerged from the fiery pool was a deeply scarred and burnt husk of a man carrying in him both hatred for Kenobi and the power of the dark side. In that black moment, Anakin skywalker became Darth Vader.

Reborn to the darkness, Darth Vader joined with Emperor Palpatine, whose New Order and Empire were the nightmare of many of the Jedi. Palpatine was able to continue Vader's training in the dark side, allowing him to learn an angry control over the Force. Vader eventually gained the long-dormant title of Dark Lord of the Sith, allowing him to tap into the evil forces of tens of thousands of years.

Yet for all his dark-side power, Vader had his weaknesses. Unable to breathe on his own without great difficulty, Vader was forced to wear a breath mask and life-supporting body armor. Over time, Vader custom designed a new mask unit that was terrifying and imposing in person. Made of shiny black durasteel, the fearsome helmet covered his head and hid his eyes behind all-seeing lenses.

Built into the mask and helmet were visual-enhancement systems, hearing-augmentation devices, a Vocoder electronic voice synthesizer, and air intake/output vents. The death's-head look of the mask became shorthand for Vader among the Imperial forces. The only places Vader could be without the helmet were in specialized "meditation chambers" in his quarters or on his ships.

Vader's system of body armor included a life systems–control computer, temperature-regulation systems, and a respiratory sensor matrix on his belt. His shoulders, torso, and shins were covered by shiny black durasteel armor, while his insulated gloves and bodysuit protected his scarred body. A floor-length black cloak and two shoulder-draped capes helped hide other hardware that allowed him to function.

As Darth Vader aligned himself with the self-proclaimed Emperor and his New Order, Obi-Wan feared for the future of the Republic. He changed his name to Ben Kenobi, and moved from the forefront of the Jedi into retirement. He kept in contact with Anakin's recently estranged wife, who, unbeknownst to Vader, was pregnant with twins. Obi-Wan knew the children had tremendous potential as future Jedis.

On the day the twins, Luke and Leia, were born, Kenobi and their mother separated them. Leia remained on Alderaan, where she was adopted by Bail Organa into the Royal House as his daughter. Obi-Wan brought the infant Luke Skywalker to his brother's home on Tatooine. There, Owen and Beru Lars promised to raise the child as if they were his aunt and uncle.

Obi-Wan's precognition was correct. Soon enough, Palpatine had Vader and his troops instigate a great Jedi Purge. The men, women, and aliens of the galaxy who wielded the light side of the Force soon found that

their lightsabers were no match for those who could wield the dark side against them or greatly outnumber them. The Jedi were all hunted down and killed. When Vader couldn't find Obi-Wan, he assumed the old man was already dead. His ex-teacher surely wouldn't run from a fight.

Tall, black, and imposing, Vader became one of the most visible symbols of the Empire. His severe command structure was legendary, if not horrifying; displease him and the *least* that would happen was physical unpleasantness; disappoint him, and accept death as punishment. Vader seemed to relish killing his own "incompetent" officers, but it did little to gain him respect—only fear. Even Grand Admiral Thrawn once said, "I am not reckless with my men, and I do not take their deaths lightly, unlike Lord Vader."

As he himself gained in strength and pride, Vader trained many of his own students in the dark side of the Force. Some, like Hethrir, would succeed in their powers. Hethrir had become a Procurator of Justice, who destroyed his own planet at Vader's command. Hethrir's mate, Rillao, was a disappointment. Her Force talents in healing could not be easily corrupted.

The Dark Lord gained a powerful ally, for both himself and the Empire, when a space battle above the planet Honoghr resulted in a Rebel ship crashing onto the world below. Vader and the Imperials who investigated found the short, gray-skinned populace of Noghri to be very deadly. Rather than instigate a fight, Vader offered them help in restoring the ecosystem of their world. Grateful to him, the Noghri pledged their servitude—and that of their descendants—to Lord Vader.

Many of the deadly Noghri were then used throughout the galaxy, performing Imperial assassinations or bodyguard duties. Meanwhile, Vader's scientists poisoned Honoghr further, blaming the resulting blight on the fallout from the crashed Alliance ship. The Noghri wouldn't find out Vader had lied to and betrayed them until

decades later, when one of their assassins encountered the Mal'ary'ush—Lady Vader—Princess Leia Organa Solo.

When not on a mission for the Emperor, Vader meditated in his castle stronghold on the planet Vjun. He never meditated on his past, and regretted nothing other than not having killed Kenobi before their final battle. He honed his lightsaber skills, wielding the blade with blinding speed. He practiced levitation and Force shielding, allowing him to move objects or deflect laser fire with simple gestures.

The Emperor eventually assigned Vader to watch over the construction on his deadly new battle station known as the Death Star. Developed by Bevel Lemelisk and others, the station was being constructed under the control of the cadaverous Grand Moff Tarkin. All went well until Rebel spies stole the Death Star plans and fled across the galaxy.

Shortly thereafter, Darth Vader encountered Princess Leia of Alderaan on Ralltiir, where her ship, the Corellian Corvette blockade runner *Tantive VI*, was supposedly on a diplomatic mission of mercy. Leia had never liked him, nor made much pretense of support for Palpatine's ways or strong-arm tactics. Still, Lord Tion, the pompous bachelor who governed Ralltiir, allowed her to leave the planet.

Leia was dispatched to intercept the battle plans from the Rebels and to find the lost Jedi, Obi-Wan Kenobi. Finally, she was to deliver him and the Death Star plans to the Alliance. It was to be an ill-fated mission. Although they got the plans, the *Tantive VI* was caught by the Star Destroyer *Devastator* and tracked to Tatooine.

Vader was on the *Devasator* when it caught up with and boarded the *Tantive IV*. But his men were too late to stop Princess Leia from placing the plans inside an escape pod and sending it to the surface of the planet below. Vader ordered the troops to find the pod, then departed with Leia for the Death Star.

Leia was able to resist the probes Vader used on her. He thought this odd, as his Force powers should have been able to penetrate any barriers in her mind. He assigned an Imperial interrogator droid to make her reveal the location of the main Rebel base, but it too was ineffective. Vader and Tarkin discussed matters and decided that Leia could be persuaded to help them if they raised the stakes.

Brought to Vader's side in a main control room of the Death Star, Leia felt her defiance melt away when Tarkin threatened to destroy her home planet of Alderaan unless she told them what they wanted. Quietly, she admitted that the base was on Dantooine. And then, when Tarkin ordered Alderaan destroyed anyhow, Vader forced Leia to watch.

When the Death Star tractor beam pulled in a freighter ship entering the Alderaan system, Vader felt the presence of Obi-Wan Kenobi. The ship checked out as empty, but Vader knew Obi-Wan had been—or was—near. He was correct. Even as Han Solo and Luke Skywalker helped Princess Leia escape, Vader met his old Master in a hallway.

"I am the Master now," Vader said, igniting his lightsaber.

"Only a master of evil, Darth," Kenobi replied. The battle that followed was fierce, with lightsabers clashing and igniting, no quarter asked or given. And then Kenobi warned him, "If you strike me down, I shall become more powerful than you can possibly imagine." With that, Obi-Wan deactivated his lightsaber and stood waiting. In a rage, Vader swung his own lightsaber, cleaving Kenobi's robes into pieces. The noble Jedi Master's body had disappeared, becoming one with the Force.

Later, as Rebel starfighters attacked the Death Star, Vader boarded his prototype TIE interceptor. Joining the battle, he noticed the Rebels making attack runs down the station's equatorial trench, so he and his wingmen concentrated on these teams. Vader felt the Force strongly ema-nating from one X-wing in particular, and Vader set his sights to blow him up.

Then, from out of nowhere, a laser blast caught the TIE fighter next to him, blowing Vader's interceptor out of the trench. He spun helplessly into space, tumbling, as the Death Star exploded in a blazing rage.

When he finally regained control of his ship and found his way back to an Imperial base, Vader was determined to put his anger to good use. So was the Emperor. He gave Vader one main objective for the future: hunting down the Rebel High Command and destroying them.

As powerful as he was, Vader still managed to allow the Alliance leaders to slip through his grasp. The two most vexing to him were Princess Leia and the young man she traveled with. One of their encounters ended badly for Vader. On the jungle planet Mimban, Imperial Supervisor Grammel had caught Leia and her male friend. Grammel contacted Vader, who was already on his way to the planet to find the Kaiburr Crystal. The mysterious object supposedly had the power to enhance the powers of the Force.

Leia and the boy escaped, and later faced Vader at the Temple of Pomojema. Surprisingly, Leia used the boy's lightsaber to defend them, but Vader wounded her badly, burning and stabbing. The trapped youth finally freed himself and dueled Vader.

The Dark Lord knew the boy was strong in the Force, but he didn't expect what happened in the battle. He managed to slice off Vader's right hand, forcing him backward. Vader fell into a pit in shock. By the time he extricated himself, the boy had used the powers of the crystal to heal Leia and they both had disappeared.

After several more brushes with the Rebellion, Vader finally learned who the boy was. He was Luke Skywalker, from Tatooine. Could he be a relative? Could his wife have borne a child? Vader had yet another reason to find the Alliance.

Utilizing probe droids, Vader did finally locate the Alliance's Echo Base on Hoth, where he came tantalizingly close to capturing Princess Leia and her friends aboard Han Solo's ship. Vader knew that if he captured Solo and Leia, he would be able to lure Luke to him. So he hired several bounty hunters, including Boba Fett, whom he had worked with before, to find the *Millennium Falcon*.

Fett came through, and Luke was lured to Bespin's Cloud City to rescue his imprisoned friends. But he found Vader instead. The two engaged in a tremendous lightsaber duel as the Dark Lord tried to lure Luke into the carbonite-freezing pit. Luke was too well trained, though, and the battle raged on.

Vader finally drove Luke out onto a gantry above a reactor shaft and distracted him long enough to slice off his right hand. Defenseless and in shock, Luke could only scream denials as Vader revealed, "I am your father. Search your feelings. You know it to be true."

Vader offered his hand, telling Luke that they could overthrow the Emperor and rule the galaxy together as father and son. Luke didn't even reply. Looking at the monster his father had become, he calmly stepped off the platform and fell. Vader watched until he saw Luke sucked up by an exhaust pipe.

Vader found Luke's severed hand and his lightsaber in Smelting Core D, where an Ugnaught named Groggin had rescued them. Killing the Ugnaught, Vader took the hand and the saber and left aboard his Super Star Destroyer *Executor*. He fleetingly caught Luke's mind as the *Falcon* fled into hyperspace.

The Dark Lord delivered the hand and saber to the Emperor on Mount Tantiss of Wayland. Palpatine immediately started cultivating the cells for a clone of Luke.

In the end, Luke surrendered to Vader's troops, on the forest moon of Endor. The Emperor had set an elaborate trap for the Alliance, centered around the second Death Star. Still under construction, the Death Star was operational. It could also have meant the end of the Alliance fleet if fate hadn't intervened.

Luke appealed to his father, trying to find the bit of Anakin he knew was inside. Vader steeled himself and brought his son to the Emperor. Laughingly, Palpatine goaded the boy about the fate of his friends until he attacked. Vader defended the Emperor, and father and son were soon locked in deadly combat. And then Luke refused to fight; he had gained control of his anger.

Vader probed his son's feelings, to make him fight. As he did so, he sensed something he had never seen before. Luke's twin sister—his daughter—was Princess Leia. "If you will not turn to the dark side, then perhaps she will," Vader threatened. It was the catalyst that broke Luke's Jedi calm. He attacked again, hacking and stabbing with the lightsaber. He finally beat his father down, chopping off his cybernetic right hand. The hand and the lightsaber tumbled down a reactor shaft.

Turning his back on the crippled Dark Lord, Luke confronted the Emperor. "You've failed, Your Highness. I am a Jedi, like my father before me." Palpatine knew then that the younger Skywalker would never turn against him. He attacked Luke with blue Force lightning, and was prepared to deliver the killing bolts when Vader betrayed him for the final time.

The Dark Lord lifted his Master into the air and threw him into the burning shaft of the power core. As Palpatine disappeared into the abyss, Vader tried to throw himself after him. Luke stopped him, and pulled him toward an Imperial shuttle. They both knew that the Death Star was in danger.

Vader couldn't go on. He asked Luke to take his helmet off so he could look at his son with his own eyes. As he struggled to breathe, he assured Luke that he did have goodness left in him. And then, Anakin Skywalker—not Darth Vader—died.

Luke took Vader's armor to the moon of Endor and burned it on a funeral pyre. Later that night, as he slipped away from a joint Rebel and Ewok celebration, Luke was surprised by a vision of Obi-Wan Kenobi, Yoda, and Anakin Skywalker, all smiling to

him. Kenobi and Yoda's pupil—and Skywalker's son—was, now and forever, a Jedi. And Anakin was part of the light side of the Force once again.

Luke later saw the trio of Jedi in his dreams. Yoda and Ben told him that dreaming was a conduit for the Force, while the spirit of Anakin helped reveal to his son who the Dark Lord of Beldarone really was—a prospective Jedi named Flint, who had been slighted by Luke and trained in the dark side by Vader. It was the final time Luke would converse with the spirits of Yoda and his father.

Five years after his death, Vader's legacy was finally snuffed. The cybernetic hand Luke had cut off had somehow become encased in metal and had survived the explosion of the Death Star. The molten space garbage eventually found its way to Calamari, where it plunged into the seas. The remains were found by a pretender to the throne of Palpatine, Trioculus, who was attempting to fulfill a prophecy given by the prophets of the dark side. With Vader's glove, he was supposed to be able to overtake the galaxy. It didn't work. The whereabouts of the glove are unknown.

Anakin's spirit did appear again, though this time it was to Leia in her suite on Bakura. He begged her forgiveness, trying to take away her anger. "Anger is the dark side," he cautioned, adding, "I do not ask for absolution. Only your forgiveness." Leia didn't want to listen, refusing to forgive the man who had tortured her, helped destroy her world, and frozen Han in carbonite. Anakin disappeared, telling her he would never be able to see her again, but that he would hear her if she called.

Eventually, in the heat of the Bakuran battle, Leia did come to at least forgive her father. Even if she would never forget, every world she took from the Empire would help ease the pain of her memories. In that forgiveness, Anakin Skywalker, the man who had once been Darth Vader, was finally freed.

LADY VALARIAN

SPECIES:
Whiphid

SEX:
Female

HAIR COLOR:
Golden and white, with red tints

EYE COLOR:
Unknown

HEIGHT:
2.5 meters

HOMEWORLD:
Toola

POLITICAL AFFILIATION:
None

WEAPON(S) OF CHOICE:
Unknown

VEHICLE OF CHOICE:
Unknown

FIRST APPEARANCE:
Star Wars: Galaxy Guide 7 —Mos Eisley

At the age of twenty-four standard years, the tall and imposing Whiphid woman Valarian took the biggest gamble of her life . . . challenging Jabba the Hutt.

Whiphids come from the planet Toola, a bitterly cold world in the Kaelta system. Her people have adapted to the changing temperatures, shedding fur and fat during the hot but short summers. The nomadic Whiphids live in small tribes, hunting craboose, mastmots, sea hogs, and ice puppies. With the discovery of their planet by the Empire and by traders, Whiphids have begun to appear throughout the galaxy.

The daughter of Whiphid gangsters, Valarian knew nothing other than a life of crime. Her record began when she was young, and when her parents committed a crime so grievous that they were locked up, Valarian struck off on her own.

Years later, her criminal empire burgeoning, Valarian decided to make an investment on Tatooine. At Mos Eisley spaceport, a battered cargo hauler called the *Lucky Despot* had been sunk into the desert and refitted as a luxury hotel, then abandoned. Calling herself "Lady" Valarian, she bribed the right officials and the *Lucky Despot* was hers.

Jabba the Hutt, Tatooine's biggest crime lord, was not pleased with Valarian's decision. Soon, officials were charging her huge taxes and Jabba's thugs began harassing her customers. Valarian eventually negotiated a truce: She would pay Jabba off and would not allow her operation to grow too large. Still, when she tried to get a gambling license, Jabba blocked it. Knowing that she had set up illegal gambling anyway, Jabba warned her of Imperial raids . . . for a price.

Those who work for Valarian are generally happier than most criminals. Despite her fearsome appearance, Valarian is often happy and positive, and is thus respected by her employees and the public. Even the smugglers who worked for her over the years knew that if they messed up, they were more likely to be forced to fly free missions than to be fed to the rancor.

Eventually Val found a Whiphid mate from her homeworld and planned a wedding at her Lucky Despot Hotel. The mate was D'Wopp, and he was an expert hunter. During the reception, as Figrin D'an's band played on stage, one of Jabba's Duro lackeys approached the new groom. Complimenting D'Wopp on his excellent hunting abilities, the Duro told him of a record bounty Jabba had posted . . . for a Corellian smuggler named Han Solo.

Before D'Wopp could leave the reception to collect Solo, Lady Valarian was on him for taking her competitor's bounty. A huge fight ensued, with Imperial stormtroopers arriving to raid the place and shut down the illegal gambling. Days later, D'Wopp was shipped home . . . in pieces. Some pieces were missing, but only Lady Valarian and her cook knew what had happened to them.

Four years later, when Jabba was killed by Luke Skywalker and his Rebel friends, Lady Valarian forged ahead to recapture Jabba's business on her own.

VIMA-DA-BODA

SPECIES:
Human

SEX:
Female

HAIR COLOR:
Unknown

EYE COLOR:
Unknown

HEIGHT:
Unknown
(hunched over)

HOMEWORLD:
Unknown

POLITICAL AFFILIATION:
Alliance

WEAPON(S) OF CHOICE:
Lightsaber (blue blade with white core)

VEHICLE OF CHOICE:
None

FIRST APPEARANCE:
Star Wars: Dark Empire #3

Neema into—the power of the dark side. And despite Vima's distraught protestations, Neema betrothed herself to a barbaric Ottethan warlord who ruled twelve outer-perimeter systems.

Neema had chosen poorly. Her husband beat and abused her, and the dark side of the Force did not seem to affect him. Placed in chains and thrown into the dungeons, Neema sent a Force call to her mother, begging her help. Vima arrived soon, but she was too late. The warlord had fed Neema to the rancors that overran the Ottethan forests.

Vima had been pushed too far. Despite her Jedi training, rage drove her to ignite her lightsaber and cleave the barbaric warlord in two. Rage gave way to despair, and Vima realized that not only had she lost her daughter, but she was now losing her deep connection to the Force. Unable to outrun her conscience, she slipped further and further into desolation.

When Emperor Palpatine commanded Darth Vader to destroy the Jedi Knights, Vima retreated, masking herself and hiding away on a succession of worlds. Impoverished and alone, her Force skills faded to almost nothing, Vima survived the Jedi purge.

Decades later, imprisoned for some crime real or manufactured, Vima was sentenced to Kessel's gigantic Imperial

The history of the Jedi Knights is long and illustrious, filled with triumph and honor. It is also filled with tragedy and betrayal, as the fierce Jedi woman Vima-Da-Boda was to learn—to her eternal regret.

Vima-Da-Boda was a human woman who had become a prominent Jedi Knight. Part of an illustrious line of female Jedi, Vima was the great-great-great-granddaughter of the legendary Vima Sunrider, herself the descendent of Nomi Sunrider. Vima served the Force for one hundred

years, during which time she raised one daughter, Neema. Knowing she had passed her aptitude for the Force on to her child, Vima trained Neema in the ways of the Jedi.

The girl was powerful, but hungered to learn more, in the fastest, easiest way possible. She discovered that her impatience and ambition actually *aided* her in her learning; what she did not know was that she had tapped into the dark side of the Force. Neema was easily swayed, and soon fell in with a rebellious crowd of young Jedi who experimented with—and brought

Correctional Facility. Sent to work in the underground glitterstim spice mines, she met a young man named Kyp Durron, in whom she could feel incredibly strong aptitude for the Force. She taught the young man some lesser Force skills, but one day the Imperials came and took her away. Kyp Durron never saw her again.

Somehow, Vima ended up free from the Imperials—though still not free from her conscience. She retreated to the dark and byzantine lower levels of the Corellian sector on the smuggler's moon of Nar Shaddaa. Hiding in corners, she used the Force to pull shadows around her and make herself go unnoticed.

Six years after the destruction of the second Death Star, Alliance hero Han Solo brought Leia Organa Solo to those same labyrinthine levels. Now two hundred years old, Vima was surprised to recognize the Jedi potential in Leia. Kissing the Alderaanian's feet, Vima begged forgiveness for her crimes. As Han pulled Leia away from the filthy old creature, Vima gave Leia a boxed gift. Leia later discovered that

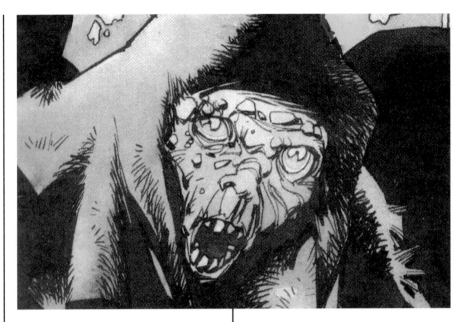

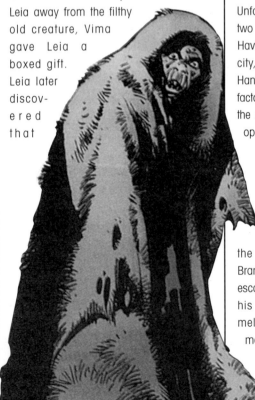

it contained an ancient lightsaber—Vima's own.

Months later, Leia and Han returned to Nar Shaddaa, in order to find the old Jedi woman and bring her from her despair into an Alliance that needed all its Jedi. Unfortunately, Vima was on the run from two Imperial Dark Siders, Zasm and Fass. Having escaped into the lowest levels of the city, Vima was surprised when Leia and Han tracked her to an abandoned sail-barge factory. Leia insisted Vima go with them on the *Millennium Falcon*, and they took off for open space.

Subsequently pursued by Boba Fett and his ship, *Slave I*, the *Falcon* escaped into an interstellar gas cloud, where they found the giant Ganathan city-ship, the *Robida Colossus*. There, Vima and Leia recognized that the ruler of Ganath, King Empatojayos Brand, was another former Jedi. Brand had escaped one of Vader's attacks, but had lost his limbs in the process. Now, he was melded into a set of floating prosthetic machinery.

Brand's doctors treated Vima even as his technicians helped Solo modify the *Falcon*. The Ganathan king then decided to join Leia and Vima

as they traveled to meet Luke Skywalker on New Alderaan. The new generation of Jedi would be united with two of the old!

Vima and Brand aided Luke in the training of his Jedi students Jem and Rayf Ysanna, and Kam Solusar. When two Dark Siders managed to infiltrate the settlement on New Alderaan, they used Scarab droids to inject Luke with poison. Although he was able to fight it off, Jem was less fortunate—having been caught by a laser blast from a Dark Sider. Despite Vima's attempts to heal her, Jem died.

Soon after, when the Dark Siders attacked the settlement in AT-ATs, Salla Zend's gang of smugglers joined with the *Falcon* and three Alliance X-wings to defend New Alderaan. In the midst of the carnage, Salla touched down her ship, *Salvager Three*, to rescue Leia and her children, Luke and his Jedi initiates, Winter, and Vima-Da-Boda. The squadron of ships evacuated the entire group to the abandoned floating space city Nespis VIII in the distant Auril system. There, the Alliance had formed a new base.

The future of the ancient Jedi woman was unknown, but with a hope for tomorrow, and a surrogate daughter in Leia Organa Solo, Vima-Da-Boda could feel the Force was with her . . . once again.

WEEQUAY

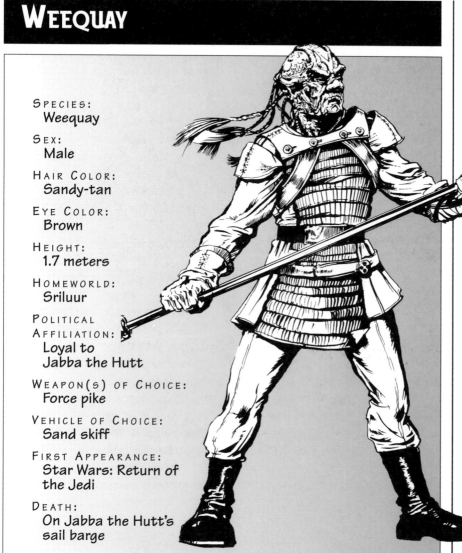

SPECIES:
Weequay

SEX:
Male

HAIR COLOR:
Sandy-tan

EYE COLOR:
Brown

HEIGHT:
1.7 meters

HOMEWORLD:
Sriluur

POLITICAL AFFILIATION:
Loyal to Jabba the Hutt

WEAPON(S) OF CHOICE:
Force pike

VEHICLE OF CHOICE:
Sand skiff

FIRST APPEARANCE:
Star Wars: Return of the Jedi

DEATH:
On Jabba the Hutt's sail barge

planted near the final set of banthas to put suspicion on the humans.

Only one Weequay was given a name—Ak-Buz, the Weequay commander of Jabba's sail barge. After Barada the mechanic discovered that Ak-Buz had been murdered, the Weequay gathered to discuss finding the murderer. Eventually they decided to ask their chief god, Quay, god of the moon, who gave birth to their name. Weequay means "follower of Quay."

The Weequay questioned their god all day, trying to ferret out who had murdered Ak-Buz and the many others who had been found in Jabba's palace lately, and how. And would it happen again? Jabba was sailing his barge that day to the Pit of Carkoon, and they were concerned.

Several Weequay went out on sand skiffs with the trio of doomed prisoners that were to be fed to the Sarlacc. Soon, the Weequay aboard the sail barge were startled to see that the trio of prisoners were killing the other Weequay and making their escape. Many of the Weequay died in the battle that followed, and the rest were killed when a rippling explosion shook the sail barge.

Silent and stupid, the brown-skinned Weequay were some of the cruelest and most efficient of Jabba the Hutt's enforcers. Several Weequay resided at Jabba's palace, but no one knew who—or what—the Weequay were. The only way to tell them apart was by their ceremonial topknots, as their burnt-looking, pitted, brown faces were so similar.

The Weequay were almost as feared as the rancor. Rumors abounded among newcomers of a savage Weequay killing spree of Tatooine's banthas as part of their religious rituals. The slaughter of the banthas was making the Tusken Raiders angry, so Jabba ordered the Weequay to stop the rituals, and had a dead moisture farmer

WICKET W. WARRICK

SPECIES:
Ewok

SEX:
Male

HAIR COLOR:
Brown

EYE COLOR:
Brownish black

HEIGHT:
.8 meters

HOMEWORLD:
Endor

POLITICAL AFFILIATION:
None

WEAPON(S) OF CHOICE:
Spear

VEHICLE OF CHOICE:
Glider

FIRST APPEARANCE:
Star Wars: Return of the Jedi

sense of smell, and a rudimentary awareness of the Force, help warn them of impending danger. And though they are technologically primitive, the Ewoks are amazingly inventive, using bows and slings with greater accuracy than an aimed laser pistol.

High in their vine-and-wood villages, the Ewoks worship the guardian spirits they believe live in the trees. They joyously play music, drumming and chanting and dancing, passing down songs and stories from generation to generation. Although completely loyal to his tribe, Wicket has always shown a curiosity to explore the unknown, which has resulted in many adventures shared with his brothers, his friends Teebo, Logray, Paploo, Latara, and Malani, and his best friend—Princess Kneesaa.

In his younger days, Wicket and his companions had many skirmishes and battles with the warlike Duloks, cousins to the Ewoks who are taller and thinner. The Duloks were led by King Gorneesh, a one-eyed, red-footed tyrant. The Ewoks also faced the evil Morag, the Tulgah witch; her giant pterodactyl-like mantigrue; the giant green Phlogs, the reptilian, carnivorous Froschs; and the semisentient Dandelion Warriors.

The forest moon of Endor is teeming with life-forms, some predatorial, some peaceful. The short, furry, biped omnivores known as Ewoks are among the peaceful, and as far as the Alliance is concerned, the most heroic of those Ewoks is Wicket W. Warrick, a mere teenager when he helped Rebel heroes Leia Organa and Han Solo in their mission to destroy the second Death Star.

Wicket lives with his family in Bright Tree Village, built fifty meters up among the boughs of the three-hundred-meter trees that forest the world. His father is Deej, and his mother is Shodu. Wicket is the youngest of three brothers, including Weechee, the oldest son, and Widdle, in the middle. Wicket also has a baby Wokling sister, Winda. He is the great-grandson of Erpham Warrick, a famous Ewok who fought the Duloks years earlier, using a weapon-laden War Wagon.

Like the other Ewoks, Wicket is brave and loyal, though suspicious and cautious of strange things. Too many close calls with predators have kept all of the Ewoks alert. Though their sight is poor, their heightened

Wicket's life wasn't always filled with conflict, though. He gathered rainbow berries for the Harvest Moon Feast, shot in the archery contests at midsummer festival, went hang gliding with Teebo, fished in nearby streams and rivers, and rode Baga, his horselike pet bordok. He also made friends with the shape-changing, elflike Gupin.

Wicket and Kneesaa helped save the ancient trees of the forest when the giant Phlogs came from the other side of the moon to chop them down. The Phlogs journeyed from a land called Simoom, long ago the home of the Ewoks, and with Logray's help, Wicket and Kneesaa drove the invaders back there. As a reward, the Council of Elders made Wicket and Kneesaa honorary council members. Although this title held no privileges, the young Ewoks were nevertheless overjoyed. Logray was also named medicine man for the tribe.

Despite Wicket's heroism, when he decided to become a medicine man, and asked to be Logray's apprentice, the older Ewok turned him down. Logray found Wicket too headstrong and hasty, but when Wicket proved himself by gathering fuzzynettles to save the sick Latara's life, Logray reconsidered and accepted Wicket as his apprentice. The apprenticeship was not to last for long, though, and Wicket and Logray went separate ways.

One evening thereafter, Deej was out looking for his sons, Weechee and Widdle, when he spotted a crashed star cruiser. Inside, the trio found the young human children Cindel and Mace Towani. The Ewoks took the children back to their village, where they nursed Cindel back to health. Cindel and Wicket became good friends while she was healing.

When the human children found out that their missing parents were captives of the giant Gorax, they asked the Ewoks to help them rescue their mother and father. Deej

and his three sons struck off with the Towani children, and were soon joined by the stocky Ewok lumberjack, Chukha. Later, an Ewok priestess named Kaink joined them, as well.

The eight adventurers found many obstacles and new experiences along their way, from Borra monsters to deadly pools of water, to the fairylike Wisties—one of whom befriended Mace. Wicket saved Mace's life using a magic stick Logray had given him. Despite the young Ewok's bravery, when the group got to the entrance of Gorax's stronghold, Deej made Wicket stay with Widdle just inside the cave entrance, to protect Cindel.

In the dark cliffs of the stronghold, Mace and the remaining four Ewoks encountered a giant spider, then faced the giant Gorax itself. Meanwhile, down below, Wicket also faced a giant spider, and bravely used his spear to kill it, saving Cindel and his own brother. Up in Gorax's cave, Weechee and Mace's Wistie friend, Izrina, distracted the giant, while Chukha and Mace freed the human parents, Jeremitt and Catarine. In the ensuing battle, Chukha was killed.

Wicket's family took the reunited Towani family back to the village, where they celebrated their good fortunes. Logray presented all of the heroic Ewoks, including Wicket, with white ear-wing headdresses of hope, like those worn by the warrior father, Deej.

Several months later, Jeremitt managed

to repair the ship enough that the family could leave Endor. By this time, Cindel and Wicket had become the best of friends, and Wicket had even learned the rudiments of Basic language.

One day, as Wicket and Cindel returned to the village, they were shocked to find it under attack by seven-foot-tall Marauders. Mace and Catarine were killed in the battle, and Wicket was captured.

A short while later, Cindel was captured as well, and was put in the caged wagon with Wicket and many other Ewoks. They escaped and were chased into a cave by Marauders, where Wicket and Cindel slipped out the other side, only to face a sheer cliff and a hungry condor dragon. Using a hastily constructed hang glider, Wicket rescued Cindel from the dragon's claws.

The next morning, Cindel and Wicket met the odd, superfast creature known as Teek, and his human master, a hermit named Noa. The old man's own star cruiser had crashed on the planet years earlier, and he needed a crystal oscillator if he was to leave Endor. Noa found himself bonding to the orphan Cindel in an almost grandfatherly way, and he tolerated the fuzzy little Ewok.

Days later, Cindel was caught, this time by Charal, who took the girl to the castle of Marauder King Terak. Noa, Wicket, and Teek rescued Cindel and the other Ewoks from Terak's dungeons, but Charal overheard their plans. She led Terak and his soldiers to Noa's star cruiser, they engaged the Ewoks in a bitter battle, and Wicket was caught in a trap. He was rescued by several of the other Ewoks and Cindel, but shortly thereafter, Terak was able to capture Cindel.

Wicket's sharp aim with his slingshot broke an enchanted ring around Terak's neck, turning the king to stone, in the process trapping Charal in the form of a raven. The disorganized Marauders fled into the woods.

After all the other Ewoks had been freed, Cindel decided to accompany Noa off planet in his star cruiser, using the crystal oscillator from the Towani ship, while Teek stayed behind with his new Ewok friends. Cindel promised the brave Wicket that she would one day return.

Perhaps because of his many brushes with dark magic over the years, Wicket had begun to distrust magic. To the consternation of his tribe, he objected to Logray's dark rituals, in part because many of them involved the sacrifice of living creatures. Since the young Wicket held little sway with the tribe, the angry Logray was able to ridicule and abuse him. Eventually, Logray talked the tribal elders into banishing Wicket from all rituals, even the pleasant festivals of the rain and sun. Shortly thereafter, Logray took Teebo as his new apprentice.

When the Imperials first came to Endor, the Ewoks were alarmed and frightened. Although many of them wanted to wage war on the Imperials and their "not-animals"—AT-STs and other machinery—Chief Chirpa reminded them that their spears couldn't hurt the Imperial fortresses, and that the invaders had machines that could fly through the air or burn the forests. One night, as the villagers gathered around the fires with their latest news, young Wicket came forward. He had seen an AT-ST stumble on the rocks, fall, and explode. Now, the Ewoks had a way to fight back against the walking beasts, and the small, furry creatures began building traps.

On a foraging expedition, Wicket came across the unconscious Princess Leia, who had been thrown off a speeder bike during a chase. Although she initially frightened him,

Wicket could sense her innate goodness. He returned with her to the village, only to find that Leia's companions, Han Solo, Chewbacca, Luke Skywalker, R2-D2, and C-3PO had been captured in an Ewok hunting net. Even though Wicket pleaded Leia's case to Chief Chirpa, it took some Jedi tricks from Luke to free the Rebels. Using the Force, Luke levitated C-3PO, making the Ewoks believe that an old legend about a golden god had come true.

Although C-3PO had told the Ewoks the story of the Rebellion, the tribal elders didn't see why they should get involved. First Han, then Luke, then Leia tried to reason with them, each explaining the fight in their own way. Finally, Wicket stepped forward, arguing that both the Ewoks and the Rebels were like leaves on the large forest trees, ready for the season of change. Finally, having heard from one of their own, the furry creatures rallied behind the Rebels.

Wicket and the others joined with Chewbacca in a battle against the Imperials and their AT-ST "chicken walkers." In doing so, they helped free Han, Leia, and the droids to shut down the Death Star's shield generator. After Alliance pilots destroyed the second Death Star in orbit above Endor, the Ewoks held a celebration for the brave Alliance members. They made many of them "leaf brothers."

Chief Chirpa insisted that Princess Leia preside over a ceremony that gave

Wicket the rank of lead warrior, thus rewarding him for his bravery. That day was the proudest in the young Ewok's life. Soon, tribal elders were talking about the young Wicket as the likely replacement for Chief Chirpa when the aging Ewok finally decided to retire.

Wicket and several of his friends decided to make the remnants of the Empire a part of their world. Using vines, wood, sap, and leaves, they wove organic life through the ruins of the Death Star's shield generator. Wicket decided to make a second home there, using the burnt-out husk of an AT-ST cockpit as his fireplace, and biker-scout helmets as his food bowls. He carved trinkets for the village children, communed with animals and the forest, and dreamed of the wonders that the Alliance had introduced into his life.

Although many of the Ewok females in the tribe left him gifts and weaponry, showing a desire to court him, Wicket was much more intrigued by the occasional Alliance visitor. The inherent "cuteness" of the Ewoks made Wicket almost irresistible to off worlders, and his curiosity about the world beyond Endor grows with each visitor. It's entirely possible that Wicket may one day accompany one of the visiting Alliance members off the moon of Endor, and into a whole new galaxy of adventure.

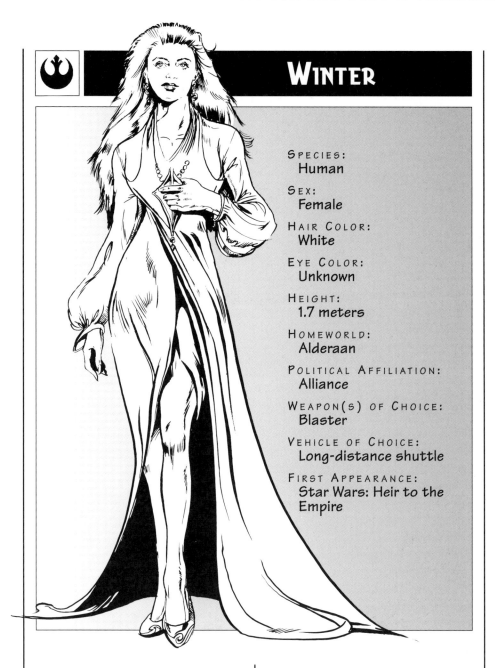

WINTER

SPECIES:
Human

SEX:
Female

HAIR COLOR:
White

EYE COLOR:
Unknown

HEIGHT:
1.7 meters

HOMEWORLD:
Alderaan

POLITICAL AFFILIATION:
Alliance

WEAPON(S) OF CHOICE:
Blaster

VEHICLE OF CHOICE:
Long-distance shuttle

FIRST APPEARANCE:
Star Wars: Heir to the Empire

The tall, regal woman named Winter has proven that beauty can also be a beast. She takes very seriously her job as Princess Leia Organa Solo's assistant and the Solo children's nanny. Seriously enough to kill, if need be.

Winter grew up living as one of the Royal Family of Alderaan. She was a constant companion and playmate for the young Princess Leia; they were inseparable and became closer the older they grew. Visitors often mistook Winter for the princess, as she had the air of royalty, whereas Leia generally had a more rough-and-tumble attitude.

As Leia entered into adulthood, her duties involved more politics and less play. Still, Winter accompanied her everywhere, and was assigned as her royal aide and personal assistant. Leia became a senator, and so was swept up along with her father, Viceroy Bail Organa, in the growing Rebellion against Emperor Palpatine.

Bail had learned to value the special talents Winter possessed, and began assigning her to Alliance missions. She was making a supply run with Rebel agents when Leia was captured by Darth Vader and taken to the Death Star. Had Winter been on Alderaan, she would have been destroyed by the Death Star's superlaser, along with everyone else on her world.

Unlike Leia and the other survivors of Alderaan, whose memories of the destruction faded over time, Winter possesses a holographic and audiographic memory that forces her to vividly remember everything she has heard or seen. This made her an invaluable assistant in Senatorial or Provisional Council meetings, but has made it impossible for her to forget the life and friends she lost with the destruction of Alderaan. Although she rarely has shown emotions, the loss of her home and culture has often seemed more than she could bear.

Winter worked in the background of the Alliance from the time of the Battle of Yavin to the Battle of Endor, and was assigned to the Alliance procurement and supply division. She would find ways to enter private or Imperial military supply houses, memorizing every detail and preparing maps for Rebel strike teams to utilize. She earned her place on the Imperial death lists under several aliases, but none was more accurate than one short-lived name, "Targeter."

Following the destruction of the second Death Star, Winter and Princess Leia were reunited. Winter once again became her top aide, shadowing her to the meetings of the Alliance's Provisional Council. Leia often wondered what the other Council members would think if they knew that Winter was effectively recording everything that was said and done in the meeting. Few knew of the white-haired beauty's powers. Luke Skywalker did, but he had already ascertained that they were not Force related.

As the Alliance steeled itself for confrontation with Grand Admiral Thrawn and his fleet, Winter was instrumental in ferreting out the Delta Source, a security leak at the Imperial Palace on Coruscant, which was serving as the new Alliance headquarters.

She and the computer slicer Ghent found that Delta Source was actually a system of organic microphones hidden in the ch'hala trees that lined the Grand Corridor outside the Council chambers.

But Winter's greatest help was to her oldest and closest friend. During Leia's pregnancy with the twins, Jacen and Jaina, she was an invaluable assistant. When Leia was forced back into service, Winter accepted the aid of Mobvekhar and two other Noghri who were indebted to Leia. For a short time, they joined Winter as the twins' bodyguards.

After the battles against both the mad Jedi clone Joruus C'Baoth, and the equally mad clones of Emperor Palpatine, Leia and Han realized the danger to which their children could be exposed on any of the Rebel bases. If someone using the dark side of the Force came near, the children could be warped permanently.

Rebel leader Mon Mothma found an exotic world on which Winter could sequester and raise the children. Han and Leia called it New Alderaan, but its beauty was soon to be spoiled by a group of the Emperor-clone's Dark Siders. With the aid of Salla Zend and the Millennium Falcon, Winter and the other settlers of the planet were evacuated to the distant Auril system and the abandoned floating space city Nespis VIII, where the Alliance had formed a new base.

Next, Admiral Ackbar and Luke scouted out a faraway world called Anoth, which could support life. A heavily guarded facility was constructed in which Winter would reside, teaching the Solo children and taking care of them. She was aided only by a TDL nanny droid and a GNK power droid.

No one except Luke, Ackbar, and Winter knew Anoth's location. Several times a year, Winter would bring a long-distance shuttle to Coruscant, allow Leia and/or Han to board, and then take multiple hyperspace jumps to cover its path. Thus, even the two parents were protected from knowing where Anoth was.

When Jacen and Jaina were two years old, Winter brought them back to live on Coruscant, keeping the infant Anakin back on Anoth. Months later, Ackbar himself visited; he was planning to leave the Alliance after a particularly disastrous incident, but he declined Winter's personal invitation to stay with her on Anoth while he healed his spirit.

Ackbar's ship had been tracked by a Mon Calamari traitor named Terpfen, who had relayed Anoth's location to Imperial Caridian Ambassador Furgan. An attack force arrived aboard the Dreadnaught Vendetta, carrying assault teams and eight Mountain Terrain Assault Transport "spider walkers." Winter used the multiple-tentacled Foreign Intruder Defense Organism— FIDO—to eliminate four of the MT-ATs, but four others gained access to the landing grotto.

Winter fired her own blaster as the troopers disgorged from their MT-ATs, killing one. Six remained, along with the squat Ambassador Furgan. Winter could go back to Anakin and defend him with her life, or she could draw the troops away from the child. She chose the latter.

The fortress was a labyrinth of passageways and blast doors, and Winter was able to delay the troopers significantly. She finally lured them to the subterranean generator room and computer core. As the troopers closed in on her, the walls shimmered and moved, revealing their true nature as burly assassin droids. The white-armored Imperials were immediately cut down by laser fire.

One trooper and the ambassador still survived, and Winter realized that they hadn't followed her. Above, in Anakin's bedroom chamber, TeeDeeEl had given her "life" to protect the child, killing the stormtrooper in the process. Furgan however, had gotten away with the baby Anakin.

Luckily, Ackbar, Leia, and a contrite Terpfen arrived in the Galactic Voyager, and made their way to the citadel. Terpfen managed to take Anakin from Furgan, then pur-

sued the fat ambassador. As Winter came up from below, Terpfen and Furgan were engaged in a battle, both housed in Imperial MT-ATs. Furgan's spider walker fell to the rocks below the fortress, but Ackbar was able to stop Terpfen before he could kill himself for his betrayal of Anoth and the Alliance.

After careful consideration, Leia and Han decided that Anakin would be just as safe on Coruscant with them. Shortly thereafter, Winter accompanied Admiral Ackbar to the planet Vortex for the reopening of the Cathedral of the Winds. She expressed her happiness that Ackbar had returned to the Alliance. He in turn, expressed his own pleasure that Winter would no longer be exiled on Anoth.

The white-haired beauty and Ackbar enjoyed each others' company a lot over the years, both in their tasks for building the New Republic, and in private. Winter also continued to be a boon to Leia and her children, ever loyal to her longtime friend and princess.

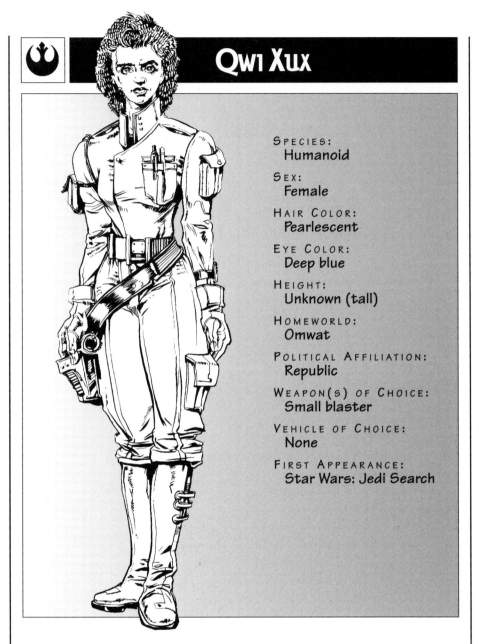

QWI XUX

SPECIES:
Humanoid

SEX:
Female

HAIR COLOR:
Pearlescent

EYE COLOR:
Deep blue

HEIGHT:
Unknown (tall)

HOMEWORLD:
Omwat

POLITICAL AFFILIATION:
Republic

WEAPON(S) OF CHOICE:
Small blaster

VEHICLE OF CHOICE:
None

FIRST APPEARANCE:
Star Wars: Jedi Search

The frail and willowy, light-blue-skinned Omwati woman known as Qwi Xux hardly seemed a threat, but from her analytical mind sprang some of the most terrifying weapons the galaxy would ever see.

The course of Qwi Xux's life was set for her by the power-hungry Grand Moff Tarkin, then a governor of the Seswenna sector, deep in the wild frontiers of space known as the Outland Regions. His ruthless Tarkin Doctrine, taught by the Imperial Navy, was "Rule through the fear of force, rather than the force itself." Nowhere was this more evident than in his experiments with the Omwati people.

Knowing that the willowy race had a genetic capability toward breeding brilliant designers, Tarkin kidnapped ten ten-year-old Omwati to tutor and test. Among them was Qwi Xux, taken from one of the Omwati honeycomb settlements to an orbiting Imperial educational sphere. For two years, the children were pushed harder and harder to solve problems, forced to learn engineering, constantly subjected to training and tests.

At the end of the two years, Qwi was the only survivor of her "class." Tarkin rewarded her by giving her a place in his hierarchy, at a new top-secret project of his located deep in the black-hole fields outside Kessel, in the area known as the Maw.

Tarkin had placed his beautiful lover—Admiral Daala—in charge of the secret project known as the Maw Installation. It was a thinktank of brilliant scientists, weapons designers, and inventors, who were brought together to create horrifying weapons for Tarkin to take to the Empire. The Grand Moff placed Qwi under the tutelage of top Imperial designer Chief Bevel Lemelisk, and she excelled at her design and engineering assignments.

It was in the early days of the installation that administrator Tol Sivron, Chief Lemelisk, and Qwi Xux created the plans for the first Death Star. They also created a prototype of the space station, which orbited the installation. Another of their creations was the mobile recycling/manufacturing engine of destruction known as the World Devastator.

When the Emperor approved the Death Star plans, Tarkin took Lemelisk from the Maw to supervise its construction. Qwi never saw Lemelisk or Tarkin again, and she was too busy to care. Her one creative outlet came when she developed a computer program that allowed her to do research and make music at the same time.

Her most powerful superweapon was the Sun Crusher, an indestructible ship that carried resonance torpedoes that had enough firepower to snuff out a sun. Qwi naively told herself that the Sun Crusher would be used for some sort of useful purpose. After all, she had previously reasoned that the Death Star would be used to break up dead planets for mining, while she believed the World Devastators would become autonomous, nonpolluting factories.

Years of isolation passed, until the day when an Imperial shuttle burst into the Maw. Qwi was excited; finally, news from the outside was imminent. However, the shuttle was piloted not by Imperials, but by Han Solo and Kyp Durron, with the giant Wookiee, Chewbacca, also aboard.

Daala's men captured the shuttle, and brutally interrogated the trio. Daala gave Qwi Xux an edited transcript of the "interview," but Qwi wanted to know more, especially concerning the way in which the first Death Star was destroyed. She had Han brought to her laboratories, where she questioned him herself.

Han was belligerent. He stated that, if she wanted information, she would first have to tell him where his friends were. He questioned her about her *own* motives, goading her into looking at the uncensored transcripts of his "debriefing" by Daala.

After Han was taken away, Qwi activated her security locks and checked the video of Solo's interrogation. It dawned upon her that she had been fooling herself, manufacturing ethical purposes for the superweapons she had created. Now she learned she had also been willfully deceived by Daala. As Qwi heard the broken Han telling about the destruction of Alderaan, the attacks on Yavin Four and Endor, and the fight against the two Death Stars, Qwi became more and more horrified. She knew that her own creations had caused more destruction and death than even Tarkin's turbolasers had rained down on the Omwati.

When Admiral Daala summoned Qwi to her offices, the Omwati scientist was stunned to hear that the Imperial planned to take the Sun Crusher into open space and use it against the Alliance. At this point the designer made up her mind. Qwi knew that she must aid Han Solo and his friends, and stop Daala from having access to the superweapon—no matter what the price.

Forging authorizations from Daala and Sivron, Qwi freed Han, Kyp, and Chewbacca. The quartet commandeered the only working model of the Sun Crusher and left the installation, and the Maw.

Qwi and the Sun Crusher were taken to Coruscant, site of the Alliance headquarters. The Alliance impounded the Sun Crusher for immediate study, but the nervous Qwi Xux refused to reveal its secrets, fearing that it might someday be used. The New Republic Council assigned General Wedge Antilles to be Qwi Xux's bodyguard and escort. They were concerned that Daala or some other Imperial would try to recapture or kill her.

Shortly thereafter, Qwi spoke before the New Republic Assembly. She urged the Assembly to allow the superweapon to be destroyed. They agreed, deciding that since no conventional methods could break its invincible shields, it should be disposed of in the heart of the gas giant of Yavin.

Kyp Durron was drafted to fly the Sun Crusher to Yavin, accompanied by Wedge and Qwi in an Alliance transport. As the trio watched the deadly weapon disappear into oblivion, Qwi experienced a variety of emotions. Afterward, they dropped Kyp off on the Yavin Four moon, where he was to begin his Jedi training with Luke.

Wedge and Qwi Xux next went to Vortex, to watch the repair work on the shattered crystal Cathedral of the Winds. Wedge worked with the cleanup crews, while Qwi walked through the glassy debris, watching the lacy-winged Vors as they navigated the strong winds of their world.

In the rubble, Qwi found a small unbroken windpipe from the cathedral. She put the dainty flute to her mouth, and began to play music for the first time in much too long. The Vors stopped their rebuilding efforts and listened to her, but when she finished, a clan leader came forward and crushed the flute. There would be no more music until the cathedral was finished.

Wanting to ease Qwi's conscience, Wedge took her to the paradise world of Ithor. There, they were surprised to find themselves greeted by Momaw Nadon, the "Hammerhead" Herd Leader of the floating city *Tafanda Bay*. Mon Mothma had asked him to make their stay a pleasant and comfortable one. Tentatively, Wedge and Qwi began to fall in love.

Just when it seemed she was entirely safe in the arms of her Alliance hero, Qwi's world came crashing around her. Kyp Durron came to Ithor and broke into Qwi Xux's quarters. The untrained Jedi had decided her knowledge of weaponry was too dangerous, so he used the Force to fillet her memories.

When Wedge found Qwi the next morning, she could barely remember him. Kyp's' mindwipe had destroyed more than just her memories of weapon plans; it had erased most of her life.

With Wedge's aid and her participation in the Alliance's strike raid on the Maw Installation, she began the long healing process. She could start her life again, free of the haunting knowledge of the weaponry she had created. Alongside Wedge Antilles, Qwi Xux had finally found a future to explore, and someone to explore it with.

YODA

SPECIES:
Unknown

SEX:
Male

HAIR COLOR:
White

EYE COLOR:
Brown

HEIGHT:
.65 meters

HOMEWORLD:
Dagobah

POLITICAL AFFILIATION:
Alliance

WEAPON(S) OF CHOICE:
None

VEHICLE OF CHOICE:
None

FIRST APPEARANCE:
Star Wars: The Empire Strikes Back

DEATH:
Just prior to the battle against second Death Star

One of his more famous students had been the young and reckless Obi-Wan Kenobi—his *final* student before the coming of Luke Skywalker, decades later. Kenobi was one of the last Jedi to survive under Emperor Palpatine's rule. Another Yoda-trained Jedi who survived the purge was Brand, who escaped with his life—but not his limbs.

Yoda taught his students that affinity with nature enhanced an affinity with the Force. He gave them endurance tests, had them run marathons, jump wide lagoons, fight seeker balls with their lightsabers, balance in seemingly impossible ways, meditate for long periods, and levitate objects. Yoda made his students *unlearn* that which their upbringings, and their own eyes and ears, had taught them.

"A Jedi uses the Force for knowledge. Never for attack." Lessons such as these made training easier; they also became good advice to pass along to future Jedi.

When Palpatine ordered the Jedi Knights purged from the galaxy, Yoda went deeper into hiding on Dagobah. Using the Force and the planet's natural defenses, Yoda was able to discourage visitors, even as his students and his students' students were slaughtered by Darth Vader and Palpatine's men. Since Vader had been trained solely by Kenobi, he seemed not to know of Yoda's existence, and Palpatine either forgot about

For more than eight hundred years, the diminutive creature known as Yoda trained only the most serious and committed students in the ways of the Force.

Yoda's origins are steeped in mystery. His species is unknown, but he was green-skinned, with large bulbous eyes and long ears. Although he walked on two feet, they were reptilian tridactyl feet. His hands likewise were claws. And by the time Luke Skywalker met the Jedi Master, Yoda was nine hundred years old, walking with the aid of a gimer stick.

Yoda built his home of mud, sticks, stones, and other natural materials from Dagobah. The windows were made from transparent gems. Yoda lived near a lagoon so he could listen to the lulling sound of rain falling on water. He ate plants, fruits, and fungi, subsisting on the things nature offered.

Yoda or thought he had already died. Either way, Yoda escaped the purge.

Yoda kept a Force watch on Luke Skywalker and Leia Organa as their destinies took shape. Obi-Wan wanted to tell Luke about his father early in Skywalker's teen years, but Yoda told him to wait. But after Kenobi's temporal death, Yoda knew the training of his last Jedi student must commence soon.

On Hoth, an injured Luke Skywalker was visited by the life force of Obi-Wan Kenobi. Ben told him to go to the Dagobah system to learn from Yoda, "the Jedi Master who instructed me." So when the Rebels evacuated the ice planet, Luke flew his X-wing to the boggy planet. It crashed into the swamps, leaving Luke and R2-D2 only a few supplies to help them survive.

Yoda approached the duo, offering help, but not revealing who he was. When Luke admitted he was looking for a great warrior, Yoda chuckled, telling him that "wars do not make one great," then offered to take them to see Yoda.

Back at his cramped hut, Yoda tried to be hospitable, giving Luke some rootleaf stew, but Luke was impatient. Frustrated, Yoda complained that Luke was unteachable and full of anger and recklessness. "Was I any different when you taught me?"

the nearby spirit of Ben Kenobi asked. Then Luke realized he was in the presence of Yoda, and promised that he would do whatever it took to become a Jedi.

Yoda commenced training Luke immediately, lecturing him about the Force while Luke performed rigorous physical and psychological exercises. He especially warned Luke against the easy path of anger, and the lure of the dark side. He tested Luke by allowing him to go into a tree that was filled with dark-side energy. There Luke dueled with an apparition that resembled Darth Vader, until the helmet cracked and Luke saw his own face. The young Jedi had learned a valuable lesson about the dark possibilities that lay in his future.

Luke learned two other valuable lessons. Once, when Yoda had him practice levitation, Skywalker was distracted when his X-wing sank in the bog, and he gave in to despair. Yoda ordered him to use the same levitation powers to raise his ship. Luke said he'd try, but was cut off curtly by Yoda. "No! Try not. Do. Or do not. There is no try."

Lacking belief in himself or his powers, Luke was unable to raise his ship, complaining that it was too big. "Size matters not," Yoda told him, reminding him that the Force flowed through everything . . . through Luke, through the bog, and through his ship. Then Yoda concentrated, and grandly raised the X-wing out of the marsh and onto dry land. "I don't believe it," his astonished student said.

"That is why you fail," Yoda told him.

Days later, Yoda instructed Luke to open his mind to memories of old friends, and to the possibilities of the future. Jarred by visions of Han Solo and Leia in pain on Cloud City, Luke determined to rescue them. Yoda and the spirit of Kenobi both warned Luke that the decision could destroy everything they

had fought for, and that he was still much too susceptible to the dark side.

Torn between this knowledge and the visions of his friends in danger, Luke decided to leave Dagobah. He promised to return to complete his training, and took off in his X-wing. After Luke left, Yoda and Ben discussed the future of the Jedi, with Yoda reminding Ben that there was "another" hope. He was referring to Leia.

Luke was not lost to the dark side, and the following year he returned to Dagobah, as he had sworn to do. But he found that Yoda was dying. Yet the diminutive Jedi Master joked that Luke would not look nearly so good at nine hundred years old.

Then Yoda offered his final advice. He once again warned Luke to beware the dark side, even though a confrontation with Darth Vader would be a necessity. Reminding Luke that *he* was now the last of the Jedi, Yoda's final words were to reveal that there was another Skywalker. Then Yoda breathed his last and disappeared, becoming one with the Force.

When Luke and the Alliance were victorious in the Battle of Endor, a celebration was held. There, for a few moments, Luke saw Obi-Wan Kenobi, Yoda, and Anakin Skywalker, all smiling to him. Kenobi and Yoda's pupil—Skywalker's son—was, now and forever, a Jedi.

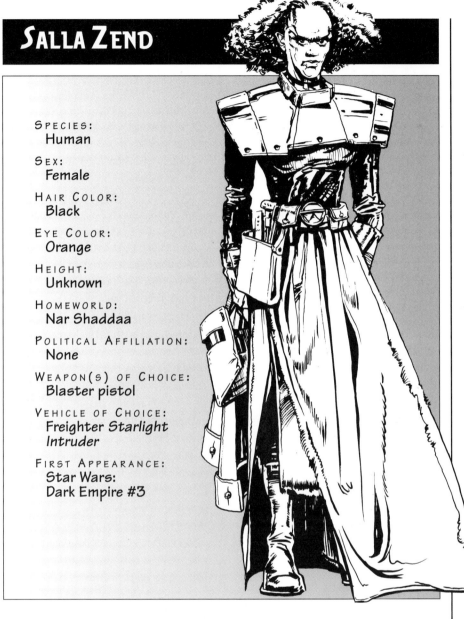

SALLA ZEND

SPECIES:
Human

SEX:
Female

HAIR COLOR:
Black

EYE COLOR:
Orange

HEIGHT:
Unknown

HOMEWORLD:
Nar Shaddaa

POLITICAL AFFILIATION:
None

WEAPON(S) OF CHOICE:
Blaster pistol

VEHICLE OF CHOICE:
Freighter *Starlight Intruder*

FIRST APPEARANCE:
Star Wars:
Dark Empire #3

Little is known of the past of former smuggler Salla Zend, a statuesque and exotic woman whose hard personality hides a softer side.

In her early twenties, Salla was a technician on a corporate transport. Her innate understanding of machinery made her an invaluable technician, and she loved the limitless promise offered her by the planetary ports the corporate ship visited.

Salla saved up enough of her earnings to secure a legitimate loan and buy her own ship. She drifted into smuggling, and met half-breed Corellian master mechanic Shug Ninx, gambler pilot Lando Calrissian, his roguish Corellian pilot friend Han Solo, and Solo's copilot, a Wookiee named Chewbacca.

Han and Salla developed an almost immediate rapport as they traded technojargon and smuggler's tales. Both ran spice to the Stenness system, competing to see who could make the Kessel Run the fastest, or who could cut the tightfisted 'Nessies' the best deal on spice prices. After he lost the *Millennium Falcon* to Solo, Lando was often Salla's copilot on the Kessel Run. Years passed, Han and Salla enjoyed each other's company more and more, but no commitments were discussed.

One time, while making a solitary run, Salla's hyperdrive cut out and her ship made the reversion to real space. Unfortunately, she discovered it was on a collision course with a neutron star! She ejected in time to save herself, and was rescued by Han Solo, but her ship was lost. Badly shaken by the experience, Salla carefully considered her future, and saw it in the arms of Han Solo. She wanted to retire from smuggling, and wanted Han to retire with her. But Solo didn't want to be tied down so early in his adventurous life, and bid goodbye to Salla through a holomessage.

Over the next decade, Salla hooked back up with Shug Ninx at his ship repair space-barn on the smuggler's moon of Nar Shaddaa. Deep in the Corellian sector of the mazelike city, Salla made a good living as a welder and occasional gunrunner. In between jobs, she constructed a massive freighter that she named the *Starlight Intruder*. Cobbled together from spaceship parts scavenged across the galaxy, Salla's ship wasn't a pretty sight, but its size meant it could carry large loads, and it was registered for Deep Core freight hauling. Salla was overhauling the hyperdrive engines when Ninx's shop received very familiar visitors: Han Solo and Chewbacca, accompanied by Leia Organa Solo and droid C-3PO.

Solo offered Salla and Shug 100,000 credits for transport into the Deep Galactic Core. As Solo and Leia left to get replacement power couplings, Salla, Chewbacca, and Shug worked to finish installing the hyperdrive. Word reached them that Han had been betrayed to bounty hunters by Mako Spince, and Salla and Shug took off with the *Intruder*, the *Millennium Falcon* magnetically adhered to its hull. Dodging pursuers, Han and Leia rendezvoused with the *Intruder*, and the ship left Nar Shaddaa. Boba Fett and Dengar pursued aboard the *Slave II*.

The *Intruder* arrived at Byss, location of the Empire's new command center. Followed by the *Slave II,* the *Intruder* was allowed through the planet's security shields, but Fett's vessel did not fare so well: it was damaged and sent spinning away from Byss. The *Intruder* docked at the Imperial freight complex at the outskirts of Emperor Palpatine's ruling city.

Back aboard the Falcon, Salla and Shug accompanied the others to Palpatine's Imperial Citadel, where they were surprised at the boldness with which Leia and Han allowed themselves to be captured. Hiding in the ship while the two were taken away, Salla then took command of the *Falcon,* using the blasters to help disable the guards that were escorting the Alliance heroes, enabling them to flee. Salla took off, piloting the *Falcon* to a hiding place inside a fellow smuggler's ship, the *Hyperspace Marauder.*

The Empire had impounded the *Starlight Intruder,* leaving Salla and Shug shipless. While having drinks with the *Marauder's* captains, Salla and Shug received coordinates from Han as to where to pick them up. The Alliance plan seemed to have hit some snags, but Salla and Shug took off anyway. Unfortunately, as the *Falcon* took off, it was spotted by a giant Arakyd Hunter-Killer probot droid, and was swallowed up inside the droid's holding area.

Salla and Shug escaped into the Hunter-Killer's innards, and Shug hot-wired its circuits, thus enabling them to control the droid. They used it to free Solo

and Chewbacca, and soon, Leia, Luke, C-3PO, and R2-D2 joined them. As the giant probot droid sped away, the Emperor's security patrol fired on them, but failed to stop them. Everyone boarded the *Falcon,* which fled through the atmosphere, jumping into hyperspace moments before it would have collided with the planetary shields.

Carrying security codes provided by Luke and stored in R2-D2's memory circuits, the *Falcon* sped toward Calamari, where the immense World Devastators were destroying the planet. The transmitted codes allowed the Alliance to disable and destroy the World Devastators.

Weeks later, Salla and Shug accompanied Han, Chewbacca, and Leia to Nar Shaddaa to find the ancient Jedi Vima-Da-Boda. When a Star Destroyer tracked the *Falcon* on its approach, Salla guided the modified freighter through the ruined Duros sector of the smuggler's moon. When they arrived at Shug's repair facility, they found Darktroopers interrogating Shug's mechanic, Warb, and his repair droids. A firefight ensued, in which Shug's starfighter was blown up by the *Falcon's* lasers.

While Leia and Han hunted for Vima-Da-Boda, Salla and Shug were caught in *another* firefight with the Imperial Dark Siders. They left the smuggler's moon, taking the ship the *Salvager Three* on a return trip to Byss in an attempt to recover the *Starlight Intruder.* When Han and Leia returned to Shug's garage, a droid passed along Salla's final message: they should give up the Rebellion and think about making some money.

Arriving at Byss, Shug

bluffed his way through the Imperial gauntlet by posing as a maintenance worker with an order of obsolete parts for Lo Khan. In orbit around the planet, Salla spotted a massive orbiting dry dock with a superweapon under construction. It was the Emperor's fearful new device of destruction: the Galaxy Gun.

Lunching in the Byss Bistro with Lo Khan and Luwingo, Salla and Shug tried to figure out how to get the *Starlight* back. They were surprised when the Alliance made an attack on the Emperor's citadel, using hijacked Viper Automadon war droids.

Salla decided that she had a responsibility to aid the Rebels, and gathered a team of smugglers. Using three starfighters, the ragtag crew joined the attack on the Emperor's citadel. Shug's space-truck cargo ship, *Starhook VII,* rescued several Alliance heroes, including Lando Calrissian, Wedge Antilles, R2-D2, and C-3PO. Surviving an attack by a Warbeast, the *Starhook VII* escaped into the skies, flying perilously close to the orbiting Galaxy Gun. The smugglers and Rebels were surprised to find they weren't fired upon. The Emperor, having assumed they would be killed when the gun was fired, had ordered that they were to be allowed to escape into hyperspace.

Soon after, Salla and her gang of smugglers joined with the *Falcon* and three Alliance X-wings to defend New Alderaan from the Dark Siders and their AT-ATs. Salla touched down amid the carnage, to rescue Leia and her children, Luke and his Jedi initiates, Winter, and Vima-Da-Boda. They evacuated to the abandoned floating space city Nespis VIII, where the Alliance had established a new base.

Remaining with the Alliance seems a remote possibility for Salla and Shug, but they may now have an even more difficult time retrieving the *Starlight Intruder.* Once again, Han Solo has come into the life of Salla Zend, and once again, he has left her future in question.

ZUCKUSS

SPECIES:
Gand

SEX:
Male

HAIR COLOR:
None

EYE COLOR:
Unknown

HEIGHT:
1.5 meters

HOMEWORLD:
Gand

POLITICAL AFFILIATION:
**Free-lance
bounty hunter**

WEAPON(S) OF CHOICE:
**Blaster pistol, vibro-
blade, stun grenades**

VEHICLE OF CHOICE:
Mist Hunter

FIRST APPEARANCE:
**Star Wars: The Empire
Strikes Back**

The insectoid bounty hunter Zuckuss was one of his planet's most successful findsmen, but the elusive quarry assigned him by Jabba the Hutt and Darth Vader still managed to slip from his grasp.

On the gaseous planet of Gand, the inhabitants had formed a series of pocket colonies, establishing a totalitarian monarchy. Like the Rodians, the Gand honored the tradition and skills of bounty hunting. Their hunters—called findsmen—were largely used to corral fugitive criminals and runaway slaves.

The findsmen were highly superstitious. Their sect worshipped the swirling mists that hid the planet, performing ancient rituals handed down through generations. In the gases, the findsmen believed they could divine signs and omens, leading them to their prey. Unfortunately for the hunters, the Empire insinuated itself into the Gand's slave trade, and Imperial technology made obsolete the findsmen and their rituals.

Although many of the findsmen retired, a few of the younger ones left for the stars. One of those who left the planet was

Zuckuss, a young Gand descended from a long and illustrious line of successful findsmen. He used the elaborate and arcane rituals in his hunts, becoming a tireless tracker with an affinity for intuiting his quarry's moves; he was called "the uncanny one."

Off planet, Zuckuss was forced to wear a special breathing apparatus that protected him from harmful oxygen and provided supplemental gases necessary to his species. He adopted battle armor under his heavy cloak, and hung a computer and sensor array on straps around his neck. He dared any terrain or environment in pursuit of his prey.

Zuckuss was eventually hired by the Tatooine crime lord Jabba the Hutt. Although he worked solo on several missions, it was when Jabba paired him with a brilliant rogue protocol droid, 4-LOM, that Zuckuss found the missing piece to his hunting procedure. Zuckuss's intuition and ability to outguess his opponents worked perfectly in combination with 4-LOM's analytical skills. For a time, they were two of Jabba's favorite hunters.

A year after the destruction of the Empire's first Death Star, Jabba sent 4-LOM and Zuckuss as "nonofficial emissaries" to Darth Vader's Super Star Destroyer *Executor*. The Dark Lord of the Sith had sent out a call for bounty hunters to find Han Solo and the *Millennium Falcon*. Zuckuss and 4-LOM saw that their competition would be fierce; the four other bounty hunters were Boba Fett, Dengar, IG-88, and Bossk.

Unfortunately for Zuckuss and 4-LOM, Boba Fett was the one who tracked the *Falcon* to the Bespin system. Fett received not only the bounty from Vader, but also the carbon-frozen body of Han Solo to deliver to Jabba the Hutt.

Zuckuss had lost one of the biggest quarries of his career, but that didn't concern him. There would be others, and he and 4-LOM would keep alive the tradition of the findsmen for many years to come.

BIBLIOGRAPHY

FILMS

Brackett, Leigh, with Lawrence Kasdan and George Lucas. *The Empire Strikes Back* (Twentieth Century Fox, May 21, 1980)

Kasdan, Lawrence and George Lucas. *Return of the Jedi* (Twentieth Century Fox, May 25, 1983)

Lucas, George. *Star Wars: A New Hope* (Twentieth Century Fox, May 25, 1977)

TV SHOWS

The All-New Ewoks (Lucasfilm Ltd. and Nelvana, ABC-TV, November 1, 1986–September 5, 1987)

Burrt, Ben. *The Great Heep* (Lucasfilm and Nelvana, ABC-TV, June 7, 1986)

Carrau, Bob and George Lucas. *The Ewok Adventure: Caravan of Courage* (Lucasfilm Ltd. and Korty Films, ABC-TV, November 25, 1984)

The Ewoks and Star Wars Droids Adventure Hour (Lucasfilm Ltd. and Nelvana, ABC-TV, September 7, 1985–November 30, 1985)

Star Wars Holiday Special (CBS, November 17, 1978)

Wheat, Ken with Jim Wheat and George Lucas. *Ewoks: The Battle for Endor* (Lucasfilm Ltd., ABC-TV, November 24, 1985)

NOVELS

Anderson, Kevin J. *Star Wars: Champions of the Force* (Bantam, October 1994)

Anderson, Kevin J. *Star Wars: Dark Apprentice* (Bantam, July 1994)

Anderson, Kevin J. *Star Wars: Jedi Search* (Bantam, March 1994)

Anderson, Kevin J., editor. *Star Wars: Bounty Hunters* (Ballantine, Late 1996)

Anderson, Kevin J., editor. *Star Wars: Tales of Jabba's Palace* (Ballantine, Early 1996)

Anderson, Kevin J., editor. *Star Wars: Tales of Mos Eisley Cantina* (Ballantine, Summer 1995)

Anderson, Kevin J., and Rebecca Moesta. *Star Wars: Young Jedi Knights #1—Heirs to the Force* (Berkley Books, June 1995)

Anderson, Kevin J., and Rebecca Moesta. *Star Wars: Young Jedi Knights #2—Shadow Academy* (Berkley Books, 1995)

Daley, Brian. *Han Solo and the Lost Legacy* (Del Rey, 1980)

Daley, Brian. *Han Solo at Stars' End* (Del Rey, April 1979)

Daley, Brian. *Han Solo's Revenge* (Del Rey, November 1979)

Davids, Paul and Hollace Davids. *Star Wars: The Glove of Darth Vader* (Bantam Skylark, July 1992)

Davids, Paul and Hollace Davids. *Star Wars: The Lost City of the Jedi* (Bantam Skylark, July 1992)

Davids, Paul and Hollace Davids. *Star Wars: Mission from Mount Yoda* (Bantam Skylark, February 1993)

Davids, Paul and Hollace Davids. *Star Wars: Queen of the Empire* (Bantam Skylark, March 1993)

Davids, Paul and Hollace Davids. *Star Wars: Prophets of the Dark Side* (Bantam Skylark, May 1993)

Davids, Paul and Hollace Davids. *Star Wars: Zorba the Hutt's Revenge* (Bantam Skylark, August 1992)

Foster, Alan Dean. *Splinter of the Mind's Eye* (Del Rey, February 1978)

Glut, Donald F. *The Empire Strikes Back* (Del Rey, May 1980)

Hambly, Barbara. *Star Wars: Children of the Jedi* (Bantam, April 1995)

Kahn, James. *Return of the Jedi* (Del Rey, June 1983)

Lucas, George. *Star Wars* (Del Rey, December 1976)

McIntyre, Vonda M. *Star Wars: The Crystal Star* (Bantam, December 1994)

Smith, L. Neil. *Lando Calrissian and the Flamewind of Oseon* (Del Rey, October 1983)

Smith, L. Neil. *Lando Calrissian and the Mindharp of Sharu* (Del Rey, July 1983)

Smith, L. Neil. *Lando Calrissian and the Starcave of ThonBoka* (Del Rey, December 1983)

Tyers, Kathy. *Star Wars: The Truce at Bakura* (Bantam, January 1994)

Wolverton, Dave. *Star Wars: The Courtship of Princess Leia* (Bantam, May 1994)

Zahn, Timothy. *Star Wars: Dark Force Rising* (Bantam, June 1992)

Zahn, Timothy. *Star Wars: Heir to the Empire* (Bantam, June 1991)

Zahn, Timothy. *Star Wars: The Last Command* (Bantam, May 1993)

CHILDREN'S BOOKS

Bogart, Bonnie. *Escape from the Monster Ship: A Droid Adventure* (Random House, 1986)

Dubowski, Cathy East. *The Ring, the Witch, and the Crystal: An Ewok Adventure* (Random House, 1986)

Dubowski, Cathy East. *The Shadow Stone: An Ewok Adventure* (Random House, 1986)

Ehrlich, Amy. *The Ewoks and the Lost Children* (Random House, 1985)

Gerver, Jane E. *Three Cheers for Kneesaa! An Ewok Adventure* (Random House, 1984)

Goodwin, Archie. *Star Wars: Droid World*. Art by Dick Foes. (Buena Vista Records, 1983)

Herbstman, Judy. *The Ewoks' Hang Gliding Adventure* (Random House, 1984)

Howe, James. *How the Ewoks Saved the Trees: An Old Ewok Legend* (Random House, 1984)

James, Emily. *The White Witch: A Droid Adventure*. Illustrated by Bunny Carter. (Random House, 1986)

Johnston, Joe. *The Adventures of Teebo: A Tale of Magic and Suspense* (Random House, 1984)

Luke, Melinda. *The Baby Ewoks' Picnic Surprise* (Random House, 1984)

Luke, Melinda. *Wicket Finds a Way: An Ewok Adventure* (Random House, 1984)

Luke, Melinda. *Wicket Goes Fishing: An Ewok Adventure* (Random House, 1986)

Luke, Melinda and Paul Dini. *The Red Ghost: An Ewok Adventure* (Random House, 1986)

Richelson, Geraldine. *Star Wars Storybook* (Random House, 1978)

Star Wars: The Maverick Moon. Illustrated by Walter Wright. (Random House, 1979)

Star Wars: The Mystery of the Rebellious Robot. Illustrated by Mark Corcoran. (Random House, 1979)

Star Wars: The Wookiee Storybook. Illustrations by Patricia Wynne. (Random House, 1979)

Steneman, Shep. *The Empire Strikes Back Storybook* (Random House, 1980)

Vinge, Joan D. *Return of the Jedi Storybook* (Random House, 1983)

Weinberg, Larry. *Wicket and the Dandelion Warriors: An Ewok Adventure* (Random House, 1985)

Weiss, Ellen. *The Lost Prince: A Droid Adventure.* Illustrated by Amador. (Random House, 1985)

Weiss, Ellen. *The Pirates of Tarnoonga: A Droid Adventure.* Illustrated by Carter Concepts, Inc. (Random House, 1986)

MIXED MEDIA

Anderson, Kevin J., and Ralph McQuarrie. *The Illustrated Star Wars Universe* (Bantam, Late 1995)

Attias, Diana and Lindsay Smith, editors. *The Empire Strikes Back Notebook* (Ballantine, November 1980)

Bulluck, Vic and Valerie Hoffman. *The Art of The Empire Strikes Back* (Ballantine, October 1980)

Carrau, Bob. *Monsters and Aliens from George Lucas* (Harry N. Abrams, Incorporated, 1993)

Daley, Brian. *Star Wars* radio dramatization, thirteen episodes (National Public Radio)

Daley, Brian. *Star Wars: The National Public Radio Dramatization* (Del Rey, October 1994)

Daley, Brian. *Star Wars: The Empire Strikes Back* radio dramatization, ten episodes (National Public Radio)

Daley, Brian. *Star Wars: The Empire Strikes Back—The National Public Radio Dramatization* (Del Rey, June 1995)

Gerani, Gary. *The Art of Star Wars Galaxy*, Vol. 1 (Topps Publishing, November 1993)

Gerani, Gary. *The Art of Star Wars Galaxy*, Vol. 2 (Topps Publishing, November 1994)

George Lucas, *The Art of Star Wars* (Ballantine, November 1979)

Johnson, Shane. *Star Wars Technical Journal*, Vol. 1–3 (Starlog Press, 1993–1994)

Johnston, Joe. *The Star Wars Sketchbook* (Ballantine, September 1977)

Johnston, Joe and Nilo Rodis-Jamero. *The Empire Strikes Back Sketchbook* (Ballantine, June 1980)

Johnston, Joe and Nilo Rodis-Jamero. *Return of the Jedi Sketchbook* (Ballantine, June 1983)

Kasdan, Lawrence and George Lucas. *The Art of Return of the Jedi* (Ballantine, November 1983)

Miller, Rusty. *The Jedi Master's Quizbook* (Del Rey, November 1982)

Sansweet, Stephen. *Star Wars: From Concept to Screen to Collectible* (Chronicle Books, 1992)

Slavicsek, Bill. *A Guide to the Star Wars Universe* (2nd edition) (Del Rey, March 1994)

Star Wars Blueprints (Ballantine, November 1977)

Vaz, Mark Cotta and Shinji Hata. *From Star Wars to Indiana Jones: The Best of the Lucasfilm Archives* (Chronicle Books, 1994)

Velasco, Raymond L. *A Guide to the Star Wars Universe* (Del Rey, December 1984)

various issues of *Bantha Tracks, Lucasfilm Fan Club, Star Wars Poster Magazine, The Empire Strikes Back Poster Magazine,* and *Return of the Jedi Poster Magazine.*

GAME BOOKS

Boucher, Grant. *Star Wars Galaxy Guide 1: A New Hope* (West End Games, 1989)

Boucher, Grant and Michael Stern. *Star Wars: The Movie Trilogy Sourcebook* (West End Games, September 1993)

Caspian, Jonatha, with Christopher Kubasik, Bill Slavicsek, and C.J. Tramontana. *Star Wars Galaxy Guide 2: Yavin and Bespin Planet Profiles* (West End Games, 1989)

Costikyan, Greg. *Star Wars: The Roleplaying Game* (West End Games, October 1987)

Denning, Troy. *Star Wars Galaxy Guide 4: Alien Races* (West End Games, 1989)

Denning, Troy and Chuck Truett. *Star Wars Galaxy Guide 4: Alien Races* (2nd edition) (West End Games, 1994)

Gorden, Greg. *Star Wars: Imperial Sourcebook* (West End Games, October 1989)

Gorden, Greg. *Star Wars: Imperial Sourcebook* (2nd edition) (West End Games, June 1994)

Horne, Michael A. *Dark Empire Sourcebook* (West End Games, June 1993)

Horne, Michael Allen. *Han Solo and the Corporate Sector Sourcebook* (West End Games, November 1993)

Kubasik, Christopher. *Crisis on Cloud City* (West End Games, 1989)

Murphy, Paul. *Star Wars: Rebel Alliance Sourcebook* (West End Games, October 1990)

Murphy, Paul. *Star Wars: Rebel Alliance Sourcebook* (2nd edition) (West End Games, April 1994)

Rolston, Ken and Steve Gilbert. *Strike Force: Shantipole* (West End Games, 1988)

Schweighofer, Peter, editor. *Star Wars*

Adventure Journal, Vol. 1–4 (West End Games, February–November 1994)

Slavicsek, Bill. *Star Wars: Dark Force Rising Sourcebook* (West End Games, November 1992)

Slavicsek, Bill. *Star Wars: Death Star Technical Companion* (West End Games, 1991)

Slavicsek, Bill. *Star Wars: Death Star Technical Companion* (2nd edition) (West End Games, 1993)

Slavicsek, Bill. *Star Wars: Heir to the Empire Sourcebook* (West End Games, July 1992)

Smith, Bill. *Star Wars: The Roleplaying Game* (2nd edition) (West End Games, October 1992)

Smith, Curtis and Bill Slavicsek. *The Star Wars Sourcebook* (West End Games, November 1987)

Smith, Curtis and Bill Slavicsek. *The Star Wars Sourcebook* (2nd edition) (West End Games, June 1994)

Stern, Michael. *Star Wars Galaxy Guide 3: The Empire Strikes Back* (West End Games, 1989)

Stern, Michael. *Star Wars Galaxy Guide 5: Return of the Jedi* (West End Games, 1990)

Stuart, Rick D. *Star Wars Galaxy Guide 10: Bounty Hunters* (West End Games, 1993)

Stuart, Rick D. *Star Wars Galaxy Guide 11: Criminal Organizations* (West End Games, 1994)

Trautmann, Eric. *Star Wars: The Last Command Sourcebook* (West End Games, March 1994)

Wixted, Martin. *Star Wars Galaxy Guide 7: Mos Eisley* (West End Games, 1993)

VIDEO GAME BOOKS

DeMaria, Rusel. *Super Empire Strikes Back Official Game Secrets* (Prima Publishing, 1993)

DeMaria, Rusel. *X-Wing: The Official Strategy Guide* (Prima Publishing, 1993)

DeMaria, Rusel, with David Wessman and David Maxwell. *Tie Fighter: The Official Strategy Guide* (Prima Publishing, 1994)

DeMaria, Rusel, with Jeronimo Barrera and Tom Stratton. *Super Star Wars Official Game Secrets* (Prima Publishing, 1993)

Hutsko, Joe. *Rebel Assault: The Official Insider's Guide* (Prima Publishing, 1994)

COMIC BOOKS

Claremont, Chris. *Star Wars 2: World Of Fire.* Art by Carmine Infantino and Gene Day. (Marvel Illustrated Books, October 1982)

Goodwin, Archie. *Star Wars: Return of the Jedi* #1–4. Art by Al Williamson. (Marvel Comics, October 1983–January 1984)

Manak, Dave. *Droids* #1–8. Artists include John Romita, Al Williamson, and Jon D'Agostino. (Star/Marvel Comics, April 1986–June 1987)

Manak, Dave. *Ewoks* #1–15. Art by Warren Kremer, Jon D'Agostino, and Jacqueline Roettcher. (Star/Marvel Comics, May 1985–September 1987)

Star Wars #1–107, Annuals #1–3 (Marvel Comics, July 1977–September 1986)

Star Wars 3-D #1–3 (Blackthorne Publishing, December 1987–Fall 1988)

Thorsland, Dan. *Dark Horse Comics* #17–19. Art by Bill Hughes and Andy Mushynsky. (Dark Horse Comics, January–March 1994)

Thorsland, Dan. *Star Wars: Droids Special* #1. Art by Bill Hughes and Andy Mushynsky. (Dark Horse Comics, January 1995)

Thorsland, Dan and Ryder Windham. *Star Wars: Droids* #1–6. Art by Bill Hughes and Andy Mushynsky, and Ian Gibson. (Dark Horse Comics, April–September 1994)

Veitch, Tom. *Star Wars: Dark Empire* #1–6. Art by Cam Kennedy. (Dark Horse comics, December 1991–October 1992)

Veitch, Tom. *Star Wars: Dark Empire II* #1–6. Art by Cam Kennedy. (Dark Horse Comics, December 1994–May 1995)

Veitch, Tom. "Star Wars: Tales of the Jedi," *Dark Horse Comics* #7–9. Art by Janine Johnston. (Dark Horse Comics, February–March 1993)

Veitch, Tom. *Star Wars: Tales of the Jedi* #1–5. Art by Chris Gossett, Mike Barreiro, Janine Johnston, John Nadeua, and David Roach. (Dark Horse Comics, October 1993–February 1994)

Veitch, Tom. *Star Wars: Tales of the Jedi—The Freedon Nadd Uprising* #1–2. Art by Tony Akins and Denis Rodier. (Dark Horse Comics, August–September 1994)

Veitch, Tom. "Ulic Qel-Droma and the Beast-Wars of Onderon," *Dark Horse Insider* #15–20. Art by Chris Gossett and Mike Barreiro. (Dark Horse Comics, March–August 1993)

Veitch, Tom and Kevin Anderson. *Star Wars: Tales of the Jedi—Dark Lords of the Sith* #1–6. Art by Chris Gossett, Mike Barreiro, and Jordi Ensign. (Dark Horse Comics, October 1994–March 1995)

Wagner, John. *Boba Fett: Bounty On Bar-Kooda.* Art by Cam Kennedy. (Dark Horse Comics, 1995)

Windham, Ryder. *Star Wars: Droids* #1–6. Art Ian Gibson. (Dark Horse Comics, April–September 1995)

Woodring, Jim. *Jabba the Hutt: The Gaar Suppoon Hit.* Art by Art Wetherell and Monty Sheldon. (Dark Horse Comics, April 1995)

COMIC STRIPS

Classic Star Wars #1–20 (Dark Horse Comics, August 1992–June 1994)

Classic Star Wars: The Early Adventures #1–9 (Dark Horse Comics, August 1994–April 1995)

Star Wars newspaper strip (LA Times Syndicate, March 12, 1979–March 11, 1984)

Star Wars #1–3 newspaper strip collection in hardcover boxed set (Russ Cochran, 1991)

GRAPHIC NOVELS AVAILABLE FROM BOXTREE

ALIENS
☐ 0 7522 0878 0   Aliens v Predator – Deadliest of the
Species 1   £9.99 pb
☐ 0 7522 0695 8   Aliens v Predator – Deadliest of the
Species 2   £9.99 pb

RANMA
☐ 0 7522 0851 9   Ranma Book 1   £5.99 pb
☐ 0 7522 0861 6   Ranma Book 2   £5.99 pb

SPIDER-MAN
☐ 0 7522 0107 7   Masques   £8.99 pb
☐ 0 7522 0112 3   Perceptions   £8.99 pb
☐ 0 7522 0876 4   The Return of the Sinister 6   £9.99 pb
☐ 0 7522 0808 X   Revenge of the Sinister 6   £7.99 pb

STAR WARS
☐ 0 7522 0893 4   Classic – A New Hope   £8.99 pb
☐ 0 7522 0987 6   Dark Empire   £9.99 pb
☐ 0 7522 0822 5   Dark Empire 2   £9.99 pb
☐ 0 7522 0793 8   Dark Empire/Epilogue   £6.99 pb
☐ 0 7522 0616 8   Dark Lords of Sith 1   £8.99 pb
☐ 0 7522 0804 7   Droids   £8.99 pb
☐ 0 7522 0606 0   Empire Strikes Back   £7.99 pb
☐ 0 7522 0704 0   Jabba the Hutt   £8.99 pb
☐ 0 7522 0611 7   Return of the Jedi   £7.99 pb
☐ 0 7522 0798 9   River of Chaos   £8.99 pb
☐ 0 7522 0913 2   Star Wars Classic   £7.99 pb
☐ 0 7522 0747 4   Star Wars Classic 2   £10.99 pb
☐ 0 7522 0752 0   Star Wars Classic 3   £9.99 pb
☐ 0 7522 0817 9   Tales of the Jedi and Freedom
Nadd Uprising   £10.99 pb

STAR TREK – DEEP SPACE NINE
☐ 0 7522 0928 0   Emancipation 1   £7.99 pb
☐ 0 7522 0933 7   Emancipation and Beyond   £7.99 pb
☐ 0 7522 0898 5   Hearts and Minds   £7.99 pb
☐ 0 7522 0888 8   Requiem   £7.99 pb

STREETFIGHTER
☐ 0 7522 0813 6   Street Fighter II – book 1   £6.99 pb
☐ 0 7522 0818 7   Street Fighter II – book 2   £6.99 pb

VARIOUS
☐ 0 7522 0897 7   Daredevil – man without fear   £9.99 pb
☐ 0 7522 0962 0   Necroscope   £7.99 pb
☐ 0 7522 0645 1   Marvels   £10.99 pb
☐ 0 7522 0881 0   Mask (film tie-in)   £6.99 pb
☐ 0 7522 0977 9   RoboCop: Prime Suspect   £7.99 pb

☐	0 7522 0856 X	Shadow (film tie-in)	£6.99 pb
☐	0 7522 0762 8	Species (film tie-in)	£8.99 pb

X MEN

☐	0 7522 0892 6	Adventures	£9.99 pb
☐	1 85283 390 4	Brood Trouble In The Big Easy	£5.25 pb
☐	1 85283 394 7	Essential Guide	£9.99 pb
☐	0 7522 0756 3	Gambit	£7.99 pb
☐	0 7522 0691 5	Ghostrider/Wolverine/Punisher/ Hearts of Darkness/Dark Design	£7.99 pb
☐	0 7522 0871 3	God Loves, Man Kills	£5.99 pb
☐	0 7522 0103 4	Rogue	£8.99 pb
☐	0 7522 0803 9	Sabretooth	£6.99 pb
☐	1 85283 395 5	Wolverine	£6.99 pb
☐	0 7522 0108 5	Wolverine – Triumph and Tragedy	£9.99 pb
☐	0 7522 0151 4	Uncanny X-Men: Acts of Vengeance	£8.99 pb
☐	0 7522 0161 1	Uncanny X-Men: Wolverine/ Psylocke 1	£8.99 pb

All these books are available at your local bookshop or newsagent or can be ordered direct from the publisher. Just tick the titles you want and fill in the form below.

Prices and availability are subject to change without notice.

___

Boxtree Cash Sales, P.O. Box 11, Falmouth, Cornwall TR10 9EN

Please send a cheque or postal order for the value of the book and add the following for postage and packing:

U.K. including B.F.P.O. – £1.00 for one book plus 50p for the second book, and 30p for each additional book ordered up to a £3.00 maximum.

OVERSEAS INCLUDING EIRE – £2.00 for the first book plus £1.00 for the second book, and 50p for each additional book ordered.

OR please debit this amount from my Access/Visa Card (delete as appropriate).

Card Number ☐☐☐☐☐☐☐☐☐☐☐☐☐☐☐☐

Amount £ ....

Expiry Date ....

Signed ....

Name ....

Address ....

OTHER BOOKS AVAILABLE FROM BOXTREE

STAR TREK TITLES

0 7522 0839 X	Beyond Uhura	£15.99 hb
1 85283 899 X	Captain's Log	£13.99 pb
1 85283 399 8	Captains Logs Supplemental – Season 6	£9.99 pb
0 7522 0938 8	Captains Logs Supplemental – Season 7	£9.99 pb
0 7522 0843 8	Creating the Next Generation	£9.99 pb
1 85283 388 2	Deep Space Logbook	£9.99 pb
0 7522 0848 9	Deep Space Logbook: Series 2	£9.99 pb
1 85283 571 0	Exploring Deep Space and Beyond	£6.99 pb
0 7522 0968 X	Great Birds of the Galaxy	£9.99 pb
0 7522 0868 3	Lost Voyages of Trek and the Next Generation	£9.99 pb
0 7522 0973 6	Making of the Trek Films	£12.99 pb
0 7522 0873 X	Star Trek Creator	£15.99 hb
1 85283 340 8	Star Trek Technical Manual	£13.99 pb
1 85283 398 X	Trek: Universal Index	£9.99 pb

STAR WARS TITLES

0 7522 0859 4	Guide to the Star Wars Universe	£9.99 pb
0 7522 0887 X	Star Wars Technical Journal	£14.99 pb
0 7522 0817 9	Tales of the Jedi	£10.99 pb

MAGIC - THE GATHERING

0 7522 0719 9	Whispering Woods	£4.99 pb
0 7522 0724 5	Arena	£4.99 pb

All these books are available at your local bookshop or can be ordered direct from the publisher. Just tick the titles you want and fill in the form below.

Prices and availability subject to change without notice.

Boxtree Cash Sales, P.O. Box 11, Falmouth, Cornwall TR10 9EN

Please send a cheque or postal order for the value of the book and add the following for postage and packing:

U.K. including B.F.P.O. – £1.00 for one book plus 50p for the second book, and 30p for each additional book ordered up to a £3.00 maximum.

Overseas including Eire – £2.00 for the first book plus £1.00 for the second book, and 50p for each additional book ordered.

OR please debit this amount from my Access/Visa Card (delete as appropriate).

Card Number

Amount £ ....

Expiry Date ....

Signed ....

Name ....

Address ....

STAR WARS THE SCRIPTS

* A long time ago in a galaxy far, far away . . .

   . . . With these words began one of the most magical and successful, science-fiction films ever

* *Star Wars* would go on to change not only the nature of science fiction movies but also rewrite the record books as the original film

* The two that followed, *The Empire Strikes Back* and *Return of the Jedi* – topped box offices worldwide

* Here for the first time, are the complete continuity scripts for all three Star Wars films

* These reflect accurately what you see on the screen

Available from Boxtree, 0 7522 0766 0,

priced £14.99 pb

ABOUT THE ARTIST

MICHAEL BUTKUS is an illustrator based in Los Angeles. He attended Otis Parsons in L.A. and Pasadena's Art Center College of Design, and when he left Art Center in 1986, he immediately started work in the movie industry. Since then, his involvement in over 1,500 films has covered everything from movie poster designs to set designs and animation series. Some of his works include the poster illustrations for *Cliffhanger*, *RoboCop*, and *Heaven and Earth*. He is the creator of the animation series *The Boneheads* and *Tenpin and Earl*. Currently the majority of his work focuses on the concept and development of ideas, including designs for Disney theme restaurants and illustrating characters for Lucasfilm. An avid Star Wars fan, he was tremendously excited when art director Troy Alders called him to work on this project. When Michael is not working in the film industry, he enjoys classical figurative painting. Outside of art, his hobbies include hiking, mountain bike riding, and martial arts. He lives with his dog, Bordo, in West Los Angeles.

ABOUT THE AUTHOR

Living in Portland, Oregon for the last decade, ANDY MANGELS has carved out a diverse writing career since his first published work in the book *Focus on George Pérez* in August 1985.

Since that time, his main body of work has been in the comic-book business. Past comic series he's written include the best-selling *Bloodwulf*, *Elfquest: Blood of Ten Chiefs*, *Nightmares on Elm Street*, *Child's Play: The Series*, *Annie Sprinkle Is Miss Timed*, and *Jason Goes to Hell*, as well as stories in *Quantum Leap*, *Justice League Quarterly*, *Badrock & Company*, *Ultraverse Premiere*, and the *Troll Halloween Special*. He also edits *Gay Comics*.

Another focus of his work is genre films and TV projects in Hollywood. His regular columns have appeared in *Amazing Heroes*, *Marvel Age*, *Fantazia* (England), *Edizione Star* (Italy), and *Wizard*. He currently appears every month in *Hero Illustrated* and *Cinescape*. His more politically charged work has appeared in *Gauntlet*, and in such gay-themed magazines as *In Uniform*, *The Advocate*, *Outweek*, *Frontiers*, *Bear*, *Drummer*, *The Leather Journal*, and *Oregon Gay News*.

In his free time, he participates in Civil War reenacting, gay activism, action-figure collecting, and uniform collecting. This is his first solo book, although other *STAR WARS* projects are in the works, including text for trading cards and toys, a Boba Fett comic serial for *Star Wars Galaxy* magazine, and an audio adaption of STAR WARS: NIGHTLILY—THE LOVER'S TALE.